A POPULAR ACCOUNT
OF THE
MANNERS AND CUSTOMS OF INDIA

A POPULAR ACCOUNT
OF THE
MANNERS AND CUSTOMS OF INDIA.

BY

Rev. CHARLES ACLAND

GYAN

Published by

GYAN

Gyan Publishing House
5, Ansari Road
Daryaganj, New Delhi-110002
Phone: 011-47034999, 9811692060
E-mail: books@gyanbooks.com

Distribution Network
gyanbooks.com
India, USA, Canada, UK, Australia, France

ISBN: 978-81-212-8262- 8 (PB)
First Published, 1847

2nd Impression 2023

Printed at: Gyan Press, Delhi.

A POPULAR ACCOUNT OF THE MANNERS AND CUSTOMS OF INDIA
Author: CHARLES ACLAND

A POPULAR ACCOUNT

OF THE

MANNERS AND CUSTOMS OF INDIA.

Illustrated with Numerous Anecdotes.

BY THE

REV. CHARLES ACLAND,

LATE CHAPLAIN AT POOREE, CUTTACK, AND MIDNAPORE.

LONDON:
JOHN MURRAY, ALBEMARLE STREET.

1847.

PREFACE.

The author of the present work was a clergyman, who, along with his wife, quitted England about the beginning of the year 1842, leaving behind him several young children, to whom, as appears from the letters he constantly addressed to them, he was most affectionately attached.

They left the country full of hope that they should all be reunited at some future period; but, before he had been three years exposed to the climate of India, he fell a victim to it. It is somewhat melancholy to find him at the outset rejoicing in the very circumstance which in some measure perhaps occasioned his death. The first destination selected for him was little in accordance with his own taste; and when it subsequently was altered from Assam to Cuttack, he expresses himself delighted with the change, though the first-named province was much more remarkable for its healthfulness than that to which he at length proceeded.

Mr. Acland felt the warmest interest in the education of his children, and, to improve their minds, determined, on quitting England, to send home, from time to time, accurate accounts of his progress, that they might be made acquainted with all he beheld—the places through which he passed, the aspect of the country, its climate, productions, flowers, trees, shrubs, and wild animals. Many an interesting adventure is related in these pages which the author met with in the jungle; the beating of which by the hunting parties, who go forth in bands for that purpose, is described with an animation calculated to awaken much interest.

The letters addressed by Mr. Acland to his children have now been thrown into the form of a Journal, as this method was considered best suited to the general reader. The Editor has, however, been careful to preserve throughout the easy familiar style in which the father first wrote them, that to the children of others they may be equally acceptable and useful.

The books hitherto published on India have been in general, from their bulk, confined to persons arrived at a more advanced period of life; and the Editor of the present volume hopes in some measure to familiarise the subject by bringing it down nearer the comprehension of the youthful reader. This work is intended to describe Indian manners in an interesting way, and will in some measure, it is hoped, supply a portion of the want that has long existed in our literature in this respect. To render the subject more attractive, Mr. Acland was careful to introduce anecdotes and short narratives throughout, which are calculated to amuse, while instruction is at the same time conveyed.

One distinguishing feature may be observed in the whole —viz. a fervent spirit of devotion, which breathes through every page of the original manuscript. Such passages the Editor has thought it better to omit, as the advice from a father to his children, clothed in the simple language he considered it best to employ, though beautiful and touching in itself, would scarcely appear interesting to the general reader. For this reason the substance of his counsel has been compressed into the present brief Preface.

He impresses upon his children the necessity of living ever in brotherly love, of sustaining and comforting one another, and of seeking the Divine aid in every emergency of life, whether great or small. He shows them how, by trusting implicitly in God and acting according to His commandments, they will attain a peace of mind above all the happiness which an indulgence in the pleasures of this life can bestow. He explains to them, in the gentlest terms, how necessary it is for their welfare here and hereafter that they should act ever in accordance with the expressed wishes of the Almighty; and that they must never cease to remember that He moves about them everywhere, and sees their every action, hears each passionate word, beholds each unbecoming gesture, and will reward or punish according as they indulge in or abstain from evil. In several beautiful passages he portrays the unceasing watchfulness of the Almighty in providing for our daily wants, in supplying us with every necessary of life; and inquires, with truth, Ought not every little heart to be daily grateful to Him, without whose will the sun cannot shine, or rise, or set; without whose will the refreshing showers could not force and raise up around us the beautiful and necessary things of life? Then he inquires, How can we better show our gratitude for these blessings than by acting in accordance with the wishes of Him who is the cause of so much good?

These words were spoken by a father to his own children; but I would ask those of my young friends into whose hands this little volume may fall, does it not equally touch them? Do they not feel the truth of these sentences? Coming over the many thousand miles which stretch between India and this country, these letters were cherished the more by the three little children to whom they were addressed; and now that the hand is cold which traced the lines, how much more will they be prized!

Whatever may be the fate of the volume with the public, to those whom it more intimately concerns it will be a lasting remembrance of their father, and of the melancholy circumstances connected with his early death. For their sake, the Editor trusts that the present work may meet with at least a moderate share of success; and that, in the endeavour to render more familiar to the youthful mind the names and habits of some of the inhabitants of India, he may not altogether fail.

London, Sept. 1847.

CONTENTS.

February 15.

A POPULAR ACCOUNT

OF THE

MANNERS AND CUSTOMS OF INDIA.

Madras, June, 1842.

We quitted England in the course of March, 1842, and reached Madras in the month of June of the same year. I shall give but a brief sketch of our voyage.

Soon after leaving England, having arrived near Ushant, situated on the north-west coast of France, a tremendous storm came on; the waves rose high and washed the deck, while the ship itself pitched to such a degree that the very dinner rolled off the table; in the night my wife was tossed out of bed, and thrown to the other side of the cabin. We were in the greatest danger of being drowned. I started out of my hammock, but was unable to stand upright. Towards morning, however, the wind abated.

After this storm had passed, the ship went forward rapidly until we reached the equator, where she lay becalmed for several days. The heat at this point of our voyage was excessive; we used to lie about on the deck almost all night, taking care, however, to cover our faces if the moon was shining; for it is said that, in these hot climates, if any one goes to sleep under its light, he is in danger of losing his sight, and even his life.*

* It is doubted whether the injury does not rather arise from the damp night-air than from the effect of the moon-beams.

We now proceeded more slowly until we had rounded the Cape of Good Hope, where another storm came on. Every sail was taken in; yet, without their assistance, we ran, in two days, 545 miles. The waves rose as high as mountains, and the ship seemed to toil up one side, and to send the bowsprit up into the air, then, plunging down again, seemed to bury it in the sea. I was standing with my wife at the door of the dinner cabin when a large wave burst in through the upper part of the ship, flooded the room, and shivered one of our large boats to atoms.

As we were passing the equator, too, we suffered from a tremendous thunder-storm. The heat was excessive: not a breath of wind stirred the air. About twelve o'clock a little cloud, about the size of a man's hand, rose in the horizon: gradually it spread until it hung like a huge black mass over the ship. I stood and watched its increase, when suddenly a vivid flash of lightning shot from the heavens, and almost blinded me. At the same moment a crash of thunder bellowed round the ship like the noise of a thousand cannons. The lightning slightly struck one of our passengers and the mate, but did not inflict any serious injury. The rain now descended: not a sharp thick shower, such as you may witness in England, but as it were all in one mass, and soon every trace of the storm passed away; the sun burst forth, and the ship and sails were dried in the course of a few minutes.

Calm weather was ours now until we reached Madras. During our voyage we observed many curious kinds of birds, the principal of which was the stormy petrel. These creatures quit the land, and fly many thousand miles over the sea in the track of ships, following them by night and by day. The whale-bird is about the size of a thrush, white in colour, and may be seen hovering about the great fish from which it derives its name.

The Cape pigeon is a very beautiful creature, about the size of our own pigeon, white, with black spots on its body, and a blue, glossy head. We several times amused ourselves with catching them; and the way we contrived was, to let fly from our hands a piece of thread several yards in length, which was carried out by the wind, and the pigeon, flying across it, became entangled in it. In fluttering about in the endeavour to extricate itself, it became only more firmly secured; and then, drawing the string towards us, we caught the bird, and, placing it on the deck, suffered it to walk about. The legs of this pigeon are so peculiarly formed that they are unable to spring up from the ground, and can only rise from the crest of a wave, or throw themselves from the edge of a rock. The albatross is a large white bird, which has been known to measure fourteen or sixteen feet from the tip of one wing to the tip of the other. We used to catch them sometimes by casting out a hook and line, as for a fish.

The Cape hen, which follows the ship in flocks, is large and black, measuring about ten feet from wing to wing. Occasionally we caught a glimpse of the tropic-bird, called by the sailors the boatswain, because of its long pointed tail resembling the pigtail which these men used formerly to wear.

The booby is a large brown bird, about as big as a common hen. I must not forget to tell you something about the pilot-fish. Every shark, whether old or young, is accompanied by a little fish about twelve inches long, and striped like a zebra, which keeps always near the nose of the shark, and seems to guide him to his food.

As I have in this place said so much about birds and fishes, I may as well tell you a little about the animals here in Madras. The first I shall mention is the cow, by which all the carts and many of the carriages are drawn along—sometimes, too, very swiftly. They are much smaller than English cows, and have a hump on their backs. Camels may be seen in the streets patiently carrying heavy loads of goods: the people, however, treat them very cruelly.

As I was going to the cathedral last Sunday I saw a mungoose, a little green and yellow animal, something between a ferret and a squirrel. It is said that when bitten by a snake it runs and rubs the place over with the juice of a certain plant, which immediately cures it.

My samee, or native manservant, who is a Malay, gave me one about as large as a kitten, and quite as playful. It will attain to the size of a cat; it follows me about, sleeps on the foot of the bed, and if a snake comes into the room will instantly kill it. When an Indian mother wishes to go out, she need only just tell the mungoose to mind the cradle, and then he lies down by it, and suffers neither man nor reptile to approach. This creature, once tamed, is quite wretched out of human society.

The cobra de capello is one of the most poisonous snakes with which we are acquainted. I saw a girl playing with some of them the other day, but their fangs had been extracted.

There are a great number of beautiful birds here; and green paroquets can be purchased for three pence, while an avadavad costs only one penny. The cock avadavad should, when kept, be confined along with twelve hens in a cage.

The large carrion-crow is as common here as the sparrow is in England, and is so tame that they fly close to the houses, and even look in at the windows. Nobody is allowed to shoot or hurt them, because they make themselves useful in carrying away all the dirt from the town. Large vultures are almost as numerous.

I must not forget to mention the mosquito, which is a gnat exactly like those you see in England. Great numbers fly about all the night, and some people suffer much from their bite, but they never touch me.

The flowers here are beautiful, and some smell exceedingly sweet. There are two tall trees, as large as elms, covered with red and yellow flowers about the size of a plate. In the hedges, too, we see very splendid cactuses. I shall be able, however, to tell you more about these things when I have been here longer.

The fruits are exquisite, but it is dangerous to eat them in any quantity. For a pine-apple nearly as big as your head we pay only two anas—that is, three pence; but they are not exactly like those you buy in England. Here they are quite sweet, and soft and juicy as a peach. The mango is a yellow fruit about the size of a large orange, the inside of which is full of a very rich sort of custard. The plantain resembles a dahlia-root, and has very much the same taste as cheese. The guava is in appearance like an apple, but possesses the flavour of a strawberry.

There are several other kinds of fruit, but I have not time to describe them now. I am very fond of the pine-apple and the orange, but do not care for any of the others.

Mother-of-pearl may be bought very cheap here. It is found in a particular kind of oyster-shell, of which I can get three or four for a halfpenny. Though the heat here is excessive, I do not suffer from it: the thermometer in the large room where I am sitting is now 93½°. The heat causes a kind of rash called the prickle-heat, which is very disagreeable. The sensation to which it gives rise is much the same as would be caused by running needles into the body. In every room, hanging from the ceiling, is a large fan, called a punkah, about four times the size of the door, and a boy is continually employed in swinging it backward and forward, and the current of air thus created cools the whole room. The windows are without glass. Venetian blinds serve instead, and sometimes mats, which are kept constantly wetted. The water soon turns into steam, and, evaporating very fast, carries off with it the latent heat.

When my wife goes to sleep, the little black boy, with no covering but a pair of drawers and a cap, stands near and fans her, while every now and then he sprinkles her face with water as she reclines on the sofa.

The people here are nearly all black, and wear very little clothing. The population is extensive. At dinner we have generally eight or ten men to wait upon us, but they are slow in their movements, and very lazy. The Arabian Nights mentions the fakirs. I have seen some here that have let their feet grow in one position until they cannot move them.

Some of the inhabitants of Madras are afflicted with a curious kind of disease, in which one leg swells to the size of a man's body, while the other is no thicker than the limb of an infant.

When you meet in the street with a native who is at all acquainted with you, or who wishes to express his thanks for anything, instead of merely saying "Thank you," or "How do you do?" he presses his hands upon his eyes, and says "Salaam, sahib." Some English persons, on going out for a walk, may be seen to carry a whip, with which, if the natives are at all troublesome, they lash them; but this is a cruel practice. Ladies are prevented by the heat from walking abroad here, and gentlemen seldom do so, but go about in what are called palanquins, which I will describe hereafter. When we ride out, however swiftly we go, a man called a coolie runs by the side of the carriage. We are obliged to get up here at about half-past five in the morning, and then we go out for a drive, or in the palanquin; at half-past seven the sun is too powerful even for that exercise: we then return home, take a cold bath, and breakfast. At half-past six in the evening we are enabled to go out again a little. In the middle of the day we take a nap.

July 1st.

A FEW days ago I saw a native wedding. At about nine in the evening I was disturbed by a noise of drums and squeaking trumpets. Looking out of the window, I saw a large party with torches conducting the bride to her husband's home. She was entirely covered by a white veil, and walked in the midst of her relations.

I went to pay a visit to the Newab, a native prince of these parts, but did not succeed in obtaining an interview. He is about fifteen years of age, and generally goes out in a carriage drawn by seven horses. His uncles ride by his side on elephants, while his cousins run with the carriage.

The natives are a fine athletic race of men, with every appearance of possessing talent and intellect. The tricks of the jugglers are very entertaining: they will swallow swords, throw up three or four knives or cannon-balls, and catch them on their necks, and pull balls of cotton out of their throats, and make snakes dance.

Bishop's Palace, Calcutta, July 15.

HERE we are arrived safely at this place, after a very disagreeable voyage, the worst part of which was the travelling up the river Hoogly. We were becalmed for some time, and merely drifted up a few miles a-day with the tide. However, I was much interested one day by watching a cloud, which, after moving and whirling about for a little time, began to send down a little thin point towards the river. Presently the column increased in size, while underneath the waves seemed to rise to meet it; and when they had done so a great quantity of the water was sucked up by the cloud, which grew larger in consequence, and then steered away towards the land: this was a water-spout.

The place in which we live—that is, our hotel—is a large house, three stories high, surrounding a square, and on each side are forty-two windows in a row.

Immediately after landing I went to pay my respects to the archdeacon, and to inform him of my arrival. Not finding him at home, I proceeded to the bishop, who treated me very hospitably, and invited us to his house.

On returning home I found that during my absence the archdeacon's wife and daughter had been calling on my wife, for the purpose of inviting us to their house; but having already accepted the offer of the bishop, we, of course, were compelled to decline this. In the bishop's palace we have two very large apartments assigned to us, besides a bath-room, and a verandah, about three hundred yards long, to walk in. I was scarcely located here, however, before I received an order to proceed to Gowhattie, in Assam, and to assume the clerical superintendence of the whole province. At Gowhattie there is one European lady, and there are five European gentlemen, who are the only ones within two hundred and seventy miles. My parish, if such it can be called, is about twice the size of England, and I shall be continually travelling about.

But I must now tell you something about this place. The principal animals here are buffaloes, elephants, and tigers, of whose numbers you may form an idea by the fact of the Government having offered a reward for every tiger's head. Last year, in the province of Assam, the number of heads brought in was two thousand six hundred, and yet these animals seem to be as numerous as ever.

We shall have to travel in a little boat, called a budjeon, with two cabins, up to Gowhattie. The boatmen are black, and we shall be the only passengers on board. We must be provided besides with two other boats, the one with the fowls and goats in it for cooking, and the other with the luggage. We shall be rather more than two months on the voyage, and must take with us enough provisions for a year. When we reach Gowhattie the boat must serve us for a home until we have built one with mats and reeds.

There are some large birds here called adjutants, about five feet high, with long white legs, black bodies, bare necks, and a beak like pelicans. They are generally seen perched on the tops of houses. The fire-flies are very pretty: on a fine night a number of them are seen flitting about the lanes and gardens glittering like stars.

The bull-frogs make a noise at night almost as loud as the bark of a dog. A pretty brown and white bird is to be found here, singing much like a blackbird; it is called a miner.

Calcutta is well termed the city of palaces, since every house is a noble mansion. Most of the rooms are at least fifteen feet high and twenty-six feet square, and along every story there is a verandah, supported by stone columns. The language of the people here seems to have retained many traces of the Portuguese, who were here before the English. For instance, the bishop is called de Lord Padre, and I go by the name of Padre Sahib.

We have no bells by which to summon the servants, who lie on the mat outside the room door; when we require them we call out, without rising from the sofa, "Qui hi?" (who is there?) then the sirdar, or valet, runs in. We give him our orders, which he reports to the others. Although I am staying at the bishop's, and dine at his table, and use his carriage, I am obliged to have five servants. I have one kitmajar, or waiter, who does nothing but attend at table. The bishop's kitmajars will wait only upon their own master. Then I have one ayah, or lady's-maid, for my wife; a sirdar, or bearer; and a matee-sirdar, or assistant-bearer. These men make the beds and assist me to dress. I have also a punkah-bearer—that is, a man who sits outside the room, and is constantly employed in pulling a string fastened to a punkah, or enormous fan, without which no Englishman could live in India. Besides these I pay a pooney-bearer, or water-carrier, and a matranes. When I go up the country I shall be obliged to have a consummar, or head servant; a dobee, or washerwoman; a dugay, or tailor; a syce, or grass-cutter; and one or two others. We cannot do with less, because, if I were to ask the kitmajar to fetch my coat, he would twist his mustachios, and say, "Me no sirdar;" or if I were to ask my sirdar to wait at table, he would say, "Kitmajar no do dat."

August 6, 1842.

The bishop has changed my appointment from Assam to Cuttack. The different towns I shall have under my jurisdiction are Midnapore, Balasore, and Poonee. Midnapore is situated eighty miles south of Calcutta, and Cuttack two hundred and forty. Poonee stands on the coast a little to the south of the great plain of Juggernat'h, which forms a part of my district.

We expect to leave Calcutta next week, and shall go down the river as far as Ooloberriab. Here we shall quit the boat for palanquins, and shall travel by night, it being too sultry to proceed by day. At Midnapore we shall stay for a few days at the judge's house, whilst I look about for one. Here we shall probably remain about three months, and shall then proceed to Poonee. Whichever of the two towns I discover to be the pleasantest and most agreeable I shall make my permanent abiding-place, only travelling occasionally to each of the others. Every one tells me my station is one of the healthiest in Bengal. Midnapore, standing on a high hill, will be best for the wet weather; Poonee, on the sea, for the hot months; and Cuttack, with a nice sea-breeze, for the winter.

The principal dangers we have to apprehend on our journey to Midnapore are the dacoits, or mountain robbers, the tigers, and the sudden swelling of the rivers from the rains.

Now, I must tell you a little of our mode of life here. At half-past five in the morning we have a cup of coffee, and then go out for a ramble. It is the only hour in the day in which it is possible to walk. If we were to go out for half an hour in the middle of the day it would most likely cause our death. At seven we take a cold bath, and pour great jars of water over our heads. I used to enjoy bathing in England, but here it becomes the greatest possible luxury. After this is over we read or write until nine, and then breakfast. At two we have tiffin, which is lunch, with plenty of meat. At five in the afternoon we have an hour's drive, at half-past seven we dine, at nine tea, and to bed at ten. These are the regular Indian hours, but as soon as I have a house of my own I mean to dine at three.

When on any occasion I ask for a glass of cold water it is brought to me with a lump of ice in it. This is excessively refreshing in a country like this, where the thermometer is at 90°. It is brought in shiploads from America. At new and full moon there is what is called a "bore" in the river Hoogly, that is, the tide, instead of coming up gradually, swells up in one large wave. When I saw it the other day it rose thirty feet in height.

Midnapore, September 12, 1842.

On the 14th of August I sent two boats full of furniture to Midnapore, and on the 16th we started ourselves in a boat with two large cabins and one small. I had nine Indians to manage it. Another smaller boat contained our palanquins, two servants, and a little sort of kitchen.

In going down the Hoogly river we met with an accident, and were nearly overturned; the wind drove us with great force against a large ship in a severe squall. We however reached

Ooloberriab, a native village on the Hoogly, in safety. Here we turned into a canal, up which we journeyed for some miles, and then anchored for the night. The next morning, having slept on board, we proceeded on our course, and reached the Khatah Ghat, or landing-place (pronounced gaut), at about twelve o'clock. Here we remained until four in the afternoon, entered our palanquins, a kind of square boxes, which are carried on men's shoulders, handsomely painted outside, with soft cushions inside, and lamps like a carriage. In this sort of thing we move about everywhere, and in crossing a river do not wet our feet. To each palanquin there are eight bearers, four of whom are employed at a time; one mussuaulchee, or torch-bearer, runs by the side, along with one baugh-whaller, to carry boxes made of tin, and called patarahs. Each man carries two slung to a stick over his shoulder.

My wife travels in one palanquin, and I in another. We had taken care to write beforehand that a dâk, or men, might be in readiness to carry us on at each stage; and we therefore proceeded rapidly through the whole night.

Soon after leaving Khatah Ghat we found the road for two miles under water, which reached far above the men's knees; and at one time, indeed, I was afraid it would have entered the palanquin; but the only accident that actually happened was the breaking of one of the baughley-whaller's sticks, and the tin patarah, containing clothes, floated away, but, after some trouble, was again secured. We slept most comfortably in our palanquins during our journey, and arrived at Midnapore early in the morning. Here we stayed at the house of the judge until I could choose a home for myself, in which we are now at last settled. Everybody here is most kind and hospitable, and, indeed, it is necessary it should be so, for, excepting in Calcutta, there are no inns, and travellers would fare very badly were the houses of the principal people closed against them. But when you go on a visit you must be careful to take your own servants, sheets, towels, and soap. My house is called a bungalow, which I chose as being the most economical. A bungalow is a thatched cottage, with only one ground story.

The floors of the rooms are not made of wood, but a sort of cement which looks like stone. The house stands in the midst of a large field called a compound, which belongs to me, and the servants' dwellings are scattered around.

I have a flower and kitchen garden, fowl-house and place for goats, kitchen, stable, cowhouse, and a banyan-tree. The pathways through the grass are of fine gravel, and the hedges are composed almost entirely of aloes and cactuses, mixed with a very sweet-smelling flowering shrub, and here and there a bamboo, which is a most beautiful tree, resembling a very tall weeping-willow. The sensitive-plant grows wild about the compound, and bears a very pink flower resembling that of the red cloves.

The banyan-tree is abundant here. Each branch projects stalks downwards, which take root in the earth, and after a few years one tree resembles a cluster, and covers a large space of ground. I have several aloes in my garden, which are just flowering. They have thrown up a straight stalk about twenty feet high. A large cactus is now in bloom. It is about ten feet high, and each stem or leaf is thicker round than my leg. This kind bears a very beautiful large white flower, which opens only at night. In my kitchen-garden are the mango, the plantain, Indian corn, pine-apple trees, and many others.

Carpets are not used here, but the floors are covered instead with India matting. In each room is a punkah, which I have before described.

We procure water for drinking from a large tank or pond; and as we cannot purchase meat, I have provided myself with thirty-five ducks, sixty fowls, four goats, and three kids, which last are almost ready to eat; the goats we shall keep for their milk. The judge made me a present of a beautiful fawn of the spotted deer, which is becoming very tame. I am just going to join a mutton-club. Four persons enter into partnership, and agree to keep a small flock of sheep; one of which is killed twice a-week, and then each partner is provided with a quarter of mutton, and each in turn has the liver, heart, and head. A gentleman yesterday sent me four guinea-fowls, and another has promised me six pigeons as soon as I have a place to keep them in.

I have just begun to make a collection of insects, snakes, and butterflies and moths, of the most beautiful kind. The chameleon is very common, and changes its colour according to the temper it is in. I have one which is generally of a brilliant green; but if its anger be roused, it becomes covered with large black spots, and when hungry with white spots. These are the only changes in its colour I have as yet observed: but I have seen others yellow; others, again, black, with yellow spots. It is said that each chameleon has ten different variations of colour. There is to be seen here a light-brown lizard, called the bloodsucker, which is constantly running about the walls in the rooms. Whenever we take up a paper or a book, we are sure to find two or three cockroaches under it—not such cockroaches as you may see in England, but great ones three or four inches long. The grasshoppers come into the house in numbers, and grow to an uncommon size. You may hear them chirruping half a mile off. The ants, of which there are three sorts, are a great nuisance. Every house swarms with them; and unless the legs of tables, drawers, &c., are kept constantly standing in jars of water, they attack the dinner-cloths, and in fact everything they can reach: 1st, there is a very small red ant, whose bite causes a very hard red swelling, which continues very painful for some days; 2nd, a great black ant, about the size of an English wasp, which bites, but does not sting; 3rd, the white ant, rather larger than the common English ant, which come in a swarm, and in one night will devour a table or a shelf full of books. You may come down in the morning and find your table and books apparently all right, but no sooner do you touch them than they all crumble away to powder.

There are a great number of snakes about here, though I have not yet seen one. I suspect that my mungoose or ichneumon keeps them away, as he is an inveterate enemy to all vermin. A venomous lizard, about a foot long, black, with yellow stripes down the sides, often comes into our verandah, but as soon as it hears the mungoose it disappears with all possible despatch; as do also the poisonous centipedes, of which there are several in the house. The noise of the mungoose is very peculiar, generally purring like a cat, but when angry it barks short and snappishly, while every hair on its long tail stands on end.

I have already mentioned to you that there are here the tiger, the lion, the monkey, the leopard, the buffalo, the elephant (tame), the spotted deer, the jackal, the flying fox: all these I shall describe as the opportunities offer; now I shall tell you something about the monkey.

I was walking out early in the morning, and reached a very large pepul-tree, covered with its red berries. Presently I heard some one chattering over my head, and looking up beheld an enormously long ape as tall as myself, with a white face and great whiskers. He gazed at me for a moment, and then chattered again. The noise becoming louder and louder, I ran from under the tree, and soon saw a great number of these animals of different sizes come leaping down, and, after a stare, as much as to say "don't follow us," they made a few tremendous leaps, and escaped into the jungle.

The Indian buffalo has no hump on its back. It is like an immense black cow, but exceedingly fierce. As yet I have seen only tame ones. A gentleman who lives here was walking out in the jungle the other evening, with the intention of shooting some birds, when he saw before him a large bull buffalo. When alone these creatures are much more fierce than when with the herd. He did not, therefore, much relish his close acquaintance; and, turning round, strove to creep quietly away. Hearing a loud roar behind him, he looked back, and beheld the buffalo in full chase after him, tossing his head most furiously. The gentleman scarcely knew what to do, as there was no tree near into which he might climb; but he was surrounded by low bushes. Turning suddenly round, therefore, he stood still, and, looking steadfastly at the buffalo, loaded his gun. On came the animal, nearer and nearer, looking fiercer and fiercer. At last, when about twenty yards off, he stopped one minute as if in hesitation, and then, with a loud roar, turned his head, and, tearing up the ground with his hoofs, was on the point of rushing onward, when the gentleman raised his gun as a last resource, and fired.

The ball entered through the eye into the brain, and the monster rolled over the plain.

I have since seen the skull and the horns, which are of great size. The elephants are very large, and there are none but tame ones here. The major of the regiment quartered at this place has offered to lend us one whenever we are inclined for a ride.

The jackals are a source of great annoyance at night: they come into the compound and howl round the house, and make a dreadful noise, but are not dangerous. There are swarms of wild dogs too here, called pariah dogs—quite harmless. They resemble a hairy greyhound with a fox's head. The flying-fox is a sort of bat. Its large black wings are nearly four feet from tip to tip, and the body is like a small fox. They fly about the trees at night, and pick the fruit and berries. The birds are very beautiful. There are many sorts of doves and pigeons. One sort of the last-named is quite green; as is also the fly-catcher, which has a long single feather in the middle of his tail. The mango is about the size of a pigeon, yellow, with green stripes. There are also the pretty little amadavad, and many others.

I am making a collection of large beetles.

Midnapore is situated on a high table-land, or flat-topped hill, about six miles across, and is much cooler than the greater part of India. The soil is about a foot deep, and underneath it is a volcanic rock, so porous that the rain soaks into it as soon as it falls, thus rendering the place dry and healthy. From the middle of June to the middle of October there are tremendous storms of rain almost every day. Then it is cool and pleasant till February. After that time the heat increases, and the weather is quite dry until April; from which time until June it is intensely hot, with occasional hurricanes and thunderstorms, of which we have had several most magnificent ones lately; and from the height of the hills we seem almost to be in the midst of them.

Indigo, rice, and grain are plentiful. The first is obtained by soaking the leaves of the plant in water until they are rotten, when they deposit a thick blue sediment, which is formed into cakes, and is used for dyeing cloths.

We have some wild silkworms, from which the natives manufacture a coarse sort of silk. The rice grows in fields which are under water, and looks like barley. These fields beautifully illustrate the expression in the Bible about casting your seed upon the waters, and after many days you shall find it again.

The greatest expenses here are servants and house-rent. I pay for my house, which is one of the cheapest in Midnapore, forty rupees a-month; a rupee is two shillings. I keep as few domestics as I can; but am obliged to have eleven men and one woman. The men are—

1 consummar, or headman.
1 kitmajar, or waiter at table.
1 sirdar, who attends to lamps, furniture, &c.
1 bearer, who works the punkah and helps the sirdar.
1 dirgee, or tailor, who mends stockings, and makes gowns, coats, shirts, &c.
2 maistrees, or carpenters.
2 mollees, or gardeners.
1 motee, who sweeps the rooms and keeps them in order.
1 beastee, or water-carrier.

We neither feed nor clothe them: indeed their food consists of nothing but rice, except the consummar and kitmajar, who are Mussulmans. Their pay varies from three to ten rupees a-month. Many people keep forty or fifty men. The sirdar, or bearer, sleeps on a mat in the verandah; the others in houses in the compound. They are all forbidden by their religion to do the work of any other; their fathers and grandfathers performed the same duties, and so will their sons and grandsons also. They are a thievish set, and we dare not leave anything in their way that they can steal.

There is at this moment a little grey squirrel hopping about in the verandah,—facing the gate of the compound are several tame buffaloes,—and a little beyond is an elephant lying down basking in the sun and lashing his trunk about upon the grass.

There is an insect here called the flying-bug; it resembles in appearance a very large ant with wings, and, if one of them flies through the room, it leaves so disagreeable a smell that it can hardly be borne for an hour afterwards.

September 15.

TO-DAY is a rustic festival; the carpenters and all other workmen have a holiday, and, daubing all their tools with red paint, cover them with flowers. and then kneel down and worship them, and beg them to work well and not to break during the next year. This is called the "poujah of tools."

October 9, 1842.

WE have had several thunderstorms here. A few days ago I saw a large black cloud coming up against the wind. Gradually it spread until it covered the whole sky. The wind now died away for a few minutes, and then rose again and seemed to rush from all quarters of the heavens at once, and formed a sort of whirlwind round Midnapore; then from the darkest part of the cloud flashed a vivid streak of lightning, followed almost immediately by a terrific clap of thunder. For three hours the storm continued, and scarcely three minutes elapsed between each clap, while we saw the lightning running along the ground for several yards.

The other morning two men who lived in Midnapore caught a cobra de capello, or hooded snake, and they were examining it when suddenly it bit them both, and they died in the course of half an hour. We have not yet seen any snakes in our house, although most people frequently find them. This, as I think I told you, I attribute to our keeping the mungoose, of which the snakes are much afraid.

The chikary, or huntsman, makes a large oval shield, which he covers over with leaves: in the upper part are two very small holes. When he perceives a bird he crouches down behind his screen, keeping a watch through the two little holes, and creeping on very slowly. When he has approached near enough, he thrusts forward a long thin stick like a fishing-rod, and touches the bird with one end of it, on which there is a little lime; the bird sticks to it, and then the man draws back the pole and secures the animal.

In this way a great number of partridges are taken, with snipes, woodcocks, pigeons, &c. I had two hoopoes given me the other day. The Major who commands this station has four elephants for the use of the troops under him, to carry their tents when they are marching; and whenever we like it he lends us one for a ride. On the back of the elephant is placed a large pad, and on that is a thing like a great cradle, with two seats in it. A man sits on the neck with his feet in stirrups of rope, and a pointed piece of iron in his hand, which he presses behind the elephant's ears to guide him. Another man runs by the side and encourages the animal in Hindustanee. When we want to get on his back, the man on the neck presses the iron rod on the middle of the animal's head, and he kneels down; a ladder is immediately brought, and we climb up into the seat, or houdah, as it is called, and then the huge monster rises again. His pace is very slow and very jolting. He is not allowed to pass over any bridges, lest his weight should shake them down; he accordingly goes through the water instead. Neither may he go where he is likely to meet many horses, lest he should frighten them.

My costume here would make you smile. I wear thin shoes, white stockings, white trowsers, a short black cassock reaching a little below the knees, and a hat made of pith covered with black merino—the crown is about four inches high, and the rim about six or seven inches wide. This is my out-of-door dress. In-doors, unless when any one calls, I wear a white jacket instead of the cassock. I am without any waistcoat. At a dinner-party, black silk socks, black trowsers, and my long black silk cassock.

The only coins in use at Midnapore are the pice and the rupee; the pice is worth a farthing and a half, and the rupee about two shillings. Another kind of money passes here, viz. a little shell called a cowrie, of which 120 are worth a pice. At Madras and Calcutta there are many other sorts.

The insects are a great nuisance here. If the candles were not protected by a glass shade they would be instantly extinguished. Thousands of insects of all sizes swarm, jumping and flying about the lamps, of all colours, green, yellow, blue; and many of them sting, whilst others smell most abominably.

Every morning the mollie, or gardener, brings in a basket of vegetables for us to look at, and select what we shall require for the day's consumption. The cold weather here begins about the middle of October, generally on the 15th, and we are all looking very anxiously for it; but by cold I mean only such a lower degree of heat as will enable us to go out in the middle of the day (provided we carry a great parasol), which we cannot do now.

At a dinner-party every one brings his or her own table servant. This assemblage has a very pretty appearance: the ladies are all in white dresses and short sleeves, and the gentlemen in white jackets and trowsers, except the Major and myself; he wears a red jacket, and I a black cassock. Behind each chair stands a dark-brown man with long black beard and mustachios, dressed in a sort of white tunic and a white turban, with a coloured sash wound several times round the waist. As it would be the greatest mark of disrespect for a servant to appear in the presence of his master with covered feet, they all leave their shoes outside the door. After the meat is cleared away, before the puddings are brought in, the servants go out and smoke for five minutes. There is not a man, either Mussulman or Hindoo, except of the very lowest caste, who would eat anything that came from the table of a European. They would consider it a degradation, and would not even drink out of anything we had ever used, or touch what we had cooked. The Hindoos eat only once a-day, unless on their grand feasts. Their food then is boiled rice, with perhaps an onion and a little spice in it, which they eat with their hands.

The language of this country, though confessedly a compound of two or three Eastern tongues, appears to me to have many remains of what must have been the original language of man, that is to say, those which must have existed from the very earliest time bear a close propinquity to the words of other and later languages. Several instances which came under my notice bear out this opinion.

It is curious to observe how the different castes or ranks here keep distinct, and it is this which renders so many servants necessary. The man who lays the cloth would feel degraded by dusting a chair, and he who dusts the chair would rather leave his place than dust the room. Again, two men of different castes will neither eat, drink, nor sleep together. Their bed is a mere mat, which explains well that saying of our Saviour, "Take up thy bed and walk."

The other day my basin had not been emptied. I told the carah of it, whose business it is to attend to my apartment, and he went a hundred or more yards to call the matee, because it would have been beneath his dignity to throw the water out into the adjoining bath-room. The men here are a sadly idle set; they make almost slaves of their wives. Early in the morning we may see troops of women going out into the jungle, from which they return in the evening with great fagots of wood; these fagots are about twelve feet in length, and in the middle quite two in thickness, and are carried on the head. The poor creatures are obliged continually to stop and rest.

The higher classes of the natives wear a kind of loose white gown, down to the knees, and very loose trowsers, also white embroidered slippers, no stockings, and a white turban. The lower classes wear nothing but a long white cloth tied round their hips.

Every one here, both native and European, takes a cold bath at least once a-day. When a native dies his body is burnt, and to make the funeral pile every native keeps four or five large trees growing in his garden. As soon as he dies, one, or two, or three trees, according to the man's rank, are cut down and surrounded with a great quantity of dry stubble, on which the body is placed. Formerly, his wife was burnt alive at the same time. This was called a sati. There are a great many tombs of holy men about the country, and on these the people throw little wooden images. There is one tomb here on which are placed two large dumb-bells, and the people imagine that every Sunday night the man who is buried there rises up and plays with them. There is one very disagreeable custom here, which exists more or less all over India; it is called dustoorie. Whenever anything is bought, for every rupee that is paid the seller is obliged to give the servant of the purchaser two pice; so that the more he has to buy, the better it is for the servant; and if a master were to say he would not allow dustoorie, no native would enter his service.

I have just been to look at the man who is making me some white jackets. The women here never do any needlework. The men sit down on the floor, and hold the work between the great toe and the next.

I was the other day in want of a sheet of pith, on which to fasten some butterflies, and, going into my dressing-room, where I knew I had left four pieces on a shelf only the day before, I found them apparently in good condition; but, on taking them up, discovered them to be only so much dust. I then examined the other things upon the shelf, and found them to be in the same state. This was the work of the white ant, which was swarming about. I called the carah and sent him to the bazaar, or the place where all the little shops are, and told him to procure me sixteen pice worth of turpentine, and when it was brought I spread it over the shelf, and, soaking into the wood, it destroyed the ants. If let alone they would, in about two days, have eaten the chest of drawers, all my clothes, and everything in the room. I have just been engaged in catching with a green net on the end of the bamboo a most beautiful swallow-tailed butterfly, and in doing so frightened away a jackal, who was so impertinent as to intrude into the compound in the middle of the day.

Midnapore, November 11, 1842.

A FRIEND has just made me a present of a very small kind of monkey, about nine inches high, of a light-brown colour. His antics are often very amusing. I fasten him by a chain to a thick pole in the compound, at the top of which is his house. He will sometimes turn his waterpot upside down and sit on it in the gravest possible manner. He will then perhaps stoop down and gather a blade of grass, and examine it as attentively as though he were inquiring to what species and genus it belonged.

Perhaps by this time several large knowing-looking crows, something like English magpies, will have collected round him, holding their heads on one side and looking as if they were listening very attentively to his lecture on botany. Presently you would see the sly little monkey turn his eye to see how near they are, and then with one bound he will catch hold of the nearest crow by the neck; but the crow is the stronger of the two and always gets away safe. These crows are as common as sparrows and quite as tame, for they will hop into the verandah and pick up anything the parrots drop. We have two parrots; they are of a kind very common here; so I told a man to go out and catch me a couple, as I wanted to teach them to talk. He did so, and they are now getting very tame. I gave him a few pice for his trouble. They are of a kind that I do not remember ever to have seen in England. The upper mandible is red, the lower black. From the lower mandible extends on each side a broad black stripe, to where we suppose the ears to be; and there is another black stripe from one eye to the other. These stripes give the bird a very peculiar appearance. The upper circle resembles a pair of tortoiseshell spectacles.

I had a young hyæna given to me, which I made every endeavour to tame, giving him milk and food, but nevertheless as soon as I approached he flew at me. As he has scarcely any teeth I did not fear him, but took him in my arms, being careful to keep a tight hold on his neck. He slept during the day, but showed an inclination to go out at night, but, not being permitted to do so, continued making the most extraordinary noises resembling the sobbing of a child in pain. The servants were all afraid of him. Having kept us awake that night, I resolved the next to try him outside the house, and accordingly, fastening him up, I gave him a box to sleep in. The next morning I found he was dead. The servants declared he had been killed by a pack of jackals, but I shrewdly suspected they themselves to have been guilty.

The other day I caught one of those beautiful little squirrels which I have before described. It is grey, with a broad yellow stripe down each side. The body is about as big as my thumb, and the tail the size of my middle finger. I borrowed a common squirrel's cage, but the little thing was so small that it immediately struggled through the wires, and the mungoose, perceiving it, killed and devoured it. A great many of them live in the thatch of our house.

The musk-rat is a small sharp-snouted animal, from which musk may be extracted. The scent rising from it is overpowering. All the houses here swarm with them, but the mungoose has either killed or driven away all that were here, and our house therefore is quite free from the smell. The mungoose is very destructive. I just left the room for a few minutes, and while absent it commenced demolishing some eggs which I had brought in from the fowl-house: there were eight on the table; he had broken five over my papers and then dipped his paws in the ink and ran over the table. Whilst punishing him for this fault I held him by the neck, but he nevertheless managed to give me a severe scratch with his claws. He is a thorough beast of prey, and will eat nothing but animal food except sugar.

The prawns here are most delicious, and many of them are as large as a good-sized lobster. I was crossing my compound in the dusk a few evenings ago, after feeding my fowls and ducks. I walked slowly, thinking of England and my children, when I happened suddenly to cast my eyes upon the ground. I started back on perceiving within two paces of me the dreaded cobra de capello—its head raised, its hood expanded, and manifesting every sign of anger. Two, or at most three, steps more, and I should have trodden upon it and received the fatal bite. Unfortunately I had no stick in my hand; I called the servants to bring bamboos, but by the time they came it had glided into its hole, and I went home thanking the Supreme Being who had saved me from the fearful danger. Since that time I have not been out without a large bamboo in my hand, for, although I have stopped up the hole, yet the cobra de capello is, no doubt, still in my compound. The bite of this snake is most deadly.

During the last fortnight I have heard of three persons having been killed by it in Midnapore. Two of them were hunters, the other was one of the wives of the Rajah. She put her hand into a cupboard to procure something, when a cobra, which had concealed itself there, bit her. When a person is wounded by this venomous reptile he generally expires within an hour. The only possible cure, and that is an uncertain one, is to swallow every few minutes a glass of brandy with some eau de luce, or smelling-salts, dissolved in it, while a man stands near beating you with a heavy whip. Or, instead of this, you may be fastened to a carriage and be compelled to run as fast as possible. The object is to keep you awake, for the danger of the bite consists in the heavy lethargy it produces. The remedies applied, however, are sure to bring on a violent fever, which frequently proves fatal. Few diseases in this country last longer than an hour or two. Fever, cholera, and inflammation of the liver, the three great scourges of India, commonly prove fatal within from two to twelve hours, so that no one can exist here without being constantly reminded of the uncertainty of human life. It is curious that I, who dreaded so greatly the reptiles of India, should have been at once sent to the station where they most abound, for there is probably no place in Bengal where serpents and lizards are so plentiful. Our house is infested by numbers of centipedes, which get on the chairs and on the clothes in a most unpleasant manner. However, we have neither of us yet been bitten.

I have not seen a scorpion alive. My wife and I were walking in the compound the other day, when we saw a very large snake looking at us through the hedge of aloes. It was of a light-brown, and was, I think, five or six feet long.

The other day my servants brought me in a venomous snake which they said they had killed in the compound; I took it up by its tail and carried it into my wife's dressing-room to show it to her. I laid it down on the floor, and soon it began to wriggle away, and, raising its head, turned at us. Fortunately there was a stick at hand, and, taking it up, I killed the animal with one blow. So great is the dread of them here, that no one ever sleeps without a light, lest, stepping out of bed at night, he should place his foot upon some venomous creature; most people keep a long bamboo in every room. We never put on our shoes without first examining well to see that there is nothing alive in them. The oil which we burn in the evening and at night is extracted from the cocoa-nut and has a most agreeable smell. For this purpose cocoa-nuts are brought from Ceylon and all the neighbouring islands. This oil could not be used in England, because it congeals into a sort of fat when the thermometer is at 64°.

We have a kind of root here which they call a yam, although I do not think it is one. It is brown outside and white within; about two feet long and thickest at the middle, where it is four inches in diameter. This they boil and then fry into lumps; it is exceedingly nice. Potatoes are scarce, dear, and bad, except sweet ones, which I like; they are very stringy, and taste like potatoes mixed with sugar.

I think I have described to you the graceful appearance of the bamboo-tree, but it is its extreme usefulness that renders it so precious. It is a sort of hollow strong cane, and serves for the upright posts at the corners of the native houses and also for the door-posts. To our own bungalows or thatched houses it forms the rafters to support the thatch; it is used for scaffolding and for ladders without any shaping or preparing. One joint of it makes a very good bottle; a long piece of it, with one side cut off and the stoppage at the joints cut away, makes a waterspout or watercourse, or a thing for fowls to eat or drink out of. In short, it would be tedious to enumerate the many uses to which it is put.

I had the other day an instance of the extent to which servants carry the system of doing each his own work and no one's else. I had been feeding the parrots with a little rice and had spilt a few grains of it upon the table. I called the barah, or furniture-cleaner: he said it was the parrot's food, and therefore it was the waiter's business to clean it up. I told him to do as he was bid, but he would not, and then I said that if he did not I should discharge him with a character for disobedience; this he preferred to doing what he considered was not his own work, so I sent him away at once.

None of my servants can speak a word of English, and I am sometimes rather at a loss on this account; but I always keep a dictionary on the table, and I am rapidly acquiring a knowledge of the Hindustanee language. There are no shops that Europeans can go to, except at Calcutta. In the country, which is called the Mofussil, a sort of pedlers come round with goods. I offer them generally one-third of the price they name, and they in most cases take it. The other day, my wife was making up her accounts, and asked the kitmajar how much he had given for a certain article; the man said, "Three rupees." My wife replied that she did not think he had given so much; he answered, "Yes, three rupees." She said, "Now, I don't believe you gave more than two rupees;" to which his answer was, "Yes, I gave two rupees." Still she did not credit him, and said, "Now, I am sure you only gave one rupee;" and he replied, "Yes, one rupee." And he was quite satisfied: and all this time he answered as calmly as possible, and did not appear in the least ashamed; and yet this man is one who is considered a very good servant, and whom I believe to be as honest as any one I have.

November 12.

Last night, a little before ten o'clock, my wife was gone to bed, and I was sitting up reading and writing. In this country, you may know, the servants at each house, instead of having a clock, strike a gong at every hour. It is a flat circular plate of bell-metal, which, when struck with a wooden mallet, gives forth a very loud ringing sound. Just before the gong struck ten, I heard a noise like that of a buggy (or gig with a large head to it to keep the sun off) approaching.* I thought to myself, "Why, there must be a party somewhere to-night;" at which I wondered not a little, because every one asks the Padre Sahib to their parties, and I had received no invitation. The next moment the noise seemed to increase, and become like the motion of a large heavy carriage. Almost immediately after, with a sound like rolling thunder, the whole house rocked backwards and for-

* It is the most common sort of carriage in India.

wards, while I was nearly thrown off the chair on which I was sitting.

The rumbling continued, I should think, for about a minute before the shock of the earthquake came, and for about a quarter of a minute after, while the shock itself may have occupied about ten minutes.

I was quite startled; and, proceeding to my wife's bedroom, advised her to get up and put on something warm, lest we should have to pass the night out of doors. I then went to the storeroom, and made the best provision I could for a bivouac: my preparations were, however, needless, as the shock was not repeated.

I can compare the motion to nothing so well as to the pitching of a small boat in a short cross-sea, or where two tides meet one another. My wife said her bed gave two distinct pitches up and down. While I was making my preparations for departure I heard a loud noise of crows, ducks, fowls, and all sorts of birds, cawing, cackling, and screaming, as if they were very much frightened. The natives all round started up and blew their conchs (a sort of shell, which they use instead of a trumpet); and this morning every one is talking about the earthquake.

Speaking of the natives reminds me of the subject of the population of India, which is very much exaggerated. It cannot be compared, in proportion to the extent of the country, to that of England. There are said to be 40,000 natives in Midnapore, though I much doubt the fact; and then on every side, farther than the eye can reach, extends a vast expanse of thick jungle (that is, bushes growing so close together as to be altogether impassable, and full of tigers, deer, leopards, buffaloes, elephants, &c.); and as the same is the case throughout the whole of India, I should think that nine-tenths of the country consists of thick, close jungle, or enormous swamps. Here and there, amidst all this, is found a small native village, composed of a few huts; but the population in such places is probably not above one in thirty square miles on the average; this is, of course, a mere rough guess. The jungle-men, who are nearly black, though not at all resembling the negro in feature, are said to be the original inhabitants of the country. Their religion is unknown, and I believe they possess no written language. The people were driven into the bushes by the lighter race of men, whom many suppose to have been some of the ancient Egyptians, probably not less than two or three thousand years ago. Amongst this race sprang up, even subsequently to this, the religion, or rather superstition, of Hindooism. Again, about seven or eight hundred years ago, the whole country was overrun and conquered by the Mohammedans. Seventy or eighty years ago we obtained a firm footing in a small portion of the country. Not long after, the Mahratta chiefs attacked the Mohammedans in various places; the Mohammedans called upon us for assistance; and thus we in time became possessors of almost the whole country.

The greatest difficulty in the pronunciation of the language is the letter *h*, which is always aspirated, and never pronounced as as it is in our *th*, and yet this letter often comes after a consonant.

The money in the Mofussil, or country, is a source of much annoyance. If you want to change a ten-pound note, they give you no gold, but 100 rupees; if you want change for a rupee, they give you 64 pice; and if you change a pice, they give you 24 cowries. But as there are no shops, and all the people bring their goods to the house, this does not signify much.

If you were to go to Midnapore, and to ask a native where Acland Sahib lived (sahib means white gentleman), he would not be able to tell you; but if you were to ask for the Padre Sahib, he would immediately direct you to my house.

When I came here I was going to stay with the judge: I told the palanquin-bearers to take me to his house, mentioning his name, and we were carried to almost every house in the station; until at last we met a European, who told the men it was the judge sahib we wanted, and then they soon found the place. I am called Padre Sahib; Mrs. Acland is Padre Sahib ke Mem, or Padre Sahib's lady; a married woman, mem sahib; an old maid is mem; and a young lady is bibi sahib, or white lady baby.

The weather is now, comparatively speaking, delightful; the thermometer is 76° in the middle of the day, and about 66° at sunrise and early in the morning. I assure you we find it quite chilly, and are obliged to walk very fast to get warm. Our hours are now—up at six, feed the fowls, and walk till eight; bathe and dress till nine, then breakfast; write, read, and work till four, then dinner; feed the fowls and walk till half-past six; tea at seven. My wife works and I read aloud till half-past eight; backgammon or cribbage till half-past nine; then prayers, and to bed. Sometimes, however, I have to go out and see my parishioners between breakfast and dinner, and then I go in my palanquin. One great disagreeable is, the constant change of people.

The regiment that was here, of which the Major and his wife were our chief friends, has just been ordered away, and a new one is come in its place. The Captain of Engineers has just offered to take us a trip to the mountains, fifty miles off, on elephants. I do not know yet whether we shall go or not. The historical name of my parish would be, the Ooriah district, or the Oresta. Our time is six hours earlier than in England.

Midnapore, December 13, 1842.

I AM on the point of quitting this place for Cuttack. I have sold the greater part of my furniture, as it is expensive to move; the remainder is going forward on hackeries, or native carts. I want six of these carts; about a dozen of them are come, and there is now a crowd of native savages round the door, disputing as to who shall go; and they were making so much noise that I was compelled to go out and stop the cabal. I took a good thick stick in my hand, as if I were about to beat them. I called out "Choop!" (or silence) as loud as I could. I then explained that I only wanted six hackeries. Then began a vociferation as to whose were the best. "Choop!—will ye choop?" I roared again. I then called the mollee, and desired him to turn out all the bullocks, for they had unfastened those which drew the carts, and let them all loose in the rice-ground in the compound, which was just ready for cutting. This order I hallooed out loud enough for the men to hear; and told him, as soon as he had done that, to come to me for a crowbar to break to pieces all the hackeries but six. This made them submit; and although they still continued making a great chattering, yet they soon began harnessing their bullocks. With these people we are obliged to appear very severe. They despise us as being of no caste; and were we not to be firm, they would imagine we were afraid of them.

We are now engaged in packing up our things, and shall start on the 25th, reach Balasore on the 28th, and remain there ten days, and then three days' more travelling will bring me to my head-quarters at Cuttack.

I have, with much trouble, endeavoured to persuade the people here that they ought to build a church: the Mohammedans have a splendid mosque, the Hindoos have a large temple, and yet we have no consecrated building for the worship of the true God; but, however, I hope this will be remedied. As I was passing the mosque the other day, I saw the muezzin shouting out that it was time for prayer, and stopping his ears with both hands, that he might not hear the terrible noise which he himself was making.

About a fortnight ago the judge went out shooting: he came to a large hole under the root of a tree, and heard a loud growling. He is a courageous man, so he was not afraid; but he told an Indian, who was with him, to get behind the tree, and then poke a long stick into the hole. Presently the growling became very loud and savage, and then out jumped an enormous bear, one of the most savage sort—the large black bear. The judge was ready, and shot it when it came out. On examining the hole, three young bears, only a few days old, were found. He sent for some Indians, who carried the dead body, and also the cubs, home, and then, as he knew that I was fond of animals, he sent the three little ones to me. They are very ugly, and cannot see yet. One of my goats had just had a kid, so I told the cook to make the kid into soup, and I brought the goat to the young bears. One man held the goat, another covered her eyes with his hands, and a boy held up the cubs to suck. The goat did not like it at all at first, but now she is quite contented, almost as much so as if they were her own young ones. I have given two of them away. In England you never taste goat's milk: it is most delicious; far better, I think, than cow's milk: we use it every day. Each goat, after the kid is taken from her, gives about three-quarters of a pint a-day. The judge has promised me a bottle full of the pure bear's grease.

Every one here knows that I am very fond of animals, and they are all very kind in sending them to me. I received the other day from a gentleman a present of a goat, which is quite as big as a small pony. If I were to get on its back my feet would not touch the ground; it is of a dark brown, and of the long-eared Thibet kind.

December 14.

I WENT out to tea last evening, and a lady gave me two nests made of platted grass, into which the birds enter through a hole at the bottom. They are about a yard long, and they hang swinging from the branch of a tree to which they are fastened. They are built in this form, in order to keep out the violent rains, and to preserve the birds from the monkeys.

The commonest articles of dress in Calcutta are at least three times as dear as they are in England. I bought a silk hat which would have cost five shillings at home, and paid fourteen rupees for it here; and some ribbon, which would have been threepence a-yard in England, cost a rupee and a half here. Then on the other hand many things are cheaper.

There has been no rain for two months, nor a cloud until the last day or two; now the clouds will continue to increase for a week, and then we shall have three days of rain, after that no more till the middle of June, except about three tremendous thunderstorms in April and May. The weather is now delightful:

the thermometer varies from 60° to 80°; but I am glad of cloth clothes, and at night we have three blankets and a heavy counterpane. At this time of the year we have peas, beans, &c., and every one looks happy and cheerful, not healthy, for Europeans are all of a deadly white, and most of them exceedingly fat.

December 16.

I WAS walking in the compound yesterday, and I saw something black, shaped very much like a small lobster, except that it had a pointed tail; and as soon as I went near it it turned its tail over its head and tried to sting me. I managed to get him into a bottle, which I filled with spirits.

The mungoose is very fond of serpents; he kills and eats them with great rapidity, and then jumps into my wife's lap to ask for some milk.

Balasore, Orissa, December 30, 1842.

THE ancient house in which I live here is situated, like the rest of Balasore, on a large flat plain, extending north, south, and west, as far as I can see. The vegetation is scanty, and the trees are small. But turn towards the east and the eye is arrested by a most magnificent sight. At the distance of about seven miles rises quite abruptly from the plain a splendid range of volcanic hills, about two thousand feet in height. Judging from their appearance at this distance, they must be composed of reddish lava without any grass, but here and there a stumpy bush. I never saw anything to compare with them before. In England our hills are always rounded at the top; but here there are points and peaks and edges, as if you had been trying to cut a piece of paper in zigzag lines.

About fifteen miles beyond these great hills tower a still loftier range, lifting their deep-blue summits seven thousand feet into the clouds, and forming a background for the nearer and better-defined range.

On Monday we start with a picnic party and tents, &c., to explore these hills. We shall probably be out on our expedition for three or four days.

After standing gazing at these magnificent hills, I walked towards what appeared to be the remains of some mud hut: it was about five feet high, and in irregular blunt points at the top. When I came down to it I tried to break off one of the long bits, but it was too strong, and was as hard as a wall. However, on the other side I found a smaller projection, which I broke off by kicking against it, and found it full of round passages perforating it in all directions, the smallest about the size of a quill, the largest as big as my wrist. This was the large white ants' hill. Immediately after I had broken a portion of it there came a rush of the inhabitants from all the passages to see what was the matter. They examined the parts broken, and then some of them ran back. Presently a number more came, some dragging forward the others until they got them quite to the edge, when a bigger ant took hold of each of these prisoners and bit him in the neck until he killed him. I suppose the prisoners were those who had been on guard at that spot, or else those who built that part, and so were punished for my fault. Soon, however, they turned and attacked me, for I found many of them on my clothes and experienced the smart of their bite.

I now walked forward, and the next thing I came to was a human skull. In this part of the country wood is scarce, and therefore, when any poor person dies, instead of burning his body, they wait till evening, and then throw it out of doors, and by the next morning the jackals and vultures have picked the bones quite clean, and the ants then destroy all the fibres, whilst the sun bleaches the bones. I have picked up several of these skulls in the last few days; they appear very different from the skull of an European, being smaller, and very much narrower from ear to ear in proportion to the length from the eye to the back of the head; the forehead also retreats much more. Presently I came to two bamboo-trees; between them on the ground was a pair of doves, much smaller than our English ones, and of a bright reddish purple. They were walking about, whilst out of one of the bamboo-trees poked the head of a great snake, who was quietly watching them. I frightened away the doves, as I guessed the long gentleman's intentions. It is of a kind which does not hurt men, of a dirty-brown colour, about seven feet long.

Turning towards the house again, I was struck by the very beautiful plumage of a bird; its wings were striped transversely with black and white; it was about the size of a blackbird, with yellow neck and tail, and a very long head. It alighted on the ground and opened a most beautiful round crest growing fore and aft on its head, the colour of which, like the body, was an orange yellow, but there was an edging of white and black. It was the hoopoe. The only other striking thing I saw was a great vulture, with its naked red head and its tattered-looking feathers, puffing away at the top of our house, having most likely stuffed with human flesh till he could hardly move; and when I threw a stone at him, he hopped a little way along the roof and grunted.

January 2, 1843.

YESTERDAY was New Year's day. I have just heard the origin of these hills, and will put it down while I remember it. The story is from one of the natives here.

"Many, many years ago there lived a giant in Ceylon, and this giant fell in love with the daughter of another giant at Lucknow, in Bengal, so he asked her father to let him marry her. But he said No, as the other lived in a little island, and was no real gentleman at all. Upon this Master Ceylon determined that, as her father said No, he would take her without leave, and off he started, seized the young lady, put her on his shoulders, and carried her across to Ceylon. But when the papa found that his daughter was gone, he got into a tremendous rage, and determined to go and punish the Ceyloney. So off he hurried, until he came to the straits which separate the island from the mainland. But when he tried to cross over, he found that he was not quite so tall as the Ceylonese gentleman by a few hundred yards, and that the water was too deep for him. So he stood still, and he scratched his head and wiped his forehead with his handkerchief, and thought and pondered what he should do to get across and punish the wicked thief. At last an idea struck him, and he trotted back all up India until he reached the Himalaya mountains, and, snatching up two of the largest of them, one in each hand, threw them into the straits, and thus made them shallow enough for him to pass over. But as he went along some of the rocks and earth slipped through his fingers, for you may suppose his hands were rather full; and the chains of hills which extend from Balasore for nearly three hundred miles are the pieces which he dropped as he went along." The tale does not inform us whether the giant's daughter was restored to him.

I have not been up the hills to-day, because some of the party were frightened at the number of bears and tigers which are said to be there; but I am in hopes we shall go in a few days. I have been looking about me a good deal lately, and have noticed one very curious thing. The ground for five or six miles from our house in one direction seems to be covered with mounds of earth and small bushes; on examining these closely, however, I find they are all the nests of white ants. The green ones are those that are deserted, and over which the grass has grown—the others are still inhabited. In the plain visible from my window there must be many hundreds of thousands of these hills, varying in height from three feet to ten or twelve, and many of them six feet in diameter; and all of these are formed by little insects no larger than the common English ant. One part of their manner of building is most extraordinary: their nests are always completely covered in, so that without kicking them you cannot see a single ant inside; there are one or two doors in different parts of the building, but they are seldom used.

Their mode of building is as follows:—One day, perhaps, you

will perceive a single pinnacle of an ants' nest. You go and see it one day, and you find it slightly raised, but curved, like a headstone. So it increases daily until it reaches the size I have described. It is like a man building a house—as if he made a little closet with a roof on it, and then went inside and stayed there, while the closet swelled and swelled until it became a perfect house. At the foot of these ant-hills are a number of large black ants on the watch for any straggling white ants, which they kill and eat. These creatures abound in all our houses, and run about the floors: they are about an inch in length, and bite, but do not sting.

January 3.

I OUGHT to give you some account of our voyage to this place. We quitted Midnapore, after a hard week's packing, at nine o'clock on Tuesday evening, December 27th. On the Monday we went to dine and sleep at the house of the Captain of Engineers, because our own was in such a condition from packing; and after dinner on Tuesday at nine o'clock we entered our horrible palanquin. I flatter myself that most of the people at Midnapore were very sorry when we left. We had sixteen men to carry us, two mussalchees, or men who carry mussals (torches made of long strips of cotton bound tightly together and dipped in oil), and two banghy-bearers, to carry each two tin boxes with our clothes in them.

We soon got clear of the station of Midnapore, and then the scene became most wild and romantic—a narrow road, bounded on each side by an interminable jungle, or plain covered with low bushes so thickly matted together as to afford only passage to the deadly cobra, the snarling jackal, and the ravenous tiger. On the road our own palanquins, one a hundred yards in front of the other, carried by black men with merely a cloth round their loins, the red glaring torches showing the others who ran swiftly by their side, the banghy-bearers trying to keep up with us, and all keeping up a loud monotonous sing-song tune, which was varied occasionally by the shrill cry of the jackal, the grinning snarl of the hyæna, or in the distance the deeper roar of the tiger in search of his prey—and yet in the midst of all this we both slept well, awakened only occasionally by the plashing of the men through the fords of the river or the stopping at a village to change bearers.

In the latter case we were not detained an instant, the fresh relays being in attendance with as much patience and regularity as if they were horses waiting for a coach. Thus we travelled on without interruption until we reached Danton, called Dantoon. This was about nine o'clock in the morning. At this place there is a dâk-bungalow—that is, a bungalow, or thatched house, built by Government for the accommodation of travellers. In Turkey it would be called a caravanserai. Here there is a man with fire and water, but the traveller brings his own provisions, wine, tea, bread, &c., in his palanquin, though he can generally get eggs. We stayed here about two hours, and had some tea, eggs, and biscuits, and no one who has not experienced it can have any idea of the comfort of a short rest after a night of dâk travelling. Although you lie down in the palanquin, yet every limb gets cramped, and the incessant jolting is most painful to the bones, even of one so fat as I am, and I have increased sadly in bulk since I came to India. Off we started again a little before eleven, and at about one we reached the house of an Indigo-planter at Jelasore. I never saw him before, but he received us most hospitably. His wife was rejoiced to see us—she had not seen a European lady for seventeen months, for their nearest neighbours live at a distance of forty miles, or about twelve hours' journey. Here we spent a most agreeable day, delighted with everything. In the evening I took a walk with our kind host to see an old fort.

It must have been once very strong, and was probably built by the Mahrattas as a depôt for plunder when they overran this part of the country. In the inner court is a three-domed building, resembling, except in ornament, a mosque. The walls are several feet thick, built of hard stone strongly clamped together with iron. High up in the interior of the centre dome are four niches, which I hope to explore on some future occasion. The inner enclosure is surrounded by a strong stone wall and a deep moat now dry. Beyond this is a level space of a few yards in width, and then again, in another part of the wall, there are signs of a narrow sallyport, and opposite to this, between the trenches, as if it might have been reached by a drawbridge, is a very high mound of earth. Over the sallyport there has evidently been a strong tower, and above the central entrance into the interior building is a stone with an inscription. It appears very perfect, but no one can read it; it is neither Ooriah, Hindustanee, Sanscrit, nor Persian. I have called this a Mahratta fort, because that is the general opinion amongst Europeans. I myself doubt it, and from its age and appearance think it much more likely that it was erected by the Moguls when they first invaded the country; how I wished, as I stood there, that I could have seen it as it was in former ages, with its garrison, and its horsemen, and its despotic governor. The next time I go I shall provide myself with some paper covered with charcoal, and try to take an impression of the inscription. We were in some fear, during our examination, lest we should be interrupted by the natives, as they have very recently got the idea that it was once inhabited by one of their gods, and therefore consider it a sacred place. I fancied, as well as the darkness would allow me to see, that far back in one of the niches I could dimly perceive a coloured statue of a female. Before we went to see this ruin my kind host took me into his garden to show me the India-rubber tree. We scraped the bark with a piece of rough glass, and a white sticky juice oozed out; this we took between our fingers and squeezed until it became a sort of brown gluey substance. In this state it is used by the native hunters as birdlime. After being exposed to the air for some time it gradually hardens and becomes what we call India-rubber. A large part of this garden was planted with arrow-root.

At half-past eight we again entered the palanquin, and started for Balasore, where we arrived at half-past seven the next morning, and were set down at the Circuit-house—a large house belonging to Government, and kept for the convenience of officers, including the chaplain, who have to travel the district every year. I can conceive nothing more wild than the dâk travelling; but I have described it all, except that in each palanquin we carry a brace of loaded pistols. I will relate an instance, and a very remarkable one, of the advantage of carrying loaded pistols in this country. Major M., now the second in command at Midnapore, was one day out with some friends, sitting quietly under the shade of a bank, when suddenly a tiger sprang out of a jungle, seized the Major by the leg, threw him over his shoulders, and trotted off with him. The Major's companions raised a loud shout; but the beast was hungry, and did not choose to be frightened from his meal. The Major, however, fortunately had a brace of loaded pistols in his belt; he pulled out one, and fired it at the head of the tiger as it carried him off. It flashed in the pan; and almost in despair he seized the other, and shot the tiger dead on the spot. The only injury the Major received was a broken and lacerated leg, which has rendered him in some measure a cripple ever since. This story I know to be true, both from the Major himself and from those who were with him.

A small party went out for a day's pleasure a little while ago from Midnapore. They went to the Ghape, a most beautiful spot at about five miles' distance. After rambling about they went into an old house which is there, with an excellent appetite for dinner. The "cook-room" was about a hundred yards from the house. They waited and waited, and no dinner came; so at last one of the gentlemen went to see the cause of the delay, when lo! as if watching for the dinner, there was an enormous black bear sitting half-way between the house and the cook-room. They shouted, and tried to drive him away; but no, master Bruin only growled; he did not see why he should not have something to eat. None of the party had guns; and they say that they were kept waiting five hours without their dinner before the beast's patience was exhausted and he stalked off. We were, as I before said, set down at the "Circuit-house." This I expected to have found tolerably furnished; but, alas! when we went in, we found nothing but one mat, three tables, and two chairs. We then had the palanquins taken into a bed-room, and determined to make ourselves as comfortable as we could. I then went out to make calls—for in India the new comers call upon the old residents, reversing the English custom. This did not take me long, as the whole station consists of the magistrate and his wife, the excise-officer and his daughter, the postmaster, doctor, and deputy-magistrate.

At night we slept as well as we could in the palanquins, but were kept awake the greater part of the time by the mosquitoes, and the next morning our hands and faces were most beautifully spotted over with their bites. On this the second day one or two people called; and when the excise-officer and his daughter came in, the deficiency in furniture was at once made manifest. There were Mr. and Miss B., Mrs. Acland, and I, with only two chairs amongst us, and these, like all the chairs in India, were arm-chairs, so that we could not even manage by sitting two on one chair; so Miss B. and my wife had the two chairs, and Mr. B. and I sat upon the table—rather a high one it was—so that our feet dangled about half-way between our seat and the floor. However, there was one great advantage in this evidence of poverty, for Mr. B., as soon as he got home, sent us a large bedstead, some chairs, and other things necessary to make us comfortable.

I ought to mention the chant of the palanquin-bearers; though they keep to the same sing-song tune, yet they generally invent the words as they go along. I will give a sample, as well as I could make it out, of what my bearers sang the other night; I have tried to render their words as nearly as I could into English, so as to preserve the metre. The poetry must be improved. A palkee means a palanquin: it is the Hindustanee word, though one also generally used in conversation. Each line is sung in a different voice; in the following, for instance, the first line would be sung in the usual voice, the second very high, the third in a sort of gruff tone:—

"Oh, what a heavy bag!
No; it's an elephant:
He is an awful weight.

Let 's throw his palkee down—
Let 's set him in the mud—
Let 's leave him to his fate.
No, for he'll be angry then;
Ay, and he will beat us then
With a thick stick.
Then let 's make haste and get along,
Jump along quick."

And then, suiting the action to the word, off they set in a nasty jog-trot which rattled every bone in my body, keeping chorus all the time of "jump along quick, jump along quick," until they were obliged to stop for laughing. The second sample is from the men who carried Mrs. Acland, and is in quite a different metre. I must tell you that "cubbadar" means "take care," and "baba" (pronounced "barba") means "young lady:"—

1.

" She 's not heavy,
Cubbadar!
Little baba,
Cubbadar!
Carry her swiftly,
Cubbadar!
Pretty baba,
Cubbadar!
Cubbadar!
Cubbadar!

2.

Trim the torches,
Cubbadar!
For the road 's rough,
Cubbadar!
Here the bridge is,
Cubbadar!
Pass it swiftly,
Cubbadar!
Cubbadar!
Cubbadar!

3.

Carry her gently,
Cubbadar!
Little baba,
Cubbadar!
Sing so cheerily,
Cubbadar!
Pretty baba,
Cubbadar!
Cŭbbadar!
Cubbadar!"

At this place very little wood is to be found—not enough for the people to use for their fires during what is called the cold weather. The women accordingly go out, and instead of gathering wood they pick up cow-dung. This they knead into flat round cakes about the size of pancakes, dry them in the sun, and they burn almost as well as the turf or peat which is used in England, though it is a great nuisance, for the thick smoke it emits has a very unpleasant smell.

The other day we saw a most beautiful sight on the nearer hills. Some of the jungle (or wild) men had set fire to the grass and bushes on the side. The fire spread, shooting rapidly from one part to another, and as it was late in the evening it produced a most magnificent scene. The object in doing this was to get rid of the snakes, bears, and tigers, in order that the people might go and cut down the few large trees that grew on the hill.

Last night, as my wife and I were having a game of casino, we heard a low growl in the compound, and directly afterwards a screaming amongst the fowls, and a hallooing of the servants (we carry fowls wherever we go, or we should be almost starved); the only words I could distinguish were "Bargh! bargh!" A tiger! a tiger! I jumped up; but on examination it proved to be a false alarm. It was only a large wild animal, something resembling our fox, only with shorter legs and longer body, which had attacked the fowls; and I had not so much presence of mind as the Major I told you of, for when I ran out into the compound to see what was the matter I quite forgot to take my pistols, so the thief got safely off; but I have now secured my fowls more effectually.

Just before we left Midnapore, a large flock of birds, flying in regular order, amounting, I should think, to several thousands, passed over the place. They made a great noise, and I thought they were wild geese; but I hear they were a bird called the cyris, which stands about five feet high, and is not a water-bird.

I was much amused this afternoon whilst I was sitting in the verandah with watching the crows. I think I have described them to you. They are very like the carrion-crow in England, but rather smaller. There is a law which imposes a heavy fine upon any one who kills them; this is very right, for they carry away a quantity of refuse and filth which would otherwise putrefy and cause disease; but the consequence is, that they are more numerous and more impudent than the sparrows in England. I threw out the bones of a fowl we had had for dinner; presently about fifty crows came down within a few feet of me, and began to peck away; every now and then a bird, which people here call a kite, would swoop down, and send all the crows cawing away. As soon as it rose, down came the crows again; presently one of them flew away with a large bone in his beak; the kite saw it, and was off in pursuit. Backwards and forwards, up and down the poor crow dodged, but its pursuer followed it, and had nearly reached it, when the pursued thought it best to drop the bone. The sharp eye of the kite perceived this, and, although he was some distance above at the time, yet he made a dart down and caught the bone in his mouth before it had reached the ground. I have lately seen some kites like the others in all respects, except that the body and head are white, the wings being still brown; these are rather larger than the others.

Every sort of filth here is thrown out into the fields, and in a very few hours the jackals and crows clear it away, assisted by the pariah dogs. These are the only scavengers in the country.

The rain began on the 24th of December, and we had occasional showers for two days; but every one is disappointed by the season. Instead of having nice cool weather in January, the hot weather has completely set in, although it does not in general begin before the middle of February. The thermometer in the shade is at this moment above 80°, although this is considered a cool place.

For my dinner yesterday I had some peacock-cutlets, which the surgeon of the station had sent me.

Cuttack, February 2, 1843.

I MUST return now, and give you some account of how we started for this place from Balasore. On Sunday the 8th of January we had service in the morning; and at four in the afternoon we entered our palkees to proceed to Cuttack, a distance of 103 miles.

Throughout the journey not a single European is to be met with, but the traveller is entirely in the power of the natives, excepting such assistance as he can derive from his pistols and a thick stick. The danger however is not great. The Ooriahs, as well as the Bengalese, are a small and cowardly race; so much so, indeed, that the East India Company will not allow them to be enlisted as soldiers. A Bengalee of five feet six is quite a tall man, and in shape he is as delicate and effeminate as a European lady.

We jogged on most merrily until about half-past five the next morning, when I was awakened by hearing "Sahib, Sahib;" to which I sleepily answered by inquiring what my servant wanted. He told me we were arrived at Barripore, about fifty miles from Balasore, and they wanted to know whether I meant to go to the dâk-bungalow. I said Yes: for we had determined to remain at Barripore all day, as it is not safe to travel in the sun even in January. To the bungalow we accordingly went; where we eat, drank, and read books which we had brought with us, and amused ourselves as well as we could, until four in the afternoon, when off we started again. I only remember one adventure which happened there. My wife wanted to wash her hands, and took up a "gomlah" to pour out some water; suddenly she cried out that she was stung. I ran to see what it was, and, examining the gomlah, found she had been bitten by a hornet. In comparison with other insects the sting of this creature is an object of very little dread. Her hand, however, swelled a little, and for three or four hours she suffered a good deal of pain all up her arm, but still it was fortunately only a hornet. At four o'clock in the afternoon we again started, and arrived at our own house in Cuttack at about eight the next morning.

It is customary at the end of each stage to make the palkees a present of four annas (or sixpence) for each palkee. During one of the stages between Barripore and Cuttack the men did not go so quickly as I thought they should have done; so when we changed men I only gave them four annas for the two palkees, telling them why I did so. The consequence was, that during the next stage the men not only went much faster, but invented a new song, the whole burthen of which was, "He has only given them four annas because they went so slowly! Let us make haste and go along quickly, and then we shall get eight annas and have a good supper."

My house here belongs to Government, and I am in great hope they will allow me to occupy it free of rent; it is the best in the cantonment, the compound contains about twenty acres, and there are in it several beautiful clumps of trees. In front of the house is a fine group of cedars; in one part is a hill, on the top of which are several trees: I do not yet know their names, but their foliage is of a bright green, more bright than any ever seen in England. We have an orchard containing mangoes, custard-apples, waunpearls, mulberries, guavas, &c. &c., with one chur-tree—that is, the true India-rubber tree, and, I believe, the only one in this part of India; that at Jelasore is a very inferior sort.

We have a grand house in the compound, and have, besides, a flower-garden with orange and lemon trees, &c. A river three miles broad flows near, and a ghaut, or landing-place, for pilgrims proceeding to Juggernat'h, a Hindu holy temple. We can see in the distance a range of hills, rising abruptly from the other side of the river, which are a continuation of those at Balasore. On the sands are storks, wild-geese, and all sorts of aquatic birds; even all the tanks here abound with alligators. The other day one of the officers was returning home from mess; it was dark, and in his compound he fell over something which proved to be a large alligator, making its way from the river to a tank, probably with a view of there depositing her eggs. About three weeks ago a poor woman went to fetch water from one of these places, on the surface of which were weeds; she was engaged in clearing a space with her hands, when one of these animals, with its jaws open, caught her arm and stripped off all the flesh below the elbow. She was compelled to have her arm amputated.

I saw to-day a large hyæna gliding across the compound. I suppose he smelt some dead body on the beach. The Juggernat'h pilgrims come from very great distances, and many die on the road. In my compound alone, if I were to collect the skulls, bones, &c., I think I could make up eight or ten human skeletons. The other evening one of my servants came to me, and said, "If you please, sir, there is a dead pilgrim in the compound, and the matee wants to know if he shall throw it away;"—that is, throw it down on the bank for the jackals, &c. I would not let him do this, but sent notice to the commanding officer, who sent for the body, and, I suppose, threw it away. About two hours after this my wife was gone to bed, and I was sitting reading, when I felt something on my foot; I examined, and in my stocking found a large centipede. I contrived to kill him without being stung.

The Government allow me a guard of soldiers; and a sentry, with musket and bayonet, parades up and down the front verandah; they also allow three servants for the use of the church. The soldiers present arms to me and salute; and when any one comes at night, they call out, "Hookum dar?" to which the answer is "Exprin:" these phrases are corruptions of the English. The church is very nicely fitted up; there is a door leading into it from my study, which serves on Sundays as a vestry. The greatest inconvenience here—as in all the churches in India—consists in the punkahs. Over the pulpit, altar, and reading-desk are three small punkahs, and over the body of the building three very large ones, extending over the whole breadth. These are kept constantly in motion, and they sadly intercept the voice of whoever is preaching. The house, being a bungalow, has, of course, only the ground-floor; the roof is a thick thatch, extending over the verandahs, which in England would be called porticoes, and these are supported on thick white columns. The ceilings in a bungalow are nothing but large sheets of canvass whitewashed. As in India people are glad to keep all the doors within the house open, there is placed between the different rooms a framework covered with crimson or green silk, which the natives call a half-door. The beds are nine or ten feet wide, with short posts, on which you may hang mosquito-curtains, which are a sort of large sacks made of gauze, without any opening. They are supported on the posts and tucked in closely all round, so as to prevent the mosquitoes from stinging the people in bed; the only covering, generally, is a sheet, and the gentleman's sleeping-dress is a flannel jacket and a pair of calico drawers with feet to them, to keep off the mosquitoes if they should by chance get inside the curtains. Some people also throw a gauze over the face for the same purpose. There are no feather-beds, but the mattresses are generally stuffed with the fibres from the outside rind of the cocoa-nut, called "coir." The usual plan is to leave the glass doors (French windows you would call them) all open, but to shut the Venetian blinds, and to have a punkah over your head going all night. At about six in the morning all the glass doors are closed, and kept shut all day to exclude the hot air. If, however, there should be any wind, one of them is opened and a tattie hung up in its place; the tattie is a thick mat the size of the doorway, made of the sweet-scented cuscus-grass; this is kept constantly wetted on the outside.

From the 1st to the 11th of February is the Mohammedan festival of the Mohurrun, which is a grand scene. Every night drums beat, and dancing and merrymaking are kept up among the men only, as the Mohammedan women are kept in seclusion. In the compound the other day I saw about a dozen men, one of them thumping away on the horrible native drum called a "tomtom." Two others held by heavy chains a tall sepoy (this word means a native soldier, and ought to be spelt "sepahi"), who was covered all over with a dress of calico, fitting tight to the skin—so much so that at first I thought he was naked. The calico was painted in alternate stripes of red and yellow, and he had two little yellow horns. I imagine it must have been intended to represent the devil conquered and chained by Mohammed. He made a number of antics, and ended, as all these people do, in begging for a few pice; I gave him three annas. The station of Cuttack is situated on a small island formed by the confluence of two rivers; during the hot weather this island becomes a peninsula joined to the main land by a narrow neck of sand. The advantage of this insular position is that, whilst we abound in alligators, we are free from bears and tigers, neither have we so many pariah-dogs as there were about Midnapore. The opposite bank swarms with tigers, and with a small telescope we can sometimes see them coming down to drink by moonlight. On the opposite bank, all round the island, except to the south, rise the rugged hills which dropped from Vishna's fingers. There is one great comfort here: the sea is about fifty miles from us, in a straight line towards the south, and every evening, at about five o'clock, a deliciously cool sea-breeze sets in from that direction. About seven it becomes quite gusty, and continues to blow until about one in the morning. It is necessary to have lived in such a climate as this to know how truly luxurious such evenings are after the intense heat of the day, which is now rapidly increasing; the thermometer in the shade is about 82° or 84°, and this is only the beginning of February.

A walk round the compound early in the morning is quite delightful. On each tree are three or four of the beautiful little striped squirrels, whilst in the branches are many paroquets, parrots, &c. All about on the ground are numbers of a bird of a bright green, with a red breast and head, about the size of a love-bird, and very much like it, except that the beak is straight and rather long, and from the centre of the tail project two long straight feathers of a reddish green. There is also the beautiful mango-bird with its bright yellow plumage and its glossy black head. Occasionally may be seen an alligator lying asleep, with his head and shoulders on the bank and the rest of his body in the water, while a lung-bird has just alighted on his head and twitters to its mate by the side of the tank. They are about the size of the amadavad, but shaped like the swallow, and their plumage is alternately a glossy black or a deep crimson, according as the sun shines on it. Then there is the India-rubber tree, and skulls bleached in the sun. I saw one with its little teeth in the front that had not yet pierced the gums: they are the second teeth, and the skull, which is very small, must have belonged to a mere child. The house belongs to Government, and there are therefore three wells in the compound; but the water is not good. The plan for watering this large orchard and garden is as follows:—From the edge of the wall to the cistern is a wooden trough, into which the water is thrown as it is drawn from the well. By this means the cistern is filled. A brick gutter runs from the cistern and separates it into so many branches; round each bed and every here and there are little openings which let the water run out on the bed. Suppose they only want to water one, they just take up a little earth in a spade and stop up the other branches of the gutter. Whenever it crosses a path, it is carried underneath by means of a small drain. The muller takes two long bamboos, having at one end a heavy weight and at the other a large gomlah suspended by a cord. One muller pulls one cord downward to make the gomlah reach the water, the other fills the gomlah, and, letting go the cord at the other end of the bamboo, draws it up. This work proceeds with great rapidity, and so the cistern gets filled and the garden watered. At a very short distance from our garden stand the remains of a fort. When the English took Cuttack this fort was garrisoned by the Mahrattas. They, however, soon gave it up. The angles of the bastion were rectangles, which prevents it being so strong as if they had been obtuse angles, for then the balls would have had a tendency to glance off; but its great strength consists in the ditch, which is about a hundred or a hundred and fifty yards wide, with the perpendicular side faced with bricks, full of water and swarming with alligators. The water is most foul and offensive, but the medical men say that, if they were to empty and drain it, it would make for many months a most fearful pestilence. The natives have offered us 30,000*l.* to be allowed to drain it, because they say there is a vast quantity of treasure in it.

I have just learned the origin of the Mohurrun. It is a festival, or rather commemoration of the death of Hussein and Houssein, the sons of Ali, Mohammed's nephew. These two were pursued towards the desert by their enemies; they took shelter in a well, and a spider immediately wove a web across the top. Their enemies came up, and, seeing the web, thought that Houssein and Hussein could not be in the well. However, one of them looking down observed a number of lizards all hastening up the sides, so then they thought there must be some one at the bottom who frightened the lizards, and, searching, they got up the two brothers and killed them. It is to commemorate this fact that they have instituted the festival of the Mohurrun, and in consequence the Mohammedans all reverence the spider, while they kill the lizard.

The fort here is of great extent, comprising, I should think, at least 100 acres. The walls have been demolished, and a great portion of the interior is now occupied by a botanical garden and a racket-court.

The winds have risen to-day with tumultuous fury, as though they had been long confined and in one fearful moment had burst their prison-house. There is something very grand, though awful, in these furious tempest-bursts within the tropics. A few minutes back not a leaf rustled; now the trees are waving to and fro, small branches are whirled into the air, and leaves and rubbish are carried far away by the revolving eddies of almost a hurricane. I could scarcely see the river through the volumes of sand which are tossing about mixed with the spray.

Monday, February 13, 1843.

I AM going to cross the river into the jungle in a day or two, with two other gentlemen. Our object is to plan a new village for some native Christians. We each take a gun and a brace of pistols, and have no doubt that we shall bring home some venison. We shall also look out as we go along for two tigers, which have recently committed terrible depredations about Condah, whither we are going. The other day they carried off two men.

Gold-dust is mixed with the sand of the river, but the quantity is very small, and is therefore not considered worth the trouble and expense of collecting.

Cuttack, March 4, 1843.

ONE of my servants came to me this morning, and told me that there was a boa-constrictor in the garden. I immediately desired all the men to take long bamboos, and we sallied forth to attack the monster. By the time we got to the place, however, he had retreated into his hole in the ground; we had therefore to dig him out, and as soon as he appeared all the men struck him with their bamboos until they killed him. It proved not to be a boa, but a yellow snake about seven feet long, and was not venomous. We killed it, however, lest it might endanger the poultry-yard.

On Wednesday the 15th of February we started on our trip —myself and Mr. L., a missionary: Captain W. was not able to accompany us on account of the parade, but was to join us in the evening. On Tuesday afternoon we got our guns in readiness, and sent off some camp furniture, viz. a bedstead, table, &c., which fold up so as to be easily portable. My bed, food, clothes, &c., were carried by two men, each of whom was to receive two annas, that is three pence, a-day. Chogga, and not Condah, is the name of the place to which we were going, and it would be impossible to obtain anything there to eat except what we shot ourselves.

At four o'clock on Wednesday morning Mr. L. came to my house, and we took some coffee, eggs, and toast, and then set off, my companion on a tall white horse and I on a little native pony, both of us dressed entirely in white. I had with me a bearer, a kitmajar, and a syce. Mr. L. had also a bearer, a cooly, and a syce, with several coolies carrying provisions. The syces were only to accompany us as far as the river, and then take the horses back; the others carried our guns, pistols, powder, hunting knives, which are very necessary both to kill everything that is wounded, and also to defend ourselves if thrown down by an elk, tiger, &c. It was necessary that we should cross the river about ten miles from my house, so off we trotted followed by our train. Everything was perfectly still, the moon just setting, and a cold damp fog hanging over the whole island. For the first half-mile we got along very well. We had then to turn into the bed of the river, now dwindled to a narrow stream. Our course lay over a deep bed of loose sand something like that at Weston-super-Mare, only much worse, our horses' feet sinking at every step five or six inches; the poor animals could not move quicker than a trot. As the moon set, and the fog closed around us, the scene became one of utter desolation: the narrow pathway, if you can call it a pathway, winding so as to avoid the deeper sands and quicksands, did not permit us riding two abreast. Far ahead, magnified by the mist, I could just see the tall figure of Mr. L. and his white steed; behind I could hear a low chattering, and now and then one of the black servants would emerge from the fog and then vanish again as suddenly as he had appeared. From time to time arose a shrill cry from some one who had wandered from the path, answered as shrilly by the other men. As the fog thickened everything disappeared. The path was barely discernible, and I almost wished myself at home. However I trusted to the sagacity of my sure-footed little pony, and he carried me safely over the sand-hills and through the hollows for about three-quarters of an hour, when I heard a shout in front, announcing that Mr. L. had reached the water. I soon came up with him. We waited till our servants joined us, then dismounted, gave our horses to the syces with orders to be at the same place at six o'clock on Thursday evening, and embarked in a large boat, which, to render it water-tight, or rather to keep it afloat, was filled up to the seat with bushes and brambles trodden into a compact mass.

The boatmen told us that two nights before, as three carts were going along the path to Chogga, a tiger had sprung out and carried off the man in the centre cart, and that a few days earlier two men had been carried away from the village itself. The other side of the river is a steep bank without sand, and by the time we reached it the day was just breaking, of which, to tell the truth, I was by no means sorry.

On the bank we found the coolies whom we had sent forward the evening before, and who had waited there for us, being afraid to proceed through the jungle until they had the protection of the sahibs. There we took our guns, &c., into our own hands, girded on our belts, in which were thrust our long hunting knives or daggers and our pistols, letting our servants carry our powder-flasks, shot-belts, &c. This is done in order to be able to load with greater rapidity, the servant holding the shot, wad, cap, &c., in readiness. He also carries a heavy ramrod with a round knob at the top, as the drawing the ramrod from the gun, returning it, and hammering away with it at the powder, which you must do on account of its lightness, might frequently cause delay that might be fatal. Most people, for the sake of safety, use double-barrelled guns; mine was, however, only single, but the barrel was long enough for two.

At last off we started along the regular path to Chogga. The change was most extraordinary; the fog had already cleared away; we were walking along a narrow winding path cut through the jungle. On each side of us extended as far as the eye could reach a vast plain covered with laurels and shrubs of a bright green, interspersed here and there with large flowers of a brilliant crimson or scarlet, and more rarely with trees of a stunted growth, on which numbers of little tiny doves were cooing their greeting to the sun. The bushes, which we call low jungle, grow to four or five feet in height, and so thickly that it is impossible to pass through them, except where a path has been cut, or where a natural glade or opening occurs. We walked on looking out anxiously for some opening, as we knew we should find nothing worth firing at in the open plain. Suddenly, on turning an angle in the path, we saw at the distance of about a quarter of a mile on the right a clear space with a few large trees in it. Amid the branches sat fifteen or twenty pea-fowl, and on the open glade were as many more feeding. Shortly afterwards we came to a smaller one, which enabled us to separate, so that we might approach the pea-fowl in different directions; however we could not get within shot, which we much regretted.

But I own I was not quite so eager in pushing through the jungle as I should have been the next day; it was quite novel to me, and I could not help thinking every now and then of the dreaded cobra or the scarcely less dreaded tiger. Indeed, of the last I had a fearful reminder before I rejoined Mr. L.

In a small space of clear ground I came suddenly upon the skeleton of a man, evidently lately killed, for much of the flesh was still adhering to the bones. Probably it was the poor driver of whom we had heard. I had quite lost sight of Mr.

L., but presently heard him shout from some distance behind me. I made my way towards him, and soon reached a small paddy-field (rice-field). Here was a small bull of a very dark colour, who did not seem at all pleased with our intrusion: he looked at us for a minute, and then came galloping towards us, shaking his head and tail in his anger. My two servants called out that it was a wild cow, and crouched down behind me. I felt a little nervous, but faced the animal, and drew a pistol from my belt; however, as he came near, I saw a small piece of cord fastened to one of his horns, and therefore knew it was not an "unner" or wild cow. I desired the men to shout, and myself did the same, running towards the animal and waving my hat. He stopped a moment hesitating, and then, as I rushed forward, he threw up his tail in the air and scampered off, very much to my relief.

Mr. L. now came up, and we proceeded on our road. Presently one of the men who was a little in advance stopped and pointed to a tree at a little distance. Mr. L. primed his gun and fired, and down dropped a fine hen. Wild hens abound in the jungles, and are excellent eating, possessing a slight flavour of game.

Soon after we came to a spot of ground where we beheld a number of quails. I fired and killed two. Again we went on, but met with no further adventure until we came to Chogga. The last mile and a half of our journey lay through paddy-fields with the stubble still on them. The heat was intense, and by the time we reached our destination I was thoroughly tired.

Chogga is a small native village surrounded by jungle, standing about seven or eight miles from the river. It does not belong to the English, but is in the territory of one of our tributary rajahs. Mr. L. has a bungalow there, if such it can be called, consisting as it does of a single room about sixteen feet square, built of mud, and thatched with rice-straw. He has made many converts here, and is about to erect a Christian village about his own bungalow, which is half a mile from Chogga itself, and well situated on a small spot of rising ground. The appearance and manner of these wild, naked, yet Christian savages, was to me deeply interesting.

As soon as we arrived, a number of natives, both men and women, crowded about us. Many of them were Christians, though in dress they adhered to their old habits. Mr. L. at once took off everything but his trowsers, and after some hesitation I did the same. After this we had breakfast and then lay down on our camp beds and rested for two or three hours. About one I felt hungry, so went out and shot a few doves, which abound on every tree.

About half-past three we collected as many men as possible and went out to beat the jungle, through which Mr. L. and myself worked our way until we came to a small open space. There one of us posted himself; the other went on until he found another similar spot, where he also stationed himself. As soon as the shikarree who was with us saw where we were ready, he stole out of the jungle and placed the twenty-five men in a large semicircle, our positions being the centre, and the radius about half a mile. As soon as they were all stationed, at a signal they began to roar and groan and make the most frightful noises, beating the bushes with their long bamboos, and pushing through the jungle towards the open space where we were placed. This was in a high jungle, and really the scene on such an occasion is most exciting. You stand on a small space of fifteen or twenty yards in diameter, bounded on every side by lofty trees and thick underwood, your gun in your hand, your man behind you holding the next charge in readiness. In every quarter the shrieks and yells of the beaters are heard; presently there is a whirr in the air, and a peacock flies through the open space above your head. Bang goes the gun, off runs one of the men to pick up the bird; load again! quick! hark! What a rush in the bushes! There it comes! An elk or stag, shot but not killed; and a man rushes out and cuts the animal's throat.

An alarm of "Tiger!" was now given, but it proved false, as nothing but a wild cat darted over the glade. Shouts again rend the air, and a magnificent red peacock, with a deep green tail and neck of gold, flies over our heads, his long tail streaming behind him, and the brown hen at his side. The opening above our heads was small, and an immediate fire was necessary: I fired and missed him. The beaters now approached nearer and nearer, shouting, and their dark forms soon became visible gliding one by one out of the jungle. Nothing more was to be found there; we accordingly moved on, and presently were beckoned to by the shikarree. He pressed his finger to his lips and whispered "Choop! choop!" and, pointing down a narrow opening in the jungle, showed us a large leopard, beautifully spotted, lying apparently asleep. While loading our guns the animal awoke, and was stealing off just as we fired and hit him, though he contrived to crawl off. The next day, however, we found the body, as the arrow was poisoned. The skin is valuable. The shikarree, who proudly bore off the body, would suffer no one to assist him; but that same man would not carry home the merest trifle from the bazaar, but must be followed by a coolie.

Captain W. soon met us, and we returned home to dinner, after which we sallied out by moonlight to seek some deer, but were unsuccessful.

The next morning, rising at four, after a cup of coffee we sallied into the jungle again, but obtained nothing but a few fowls. Captain W. now left us on his return home, and after breakfast a number of native Christians assembled, as this was the morning appointed for talking to them. They all squatted down on the floor, the men on one side and the women on the other. Mr. L., who is thoroughly conversant with the Oorial language, now entered into conversation with them, asking them questions and hearing all they had to say. They appear to have a very good knowledge of true religion, and to be very earnest and sincere. It was most interesting to see them all sitting so quietly with their eyes fixed on Mr. L.'s face, never attempting to interrupt either him or one another, but speaking one at a time in a low reverent tone of voice. When asked a question they would pause a moment or two in deep thought before they answered. After a little time one or two inquirers came in, that is, men who are not yet converted, but are inquiring about Christianity, or arguing concerning it and comparing it with their own religion. These sat down and behaved themselves in the same decorous manner as the actual Christians. Mr. L. very judiciously encouraged the converts to argue with the inquirers, and it was most pleasing to observe the perfect mildness and the restrained gestures of both parties when talking on so holy a subject, every eye fixed upon the two disputants, and when a pause occurred some other convert gently putting in a word in support of the holy truth.

Inquirer. "You say God gave you the Bible, I say God gave us the Shasters. The religion that is good for the white man is not good for the black. God is good, and has given us each a religion proper to ourselves. I say your religion is good and comes from God; why will you not say the same of our Shasters?"

Convert. "God gave white men the Bible because he is very good, and he told them to go and teach it to every one, because he wishes every one to be good and happy, and to go to the happy country of heaven when they die; but the Shasters do not come from God."

I. "How do you know that?"

C. "Listen, brother. Brummah (God) is good, is he not?"

I. "Yes."

C. "Should not you like to go to Brummah?"

I. "Yes."

C. "Do not the Shasters of your religion teach you so?"

I. "Ha! you are very sly. No; but our religion is good for us now. By and bye Vishnoo will come again, and then he will perhaps give us a Bible."

C. "Why not take the Christian Bible and Christian Brummah now?"

I. "Then I should lose my caste, my wife will leave me, my children will go away, my brother will not smoke with me, my hut will be empty, and the Brahmins will curse me."

C. "If the Brahmins curse you, God is stronger than they

are, and he will bless you; if your wife and children run away, Jesus will make you happy in heaven; if your brother will not smoke with you, the great God will give you his peace."

I. "Well, I will see. Lend me the book; I will read it and show it to the Brahmins. How soon shall you be here again, sahib?"

Mr. L. "In about ten days."

I. "Good: I will see you again."

This is a mere epitome of the conversation, but may furnish some idea of the mode of argument pursued. Whenever the convert brought forward a good argument, or came to a convincing point, it was curious to see the countenance of the Christians. They had been watching their champion with the greatest interest, looking more like dark statues than human beings, so perfectly still did they sit, except when a mother pressed her infant to her bosom to keep it quiet. Suddenly, as they saw the drift of what was said more clearly, their white eyes would dance amid their dark skins, and one or two of them would smile and utter gently the emphatic word "Ha!" (yes).

A nice-looking young woman brought her baby to show it. It was only two months old, and had not yet been baptized. Poor woman! I won her heart completely by taking it from her and kissing it. Mr. L. seemed a little surprised at my doing so, but both the mother and her husband were delighted. She asked me to name her child. Mr. L. wished it to be a scriptural name. I accordingly gave it the first that came into my head, which was "Benjamin." It was interesting to watch the mother's face as I named the child, she had apparently never heard the name before, and there was much amusement amongst them, all trying to pronounce it; they could not quite manage it, but, as the mother carried the little one out, several of the men patted its cheek and smiled, and said very slowly Bend-za-min. There were to have been four adults baptized on this day, but one of them came in the morning and said that his wife declared she would not live with a Christian, that she had taken her children and all his fortune, consisting of one rupee and two pice, and had gone away to her brother's house. Mr. L. advised the man to go and reason with her, which he did, and we afterwards heard that she had returned with him on condition that he would not become a Christian.

The people have literally given up father, mother, wife, children, friends, and home as soon as they become followers of Jesus. They are looked upon as utterly degraded; and the tribe to which they belong has to pay a sum of money to the Brahmins before they can be freed from the stain which attaches to them in consequence of the pollution.

Mr. L. preached in the afternoon, and in the evening the Christians again met, when he addressed them a discourse in the midst of a tremendous thunderstorm.

When we rose the next morning at four o'clock we found that the rain had been so heavy during the night that we could get no fuel to make a fire: our provisions, having been neglected, were all spoiled by the rain, excepting a small piece of thick pie-crust; our beer we had exhausted the evening before; so after a scanty meal we started on our way home. We shot a peacock and fowl upon the road along with three snipes, and arrived at Cuttack about half-past eight on Friday morning.

I have just witnessed a magnificent sight; during the last month we have had such weather as the oldest inhabitant cannot recollect ever to have seen before at this time of the year. It is generally in February and March very hot and very dry. For the last month we have had almost incessant rain, with violent thunderstorms. The days are comparatively cool, and at night I am glad of two blankets. Rumours of an approaching famine began to float abroad, but at length the mystery was solved. About half-past six I thought I observed a curiously shaped long cloud, and as the sun went down and the twilight deepened it did not alter its appearance, but at about a quarter to seven proved to be a magnificent comet. The nucleus was plainly visible even with the naked eye, and equal in brightness to a small star. The tail was at least 45° in length, and inclined from W.S.W. to E.S.E. Had it been perpendicular it would have reached from the horizon half way up over our heads, the whole distance from the horizon to the zenith being 90°. The breadth of the extremity of the tail was about 2½°, and the posterior half was divided longitudinally by a dark line. The colour was that of a pale moonlight, but it would no doubt have appeared much more red if the moon had not been shining brightly at the time. There has been no comet equal to this in brilliancy and the length of the tail since the year 1759. I have hardly any books to refer to, but my idea is, that it is the same comet which appeared in 1264 and 1556, and was expected back in 1848. If so, its period of revolution is nearly 300 years. Its light was intense, being almost equal to the moon in brilliancy. The natives say it will burn the earth; they call it "jherra tarn," or "burnt star."

The weather is most remarkable. We have incessant rain, with thunder and lightning every evening, and the clouds are too heavy to allow us to see the comet. The houses require fresh thatching every year. The lightning we have here I have never seen equalled in England; each flash spreads over one quarter of the visible heavens, whilst the roaring, or rather the deafening rattle, of the thunder is incessant. The comet re-appeared last night, though hardly so brilliant as it was a week ago.

I was calling upon the judge of Cuttack the other day, and his wife told me that a few nights before she went up stairs at twelve o'clock to see her little girl, who had not been quite well. On the floor of the room she saw what she thought was a piece of ribbon, and stooped to pick it up, when a cobra raised its head and expanded its hood and hissed at her in anger. She called the servants with their bamboos, and they soon killed it, but it was a great mercy that she had not touched it.

Cuttack, April 13, 1843.

THE other evening the mhator came to ask me for the key to unlock the fowl-house door, as one of the hens was loose. I told him to bring a light, and then went across the compound. The padlock with which the door is fastened passes through a chain and eye at the top of the door. I raised my hand to unlock it, when the mhator, who had the lantern, called out, "Sahib, sahib, samp!" (Sir, sir, a snake!) I looked, and on the very chain which I was on the point of touching was a snake. I immediately called the men to bring bamboos, and they soon killed it. On examining it we found it to be one of that sort whose bite is always fatal, so that the person bitten never lives more than half an hour, and there would be no time for the doctor to come. How thankful I should be to God for my escape! I suspect that the snake was the cobra manilla, but am not sure. It was about two feet and a half long, small head, back dark green or nearly black, with all the way along it transverse yellow stripes.

About three weeks ago was a poojah, or Hindu festival, of which I forget the name. About nine o'clock in the evening of the principal day four sepoys came to my house with the subadar major's compliments, and he would be glad if I would do them the honour to go and see the samam or show (the subadar major is the principal native officer in a regiment). I had refused them once or twice before, therefore this evening I sent my compliments and I would be there in a few minutes. When I got to the lines or houses of the sepoys I found a magnificent tent about two hundred feet long, into which I was ushered with much ceremony.

The scene was most interesting. At the upper end there were a few European officers, while down each side were ranged three or four rows of dark sepoys seated on their hams, which is the favourite position among the natives. The tent was lighted by a number of flaming torches, which threw their red light upon the swarthy faces of about seven or eight hundred gigantic up-country sepoys. The whole centre of the tent was clear for the evolutions of the nautch-girls (dancing girls): of these, who were generally young and tolerably good-looking, there were several parties of four or five. All those of one party held each other by the hand, and kept dancing backward and forward with a sort of regular motion, and singing in a peculiar cadence. The song was an invocation of blessing on those who happened to be opposite them at the time, and every now and then they would separate to point with their hands to those who were designated in the verse. The light danced upon the spangles with which their dresses were covered, whilst innumerable little bells jingled on their arms and ankles.

When I entered the subadar major immediately came to me with a long-necked brazen vessel, from which he sprinkled over my clothes a scent extracted from the sandal-wood. He then poured some into his hand and rubbed my face and whiskers with it. This they call anointing. He then presented me with two packets of spices wrapped up in sweet-scented leaves.

As soon as he retired a party of nautch-girls came up, and, after singing a song in my praise and blessing me, suddenly separated and each one threw over me a quantity of crimson powder. In a minute my face and clothes were of a brilliant red; and wherever I had been anointed the powder stuck like paint. Every one was served in the same manner, and a pretty set we must have appeared: this is the chief fun of the festival. During the three or four days that it lasts almost every native that you meet has more or less of this red powder (called akbeer) on his body or dress. Even my monkey, which is a sacred animal with the Hindus, I found covered with it every morning. I did not stay long at the tomasa, but was glad that I had seen it: however, the cassock I had on was spoiled, not by the powder, for that I managed to brush off, but by the anointing, which has left in it so powerful a scent that it is not wearable.

Last Monday, Tuesday, and Wednesday was the Chena poojah, or swinging festival. Upright poles are fixed in the earth, and at the top of each is another pole which revolves upon the first. The religious devotees are said to suspend themselves to one end of the revolving pole by iron hooks stuck into their flesh, and are then whirled round and round by a number of men. Many of these mistaken men are said to die in consequence of the tortures they endure.

At this festival it is also reported that other devotees lie on their stomachs whilst the priests press sharp knives into them until they pin them to the ground, and that this does not always kill them; but that when it does they consider they shall go to Brummah, their God, and that the deity will be pleased with such suffering. I am told they never utter a groan; but I would not go to see them, though there are strong doubts whether it be not a deception.

I now often go out with Captain W. before breakfast. An account of one morning will suffice. I was called at half-past three; dressed, and had some coffee, bread and butter, and an egg. At half-past four Captain W. and Lieutenant H. called for me on an elephant. I gave my gunpowder, &c. to two of my men to carry. The great animal then knelt down. He had no howdah, as that is not necessary, except for ladies. The only clothing on the elephant is a thick pad or cushion, covered with leather, which extends over the whole of the back. He knelt, and I climbed up in the usual manner; that is, by standing on his hind foot, then catching hold of a rope which hangs down from his pad, and scrambling up as well as one can. The mahout then told the elephant to get up; and off we started, half sitting half lying on the pad, and the servants, with the guns, &c., walking behind. It seems a fearful height, and for the first few miles I could not help thinking of the danger of a fall. However, one gets accustomed to such things.

The elephant carried us bravely over the loose sands, and down to a ford in the river. In crossing the stream he went more cautiously, seeming to feel each place before he put his foot down, as if he were afraid of getting into a quicksand. Once or twice, when the water was deep, I thought he would have been obliged to swim; but I was wrong: though it would not have mattered if he had; we should have been quite safe on his back.

After crossing the sand on the other side we went through some paddy-fields and jungle towards a jheel (or marsh), which I had mentioned as containing a great number of ducks. I had been there previously on foot with Mr. L. When we reached the jheel a heavy fog came on, and Captain W. therefore proposed that we should go on farther into the jungle, in hopes of its clearing up, when we should find some hares. You must remember that in India, where we get nothing whatever but mutton and fowls, and where we cannot buy even these, everything in the shape of meat is a treat, if not a necessary.

On we went; the fog cleared up; we got down in a jungle of low brushwood, interspersed with several open spaces. We found some men taking charge of a herd of buffaloes: for two pice each they agreed to assist our servants in beating the bushes, and we were not long before we started several hares. I only shot one; the others were more fortunate.

At half-past seven we started on our way back. As we passed the jheel I shot a widgeon. At half-past eight got home, had a cold bath, and enjoyed my breakfast; and at dinner was very glad to have the hare and widgeon, for the expense of two pice. I often go out this way. The elephant belongs to the regiment which is stationed here. The exercise before breakfast is most healthy. One time we came upon a place in the midst of the jungle which I intend to visit again in the cold weather, when I shall have more time to examine it.

April 15, 1843.

I WILL now endeavour to give you an idea of some of our arrangements. We have moved to the other side of the house in order to have our bed-room to the west; because the sea-breeze, which blows every night, is a south-west wind. The room in which I am sitting was my wife's dressing-room; the one I use is fifty feet long. Dressing-rooms are absolutely necessary in this country, because nothing is put into the sleeping apartment except the bed, because of the mosquitoes, which harbour in swarms wherever they can find shelter. The bed is never placed against the wall, but always in the middle of the room; and the feet are placed in pans of water, to prevent the white ants, centipedes, &c. from paying you a visit during the night.

The room I am now in has one French window opening into the verandah in front, another towards the church, a door opening into the next room, and another into the godown or store-room. All these windows and doors are now open, and I am sitting as near the centre as I can, to catch what little breeze there is, for the weather is fearfully hot; the thermometer at noon about 90° in-doors. It is now eleven in the evening, and my wife is gone to bed. The floor, which is of cement (wooden floors are never used here on account of the white ant), is covered with a curious sort of matting, made of the leaves of the date-tree. We always use mats instead of carpets in India, because they are much cooler. The walls and the ceilings are whitewashed, the universal substitute for paper or paint in the Mofussil. When I say the ceiling, I mean the ceiling-cloths, which are great sheets of canvas covering the tops of the rooms, and fastened up with cords.

Over my head swings a punkah or fan, about eighteen feet long and three wide, made of canvas stretched on a wooden frame, and also whitewashed. This hangs from the ceiling, or rather from some bamboos placed upon the ceiling. Suspended from the lower edge of the punkah is a sort of full flounce of white calico circling along the whole length. The punkah is swung backwards and forwards over my head by means of a long rope pulled by a bearer sitting in the verandah. This man is now fast asleep, but still he continues to pull the rope, and so he would do for hours if I required it.

The furniture of the room consists of a table, a sideboard, and a large screen of common cloth, stretched on a frame of sissoo-wood (a sort of coarse rose-wood). It is about seven feet high and seven across, and is placed before the door of the garden. On the sideboard stands a flat candlestick, with a glass shade to keep the insects from the flame. The candle is wax; we cannot use tallow for two reasons: the climate of India is so hot that the candles would not remain upright, and the sheep here have very little fat upon them. On the table are two Indian table-lamps. I hardly know how to describe them. The lower part is like an upright candlestick, on which is placed a glass cup half filled with water, the other half with cocoa-nut oil. In the bottom is a little bit of lead with two thin cotton wicks in it, which reach a little above the surface of the oil. These are alight. Over the whole is a large inverted bell-glass to keep off the insects, which at present swarm around. Every minute I hear the mosquitoes buzzing about my ears; then they settle on my face, and on my clothes, through which they are enabled to bite with ease. This keeps me in a continued fidget.

There is also an incessant whistling all around from what we call crickets, though they are somewhat different from those in England. A number of large grasshoppers, about two inches long, of a light green, are hopping about on the table, and occasionally on my paper. On the wall are several long-tailed lizards: they are only slightly venomous; and, though extremely ugly, we are always glad to see them, because they eat the mosquitoes. Round the ceiling are circling three large bats, which my mungoose, sitting in a corner, keeps watching. Should one fall, he would seize and devour him in an instant. A wild cat came through the room just now, and took a peep at me; but the mungoose growled, and it ran way. It was small; but it has been very destructive in the poultry-yard.

But I must now return to what I was telling. The place which we came upon in the jungle is called Old Cuttack; and it deserves the name, for I do not suppose it has been inhabited for the last thousand years. It appears from what little I saw of it to be a most wonderful place, and certainly proves that the population in the olden times must have been very numerous, and far advanced in mechanical arts. It consists of a deep ravine, the sides of which are composed of a dark rock of extreme hardness, and containing a great quantity of iron. On one side it has been made perfectly smooth, although certainly not less than seventy feet in height: on the other are numerous steps and staircases, cut out of the solid rock. The stone does not seem to have been broken off and then chiselled smooth, but it appears as if the steps had been cut out in solid pieces.

On the summit are the remains of houses built of large blocks, all perfectly smooth, saving from the effects of time and weather. Scattered about are heaps of rock, as if collected for building. At a little distance on the banks of the river is a sort of sea-wall, which I have not yet seen, but in which, they tell me, many of the masses of rock are sixteen or eighteen feet long.

All this appears doubly wonderful when you remember that the natives now, almost naked, build their houses of mud, without windows, and with a miserable thatch; that their fireplaces are nothing but little holes in the ground; and that in most respects they are absolute savages. Either they have very much degenerated, or, which is more probable, the race which built these mighty works is swept away.

April 17, 1843.

I WAS in doubt concerning the Chena Poojah, but it appears that the hooks are fastened to a cord, which cuts into the body, and literally causes the blood to flow in streams. They say also that it is the victims themselves that pass the spears into their bodies, and not the priests.

I may here mention that my compound and garden formerly belonged to a General Carpenter, and he planted and sowed many very rare plants—some from China, from America, and from the islands in the Pacific. There are three trees of a very particular sort, of which I very much wish to know the name. They are generally called the cotton-tree, although altogether different from the ordinary cotton-plant, and I suspect they come from America. The tree is about thirty-five or forty feet in height, not many branches, and a very smooth bark. I cannot describe the leaf, for as yet it is not out; but it has borne flowers and fruit since I have been here; of course, therefore, these were before the leaves. The flower, of a brilliant red, is in appearance half-way between a tulip and a tiger-lily; it grows from buds in the thick branches, and is about twice the size of the latter flower. The blossom gives place to a pod about four or five inches in length, and in the form of a sphere drawn out at both ends. The interior of the pod is divided longitudinally into four segments: the whole contains a great number of black seeds buried in a soft silky cotton. I intend to stuff some pillows with it: I think it will be as soft as down. The fibres are said to be too short to form cloth; but I think if they had this tree in England they would manage to use it, and the cloth would resemble very soft silk.

Juggernat'h, May, 1843.

THE first account I received of the Chena Poojah was correct. The hooks are passed through the muscles on each side the spine: for several days previously the muscles are rubbed and beaten in order to harden them. At the festival they frequently run pieces of iron through the tongue. The victims belong to the lowest castes, and generally swing and torture themselves as proxies for the Brahmins who have made a vow.

This place is marked Juggernat'h on the maps, although properly that is only the name of the idol in the temple. The town itself is called Pooree, or the City of Cities.

I left Cuttack on Thursday, April 20, and after one night's dâk arrived here, the distance being about forty-eight miles. I went to the Circuit-house, a large unfurnished residence, appropriated by Government to the use of those officers who go on circuit through the district. However, Mr. B., the magistrate and principal person here, would not allow me to remain there, but insisted upon my coming and living at his house, and sending at once for my wife to come and join me. This I gladly did. Mrs. Acland discharged most of our servants, and came down here; so she has the benefit of living at Pooree, and at the same time of saving money, for the month's wages of the servants discharged will more than pay for her journey. We have a bed-room, sitting and dressing apartments, and two bath-rooms to ourselves; and we breakfast, dine, &c., with Mr. and Mrs. B.

It is difficult to imagine the delight of coming to such a place as Pooree. At Cuttack we are obliged to keep every door and window shut, in order to exclude the hot air. We close them at six in the morning and open them at seven in the evening. One doorway is fitted with a framework, covered with matting made of scented grass. This is called a tatty, and is kept all day thoroughly wet, in order to cool the room by evaporation, the punkah continually fanning over head; but in spite of all this the heat is fearful, and still increasing; the thermometer stood in-doors at 103°.

At Pooree, forty-eight miles from Cuttack, we have no punkahs, no tatties; all the windows wide open, the waves rolling up close to the houses, a delicious sea-breeze all day, the thermometer never yet above 85°; not a mosquito to be seen, and no insects but a few English flies. Excepting among the mountains, Pooree is perhaps the coolest place in India, and I am considered most fortunate in having it in my district.

The coming here is a renewal of life and strength. When we are down on the sands in the evening, we might quite fancy ourselves in England again; and I assure you that at five o'clock in the afternoon, by the sea-side, we are glad to walk fast in order to keep ourselves warm. This is the state of Pooree at present. After the rains, that is, in October and November, it becomes extremely hot and very unhealthy; for then the sea-breeze ceases and the land-wind sets in, passing in its course over the dead bodies of hundreds of pilgrims.

The most conspicuous object here is the temple of Juggernat'h, to which devotees come from every part of India. It is an immense pile of massive buildings. There are at times as many as one hundred thousand pilgrims here at once. No European is allowed to enter even the court.

The sea is most magnificent. The beach is composed entirely of sand, something like that at Weston-super-Mare; but there is only a few yards' difference between high and low water. There is an incessant surf extending almost to the horizon—one line behind another of enormous breakers. Some people used occasionally to bathe, but the surf rendered it very dangerous, and at last one of them had a leg carried away by a shark, since which every one is afraid; we therefore have salt water brought up to the house.*

Cuttack, August 7, 1843.

I MUST now give an account of Mofussil society. We will suppose a married couple going to a new station,—as, for in-

* A gap occurs here in the narrative, from a portion of it having gone down in the "Memnon" in the Red Sea.

stance, my wife and myself coming to Cuttack. Well, we arrive wretched enough about eight o'clock in the morning, after a long dâk journey. All that day we are engaged in setting things to rights. The next morning I order my carriage, and go out to make my calls; for in India, unlike England, the stranger calls first. The hours for calling are from half-past ten to one, after which time you would not be admitted anywhere, as it is supposed that the lady of the house is just going to tiffin (lunch), which she takes at two, and then goes to sleep for two or three hours.

Of course the first person I call on is the commanding officer. I drive in at the gate of the compound, and under some trees, up to the house door, and so under the portico; for every house has a very large carriage portico to protect the horses from the sun. My carriage is a phaëton—the britska, phaëton, and buggy being almost the only vehicles used in India. The britska does very well for a judge, and the buggy a sort of carriage for a single man. Mine is a phaëton with two ponies. On the box sits the coachman—dark-brown face, large black mustachios, white calico tunic and trowsers, white turban, turned up with pale blue, as livery, and blue and white cummerband round the waist; except only when it is wet, and then he wears a crimson skull-cap, and a scarlet full cloak with sleeves. A syce or groom runs by the side of the ponies.

Arrived at the door, I call out "Sahib hy?" Gentleman in? meaning, Is your master at home? If not, I leave a card: if he is, I enter the house, and follow the servant who has answered me. I should have told you that there are no such things as knockers or bells here. Every door is open, unless in the very hot weather, and there are always six or eight servants lounging about in the verandah. As I step out of the carriage, each one of these stoops down, touches the ground with the back of his hand, and then pats his forehead three or four times, signifying, I suppose, that, if I were to order him, he would even throw dirt upon his own head.

In reply to the question "Sahib hy?" one of the men answers, "Hy, khadawum"—He is, O representative of God;

at the same time holding his hands pressed together as i he were saying his prayers. He precedes me into the house, still in the same attitude. He sets me a chair, whilst another man comes in, unfastens the rope of the punkah, and, taking the end of it out into the verandah, sits down and pulls it, and very soon falls asleep, still, however, continuing his occupation.

Presently in comes the master of the house, dressed in white jacket, black neckerchief (if any), white shirt, white trowsers, white stockings, and shoes made of some white skin. I should have told you that the servant who shows me in takes my card to his master, with which card his master plays the whole time I am there. In a few minutes in comes the lady, in clothes hanging loosely around her; she probably does not wear stays in the morning: her dress is white muslin, and her face, as well as those of her children, if she have any, is of a ghastly pale colour. This is universal in India.

There is not much conversation at a first visit, so I soon rise and go to some person to whom I have a letter of introduction, when he at once volunteers to accompany me on the rest of my calls. These first visits are made by the gentleman only; his wife does not accompany him. In the course of a few days the gentlemen return the call, bringing their wives with them. Daughters are out of the question: beyond the age of six they are a genus unknown in India. They go to England at that age, come out again to India at eighteen, and probably marry in Calcutta, and settle at once some four or five months' journey from their parents, who have been so anxiously looking forward to seeing them.

A few days after the form of calling has been gone through, some half-dozen different persons send you invitations to dinner, kindly wishing to welcome the stranger to the station. From half-past seven to eight is the usual hour in India; for if people dined earlier they would necessarily lose their evening drive. The carriage enters the compound; a servant runs in to the sahib, and, pressing his own hands together, says, "Ghairee ata" (carriage comes). Out issues the sahib into the front verandah: the lady is handed out; the gentleman offers his arm, and walks off, leaving me to follow as best I may.

From the verandah we enter the dining-room. There are no halls or passages or cupboards in the Mofussil. Down the whole length of the room is a long table laid for dinner, round which we must wind to get to the opposite door leading into the drawing-room. Here are a number of ladies seated on one side the room, on the other side the gentlemen. After a little while an old Indian with a long silvery beard, and dressed completely in white, comes in, and, pressing his hands together, says, "Canna mig" (dinner on table).

Then the master of the house gives his arm to the most important lady present; the others do likewise, according to the most strict precedence of rank, the lady of the house being taken first. She does not take the top of the table, but assigns that place to whoever has led her in, herself occupying the seat next him on his right hand. Each person brings his khitmutgar; accordingly, behind each chair stands a man in white, who, as you sit down, unfolds and hands you the napkin which was on your plate; he then falls back a step, and crosses his arms over his chest. As soon as grace has been said, the cover is taken off the soup-tureen, and those who like it are helped to a rich sort of chicken-broth.

After that, you hear on every side—"Mrs. So-and-so, may I have the pleasure of taking a glass of wine with you?" "I shall be very happy." "Which do you take, beer or wine?" "Thank you; I will take a little beer," or "wine," as the case may be. Suppose the former, and myself the speaker, I turn round and say to my khitmutgar, "Beer, shraubs meem Sahib, ki do" (beer-wine, Mrs. Lady, give).

In the mean time they are uncovering the dishes. At the top is a pair of fine roast fowls, at the bottom a pair of boiled ditto. At the sides, fowl cutlets, fowl patties, fowl rissoles, stewed fowls, grilled fowl, chicken-pie, &c. &c. No ham, no bacon, and little tiny potatoes not larger than a cherry, with stewed cucumbers, and some sticky Indian vegetables, are handed round. But for the second course a great treat is reserved. Six or seven mutton-chops, each equal to one mouthful, are brought in, and with much ceremony placed at the top of the table; at the other end are slices of potatoes fried. Your hostess tells you how glad she was that Mr. So-and-so had sent her the loin of a Patna sheep to-day: she hoped we should like it. Then comes curried fowl and rice; then pine-apple pie, custard, jelly, plantain, oranges, pine-apples, &c. &c.; but directly these sweets appear, there appear also, behind the chairs of many of the gentlemen, servants carrying a little carpet, with a neat fringe to it. These they place at the back of their masters' chairs, on the floor, and then each servant brings in a large hookah, places it on the little carpet, and, whilst the ladies and others are eating the custards, pies, and fruits, you have all around you the incessant bubble from the hookah, and smell the filthy smoke from an abominable compound of tobacco and various noxious drugs.

The ladies rarely sit for above one glass of wine, when they retire and leave the smokers to themselves. Cigars are then produced for the use of the other gentlemen; and, after they have all smoked and drunk a little more wine than enough, they join the ladies. Then there is a little general talking, then a little music: then come cards—I never play—and then the good-byes, and so home to bed—a nightmare during one's sleep, and a headache in the morning! When alone, we always dine at four.

Cuttack, August 29, 1843.

I HAD been sitting in the verandah reading, and went away for a few minutes to speak to my wife. When I came back my chair was occupied. There, sitting as quietly and demurely as possible, was an enormous ourang-outang, or monkey of some sort. When I first caught sight of him he had my book in his hands, and was to all appearance reading. It happened, however, to be rather a stupid book, and he very soon threw it down; he then placed his hands upon his knees and sat perfectly still, just as if he had been meditating on what he had been reading. I should say, as nearly as I could judge, that he must have been above five feet in height, supposing him to stand erect. He sat as upright as any man.

After watching him for a minute or two, and observing that the calves of his legs were thicker and more like those of a man than monkeys' legs usually are, I stepped quietly back and called my wife. All this time I had not seen his face; however, as she came, one of the parrots screamed, and the old gentleman turned his head. His face was very dark, with large whiskers and beard, and hair all perfectly white; his body a light-brown, and his face and hands peculiarly large. As soon as he saw me he half rose, laid both hands on the elbow of the chair, and began to grin and show his teeth and spit at me. I did not quite like it, as I was afraid he might make a spring in my direction; yet I knew that my voice would at once frighten him away, if I raised the horrid unearthly yell used by the natives to scare wild beasts, and which even the tiger will hardly resist unless much pressed by hunger.

Still I felt more inclined to watch him. Once I thought of going round the other way and getting my gun, but really he looked so much like a man that I could not have shot him. He continued to grin and spit until I turned away, hoping he would resume his former sedate position. As soon, however, as he thought my eye was off him he rose leisurely from his chair, stepped slowly out of the verandah, caught hold of a branch of the banian-tree, and swung himself up into it. As he did this I saw that he had a long tail, so he could not, I believe, have been an ourang-outang. Indeed I never heard of them coming into this little island, nor, I think, into the district. I went into my study, and immediately afterwards heard him scuttling away over the roof of the house. I have not seen him since, but if he comes back I shall try to make friends with him by giving him food, though I believe he belongs to rather a treacherous family.

Whilst on this subject, I will mention another monkey which I saw a few days ago. It is almost two feet in height, quite black, except a circle of light-brown hair round its face, and is held in high veneration by the natives. They come chiefly from a place up the country called Brinderbund, where it is said there are nothing but Brahmins and monkeys.

I was once driving with a friend when we met a party of pilgrims, who had two or three monkeys with them. We stopped and spoke to the people, and one of the monkeys came into the carriage and perched himself on my lap. I offered the people two rupees for him, but they said they were going to take the two to Juggernat'h, where the Rajah would buy them. I asked how much they would take for them; they said fifty rupees for the pair. This I could not afford, and I told them so; they then said I might have them both for twenty-five rupees. This, however, was more than I could give, and we therefore drove on, though I was very unwilling to part with the little fellows, that seemed to have taken quite a fancy to me.

The manner of reception at the judge's is much the same as I described in my last; but here there are, however, two or three different additional servants, who with long chouries keep flapping the insects off the table and the faces of the company. Here is also plenty of mutton; and cheese from England. All the side dishes are of silver.

In the drawing-room most of the tables are marble. From the ceiling is suspended a number of small plated chandeliers with glass drops; in another room is a good piano-forte, and after dinner some very tolerable music and singing. There is also a little rational conversation.

But now let me describe a bachelor's party at the commissioner's, who, by the way, is above the judge in rank and in salary. I say a bachelor's party, because his wife is gone to England for her health, and he cannot therefore invite ladies. Before dinner there is much general conversation about races, church-building, hunting, the paucity of chaplains, &c. &c. Some magnificent prints are brought forward; a set of splendid silver medallions of sacred history are examined and admired; some ancient coins and inscriptions are submitted to the inspection of the unlearned; the last English reviews are brought under discussion.

In the mean time the gentlemen are lounging upon ottomans

about a large marble table, the host going from one to another, speaking to and trying to please all. To the sportsman he speaks of his gun, to the chaplain of a project of building a new church, to the engineer of the aërial steam-ship, and, in short, makes every one pleased both with himself and his neighbours. I need hardly tell you that our commissioner at Cuttack is a most agreeable man; his great object is to make others happy, and his kind good-natured face is welcome everywhere. He is about thirty-six years of age, fond of sporting, fond of reading, fond of children—although he has none himself. Every one likes him, from the judge to the faquer, from the highest to the lowest—unless, indeed, the lawless, and those he does not spare. He has the grand tact of rendering himself agreeable to everybody, and the means by which he does this is the exercise of a kind heart. He does not obtrude his concerns, but listens patiently and with interest to the remarks of others; and this, remember, with cheerfulness and pure morality, is the means by which any person may make himself beloved.

But to return: the conversation turns upon church music. "You have an organ, Commissioner, have you not?" says one. "Yes, but I very seldom use it."

"You should send it to the church," said I.

"Well, I have sometimes thought I would, but I am afraid you have no place for it; and, besides, I don't know whether the tunes would do."

"Let us judge of that," says the magistrate; "give us a tune whilst they are putting the dinner on the table."

"Very well; and I am sure, if the padre likes it, he is very welcome to have it till Mrs. M. comes back."

Thereupon we adjourned to an adjoining room, where there was a very large upright organ, but, as Mr. M. said, "only a grinder." He puts in the church barrel, and, turning the handle, plays, one after another, several really beautiful psalm-tunes, whilst every one stands serious and attentive. At last dinner is announced. The style is much the same as at the judge's, except that almost all the dishes are silver, and there is a magnificent racing-cup of the same metal in the centre. The eatables, however, are many of them English. There is fresh salmon brought from England, English soups, English potatoes, carrots, oysters, cheese, &c. &c., all brought out in canisters hermetically sealed.

Of course, as everywhere else, the beer, wines, &c., are from England, for so devoid are we of any trading community, that in this splendid climate no attempt has ever yet been made to manufacture wine. Beer we could not make, at least so they say, for want of barley;* but I believe that pine-apples, of which we get three or four young juicy ones for a penny, would make splendid wine. England has no pine-apples at all like ours. Then there are preserves and pies made of green-gages, apricots, &c., all from home. Here also, as at the judge's, there is abundance of champagne, or, as we call it here, tokay. After dinner, at all houses, each person takes a small glass of liqueur.

At the commissioner's, being a bachelor's party, we remained in the dining-room. Cigars were introduced, with coffee and brandy-and-water for those who liked it. I will now relate an anecdote I heard there:—

"Why, B.," said Mr. M., "I heard you had an adventure yesterday. What was it?"

"Oh! don't ask me; it makes me almost sick to think of it."

"Oh, nonsense!" from all present.

"Well, if I must, here goes." Then drinking off a glass of wine B. began: "I suppose I must make a regular history of it, so I will commence at the beginning. Last evening, in the bright and balmy, or I should say gorgeous, splendour of an oriental sunset, when the brilliant tints of—"

"Bah! B., don't be too absurd," cried some of us; "tell us what it was without all this brilliant balmy nonsense."

"Why, I thought I was poetical; but I see you have no poetry in your souls; so I will condescend to prose. I was obliged yesterday afternoon to go down the river for a short distance; I had a boat and three natives. When I had completed what I wanted I returned, and was paddling along, not far from the bank, just on this side of those enormous blocks of iron rock

* Plenty of barley is grown in Bhootan.

which keep the river from overflowing, and form such a splendid monument of the great mechanical powers of the ancient Hindus—"

"Come, never mind the antiquities; we will have them another time. Let us hear your own adventures now."

"Well, I had just rounded this point when one of my men called out most vehemently, 'Look, sir, look; there is a tiger!' My eyes were instantly turned in the direction towards which he pointed, and there I saw a most fearful sight. A man was tearing, springing, bounding towards the river, and a hundred yards behind him followed a large panther, pursuing him with those rapid leaps for which that animal is so famous. I instantly ordered my people to pull towards the shore, in the hope of rescuing the panting wretch who thus struggled for his life. Before we reached the bank the man had made a bound into the water, and stood immersed up to his neck. I suppose he was too much exhausted to swim, for we could hardly hear his voice as he called to us to make haste.

"At this instant I saw the dark blunt snout of an enormous alligator rising slowly above the surface, as he made his way towards his intended victim. I shouted to the man, "Crocodile! crocodile!" He heard me, hesitated an instant, then rushed back to the bank. This sudden movement disconcerted the panther, who started back a few paces, and the next moment our boat shot within reach. "Come hither," I exclaimed. The man made a spring; the panther leaped forward, and, as I seized the former by the arm, the latter seized him by the leg.

"Oh! the shriek of the poor victim! I shall never forget it. Foolishly I had not brought my rifle, but I shouted to the men to strike the beast with their oars. No; the cowardly wretches shrank down in the farther end of the boat, and would not move. I could do nothing, therefore, but pull at the man's shoulder, whilst his horrid shrieks were ringing in my ears. Had I let go, the panther would instantly have carried him off; had there been another European with me, the man might have been saved.

"This takes long to describe, but it was all the work of a few seconds. Presently I felt that I was drawing the man more towards me; I looked, and saw the flesh of the leg peeling off in the jaws of the panther until it came to the ankle, where, with one crunch, the bone was severed, and the beast galloped off with the fearful mouthful. I now drew the man, who by this time was quite senseless, into the boat. I tied my handkerchief tightly round the upper part of his leg, and with a piece of wood formed a sort of tourniquet. We brought him to Cuttack, and sent him at once to the hospital; but he died in the course of a few hours."

"What a horrible affair!" exclaimed several voices.

"But I thought," said I, "that the voice, or even the eye, of man was sufficient to make any beast quail."

"So it is, provided they are neither very hungry nor very much excited. This beast had been engaged in a long chase, and nothing could have frightened him from his prey."

"Ah! of course that would have made a difference," I replied; "but Mr. L. had a little adventure the other day which seems to prove the power of the eye of man."

"Oh! there is no doubt that man is master of all, and I believe many natives have been preserved by the power of the human eye, and many more might be saved if they only had the coolness to exercise the power which has been bestowed upon them. But what was the adventure of L.'s?"

"It was nothing very wonderful or exciting. He was staying at Chugga for a few days; and one morning he went out with his gun, accompanied by a native Christian of the name of Perswa. Whilst they were in the jungle they suddenly heard a distant shout, as of some one calling 'Perswa, Perswa!' They sat down and bent their ears to the ground to listen. Presently the cry was repeated, 'Perswa, Perswa!' Again it was renewed, 'Perswa, Perswa!' 'It is a tiger,' cried his follower. They immediately hastened back to the village, but found no one there but four old women, who told them that one of their people was hurt by a tiger. Mr. L. started instantly to his rescue, and as he left the village he was joined by at least fifty men, who in their fear were hiding, but, being now encouraged by the presence of a white man, sallied forth with him. Following the direction of the cries of the poor wretch, they soon came to the spot where he stood facing a large tiger.

"It seems that the man, whilst in the jungle, had suddenly caught sight of it on the very point of springing upon him. With great presence of mind he stood perfectly still, and fixed his eyes steadily on the monstrous brute. The tiger wavered for an instant, then, quailing before his eye, he slunk behind a bush. Still the man kept his eye upon him, whilst the tiger every minute peered forth to see whether that dreaded eye was withdrawn.

"From bush to bush the tiger moved, as if seeking to avoid the gaze, in order that he might spring out to seize his prey. Slowly the man turned from side to side, still facing his dreaded foe, and calling upon Perswa and the Padre Sahib to come and save him; and this he continued till the party came up, who by their shouts forced the tiger to abandon his intended meal. Now this seems a strong instance of the power of the human eye."

"It does indeed," replied F. "I have known it exercised with equal success in another case. A young officer was walking through the jungle; he foolishly had nothing but his pistols with him. Suddenly he heard a noise, and observed the branches shaking near him; he crept forward on his hands and knees, to see what animal was there. Presently he found himself face to face with a huge bull bison. He started to his feet, drew a pistol from his belt, and fixed his eye upon that of the animal. The bison tore the turf with his teeth and horns, stamping furiously, but yet he dared not charge while the human eye was fixed on his. Presently the beast appeared to become uneasy, moved his enormous shaggy head from side to side, and at last slunk off to join the herd that were feeding in the distance; and so my friend was saved by his own presence of mind and the power of the human eye."

But we have been long enough at the commissioner's dinner-table; so let us go home and to bed. It is ten o'clock, and for the people in the Mofussil that is a very late hour. I have told you what a nuisance the mosquitoes are, and also the white ants.

There is another creature from which you are comparatively free in England, and that is the bat. Numbers of all sizes make their nests up above the chats or ceiling-cloths in the bungalows, some not bigger than the humming-bird, others, as I have told you, so large as to deserve the name of flying foxes. Often at night they come into the rooms. One evening, when my wife was going to bed, she found five large bats wheeling round and round in her dressing-room.

On such occasions as this I post myself in one corner of the room, and my chokedar or watchman in another, both armed with long sticks, with which we keep hitting at the bats until we knock them down, and then we throw them out of doors. Often, as they whirl round the room, one will hit himself against the punkah, and fall to the ground. Instantly the mungoose springs upon him, and we hear the bones crushing in his jaws.

One night I was suddenly awakened by something moving and scratching about my head; I raised my hand, and found a large bat clinging to my hair; dreading a snake, I had started up—there was a weight upon my head. I dashed him off, and soon went to sleep again; but he appeared to have taken a fancy to me, and I was again awakened in the same manner; this time, therefore, I got out of bed, knocked the animal down, and killed him. I have several times been roused at night by a great cockroach, three or four inches long, crawling over my face. The other evening a flight of large maulises came into the parlour, and soon drove us to bed. I have two cobras, which were both killed in my own house; also a tarantula, which I caught in my dressing-room.

To turn to another subject. I have been endeavouring to render society here more friendly and agreeable than it can be at large formal dinner-parties, and I am happy to say it has been followed by some of the most influential, and I trust that the custom may become general. The plan is to invite about eight, and those all friendly and intimate, to a quiet dinner at four o'clock. By the time this is over the sun is getting low; and, instead of sitting for a couple of hours over the wine, we soon follow the ladies into the drawing-room. The carriages come to the door for those who like a drive. Some stroll into the wood with their guns; some talk; and so the time passes for about an hour, when the sudden darkness falls upon us almost without warning. We all reassemble at seven for tea and coffee; then spend a pleasant chatty hour or two, or disperse at about half-past nine, having had more amusement than can be enjoyed at a mere dinner-party.

We are making rather a large flower-garden between the house and the river. The wages to a good gardener are about two pence a-day—to a coolie, or labourer, a penny three farthings. My mollee, or gardener, is a very good one; but I must explain what we mean by a good gardener. It signifies neither more nor less than a good thief. I plan my garden and lay it out, showing the man where the paths are to be, where the beds, and where the lawns. Within a few days after it is laid out I expect to find it tolerably full of flowers and shrubs. Where they come from I do not know: you cannot purchase any such things here. Of course, then, everything must come from the gardens of my neighbours. In England this would be considered, and would in fact be, a very dishonest mode of proceeding; but in India it is the custom.

The mollees have the charge of the gardens, and they mutually supply one another. If after a time I should have anything very choice in my garden, my mollee would give cuttings or small plants of it to any of the other mollees who wished for them, and thus every garden would be improved. A person must be very churlish indeed to interfere with this system of general accommodation, which in the end is equally advantageous to all. The system, however, is liable to abuse, and therefore I do not think I altogether approve of it myself. I was once dining with a young officer, and we had some remarkably fine peas. After praising them, I observed that I did not know he had a garden. "Why, no," he replied, laughing; "but I keep a very good gardener." Now this was decidedly most unjust. This young man would not be at the trouble or expense of a garden himself, but chose to take an unfair advantage of the industry and liberality of others. I was not at all surprised to hear, shortly afterwards, that a court of inquiry had been sitting to examine into the circumstances of a most dishonourable action which he had committed, and for which, if it had not been for the leniency of his commanding officer, he would most probably have been cashiered.

I think I have told you how cruelly some of the people here beat their servants. I was standing with an officer in the porch of his house when I was last at Midnapore, when his syce, or groom, brought his horse to the door. Captain L. turned to me, and said, "I have not given that fellow a thrashing for a long time, and he'll forget what it feels like, and grow lazy." Now the fact was, the man was so attentive and industrious that Captain L. could not possibly find any fault with him. However, he went down the steps, and, on the pretence that the man did not hold his horse properly, gave him several violent blows on the face and head, kicked him three or four times with all his force, and struck him on the back with a two-foot rule with such violence that the man was obliged to have his back plastered and bandaged up: and all this without the slightest fault on the part of the servant.

Much as has been said about slavery, I do not believe that any of the slaves in Jamaica were ever worse treated than are the servants of some of our officers here. The excuse is, that it is impossible to manage the Hindus without the whip; but I never use it, and I am certainly quite as well served by all, excepting two. With these I am going to part, for they have been spoiled by living with a very violent man. I will give you an instance of the punishments I employ.

My sirdar always goes home to his supper at nine o'clock. The other evening, after he was gone, I found that he had neglected to get the night-lamp ready, so I was obliged to do it myself. The following morning, instead of thrashing him, I made no observation whatever on the subject; but at nine o'clock in the evening, when he came to ask whether he might go home, I said, "You did not bring the night-lamp last night; I may want something else that is not ready, so for the next week you will not go till eleven." This was a great punishment to him, and yet it did not degrade either the man or myself as a beating would do. At the same time I fully admit that the natives, by their slowness and inactivity, are sometimes very provoking; but surely that is no excuse to the Christian who gives way to angry feelings.

Cuttack, October 12, 1843.

I RETURNED to Cuttack yesterday from Midnapore. It was a most wretched journey, raining incessantly—not such mild gentle rain as you have in England, but regular blinding torrents. The roads were so desperately bad that, although I engaged two extra bearers at each stage, yet each day's journey of fifty miles took me twenty-four hours instead of fifteen. My last day's journey was from Barrapore to Cuttack—fifty miles. I started at two in the afternoon, and arrived at home at half-past two the next day.

About eight o'clock in the evening the rain came down almost in one sheet of water: the men could hardly stagger along with their burden. The rain was driven by the furious gusts of wind violently against the doors of the palanquin, but they were closed and bolted. I was smoking a cigar, and thinking about dear England, when suddenly it struck me that it was becoming very cold. I wondered at it, so closely shut up as the palanquin was. Still it became colder and colder. I was lying on my back. I laid my hand on my face—it was quite warm. I touched my chest—it was warm also. Suddenly I jumped up—it was only the side of me underneath that was cold. My trowsers, shirt, flannel waistcoat, &c., were all soaking. The rain had found its way in at the crevice between the doors, and formed a little puddle just where I was lying.

A severe cold is a very dangerous thing in this country, often bringing on jungle-fever. I first stripped off my wet clothes, then sopped up the puddle as well as I could, and stopped the leak. I then wrapped myself up in a warm blanket. After these preliminaries I got out of my canteen a small spirit-lamp and kettle, then hung them to the top of the palanquin, struck a light, and boiled some water. This I poured into a tumbler, and, adding a little brandy and a little essence of ginger, drank it off, and then composed myself to sleep. I dozed a little; awoke again; tried to go to sleep; could not; changed horses—I mean men; on again; the blanket wet through; moved the blanket so as to have a dry part next me; soon wet through again. At last the blanket was soaking; felt my clothes, which I had hung up to dry; still very wet, but they nevertheless seemed better than the soppy blanket, so I dressed again.

I dared not call the man for my patarahs, or tin boxes, and get out fresh things, for they would have been drenched in an instant. So I dressed in the wet ones; stuffed the blanket up against the leak; lighted another cigar, and puffed away until the palanquin was quite filled with smoke. This created additional warmth, helped to dry my clothes, and by its effects upon myself I have no doubt assisted in keeping off fever.

But as I live so much in my palanquin, I think I had better give a more accurate description of it than I have done. It is made of wood, painted as an English carriage, and having arms, crest, &c., if you choose. The top is covered with a white cement to prevent its leaking, and is slightly curved, so that the rain may run off. The bottom is open wicker-work, on which is laid a mattress and other cushions, covered generally with thin leather. The sides, top, &c., are lined, often with crimson silk. I have had my mattress and other cushions covered with white drill; it is much more serviceable, and will wash: my lining is of the same. The interior length of my palanquin is six feet six inches, the breadth three feet three inches, and of the same height.

The wicker-work of the bottom extends from the head to within one foot three inches of the foot; then instead of wicker-work is a wooden box, which in mine is covered with part of a leopard's skin. In it I carry a few bottles of soda-water and beer and a bottle of water. Over my feet, resting on brackets, is a box, an invention of my own, which I find most useful. It is three feet long, one foot and a quarter broad, and one foot high. In this I keep a great variety of things that I may need.

Whenever I halt I have nothing to do but lift this box out, and there is all my apparatus on the table. Most people have only a shelf, on which they place their medicine-chest, dressing-case, pistols, &c.; but I found this so inconvenient, that I resolved to have the whole in one moveable box, and I find it a great additional comfort. In the lining of the palanquin are pockets for books, &c., and stuck here and there are hooks, on which to hang a watch, &c.

I have pillows especially for my palanquin. I take a blanket and a few books, and then I can start in tolerable comfort for a four or five days' journey. There is a place outside behind for a large brass washhand-basin; in front there are two little windows, like those of a carriage, with glass and Venetian blinds; behind there is one window, and also a lamp with a glass in the back of the palanquin, so as to show its light inside.

Cuttack, November 8, 1843.

I HAVE just been called out to see an enormous Bengal tiger which some native huntsmen shot last night. It has been long prowling about between Cuttack and Chogga, and has carried off many unfortunate men. A party of us intended to go out and look for him next week. He was wounded first by a shot in the shoulder; the second ball went through his eye and killed him at once. It was a magnificent beast.

On the 9th a large leopard was brought in, and also a wild boar. The latter animal is excessively savage and very dangerous. The usual mode of hunting is on horseback, armed with long lances or spears. His strength is very great; he is much larger and longer than the English pig. When enraged his back becomes as much curved as that of the hyæna; indeed, it is a good deal so at all times. From the top of the head to the tail extends a thick mane of bristles, not hanging down like a horse's mane, but standing perfectly upright. I have a young one now in a sty, but the men are obliged to throw his food to him, as he flies at them directly they go within reach. The tusks of the wild boar grow to several inches in length. A friend of mine was out one day when a boar charged his horse; the brute made a spring at its hinder parts, cutting right and left, and both the hind legs of the steed were severed to the bone, and his master was obliged to dismount and shoot him.

This reminds me of another anecdote. Miss D., the sister of the doctor at Balasore, was out riding a short time since; a gentleman of her acquaintance was with her. They were moving slowly along, when suddenly they heard a crackling of the branches by the roadside, and the next instant an enormous tiger sprang into the middle of the lane, just in front of them. The horses appeared paralysed; they could not move, but stood trembling in every joint. The tiger turned round, glared upon them, opened his mouth wide, and gave that horrible ya a-a-a, then made a spring, bounded into the jungle on the other side, and disappeared.

The tiger which they brought in the other day measured ten feet six inches in length, and one foot two inches round his ankle. This species possesses enormous strength; a single blow from his paw is sufficient to crush a man's skull into one frightful mass.

The adjutant of the 8th Bengal Native Regiment told me of a case which he had seen. A tiger seized a large English bullock, tossed it over his shoulders, and then sprang at one bound over a fence several feet in height: so you may easily imagine that a wild tiger is not a very pleasant companion.

We had a sad loss the night before last. I have already mentioned our beautiful little antelope, which used to come and lie at my feet while I was writing. The other night I heard him give a faint scream, and hastened to see what was the matter; he had been bitten by a cobra, and was dead in ten minutes. Poor little fellow! I could have cried,—my wife *did.* I have seen many, but never knew one so tame before. I doubt whether any of the servants had dry eyes as its body was thrown into the river. The bite of the cobra causes the body to swell to a frightful size.

The other day my wife was walking in the garden, when a large cobra glided past her; she called some of the men, who soon killed it, but it was too large to put into a bottle. A gentleman, happening to call just then, asked me whether I had seen the poison. I said, "No." He took the head between his fingers and squeezed it in such a way as to open the mouth. In the upper jaw were two very large white fangs, corresponding as it were to our eye-teeth. As he squeezed with more force, a tiny drop of perfectly transparent colourless fluid issued through the point of each fang—these were drops of venom that pass into the wound. The gentleman who showed me this was a medical man, and he said that he would not for a lac of rupees have the half of one of those drops get into a cut in his finger.

Last June, when the weather was intensely hot, after we left Pooree, where we had resided for six weeks with Mr. and Mrs. B., I went to Chandapore, a delightful place on the sea-coast, about seven miles from Balasore. The thermometer was 105° in-doors at six o'clock in the evening. When I started from Cuttack the thermometer in my palkee stood at 126°. At Chandapore I was glad to put on a cloth coat and cloth trowsers. That is one great advantage in my station; I have almost every variety of climate, except extreme cold. Indeed, when the bishop asked me how I liked my station, I told him I would not change with any chaplain in India.

At Chandapore four of us one morning started for a walk over the sands. We took no shoes nor stockings, and had our trowsers tucked up to the knees. How we did laugh at eyeing ourselves! we were like a set of merry boys. Every now and then one of us would step upon a quicksand and sink down half up his legs, and have to scramble out. Then, as we ran along in the water about six or eight inches deep, we would suddenly see two or three sea-scorpions, and run away, or perhaps slip or stumble over a piece of rock, and then down we came, and all roared with laughter, and then the magistrate sang out,—

> "There was an old man at Barbago,
> He lived upon nothing but sago;—
> Oh! how he did jump,
> When a doctor said, plump,
> 'To a roast leg of mutton you may go.'"

I caught a couple of the sea-scorpions; they do not sting, but cut with the edge of their tails, and it is said that the wound is incurable. They are covered with a hard shell.

There is a great deal of illness about now, although the weather is most delightful: the thermometer seldom above 80°; the morning quite chilly. I am very well; the only complaint I have is that of getting exceedingly fat. I think I have mentioned our relief fund. There are a number of poor Christians here who have lived by beggary, stealing, and all sorts of wretchedness. We are trying to induce them to work, and give them materials, and purchase at a high rate what they produce, and I quite hope our plan will succeed.

You would have laughed to have seen me to-day, surrounded by a crowd of half-black women, measuring out prints and calicoes for dresses, &c.; I being obliged to do it, as my wife was poorly. The things they make are to be given, as rewards, in our new Christian school.

Barripore, November 28, 1843.

How extraordinary does this utter solitude appear! I have just been outside the bungalow: there is none of that confused murmuring sound which is almost universal in England. Every noise is distinctly heard: a child's voice, or a dove's coo, appears to break the intensity of the silence. And then, the thought that, excepting a few barbarians, there is not a human being within a day's journey! The whole feeling is exciting, but oppressive. Millions of black heathens interpose between me and a single European; and yet, with one brace of pistols and a good thick stick, I feel myself perfectly secure. But I will give an instance of the power which each European possesses over these people.

When I went to Balasore with the L.'s, we had four palanquins, and consequently forty bearers. At one place, where we stopped to change men, Mrs. L. sent a man to my palanquin to say that she wanted to speak to me. I at once walked across to the spot where her palanquin stood. The night was as dark as pitch, with a nasty drizzling rain. The red flaming torches disclosed a group of from eighty to a hundred natives, with their long black hair and immense mustachios, naked, except a cloth round their loins.

As we changed bearers here, there was of course a double set present. We had four palanquins—one containing a native nurse and three of Captain L.'s children; another, Captain L. and one child; another, Mrs. L.; and the fourth was my own. On one side of the road was a dense thicket, or jungle; on the other, a deep canal, called by the natives a "nullah;" and these, as well as the dusky group, were flittingly lighted by the torches of the mussalchees. Every man, as is the custom, had a long stick in his hand. We were many hours' journey from any European; Captain L. was totally enfeebled by sickness; and, in short, I was the only person who could have attempted to knock a man down.

But mark the power of white skin (not but that mine is getting somewhat mahogany colour): when I bent down to learn what Mrs. L. wanted, she was too faint and weak to speak loud, and the abominable babbling of the hundred men about us prevented the possibility of my hearing what she said.

"Choop ruho!" (keep quiet) I called out, but to no effect. "Choop ruho!" I bawled, but still to no avail; I could not hear what Mrs. L. said. Suddenly I snatched the stick out of the hand of the man next me, just gave it a little flourish, and jumped into the middle of the crowd. "You want the whip, eh?" I shouted. "Choop ruho, will you?" (for a word or two of English generally slips in either at the beginning or the end of a hasty sentence). In one instant there was a dead silence: not a word of resistance, or even insolence. Mrs. L. was weak and faint, and it seemed she wanted a glass of wine-and-water; this detained us a little time, but as long as we remained there

I found that, even if a whisper arose, the single word "Choop" was sufficient to quiet it directly.

Now, some people may say, here is a long story about nothing, or rather about getting a glass of wine-and-water; but I wish you to observe everything that takes place. Now, the nullah and the jungles, and the torches and the palanquins, are no great wonders in themselves, but together they make a pretty picture, or rather a striking one; and so through life you will find that every half-dozen things that you observe will either form, or assist in forming, some picture in your minds, which will certainly prove amusing or useful, or both.

Then, again, suppose I had told you that I desired the men to be quiet, and they obeyed me: that would have been much shorter, but it would not have led the mind on to any other train of thought; whereas the narrative, as I have related it, suggests many ideas which, if followed up, would fill whole pages; for instance—

1st. Why did the men dread the whip, when they were equally well armed?

2nd. Are they accustomed to feel it?

3rd. Are they generally oppressed, and in what way; and would a native government be an advantage to them?

4th. In what does that superiority consist which makes one hundred Hindus afraid of one European?

5th. What is civilization? What is the difference between *real* civilization, and that knowledge of arts and sciences, of railroads and balloons, which is commonly dignified with the name? And also what is the connexion between real, true civilization and religion?

Here are a few out of numberless trains of thought and questions which might arise, and do naturally arise, from the little anecdote I have given. Now, suppose I had said, "At one stage Mrs. L. said something to me which I could not well make out on account of the noise the men made; however, I soon quieted them, and then found that she wanted some wine-and-water." That description would have given no idea of what actually took place, neither would it have afforded any subject for after consideration.

It was bitterly cold last night. I had on cloak, trowsers, a flannel jacket next my skin, a thick coat buttoned up to my neck, a double blanket over me, and both doors of my palkee shut. Yet I awoke about four o'clock this morning shivering with the cold, and was glad to get out and have a good run of two or three miles, flapping my arms against my sides, to restore the warmth. Mrs. Acland has complained of the cold for the last two days, even at twelve o'clock at noon. The fact is, people here become so accustomed to intense heat that they often find the cold weather very trying, and the hot season is notoriously the most healthy part of the year, though I fancy it is now as warm as an English summer.

Poor Mr. B., with whom we stayed while at Pooree, has had an attack of the terrible jungle-fever, and will, I fear, be obliged to return to England. A sick person, at least in my district, is quite a rarity: all the diseases are so rapid in their operation, that a week's illness is considered a long time. If it is violent, the patient generally dies in a few hours, or at most in two or three days; if slight, he is by that time convalescent, and generally proceeds at once either to the Cape of Good Hope or to England.

Cuttack, December 10.

I HAVE been to Midnapore and back again. Whilst I was at Balasore information was brought in that one hundred and fifty or two hundred elephants had come down into the paddy-fields about twelve miles from Balasore, and that they were destroying the crops. Two or three of the Europeans there wanted to make up a party to go and attack them; I should very much like to have gone with them, but could not afford the time; so the proposition fell to the ground.

It is dangerous sport, but very exciting. The elephant is invulnerable except at one point, and that is a small hollow in the middle of the forehead. I said invulnerable, but that is an improper word; I mean, that that little spot is the only point where you can hit him fatally. Fancy an enormous elephant charging at full speed down a narrow path, with dense jungle on either side, and the sportsman standing still till he comes almost close, and then aiming at the forehead. Suppose he misses the one little spot—the elephant seizes him with his trunk, dashes him to the ground, and then kneels upon and crushes him; that is to say, if it is a fierce male elephant. The tusks of a large one are worth fifty pounds.

The sight of the dead pilgrims by the roadside in this part of India is very dreadful; they go to Juggernat'h by hundreds, or rather by thousands. At the grand festival in June this year, when the car of Juggernat'h is dragged from the temple to his country house, there were present at least eighty thousand pilgrims from all parts of India, who each make large offerings to the idol, and during their stay are not allowed to eat any food but what has been prepared in the temple by the priests. Of course, for this food a most exorbitant price is charged, and at the same time it is of so inferior a quality that numbers died of cholera in consequence of eating it. Many of the pilgrims when they leave Pooree have not a pice left, and literally lie down and die of starvation by the roadside. The instant they are dead they are surrounded by jackals, dogs, and vultures, who quickly peel all the flesh from the bones: it is a horrid sight, but one which is too frequent to create surprise.

To the support of this temple our Christian government pays 6000*l.* a-year, whilst at other places it supports one, two, or more priests. Some will scarcely understand all the arguments by which this pernicious support of idolatry is defended. The principal reason given is, that, when we took possession of the country, we found a number of heathen temples, supported out of the produce of certain lands which were appropriated to their service; and that we, having taken possession of those lands, are bound to support the same temples by money derived from our own revenue. When the Roman Catholics conquered a country, their first object was to extirpate idolatry; when the Mohammedans waged war, they did it in order to destroy the idols of the heathens; but we encourage and protect all those wicked and evil superstitions.

Terrible as is the sight of the mutilated bodies of the pilgrims, it is not to me half so shocking as their thanks when they are relieved. As I travel, some poor wretch, who has more the appearance of a skeleton than a human being, comes to the side of the palanquin, and cries in Hindustanee, "Oh, great king, have mercy! I have been to Juggernat'h, and I have no rice. I have not tasted food, O great king, for three days. Oh, great king, give me some cowries to buy some rice!" I give the man a pice or two, and then he exclaims, "May Juggernat'h bless you, O great being! May Juggernat'h make you prosperous!" This invocation of a blessing from an idol sounds most frightful. The horrors of the roadside scene I will not describe—they are too fearful.

The above account reminds me of the exaggerated manner of expression in use among the Eastern nations. I will give another instance of it, premising that it is the usual style of language employed by the natives towards their European masters. At Midnapore, the other day, I wanted to call on the commanding officer; I accordingly got into a tanjore,—that is, the body of a gig, supported on two poles, and carried by men. As they took me up, I told them to go to the Colonel Sahib's; they spoke together for a few minutes, and then one of them said in Hindustanee, "O representative of God, your slaves do not know where the Colonel Sahib lives."

"Well, do you know where the Salt-Agent Sahib lives?"

"Yes, O representative of God."

"Then take me there."

I had turned away a domestic for being impertinent—a case of very rare occurrence amongst the natives. He was my own personal attendant, and an excellent servant, but I would not allow him to be insolent, and therefore discharged him at once. For weeks this man stood at the gate of my compound, ran for miles by the side of my palanquin when I went out in it, and, if he saw me walking, threw himself on the ground at full length before me, extending his hands clasped over his head, and then crept or rather glided on his stomach close to me, kissed my feet, placed them on his head, and, whilst the tears ran from his eyes, exclaimed in Hindustanee, "O great being! O representative of God, have pity on your slave! punish me, whip me, but let me be your slave, O great king!" One day he brought his two little boys with him, and made them also kneel at my feet. He was an old man with a long beard, and he rubbed it in the dust, and cried and sobbed. I looked at his sons, and thought of my own children, and, as I considered he had been sufficiently punished, I told him to get up and I would try him again. He raised himself on his knees, and kissed the hem of my garment.* He is now the most useful servant I have. He is a sheikh—Sheikh Ibrahim is his name, and he had served every one of my predecessors, the chaplains at Cuttack.

I do not know the names of all my servants, but I will mention a few. Ibrahim is my sirdar, or valet, and chief man; my bearer is Maqua (which, by the way, is a name in use amongst the Indians in North America); my water-carrier is Rangore; my watchman, or chokedar, Sieboo; my sweeper, Ramoo. These last four are allowed me and paid for by Government: I give them a trifle in addition to their regular pay. The cook, or bowachee, is Callipar; and the table-servant, or khitmutgar, is Pekhoo. We only keep one table-servant; every one else keeps two, and many four or five. My syce, or groom, is Saitor; I do not know the names of the coachman, grass-cutter, tailor, and carpenter, nor of my wife's woman-servant, or ayah, as she is called. I think these are all our domestics, except the dobee, or washerman, but I do not know his name.

I believe every one in Bengal keeps more servants than I do. In the Madras presidency not nearly so many are required, as one there will do the work of three here. I do not know how it is in Bombay. I suppose it is on this account that in the Bengal presidency we receive higher pay than in the other parts of India. I said that I kept fewer than most people, but I certainly think I am better served than those who keep double the number, and I attribute it to this: I never beat my servants; I scold them, but do not strike them: and I be-

* This man continued most faithfully attached till his master's death, and was then inconsolable.

lieve that they exert themselves very much in order that they may remain with me on that account, for the cruelty practised by many towards their domestics is most shocking. Yet I firmly believe that I am better served, and, if I may use the expression, really loved, for that very reason.

When a servant is ill it is usual to stop his wages entirely: this I think wrong, and I therefore only stop half, which is another inducement to them to exert themselves in order to remain with me. I will give an instance of the sort of exertion to which I allude. When I packed the last box for England, my carpenter was ill; my cook is a very handy sort of man, so I called him, and desired him to nail up the box; he did it without a moment's hesitation. Almost any other cook would rather have left his situation than have done what he did not consider his work.

Again, I do not know any other person who can get one man to wait on both the sahib and the mem. My khitmutgar not only does this, but also cleans my gun, and sometimes goes out shooting with me; when he is thus engaged the cook supplies his place. These are the advantages of kindness.

It is a common saying that the Hindus have no sense of gratitude, that they have not even a word to express that feeling in their language. I do not believe it, and will give you a case in point. When we are going to travel we pay the money for the bearers into the hands of the postmasters beforehand; he then orders the men to be ready at each stage, and he subsequently sends them their pay. At one stage, as I was going to Midnapore some time ago, the men complained to me that they had not received their money for many months. I questioned them, and, finding their story probable, I promised to speak to the postmaster, and also offered to carry a petition from them to him. This I did; there had been a fault somewhere, but not, I believe, with the postmaster. However, the poor men got their money.

Since that time, whenever I go along the road, as soon as I come to that place a man calls out, "Here is the kind sahib that took our letter for us;" and although the stage is ten miles in length, yet they carry me over it in less time than it takes me to go a six-mile stage elsewhere. My palkee is a heavy one, but they literally run as fast as they can the whole way; and two additional men always go with them without asking for any pay. Is not this something like gratitude?

They are said to be extremely dishonest—I mean the natives generally. This also I deny; although their treatment by individuals is enough to make them so; for on the part of Government the error—if any—lies in an excess of mildness and lenity. I would not hesitate, if it were necessary, to intrust a thousand rupees to a servant to take to Calcutta: that is for him a fifteen days' journey. Yet, if he chose, he might easily get beyond my reach; and such a sum would be sufficient to purchase an estate which would render himself and his descendants landed proprietors and gentlemen. I doubt whether you could say more than that for English honesty; although, of course, there may be exceptions here as well as there.

After I left Jelasore the other day, I remembered that I had omitted to lock my patarahs or tin travelling-boxes. There were many valuable things in them, and when I reached the first stage they had not then come up; yet I proceeded day after day for one hundred and fifty miles without the slightest uneasiness; and these patarahs, which had passed through the hands of sixteen men successively, all of the poorest class and each one alone, arrived at Cuttack in safety one day after myself. I should not have felt so easy had this occurred in England. But enough of this subject for the present.

I was riding out with two friends a few days ago near Balasore, when we saw a cavalcade approaching, consisting of several armed men, some on horseback others on camels. We inquired who they were, and learned that it was the escort of Bheere Singh, who had been on a pilgrimage to Juggernat'h. We joined the Rajah and had a long gossip with him.

The first salutation was a salaam on both sides, that is,—we bowed almost to the necks of our horses, pressing the palms of our right hands against our foreheads. The Rajah, being more polite, or having better command of his horse, salaamed with both hands. I shall describe the man, because, judging from the present state of his country, it is possible that he may hereafter figure in the history of India. He appeared about forty years of age, strongly built, but not very tall; large black whiskers, and the universal moustache, which however was smaller than usual. There was much fire and animation both in his eyes and gestures; I should say also that his look betrayed a cunning and intriguing spirit. He was evidently unwilling to say much concerning the disturbances which have recently taken place in his country, but was most anxious to hear our opinions. He said he had seen the burra lord (great lord), Ellenborough, as he came through Calcutta; and I wondered whether the real object of his journey might not have been to see and speak with the Governor-General rather than to perform his devotions at Pooree.

But one thing struck me especially, and it is a thing highly to the credit of our Indian Government. Pointing to his retinue, he said, "This I very much admire. In my own country and all the native states (that is, states governed by native rajahs), if I were to go to sleep, I must set my guards round me with their arms in their hands, and I dare not ask a stranger to carry a thing for me lest he should run away with it. But directly I come into the Burra Beebee Company's territories" (the East India Company is called the Burra Beebee, or the great lady, by all the natives), "directly I come into their territories, although they are so vast, so immense, from sea to sea" (and he stretched forth his hands in every direction), "directly I come there, if I am weary, I can go to sleep under any tree by the roadside, and I can tell all my guards to go to sleep also. If I want anything carried, I can say to the stranger 'Carry it,' and I know it is safe. Oh! the Burra Beebee Company is a very good great king."

And most assuredly it is so. Wherever we come we give sound laws, and the people find peace and comparative happiness. Under the native rajahs all is anarchy, bloodshed, and oppression. Would that the whole of India were under our sway, and that our Government would seek, by firm and decisive measures, to introduce the blessings of Christianity amongst the thousands and millions of their heathen subjects! I consider these few words of Bheere Singh to confer far more real honour on our Government than all their victories.

How little one knows in England of the pleasure of meeting with an acquaintance! The other night, as I was travelling and just dozing in my palanquin, I was roused by a loud voice—"Hulloh, Acland! what, is that you?" I was out of my palkee in an instant, and Mr. C., of Talacore, jumped out of his. What a break in the monotony of the road! and yet there was one great unpleasantness about it, and that was, we were obliged, after a few minutes' gossip, each to return to his own solitary palanquin. He produced some oranges; we sucked one or two, and then separated.

Cuttack, December 25, 1843.

YESTERDAY morning Captain W. sent to ask me whether I would go out into the jungle with him and try and get some hares. I did not feel much inclined, as my yearly supply of stores, such as wine, beer, candles, vinegar, &c. &c., had just arrived from Calcutta. However I thought that perhaps I should see something which might amuse me, so I went. At three we started on our ponies across the tedious sands to the river. The water we crossed in a boat, and then remounted and rode for some distance into the jungle: at last down we got. We had fourteen men with us to beat the jungle.

We walked along through the wildest scenery, looking for hares, until we arrived at Choudwar—at least that I believe to be the name of the place I described once before, which I said reminded me much of the ancient Petra. There are several long deep ravines filled with dense jungle, the sides composed of perpendicular black rock, a sort of iron-stone, in some parts of which steps have been cut, and in other places great blocks are lying about irregularly, or forming the foundations of the houses of the ancient inhabitants.

We had found no game of any sort except porcupines, which

abound here. At last we came to a ravine of the shape of an acute triangle. The lower line was a perpendicular face of rock of perhaps forty feet in height, the other line was a steep slope, and all the hollow was filled with thick jungle. Captain W. and myself were standing about the middle of the lower line, and we ordered the men that were with us to go down and beat the bushes in the hollow.

As they went down I observed to Captain W. that I thought it looked a likely place for something rather larger than hares. He replied that the men said there were no wild beasts about here. He had hardly done speaking when we heard the most frightful snarling growl proceeding from the bushes down at the farther point of the angle. "A tiger!" screamed the men, and ran off in every direction as fast as they could. "Give us the guns with ball," shouted we; for those in our hands had only small shot, and the men behind us held our other guns. "It is a great hyæna!" shouted I, as with another growl an enormous one sneaked out of the bushes up the bank opposite to that on which we stood. Bang! went the Captain's gun and mine at the same time;—down fell the brute, up again, turned round, yelled, and screamed, inclined to make a rush at us. Bang! bang! again with the other barrels, and with a scream the animal bounded off on three legs, his hind thigh having been broken by one of our balls. "Powder! powder, quickly!" was the cry, and our men handed us the powder and balls: we reloaded as quickly as possible, our hands trembling with excitement.

"Give chase!" I shouted, and off we set as hard as we could run towards the other bank, where the beast was still running, and turning every now and then to snarl at us. "Coolies, drive him hither!" cried Captain W., and on we bounded; but the coolies were not at all willing to obey the command, and so we had a long chase. "I'll fire; you mind him if he turns," exclaimed W. Bang! A yell from the hyæna; and down he rushes towards me. Bang! he's down—no—up again. Another shot from Captain W., and over he tumbles and is dead in a few minutes.

The excitement of such a chase is very great. I was hot and

tired, and also fat; but when I saw the enormous brute all was forgotten, and I leaped down the rocks, scrambled up the hills, and bounded over the bushes, as if I had been a boy.

The hyæna is a cowardly animal, although he has immense strength both of jaw and paw. Had this been a tiger, he would at the first wound have flown at us, and perhaps killed us before we had time to load again; but the hyæna rarely turns upon the hunters unless he sees that all escape is hopeless. I had no idea that these animals were so large. This was little if at all less than a full-grown tiger. He did not spring out like the latter would have done, but sneaked along as if he thought his horrid ugliness would protect him.

As we were coming home over the sands, I asked Captain W. if he did not mean to discharge his gun before he went in. "Yes," said he, "and there is a target," pointing to a large black pariah dog, which was feasting on some rotten carrion at a considerable distance. We dismounted, took our guns, and Captain W. fired. The ball struck the sand between the animal's legs, and he stared round him as if to know what it meant. Captain W.'s next shot struck the sand close to the dog's nose. Off he started, when I raised my gun and fired, and he rolled over dead. This was a useless piece of cruelty; the killing the hyæna was right, because these animals do much mischief among the cattle, and will also carry away young children; but the dogs are in a great measure our scavengers, and carry off all sorts of filth.

The only other things we fired at were some jackals and a white-headed falcon. The former we missed; the latter I killed. The miner is a pretty bird, of which I have before spoken. I consider it good eating, although most persons have a prejudice against it, as not being a very clean feeder. They fly in large flocks. The other day, with a small charge of shot, I killed five at once. The parrots are very destructive to the fruit, especially the custard-apple; I therefore frequently shoot them in my own garden.

Cuttack, January 2, 1844.

I HAVE been to Pooree; but what I am going to relate now is an adventure, not of my own, but of some valiant officers of the regiment stationed here. The Captain, the Lieutenant, the Ensign, and a Serjeant, went out for a day's shooting; and I had the story from two separate individuals of the party. They rode to the ground, and then skirted for some time along the side of the dense jungle. At last the Captain says—"Well, I am tired; I shan't go any farther. Bring me my camp-stool." Fancy a man's taking a camp-stool when he goes out to hunt or shoot! However, down he sat; and the other three proceeded some way farther. At length the Lieutenant says—"Well, *I* am tired; I shan't go any farther. Give me my camp-stool." Down he sat; and on went the other two, until the Ensign said—"Well, I am tired; I shan't go any farther. Give me my camp-stool." And he sat down.

The Serjeant, with one native, now proceeded down a narrow path which led into the jungle. He had not been gone more than five minutes when the Ensign heard the report of a gun, and the next instant the Serjeant rushed out of the jungle, without his hat, without his gun, with his mouth wide open, eyes staring, and hair all on end. "What's the matter, Serjeant?" cries the Ensign. "A tiger, sir," says the other, without stopping. "A tiger?" "Ay." Down goes the Ensign's gun over his camp-stool, and off he starts after the Serjeant as fast as his legs can carry him. "Hulloh!" exclaims the Lieutenant, as they came rushing towards him: "why, what's in the wind now?" "A tiger! a tiger!" they shout. Down goes the Lieutenant's gun, and he quickly joins in the race. "What in the world are you all after?" cries the Captain, as they came to where he was comfortably sitting, drinking a bottle of beer, and smoking a cigar. "A tiger! a tiger! a tiger!" is again the reply. "Pooh, pooh, nonsense!" said the Captain, moving slowly towards his horse. "Nonsense!" answered the fugitives; "we tell you there is a tiger down there: go and see yourself." "No, I am tired," says the Captain; "I shall go home." And he jumped on his horse, and, followed by his brave comrades, galloped back to Cuttack. How the natives did grin and chuckle. They, too, had seen the frightful monster, and knew that it was a poor harmless jackal which had put to flight the Captain, and the Lieutenant, and the Ensign, and the Serjeant!!!

But there is moral to this tale. Another officer asked the Serjeant afterwards why he ran away? The answer was, that he ran at first because he was alone and unsupported, and that he ran afterwards because he saw the officers run. And this will ever be the case. If the officers show a firm front, so will the men: if the officers waver or hesitate, it will naturally strike a panic into the minds of those who are accustomed to look up to them for guidance. Remarkable instances of both these positions we have recently had at Jellalabad and Kabul.

I start on Friday next for Balasore. I go principally for the sake of exercise and shooting. There are a great many bears there. My wife has just hired a new woman-servant. She is of the Ooriah Mehanee caste, and therefore may not wear petticoats, but only the common native dress. Now, all ladies like their own personal servants to wear petticoats; but here it is so strictly forbidden, that the woman, if she were once to put them on, would be deserted by her husband and children, and never be suffered to eat with any of her tribe. But then the Hindu law, whilst it is thus severe on any breach of caste, provides an easy mode of getting over the difficulty. My wife gives the woman eight shillings: the woman gives half of this to the priest, and with the other half she provides a feast for her tribe. After this she may wear her petticoats in peace and security.

Barripore, January 5, 1844.

THERE is one part of the sands at Pooree, on which if you stand about the middle of the day, and look towards the north, you are surprised to observe in the distance an English town. You see several three-storied houses, with doors and windows: interspersed here and there are several very English-looking trees; and at a short distance, standing on a small hill, you see the ruins of a large castle, with the green ivy clinging to it in many parts. Often have I stood and gazed upon this scene, for it reminds me of dear England. And yet, if you go to the place, what do you suppose you find? Nothing but one long flat bed of loose sand, without one vestige of a tree.

The appearance is caused solely by the refraction of the rays of light. To explain this I will give an example. If you hold a stick so that the lower part is in the water and the upper part in the air, the stick will appear to be bent at the point where it passes the surface of the water; or, place a shilling in a cup or basin, so that you cannot see it because the side of the cup hides it from you, fill the cup with water, and then you will see the shilling, although it is still in the same spot it was in before. This bending of the rays is what is called refraction, and is caused by the rays passing out of one transparent thing into another which is more or less dense than the first. I think that the cause of the mirage at Pooree is this. Hot air is less dense than cold air. The steam which comes from a kettle is still water, but it occupies a much larger space than the water did. One kettle of water will give much more than a kettlefull of steam, so that it is evident that the heat has made the water occupy a much larger quantity of space. Still the steam is only water; therefore it must be much less dense than cold water. If you filled a saucepan with water, and fastened the lid down, so that no steam could escape, it would burst it: the particles of heat cause the particles of water to be less closely connected together. But that is a subject too abstruse for this work.

Well, hot air, like hot water, is less dense than cold air; also water is more dense than air. You could not run along as quickly in the water as you could in the air; you could not strike a person with your hand under water hard enough to hurt him; and this is because the water is more dense or solid than air: therefore, air with a good deal of moisture in it is more dense than when dry. But along the hot sands of Pooree, close to the sea-shore, there must be a great deal of heat and also a great deal of moisture.

In the direction in which you look to see the mirage I mentioned, there is a small piece of stagnant water from which much moisture must arise under the burning heat of the sun; consequently there must be much refraction in all directions. And this is seen in looking the right way from all parts of the Pooree sands; and from the particular point to which I have alluded, this picture, owing, I suppose, to certain marks in the sand, assumes the appearance of a castle, houses, &c. All this is a very rough explanation; but it may serve to give you some idea of the probable cause of the mirage. Ships have sometimes appeared to be sailing in the air from the same cause; and distant coasts, which were far below the horizon, have been distinctly seen by means of the refraction.

Guzzeepuddee, 8 miles from Balasore, January 12.

YESTERDAY morning about four o'clock we started from Balasore on horseback. The party consisted of the magistrate, the surgeon, and myself. It was a brilliant moonlight, but somehow I thought I should like to finish my night's rest, and therefore soon got into my palanquin, and had a most comfortable nap. I was awakened at daybreak by my bearers stopping and telling me that they did not know the way to Guzzeepuddee. I got out of my palanquin, loaded my gun, inquired my way of the first native I saw, sent my palanquin on, and then with two servants entered the jungle. Whereabout the magistrate and the doctor were I had not the slightest idea. I had a delightful ramble through a jungle, many of the natives following me from each village through which I passed, and appearing to take great interest in the success of my sport.

I went on, with my broad-brimmer hat and brown leather gaiters, followed by twenty or thirty black fellows, forcing my way through the thickest, densest shrubberies, thinking at every instant that I might come suddenly on a large bear. Every now and then a break would occur in the jungle, and I would emerge from the tangled thicket into a broad open space of three or four acres, covered with the smoothest turf, interspersed here and there with the graceful bamboo, and surmounted on all sides with a literal wall of trees and underwood. On their branches sat the splendid wild fowls and the beautiful peacocks, whilst from all sides I heard the soft cooing of the doves.

Then again I would find myself in a similar open space; but instead of the turf there was a broad sheet of water, with the red and white lotus-flowers floating on the surface, and the glittering white paddy-bin (a sort of small stock) stretching along the edge. A little farther on I came suddenly on a large jheel (a piece of shallow muddy water), with the heron and the pelican, and I think the spoonbill, standing on the sides and busily catching their breakfast of fish. Several of the most curious of the birds I shot, in order to preserve their skins, and occasionally, as a hare darted across my path, I would raise my gun and fire. But one bird I must describe more particularly.

I was standing by the side of a large jheel, when a native called out, "A bird, very good: look, sir." I looked in the direction in which he pointed, but could see nothing, and was going to scold him, when he said, "It will come." I continued watching, when presently I saw what appeared to be a long snake rising from the water. It was some little time before I could make up my mind that this was actually part of a bird, and by that time the long neck was again drawn under water, and nothing was visible.

I continued to watch, and presently, at some yards from the spot where it had before appeared, the same snaky form was again elevated into the air. It was almost like shooting at a reed, but however I raised my gun and fired. There was an instant struggle in the water, and then I saw the body of a large dark-coloured bird floating on the surface. Wishing to obtain the body, I turned to the natives and said, "The man that wants a pice, bring that bird to me." The pice is a little more than a farthing, but enough to find a family for a day. Six or eight boys and men dashed into the water, and there was a regular race, struggling and swimming in order to obtain the prize. One boy had just reached the spot, when suddenly it disappeared; now the long neck rose in a different place, and again there was a rush to obtain the pice. The bird, which was evidently much wounded, began to move across the water, keeping its long neck about eighteen inches above the surface, no other part being visible. I was running round the banks to have another shot, when the bird suddenly rose, and, with its long legs extending behind, flew over the jungle. I saw it fall at a short distance, but the bushes were so thickly matted together that I could not get near the place.

As I advanced farther from Balasore the natives of the village appeared astonished at my appearance, many of them probably never having seen a white man before. Some stood still staring at me, others ran and hid themselves in their houses. At last I came to a large open space of a mile or more in diameter, and here a most singular scene presented itself. Throughout the whole extent of the space, large masses of black rock, perfectly smooth and rounded at the edges, rose at intervals to the height of twelve or sixteen feet, at an angle of about 70°. It appeared as if some mighty city had been swept over by a hurricane, and all the walls were tottering to their fall.

Some time after this, to my great satisfaction, I arrived at the tent, which had been sent there the day before, and found a plentiful breakfast ready, and the rest of the party anxiously awaiting my arrival. I had been nearly six hours on foot. Our tent is about eighteen feet square, with one pole in the centre, a table and chairs inside, and our palanquins, in which we sleep at night, standing under a sort of canvas verandah. There is another very small tent for a bath-room, and also a part composed of a single piece of canvas for the servants. The latter is about thirty feet long and fifteen broad.

And now let us look around the encampment. The immediate neighbourhood consists of rice-fields, from which the paddy has been cut. At about half a mile from the tents on either side is a thick jungle, and in the distance are the rugged and magnificent hills of the Neilghur, which I have already described.

At six o'clock in the evening the sun was just setting as we three sahibs returned from our day's shooting. The magistrate is just washing his hands in a chillumchee, or brass basin, at the door of the tent. In the front-ground, on two chairs, are seated the doctor and myself; the former is having his long leather gaiters or overalls pulled off. I have one foot in a chillumchee of warm water, the other resting on the black knee of one of my servants, who is shampooing and cracking each joint of the toes. Now he has done that, wiped the foot dry, put on the shoe, and is squeezing or kneading each muscle in the calf of the leg. No one but those who have experienced it can have any idea what a luxury this is when you are very tired!

Behind us stands a long-bearded turbaned khitmutgar, with sherry and glasses. Our guns are leaning against the side of the tent, our horses are picketed to a tree close by, and the grooms are busily rubbing them down. A hundred or a hundred and fifty black natives are separating into groups according to their castes, and are lighting fires all around in order to cook their dinners. Behind the servants' tent is a fire of charcoal, over which a black man is turning a hare, some partridges, a peacock, and several other results of our day's sport. Close by is another fire of wood crackling and sparkling, on which are stewpans with salmon, oysters, &c. &c., which have come from England.

It grows late: the moon rises over the hills; the fires blaze up in all directions; I see the swarthy natives moving around them, and hear them chattering or singing their low monotonous song; everything looks wild; I begin to indulge in all sorts of reveries —when a man approaches with his hands clasped together, and, bending low before me, says "Cana meg" (dinner-table). The peacock takes the place of the reverie; visions of the partridges and oysters flit across my mind; and I run to help in demolishing a most substantial and well-earned meal. I then go to my palkee. The howling of the jackals does not awake me, I am too well used to it; but at last, about two o'clock in the morning, I was aroused by a sort of sniffing and a scratch at the door. I guessed at once what it was, and debated for an instant whether I should open it a little and try the effect of my pistols, or call out so as to rouse my companions, or lie still and leave him to himself. I determined on the latter; as, supposing I had not killed him, my visitor might have come into my palanquin and killed me before I could get assistance. I therefore lay quietly with a pistol in my hand; and I felt much happier when I heard the bear at last trot off.

Barripore, January 16, 1844.

On Friday morning the magistrate and myself determined to ascend one of the Neilghur hills. The doctor did not think it worth the fatigue, and therefore shot partridges and wild-ducks for our breakfasts. We started from our tents at about half-past five in the morning. For about four miles our road lay through jungle, similar to that I have already described.

As we emerged from this the effect was most extraordinary. We had been suffering much from heat, and the sudden exclamation of both of us was, "Oh, how very cold!" A chilling blast came down from the hills, which entirely altered the temperature of the air; and, moreover, the place where we now were can very rarely, if ever, be reached by the sun. These causes produce a most singular effect upon the vegetation. Behind us was a dense jungle of bamboos, brambles, cacti, &c., through which it was most difficult to force a passage. In front of us for nearly a mile—that is, extending to the foot of the hills—the appearance was altogether different: not a bamboo nor a cactus, not a bramble, scarcely even a thorn; the turf perfectly smooth; the only plants a sort of laurel and a species of wild-apple; and no two plants growing within four feet of each other. It was like a wilderness or a shrubbery in a gentleman's park. We found several marks of bears and also of elephants; and the natives were rather unwilling to proceed. However, we led the way, with our guns in our hands, and soon arrived at the foot of the hill. It rose very suddenly, and in many places we had to climb for several feet up the face of a smooth black rock, similar to that which I have already mentioned.

We had no adventures beyond a tumble or two, but it was a most fatiguing work; and the instant we reached the top we threw ourselves down and called for a cigar and a glass of beer. This hill, which is much the lowest of the whole range, is not, I suppose, more than five hundred feet in height: it rises to a peak, the extreme top being about six feet in diameter. Here we fired off our guns as a signal to the doctor, and then commenced our descent.

At the bottom we were very glad to mount our horses and ride back to the tent. It was a very clear morning, and you can hardly imagine the wild magnificence of the scene from the top. Behind us lay the thick jungle through which we had passed, with Balasore in the distance, and the sea forming the background; in front, a wilderness of brushwood, extending as far as the eye could reach; to the right was a winding river, bordered by the graceful bamboo, with native villages and patches of rice-fields on its banks; whilst to the left, from the midst of the thickets, rose abruptly the other hills, towering to the height of several thousand feet. All these ranges belong to tributary rajahs, and are not the property of the English. We were delighted with our excursion, and it has led to the proposal of another, which we hope to accomplish, with the addition to our party of the doctor and the master-attendant, as soon as I return from Cuttack.

This second expedition is to be to the highest point visible from Balasore. No human being has ever yet ascended it, and the natives pretend that it is impracticable; however, we mean to try. I should like to set my foot where no man has ever trodden. We shall go well armed with guns, pistols, and swords; we are also each to carry a hatchet and a billhook, to cut our way through the jungle.

We intend to take a barometer and thermometer in order to measure the height, and go well attended by natives. It is said that this hill is tenanted by all sorts of wild beasts, but we shall be too well armed to fear them. The inhabitants are a very savage race, and offer up human sacrifices; but they will hardly dare to attack white men. I am very fond of these excursions; the exercies I consider good for me—whilst at Guzzeepuddee I was ten or eleven hours on my feet each day; and another great advantage is, that they cost nothing beyond the price of powder and shot. I must now start for Cuttack. I found in the jungle the skeleton of a small boa constrictor: it is perfect except the lower jaw. I told one of my servants to take care of it. When I returned to Balasore he had lost it; I said, if he did not find it again I should deduct a rupee from his month's wages. His answer was, "O representative of God, you are the father and the mother of your slave, and you must do with him as you think fit." However, he managed to find the skeleton.

Midnapore, February 1, 1844.

WHEN I returned to Cuttack the last time I found that my wife had been rather poorly for some days; I therefore determined that I would take her out for a little excursion. We accordingly sent out a tent and all necessary apparatus, and then started with some friends of ours—a Captain of Engineers and his wife, and a couple of children—to explore two of the most extraordinary places in India, Bhabaneswar and Cundeganee. At the former there are nine hundred and ninety-nine temples, besides numerous tombs, &c.: at the latter place some very high hills, perforated in every direction with artificial caves; a palace, statues, and animals, cut out of the solid rock; long inscriptions in some language now forgotten; images of gods, of which the Hindus know nothing.

The trip did my wife a great deal of good; but almost immediately after our return to Cuttack I was attacked by one of the fearful diseases of the country. Fortunately I knew what it was by the very first symptoms, and therefore went to the doctor at once. The disease is what we call *liver;* in England it is called, I think, inflammation of the liver. It is accompanied by a soreness in the side and acute pain in the shoulder. The doctor immediately took most energetic pains to reduce me both in size and in strength, and he succeeded so well that all danger was soon over. Directly I was better I was ordered change of air, starvation, and exercise.

February 15, 1844.

I FEEL quite well again: we start for the hills this afternoon. The party consists of seven Europeans and about one hundred natives. It happened rather curiously that the Rajah to whom the hill belongs called here this morning on business: he is a very intelligent young man. He has volunteered to accompany us, to supply us with elephants if we wish to hunt upon the plain, and to provide us an escort of five hundred men; so we shall go in state. He rode a magnificent white horse with *pink eyes.* We each take a small axe, a pair of pistols, and two guns.

But before proceeding I would enter into more particulars concerning the excursion that we took for the benefit of my wife's health. On Monday we all started at half-past five in the morning—Captain R. and myself on horseback, and Mrs. R. and my wife in palanquins, having their ponies led by their side. We had about one hundred and twenty servants with us, Captain R. having a good deal of surveying and other work to do.

As we went along the road he stopped to inspect the different bridges, &c. We had one little adventure this morning. It seems that some months ago a beyraghee, or mendicant, sat himself down by the side of the road, a few miles from Cuttack, with nothing but an umbrella to shade him from the sun. There he remained for some weeks, subsisting on the charity of the pilgrims who were proceeding to Juggernat'h. I should have mentioned that our road lay, for a considerable distance, on the direct route for Pooree. After some time the beyraghee made himself a little hut of wickerwork, after the fashion of many of the Indian devotees. These baskets, as I may call them, are just large enough to contain a man in a lying-down position; they are, in fact, mere coverings.

By degrees the basket became a good-sized mud hut; then the beyraghee began to enclose a small piece of ground, which he cultivated, and built himself a granary of bamboo to contain the rice given him by the pilgrims. Now, although a man with an umbrella does not much matter, yet a hut with a little field, around which a village is likely enough to spring up, cannot be allowed upon the roadside, which belongs to Government.

The man had been warned, but paid no attention to what was said; and accordingly, when we reached the spot, Captain R. directed the chuprapees, or Government messengers, to pull down the fence and destroy the hut, granary, &c. We sat on our horses while these men obeyed the order. In a quarter of an hour the whole was level with the ground. I knew that Captain R. was perfectly right, yet I could not help pitying the poor man, who came and laid himself down at our horses' feet, with his hands clasped over his head. Like many of the beyraghees, he was entirely naked. They are a worthless, wicked set of men, and peculiarly obnoxious to Europeans. It was a singular scene. Captain R. and myself, with our broad-brimmed hats, sitting quietly on our sturdy ponies; a half-naked groom at the head of each; the naked beyraghee at our feet; and a dozen chuprapees, in the white native dress, with red badges, hewing the house and fence to pieces, and scattering the remains on all sides under the grove of mangoes with which the road was bordered. In the distance were the palanquins, whilst the wild song of the bearers faintly reached our ears.

Nothing of interest occurred after this until we arrived at Bengwharrie, a small village, where our tents were pitched under a grove, or, as we call it, a "tope," of splendid trees. I have already described the appearance of a private encampment; the only difference here was that we had a greater number of men about us, and more tents. Mine contains one room, about twenty-four feet square; in the centre rises the high pole which supports our canvas house. At each end are cloth doors, made to roll up. The tent has a double fly or covering, one much larger than the other; it is like a small one inside a large one. This tends to keep it warm at night, and cool during the day; the outer fly forms a verandah round the inner room. In the latter are two small camp bedsteads, a camp table, camp chairs, &c. By camp bedsteads, &c., I mean such as will double up for the convenience of carriage. In the verandah are our palanquins, a chest of wine, beer, &c., some cooling apparatus, and various other articles. At one side there is an entrance into a small tent, which serves for a bathing-room.

After breakfast we were very much interested in watching the monkeys. The tope swarmed with a grey species, some of which appeared almost as large as men. They are peculiarly sacred in the eyes of the Hindus, who imagine that one of their gods once assumed a similar form. They are called Hunnamuns, which was the name of that deity. My wife and I stood at the door of the tent watching them for hours; they do not appear to be afraid of men. Many of the females had young ones with them, and they came and sat down close to us with their little ones in their laps. First they would suckle them, then they would hush them to sleep, or turn them over and over, pulling off all the dirt that adhered to their skins, and making them clean and comfortable.

A little farther off you would see four or five males picking the fruit off a low bush, and chattering to one another all the time. Then a half-grown one would jump down, and give a hard pull at an old one's tail, for which he generally received a good box on the ear, unless he was nimble enough to get out of the way in time; presently one of the old fellows would get angry, and spring into the tree after his little tormentor, and a regular chase would ensue. The leaps they take are tremendous; they will often spring from the top of a lofty tree into the middle of the next without falling.

I saw one of the females shot; it was a cruel sight, and struck all the natives with horror. They refused to touch the dead body. The ball did not kill her instantly, and she cried piteously, whilst she pressed her little one to her bosom, and tried to get into the tree. To the last she would not relinquish her young one, and died in endeavouring to save it. I could not shoot a monkey, their actions and their cries are so like human beings. I know of a case in which an officer shot one, and the whole herd instantly sprang from the trees and attacked him; it was with difficulty he was saved. They are most interesting creatures.

In the evening I went out with my gun, accompanied by Captain R. I got nothing, however, but some doves and some crow-pheasants; the latter are not eaten by Europeans, though much relished by the low-caste natives. It is a bird, as the name signifies, between a crow and a pheasant. The colour is black, tinged with a deep dull red. It has a long tail, and runs like a pheasant; but I believe that its food is the same as a crow's, that is, carrion and animal food.

On the Tuesday morning Captain R. was lazy, so I started by myself at six o'clock to try and get some jungle-fowl. When I say by myself, I of course mean with three or four servants. I, however, shot nothing but a few doves and one green pigeon. The latter is a large bird, of a pale-green colour, and is most delicious eating, which is more than can be said of any of the game in India. The partridges are dry and flavourless; the deer have literally not a particle of fat upon them; the hares are fit for nothing but soup. A leveret is good, and so is a very young peacock, but, old or young, they must be eaten the same day that they are killed. By the by, the black partridge is pretty good: it has a black neck, shading into deep red on the head; the back is dark; the breast and tail are most beautifully covered with minute white spots.

I may as well mention now that we shot the other day a double-spurred partridge; it was of a dingy red colour, with a crest on its head; the legs were bright red, and each armed with two long sharp spurs. As I walked along I observed a bird of a species which I had never seen before; I tried to shoot it, in order to have it stuffed, but missed, and sadly frightened some monkeys who were in the same tree. As far as I could judge, every feather was a bright blue, giving a most splendid appearance to the bird.

After breakfast Captain R. and I stood at the door of the tent amusing ourselves with his air-gun. I killed with it three or four birds, whose skins I should like to preserve; one especially, though I believe I have before described it, namely, the mango-bird. I fancy the European name is the golden oriole. It is of one uniform brilliant yellow, with the exception of the head, which is perfectly black. Its note is very peculiar, as indeed are the voices of many of the Indian birds. I cannot describe the sounds on paper, but I have learned to imitate many of them well enough to hold a long conversation with them. Once or twice, when Captain R. wanted to get near to a bird without being observed, he asked me to continue talking to it. It is curious to observe them hopping from branch to branch replying to my call, and looking round on every side for the bird from which they suppose the sound to proceed.

On Tuesday evening Captain R. and I rode about four miles to try and find some peacocks. His pony had hurt its foot, so he took one of mine. We were going along quietly enough through some rice-fields, when suddenly the pony he was on shied; he spurred it, and it immediately reared and fell over backwards. Most fortunately he managed to throw himself off, so as to escape being under the horse, though, as it was, he got a heavy tumble. It is a very nice pony, a little inclined to rear; but I am too heavy for it to do so with me. I am getting thinner now. We came at last to a beautiful bit of bamboo-jungle, where we dismounted, inside of which was a paddy-field; in the centre were two fine cocks and five hens feeding. Beckoning to the servants to stay behind, I crouched down on the ground and crept slowly forward, until I came very near to the jungle-fowl, when I cautiously raised my gun to fire; from some cause or other it did not go off, though the cap exploded, and the birds flew away. Now, a regular Indian sportsman would not fire at a bird on the ground, but would first make a noise to frighten him, and would then fire as he was flying away; however, I am not practised enough for that, and like to get what they call a pot-shot whenever I can.

A little while ago a party of officers went out from Cuttack to shoot. Their men were beating the jungle, when suddenly all the wild cry ceased, and a man came gliding to where all the sahibs were standing to tell them that there was a tiger lying asleep in his den close at hand. A consultation was instantly held; most of the party were anxious to return to Cuttack, but Captain B. insisted on having a shot at the animal. Accordingly he advanced very quickly until he came to the place, when he saw—not a tiger, but a large leopard lying quite still, with his head resting on his fore paws. He went up close and fired, but the animal did not move. This astonished him, and on examination he found that the brute was already dead. One of his companions had bribed some Indians to place a dead leopard there and to say that there was a tiger asleep. You may imagine what a laugh there was, though it was very wrong of the Europeans to encourage the natives to say what was not true.

Since then a large party has been out from Cuttack on a shooting excursion: they found five leopards, two sambres (the largest species of deer), and four of the Indian bisons or ghyal, of whose horns I have preserved a specimen. They however killed only one leopard.

But I must hasten on with my description. Captain R. and I proceeded into the jungle, where we heard several peacocks; we separated, creeping along in different directions. Presently I came to an open space where some pea-fowls were feeding, but we did not succeed in killing anything. The next evening we went to the same place, when Captain R. shot a peacock. Towards dusk I was creeping along, when suddenly I saw what appeared to me a fine peahen. I signed to my men to be quiet, got as near as I could, fired, and shouted to my followers to run and pick up the bird, for it was dead. An Indian servant rarely loses his gravity; but in this instance they could not restrain themselves when they found that instead of a pea-fowl I had knocked to pieces the skull of an old cow which had been half-picked by the vultures; in the dim light I had mistaken it for a bird.

The next day we proceeded about ten miles farther to Bhalmacottee; and on the day following, that is Friday, we started at five o'clock in the morning for Bhohoneswar. On the way we passed the remains of a very large old fort built of hewn stone. In one of the moats, which was still full of water, I saw the remains of a pier of a bridge. Bhohoneswar is a very ancient town, much more so than Pooree: it is celebrated for containing nine hundred and ninety-nine temples. The natives say that, had there been a thousand, Juggernat'h would have taken up his abode here; but as there were not he preferred having a new temple for himself at Pooree. The ancient city has disappeared, and the town only consists of a few hundred mud huts. The temples however remain—some perfect, others in ruins; some facing the street of the modern town, others half hidden in the surrounding jungle. It is a wonderful place, and I hardly know how to describe it.

At one extremity of the town is a tank, about half a mile square, and of a great depth, entirely faced with huge blocks of black iron-stone. In the centre of this stands a small temple, whilst the sides are surrounded by others of greater or less size. At the end next the town an enormous flight of steps leads down to the water, where hundreds of pilgrims were hastening to wash themselves before entering the great temple. The farther end is bordered by a dense and lofty jungle, and in the distance is a splendid background of rugged hills.

After leaving the burrah tellores (great tank) we walked through a lane of temples, many of which were ruinous, until we came to the grand sacred edifice of the place. The form of this, as indeed of most of the others, is similar to that of Pooree. The temple of Bhohoneswar is however larger, the principal tower being about two hundred feet high. Like all the others, it is built entirely of stone, and every block is most elaborately carved. The various cornices, of elephants, horses, &c., are as beautifully executed as if they had been done by the best European artists. The fretwork is most delicate in its livery, and the many images, though representing grotesque figures, are admirably carved. The whole forms one mass of most splendid sculpture.

No description would enable the reader to form any idea of the magnificence of this building. Many of the blocks of stone are fifteen, twenty, and twenty-five feet in length, and thick in proportion. It would be curious to discover by what means they were ever raised to the height of above one hundred feet. This temple is still sacred, and we were therefore not allowed to enter it, but we examined the interior of several of the others. The lofty domes were evidently constructed by a people who were ignorant of the use of the arch; they are formed of overlapping stones, approaching nearer and nearer together until they reach the top, where the whole is surmounted by one enormous block.

We breakfasted in a small tent which we had sent forward to

Bhohoneswar, and then proceeded in our palanquins to Cundeegurree, a distance of about seven miles. This latter place consists of three hills surrounded by the most romantic-looking jungle. Our palanquins were set down in what may be called a forest, at the foot of the principal hill, and crowned by a small but very pretty white temple. These hills are perforated in every direction with caves of various dimensions, and reminded me most forcibly of the ancient Petra. Many of the caves are inhabited by devotees and priests. The god whom they worship is quite unknown to our Hindu servants: he is called Persilat'h, and is the god of the Jains, who were a powerful race that existed prior to the introduction of the Hindu religion. There are very few of them now remaining. The god is represented as a naked man, standing upright, with his arms hanging down by his sides. In many of the caves are small images of this deity beautifully cut in a dark-blue stone.

At the summit is a Jain temple, which has been rebuilt within the last two hundred years. The Hindus say that the caves are the works of demons. Above the entrances to many of them are long inscriptions in a forgotten tongue. Several of the letters appear to resemble the Greek; but most of them are different from any known language. The entrance to one of the caverns is through the mouth of an enormous lion's head, cut out of the solid rock: it is exceedingly well executed. The pillars about the doorway are also cut out of the solid rock. Within the lion's mouth is an inscription in two lines, which I copied.

Many of the caves are large and lofty, others very small: there are some not high enough for a man to stand upright: of these latter several have very small entrances; and in these are devotees who had vowed never to leave them alive. The wonder seems how they could ever have managed to creep in. I saw some of these holy men: one of them had entirely lost his sight; another had his right arm shrivelled, and fixed in an upright position, with the nails several inches in length growing through the palm of his hand. What suffering do these heathens endure for the sake of their religion, whilst we are so unwilling to do even a little to please the true God! Their superstitions are most disgusting; but they are a reproach to us, both for our inertness in attempting to convert the Hindus, and also for the contrast they afford to our self-control, who call ourselves Christians.

In the solid rock of these hills have been excavated some tanks; but the most marvellous thing of all is the palace of the ancient rajahs. This, like all the rest, is hollowed out of the solid stone, and consists of two stories; the lower comprises a good-sized square court, surrounded on all sides by large excavated chambers. Into this yard you are obliged to descend from above. The upper floor is similarly cut, except that a large portion of the rock has been cut away before the entrances were made to the chambers. The consequence is that there is a broad terrace, overlooking the rooms beneath, and upon which the several apartments of the upper story open. What labour must have been employed in making these extraordinary excavations! The chambers are narrow, about twelve feet wide, but many of them are long; speaking from conjecture, I should say that one of them was not less than forty feet, the length corresponding with the direction of the side of the quadrangle. The entrance-walls (if I may call them so) seem to have been much ornamented; but what struck me most was a statue, cut, of course, out of the solid rock, and supporting one side of an ornamented entrance to one of the chambers. This statue, the natives say, is intended to represent the rajah who founded the palace: it is nearly the size of life and well preserved. The right arm hangs down by the side, the left is bent at the elbow, the hand resting on the hip. On the head appears to be a close helmet, with, I think, scales down each side of the face. The dress consists of a short shirt of scale armour reaching down to the thigh; below this hangs a cloth skirt to the knees; hanging from the shoulders behind is a short cloak resembling that worn by our modern horsemen; round the waist is a sash or loose belt; boots reaching half-way to the knees; and at the side is a double-edged Roman sword. Now, to what nation or people such a dress as this can have belonged I cannot conceive. I feel confident that no people of India have ever worn such garments; yet, when I look at this dress, and consider the Grecian nature of many of the letters in the inscriptions, and the un-Indian appearance of the pillars in the lion's mouth, I cannot help asking myself whether it is possible that, when Alexander was stopped by the Affghans, any of his people ventured still farther into the country, and after various wanderings founded Cundeegurree, as conquerors of the district. Or, if I wish to turn my speculations in another direction, I may examine the dress, carved in stone, and that statue, and think of the name of the reputed founder Lalal, India, Kesari (quære Cæsar?). All this, however, is mere speculation, as I have no sufficient data at present by which to arrive at any conclusion. There is a much longer inscription very correctly copied in Stirling's 'History of Orissa.'

After spending a most interesting day at Cundeegurree we returned to Bhalmacottee, from whence my wife and myself came on to Cuttack on Saturday. I forgot to mention an animal that we killed; the natives called it a "goodee sampsnake," and said it was very savage and very venomous, though I imagine it was nothing but a guana. It is a sort of lizard, with a very tough scaly skin, about two and a half feet in length, head like that of a snake, forked tongue, sharp teeth, short legs, armed with long claws or rather talons. I have preserved and stuffed the skin.

A gentleman has just been here who told me an interesting anecdote about an elephant. A friend of his bought one, and went out hunting with a large party. The animal behaved very well all day; but in the evening, when they were going to take off the howdah, the mahout called to the Europeans to stand farther off, as the elephant appeared to be getting uneasy. He had hardly spoken when the animal made a rush forward, seized an unfortunate native, and began trampling upon him with his enormous feet; a chuprapee who ran forward was seized by the elephant, and flung to the distance of many feet into the river; the beast then raised the poor wretch he had been crushing, and threw him into the jungle, where he was found with not a bone unbroken; every limb was crushed: of course he died almost directly. The elephant then ran off, and for weeks was the terror of the country round—going into the villages, tearing down the houses to look for corn or rice. At last he was caught, and sold to the king of Lucknow, in Upper India. I should mention that the only limestone hills in this part of India are those around Cundeegurree.

Pooree, May 26, 1844.

How little is known in England of what a thunderstorm is! At this minute (about ten o'clock in the evening) the rain is pouring down in vast sheets of water rather than in drops. For the last two hours the lightning has not ceased for a minute at a time, whilst the thunder has continued incessantly, varied occasionally by a tremendous crash which bursts immediately above the house and shakes it to its very foundation. Add to this the roaring of the sea and the howling of the wind, and some idea may be formed of the fearful noise now sounding in my ears. But the storm is, in one respect, more fearful here than elsewhere; at this station most of the European houses are blown down once in two or three years—a process which is anything but comfortable to the inhabitants, who are compelled to shiver through the night on the bleak sands, drenched with spray and rain, half covered with loose sand, and afraid to stand lest they should be blown away.

May 29.

I FIND that the depth of water which fell in the two hours and a half that the storm continued was one inch and a half, a quantity which in England, I believe, would not fall without many days of rain. But this is a delightful place. The difference of climate between this and Cuttack could hardly be conceived, and yet the distance is only fifty miles. At Cuttack, during the hot season of the year, the inhabitants are obliged to close every door and window at half-past six in the morning, in order to keep out the fearfully scorching heat, neither can they open them again till seven in the evening. Although the air is kept in constant motion by the punkahs, yet, being confined, and also much rarified by the heat, it produces a stifling gasping sensation, which is most painful. At this time of the year too the mosquitoes come into the houses in great numbers, and we are therefore compelled to use the mosquito-curtains at night, which have no opening all round, and the lower edge of which is tucked in with the bed-clothes; you might almost as well be shut up in a box. The intense heat, and the quantity of bad air which necessarily accumulates under the curtains, cause continual headaches and oppression of the lungs.

Well, you start from Cuttack in the evening, arrive at Pooree the next morning, and what a change! The doors and windows are open all day; and although the thermometer generally stands at 89°, yet the incessant breeze off the sea prevents any inconvenience from the heat; indeed, we are sometimes glad to close the doors in order to keep out the air. At night a delicious fresh wind, which frequently renders a blanket necessary, no mosquitoes, no curtains. In the morning we can remain out of doors till eight; in the afternoon we can go out at five.

How rejoiced many persons would be to be able to spend their hot weather at such a place. There are, nevertheless, two great drawbacks to the comfort of Pooree. First, the European houses are all situated on a vast plain of loose sand, extending from the sea as far as the eye can reach in every direction; so that it is considered at Pooree quite impossible to walk. My wife, like most other ladies, rides in a tonjon, a sort of small cab, carried on men's shoulders. I and almost all the gentlemen ride on horseback, or rather ponyback. At Cuttack only rich civilians keep horses; all we poor men are content with ponies. I have three beauties: two of them, Birmah ponies, for the carriage, are of a large size, thick built, very strong, and highly valued on account of their hardihood. It is usual to keep their manes cropped close, but I like to see them long. One carries me very well; the other is a saddle-pony, which does either for my wife or myself. It is bay, with long black mane and tail, very sleek, with thin ankles and arching neck. Indeed, several people who have looked at him say he is the best-built horse they ever saw. He is full of fire and play, jumps about, and every now and then stands upon his hind legs. But he will not bear to be annoyed by strangers. A friend of mine was riding him one day, and teased him so much that at last he reared and fell over backwards with him. The carriage-horses are what is called sorrel-colour.

The second drawback to the comfort of Pooree is rather a curious one, and is, I suppose, caused by the wind and the glare of the sun upon the sands. It is the impossibility for any one to keep awake during the day. Towards twelve o'clock an overpowering drowsiness comes on. Once or twice I have resisted it, and on those occasions I verily believe that in the evening, had I shut my eyes, I should have gone to sleep upon my feet. This is the universal complaint of all visitors to that place. The regular residents get over it.

Talking of the night reminds me of a general habit which would seem very odd to people in England. A person would imagine that everybody is very fidgety at night, and rolls and tosses about a great deal in the very hot weather. To render ourselves more comfortable at such times we have a number of pillows of all shapes and sizes and hardnesses scattered about the bed. At one roll you lay your leg on one and your arm on another, then you turn over to the other side, and then, throwing your feet on to one pillow, you hold another fast under your arm: that won't do, and you roll over on your back, with one pillow under your knee and another under each arm, and so on through the night. I can assure you that, however absurd it may appear, this multiplicity of pillows is a very great comfort on very hot nights, although when you awake you certainly often find yourself and them in very funny positions.

But now let us describe the journey up the hill, which is situated in the territories of the Rajah of Neilghur; that is, he pays tribute to the English, but governs his territory for himself. Just before we went there, by the advice of the masahibs or councillors, he had been into one of our villages making a great disturbance, whereupon the commissioner, a sort of governor of the district, sent for the Rajah, desiring him to come in to

Balasore and explain his conduct. I was with the commissioner when he arrived. The Rajah of Neilghur is a handsome intelligent-looking young man of about twenty. His estate brings him in a revenue of nearly sixty thousand rupees a-year. His brother, who is about two years younger, and full of fun and frolic, is always with him. They came to Balasore with a party of about thirty, three elephants, and twenty horses. The Rajah and his brother, with eight or ten of the masahibs, were ushered into the commissioner's room, where chairs were offered to the two former; the others remained standing. Of course all except the two young Rajahs took of their shoes before they entered the room. Mr. M., the commissioner, who, as I have told you, is the kindest of men, gave them a long quiet lecture, and strongly advised them to dismiss the masahibs and govern entirely for themselves; and he warned them that, if such disturbances occurred again, he should be obliged to send and take possession of the whole territory of Neilghur. They were very submissive and made what excuses they could, but which, in point of fact, amounted to none at all. At last they rose to take leave, and I with one or two others joined them.

I immediately told the Rajah that we were going over to Neilghur on the following day, and asked whether he would provide five hundred coolies to beat the jungle. The Rajah promised that he would procure us the coolies and elephants and make us comfortable. The party then mounted, and really it was a very pretty scene. Both the Rajahs and all their attendants were dressed in the purest white—full loose trowsers, white frocks open on one side of the chest, and white turbans. The younger brother wore a red sash, all the others white ones. The Rajahs had most splendid gold chains round their waists, and three very handsome rings in each ear. The eldest mounted first. His horse, which was very tall and strongly built, was an albino; it was perfectly white, with red eyes. The saddle, which for all natives is made deep and well padded, was covered and entirely concealed by a splendid crimson cloth extending from the shoulders to the haunches. It was surrounded by a deep gold fringe, and reached about half way to the ground on each side. The young man laid his hand on the horse's shoulder, and at one vault sprang into the saddle, the cloth remaining on. This was the signal for every one to mount, and then they all began to show off. Their horses played all sorts of antics; they danced, and plunged, and reared, and capered about, though still under perfect control; indeed, it was evident that all these tricks were the result of education. After some minutes spent in this way, they suddenly started off at full gallop, and tore along at a tremendous rate as long as they continued in sight. They were followed by the elephants in a rough trot.

But I must say something more about these elephants. I was walking through the town with C. the evening before, when we saw the elephants coming towards us. We were both startled, if not alarmed. One of them is said to be the largest in India, and it really did look awful. The others, which were of the ordinary size, looked like young ones by its side. I had afterwards an opportunity of measuring it, and, if I remember rightly, its height was twelve feet eleven inches. It is very old, as Tippoo Saib rode it at Seringapatam. It is quite blind, and it is most interesting to observe its manner of walking or running. At each step its trunk swings from side to side, just touching the ground in front, so that the animal may know if there is any impediment in the way. A part near the end of the trunk is much worn away and quite hardened by this constant rubbing. His tusks are magnificent, but his body is little more than a skeleton covered with skin.

Whilst at Neilghur I saw this monster bathe. A boy took him down to a pond close to our tent. He led him by one of his tusks. When he reached the water, at an order from his attendant the elephant held out his trunk and the lad climbed up it until he reached his tusks. The elephant then raised his head until they were the highest part, when the boy slipped off them on the head itself. The animal then walked slowly into the water until it reached the top of his legs; at a signal from the boy he then lay down, whilst the lad kept on the head, scrubbing both that and his back. At another signal he sank himself lower and lower, until only his trunk and the head and shoulders of the boy were visible. It seemed to enjoy it very much, and was almost unwilling to come out again.

We sent our tent on before and started from Balasore at about eleven o'clock in the evening in palanquins. Our party consisted of T., D., B., C. and his son, and myself. We arrived at Neilghur at about three o'clock, and our palanquins were simply set down on the ground that we might finish our night's rest. By the by, when the bearers of the palanquins are changed for fresh men, on taking hold they very often cry out, "Ah! my brother, my child!" but with me they generally make an addition to this—"Ah! my brother, my child, my elephant!"

When they set my palanquin down I turned to look about me. It was very dark, though the stars were shining brightly. The hill seemed to rise almost perpendicularly from my feet into the clouds; a strong blast of cold wind came rolling down its sides, and I was very glad to creep back again into my palanquin and cover myself up with a thick blanket. A little before sunrise I turned out again and roused my companions. We dressed ourselves, loaded our guns and pistols, and started on the ascent, after swallowing a hasty cup of tea and a bit of bread.

At this moment the sun rose, and none but those who have witnessed the splendour of the oriental sunrise can have an idea of the magnificence of the scene. Immediately in front of us was a broad sheet of water surrounded by dense jungle, interspersed with lofty trees, from which, as we looked, two peacocks came forth to drink. At the back of the lake the hill rose abruptly to the height of nearly a thousand feet, the sides partially covered with trees, but which were interspersed here and there with precipices two or three hundred feet in depth, composed of a dark-coloured rock. From each side of this principal eminence project as it were shoulders, of about half the height, and which, covered with the thickest foliage, inclined round to the right and left so as to enclose us in a sort of semicircle.

We had sent men the day before to trace a path through the jungle, and they had tolerably succeeded. But unfortunately I was weak and far from well, and was completely knocked up before I got half way to the top. One of our party was a medical man, and he insisted on my not attempting to go any farther. I felt deadly sick, my face was as white as snow, every pulse in my head and chest throbbed as if it would burst, my mouth was not dry but clammy, and when I lay down on a piece of rock I almost doubted if I should ever rise again. However, I soon felt better, descended the hill, got a glass of beer, and lay down in the tent for an hour or two. The others reached the top without much difficulty, though two of them avowed that, if the summit had been a hundred yards farther, they could not have reached it. They were very thankful for some beer and brandy-and-water which I sent up for them. They saw no animals, though in several places traces of bears were observed. The Rajah says there are no tigers in these parts.

We had but little hunting; while we were there one of our party killed a beautiful spotted deer. I shot some peacocks and a jungle-cock. Talking of hunting reminds me of an adventure which I must relate. The commissioner is the stoutest man I have seen in India, although my wife did insinuate the other day that I was nearly as big, but I am not.

The other day Mr. D., Lieutenant H., and the commissioner went out hog-hunting. This sport is always performed on horseback with long spears. The beaters soon turned out a magnificent boar. "A boar! a boar!" was the shout, and up galloped the commissioner and plunged the spear into the animal; but, in consequence of his horse swerving, he was unable to withdraw the weapon, and the boar ran off with it sticking into his back. Lieutenant H. now came up; the boar charged him, cut both the fore legs of his horse to the bone with his tusks, and tumbled horse and man over on the ground. In the mean time the commissioner had seized another spear from his syce, when the boar rushed at him. His horse swerved at the moment that he was making a thrust with his spear, and the poor commissioner rolled over on the ground. Fortunately the boar was nearly exhausted, too much so to charge again; but he did what perhaps no boar ever did before,—he seized the commissioner by the coat-tails as he lay on his stomach. Feeling the snout of the beast, he at once expected to be cut, if not killed, by its tremendous tusks.

He sprang upon his feet; the boar kept hold of his tail. The Commissioner faced about; he had neither pistol nor knife, so he commenced pummelling away at the boar's face with his fist. Now imagine the scene—a man of his extraordinary size with his coat-tail held up by an enormous boar; the Commissioner himself turned half round, and having a regular boxing-match with the ferocious brute. D. came up as quickly as he could for laughing, and with one good thrust of his spear put an end to the fight. The charge of the boar is fearful; he cuts right and left with his tusks, and inflicts the most dreadful wounds.

And now I must mention some circumstances which to me rendered our expedition to Neilghur very unpleasant; they relate to the manner in which our party treated the Rajah. On the morning of our arrival, after our descent from the hills, he came with a party of horsemen to call upon us. We were just sitting down to breakfast, when I observed the cavalcade approaching. I mentioned it, and proposed that, according to Indian politeness, we should go into the verandah of our tent to receive them. But the principal man of our party said, "Oh! bother the fellow, we can't see him now;" and he sent a servant out to tell him so.

In the afternoon the Rajah sent his man, corresponding to our chief gamekeeper in England, to ask when we should like the coolies to beat the jungle, and to say that he would join us in the hunt. We named the time and started accordingly, found the coolies in readiness, and saw the Rajah and his brother coming upon elephants.

Our party began to move on, when I asked, "Will you not wait for the Rajah?" "I should think not," was the reply; "we don't want the beastly niggers with us." And yet these civilized men were glad enough to make use of these beastly niggers' coolies and elephants. I stayed behind and had some talk with them.

The next day the two Rajahs called at the tent; they entered as gentlemen, and made the usual Indian salutation. With the exception of myself, I do not think one of our party even rose from his chair. In the course of conversation we spoke of the badness of the water we got. The Rajah immediately offered to send a man six miles into the hills to fetch some from a mountain stream. In little more than an hour afterwards, one of our party, feeling thirsty, sent a servant to ask the Rajah whether he had not got that water yet. In India, in speaking to a servant, you use the word "toom," which signifies "you." In speaking to a gentleman you say "ab," which means "your honour." One or two of our party made a point of saying "toom" to the Rajah, which was in fact a great insult. The younger brother called upon us. The chief of our party spoke to him on the subject of the disturbances, although it had all been settled by the Commissioner, and gave him a regular blowing up. And now remember that all this was to a gentleman—an Indian it is true, but still a gentleman, with a fine estate, and about 6000*l.* a-year, from whom we were receiving every kindness, and on whose land we were hunting. Can it be wondered at that the natives do not like us so well as might otherwise be expected?

The Rajah, I suppose, finding me more civil than the others, gave me a great mark of honour. He took me on his own elephant, while he acted as mahout, and whenever any roughness occurred on the ground he turned to warn me of it. I own that I did not enjoy the honour much. The elephant was covered with a crimson cloth, so that there were no ropes to hold by. The only way in which I could manage was to sit astride. It was really most painful, and I almost doubted whether I should ever be able to get my legs together again. I had two brace of pistols with me. The Rajah appeared very much pleased with them, and, to make up for the rudeness of our party, I gave him one of the pair. He was delighted, and I was sadly laughed at for giving anything to a nigger. His palace is a fine white building on the side of one of the hills.

Cuttack, July 4, 1844.

I HAVE mentioned the manner in which Europeans are apt to alienate the affections of the natives; I will now give you an instance of the way in which the Government seek to conciliate them. It must be remembered that salt is a Government monopoly, that is, no person is allowed to prepare or sell it except by the appointment of Government. The cost to them is about eight annas, or one shilling, per maund of eighty pounds; they sell it for four rupees, or eight shillings, for the same quantity; and yet so necessary is it to the natives, that, if any man does not buy the usual quantity of Government, which is, I believe, about half a seer, or one pound, a-month, for each individual, he is brought by the police before a magistrate and sent to gaol, on the presumption that, as he does not purchase salt, he must smuggle it.

Now the salt-manufacturers receive a portion of their pay beforehand, and the remainder when the salt is ready. They belong mostly to the poorest classes, and their mode of working is very simple, merely collecting the sea-water, and then suffering it to evaporate in the sun. When they receive the first portion of their pay, they are told how much they will receive per maund, for the price varies slightly in different years. Last year they were promised a certain sum; I am not exactly sure how much, but say eight annas per maund; and when they came to the salt-agent for their money, they found that an order had arrived from Government reducing the promised pay to six and a half annas per maund. Of course they were excessively angry, and utterly astonished; for one strong idea with the natives is, that an Englishman will never tell an untruth. I happened to be present at the time; it occurred at Pooree, in the neighbourhood of which are some of the principal salt-works, if I may use so dignified a term.

The proper course for these poor people to have taken would have been, to have brought an action against Government for breach of contract; but this they could not possibly afford. However, the magistrates of Pooree sent a strong remonstrance

K 2

to Government, and the consequence was, that they authorized the salt-agent this year to renew the contracts at the higher price, much to the delight of the poor salt-manufacturers, who still lost a part of the promised price of last year; yet it is scarcely to be credited that, before the time for the second payment arrived, another order was sent down, reducing the price as they did last year, and thus again defrauding the poor wretches of part of their small pittance, for defrauding it is in the truest sense of the word. All these things are managed by four or five men, who compose what is called the Salt Board.* I may mention that the salt-workers have been sadly disturbed this year by the number of tigers. The natives sometimes keep the claws of those which they are so fortunate as to kill, to make charms to keep off mischief.

And now I must describe Juggernat'h. To the temple are attached about *four thousand* priests and servants. Of these one set are called Pundahs. In the autumn of every year they start on a journey through India, preaching in every town and village the advantages of a pilgrimage to Juggernat'h; after which they conduct to Pooree large bodies of pilgrims for the Rath Justra, or Car Festival, which takes place in May or June—the precise time depends on the moon, as does the time of our Easter. This is the principal festival, and the number of devotees varies from about 80,000 to 150,000. About five years ago there were present, on one occasion, not less than 250,000; but that numerous meeting was owing to some peculiar sanctity which is supposed to be diffused once in 200 years. But I ought to have commenced with some account of Juggernat'h himself. He represents the ninth incarnation of Vishnoo. I have often wondered whether the Hindu religion may not, in some portions, be taken remotely from the Christian. One name of Vishnoo is Chrishna; one appellation of Juggernat'h is Sri Teo. This Teo, as Chrishna, became incarnate whilst very young; he was sought after by a king to put

* We can scarcely imagine that the Supreme Government would lend itself to such a transaction; we think it far more likely that it occurred through the culpability or negligence of some of the inferior agents, who may have misrepresented the case to Government.

him to death. Many children were killed, but he was removed from place to place in safety. He was born amongst the shepherds. The Hindus look for a tenth incarnation, when he shall unite all the world in one religion, and himself reign over them. I believe I am correct in giving these as points of faith amongst the Brahmins; and when we consider that the Hindu religion was probably established long after St. Thomas and St. Bartholomew had visited India, it certainly seems allowable to suppose that some portion of the Christian teaching became mingled with the doctrines of the Hindus. There is one objection to this supposition, namely, that Vishnoo is represented to have lived a very wicked and immoral life while on earth.

No European, Mussulman, or low-caste Hindu is admitted into the temple; we can, therefore, only speak on hearsay of what goes on inside. The idol itself is renewed every twelve years; it consists of a mere block of sacred wood, in the centre of which is said to be concealed a fragment of the original idol, which was fashioned by Vishnoo himself. The features and all the external parts are formed of a mixture of mud and cowdung painted. Every morning the idol undergoes his ablutions; but as the cowdung and paint would not stand the washing, the priests adopt a very ingenious plan—they hold a mirror in front of the image, and wash his reflection. Every evening he is put to bed; but as the idol is very unwieldy, they place the bedstead in front of him; on that they lay a small image, lock the door, and leave him to come down himself, if he can.

Offerings are made to him, by pilgrims and others, of rice, money, jewels, elephants, &c.; the Rajah of Knoudah and the priests being his joint treasurers. About twelve days before the Rath Justra, Juggernat'h goes to bathe; whilst doing so, he is supposed to be bitten by a snake, which causes him to be sick until the day of the festival. During his illness the priests take off his paint and cowdung, and give quite a new coat; so that at the end of the time he appears quite healthy and strong.

On the grand day the three cars, which, I should say, were fifty or sixty feet in height, are brought to the gate of the temple; the idols are then taken out by the priests—Juggernat'h having golden arms and diamond eyes for that one day—and by means of pulleys are hauled up and placed in their respective carriages; to these enormous ropes are attached, and the assembled thousands, with loud shouts, proceed to drag the idols to Juggernat'h's country-house, a small temple at about a mile distant. This occupies several days, and the idols, having rusticated for some time, are brought back to their regular station. The Hindus believe that every person who aids in dragging the cars receives pardon for all his past sins; every pilgrim who dies within five miles of Pooree will be greatly blessed in his next life; and every person who swims out to sea, so far as to see the top of the temple from the surface of the water, secures great blessings in another life for himself, his father and mother, his grandparents, and the three next generations descended from himself! This last experiment, however, is very rarely tried; there are too many sharks to make it pleasant. One man was drowned last year in attempting it. As to the people throwing themselves under the wheels of the car, that I believe to be altogether a European invention. Some occasionally fall accidentally, and are thus killed; but I imagine that self-immolation in this way neither is nor ever was at all a common thing.

I have very little doubt that great wickedness prevails within the temple. In two cases, lately, it is known that murder has been committed there; yet we, who have held the country so long, are not allowed to enter the building. It is said that if we attempted it we should be driven from the district; this I do not believe. Some years ago the priests declared that the god would not leave his country-house until all the English were driven from the province. The officer commanding at Cuttack directly sent word that, if the idol was not brought back on the usual day, he would come and blow both it and the temple to pieces. Juggernat'h immediately came to his senses, and was back in his temple one day before his regular time.

During the period the pilgrims remain at Pooree they are not allowed to eat anything but what has been offered to the idol, and that they have to buy at a very high price from the priests. This food is often very bad, and from that, combined with other causes, the cholera makes sad ravages amongst these poor people.

At the festival that is just past it is calculated that there were about 130,000 pilgrims. The cholera this year was very mild; but not less than 650 died at Pooree, or between that place and Cuttack. Their bodies are generally thrown out to be devoured by the dogs, vultures, and jackals. One Sunday morning, in coming home from church, we found that three bodies had been thrown out in front of our house; two of them were rapidly disappearing in the jaws of these animals, the other was tossing about in the surf. However, I sent to the magistrate, and he had them removed and burnt. A vast proportion of the pilgrims are widows. In India a widow is not permitted to marry again, but must be supported by her late husband's relations; and it is said that many of those poor women are sent down to Pooree in hope of getting rid of them, and no doubt this purpose frequently succeeds. And to support this system our Government pays 6000*l.* a-year; equal to the salaries of ten chaplains of our Church. This year an event occurred which the Hindus consider to be very ominous of evil. As they were bringing the god out, one of the chief priests was seized with cholera, and was sick all over the idol. The necessary purifications occupied so long a time, that the procession was not able to start that day.

I have just had a sad misfortune: all my cloth clothes, cloaks, &c., with two or three dozen shirts, flannels, waistcoats, drawers, &c. &c.—in short, everything but what was in actual use—were put away in a large chest. Whilst we were at Pooree my stupid man never once looked at them. When I returned I wanted something out of the chest, opened it, and found that every individual thing had been almost entirely destroyed by white ants—coats, shirts, flannels, were eaten through in all directions; and I think there was, at least, 50*l.* worth destroyed. I have fined my man two months' pay for his carelessness; but, as that is only 22*s.*, it is a very poor consolation to me.

Cuttack, August 10, 1844.

THE weather is now most fearfully oppressive; not so much from the actual heat, for the thermometer is seldom above 86° or 87°, but from a dense mass of cloud, which at the height of a few hundred feet encloses us, as it were, day and night in one vast steamy vapour-bath. The last two or three months are actually the most trying that I have felt in India.

I forget whether I have described the Brindabund monkeys. I have now a pair of them. I do not remember ever to have seen them in England. They are covered all over with long, thick, black hair; but round the face, extending from temple to temple, is a very broad, thick frill of white or rather light grey: the tail is of a middling length, the snout very short, and the animal himself remarkably docile and intelligent. Those that I have are not yet a year old, and I should say the body is about a foot in length. When on their hind legs they stand nearly two feet.

I have mine in the verandah just outside my study door, and they are so full of fun that I often sit for a long time watching them. One runs a little way up the lattice, then the other makes a spring after him, and up they both go as fast as they can. Presently the lower one catches hold of the upper one's tail, and brings him down to the bottom; then he makes a jump and gets away into his kennel and sits at the door, whilst the other wanders round and round, trying to find some place where he can get in without being observed; in doing this he carelessly turns his back, when out jumps the other and catches hold of his tail or his hind leg, and drags him round and round their cage. I should tell you that the cage is the end of the verandah at the back of my house; two sides of it are wall, and the other two are lattice. It is about ten feet square, twelve feet high at one end, and eighteen or twenty at the other.

When they are frightened they sit upright on the floor, with their arms clasped round each other; and if I take one of them out tied by a string, they both scream the whole time until they are brought together again, and then they rush into each other's arms. These two monkeys are very much admired by the Europeans at Cuttack, who have given them the name of "the gentlemen monkeys," because, from the great length of their hair, they look as if they were dressed, besides being quiet and docile. They are almost as rare here as in England. They are of the most sacred race of monkeys in the eyes of the Hindus; and indeed the only objection I have to them is, that I am afraid some of my servants make poojah to them, that is, worship them, and prostrate themselves before them, and make offerings of rice to them.

We have a great improvement in the use of our finger-glasses over those in England. One man waits behind every person at each meal, even at tea, and as soon as the meal is over he brings his master or mistress a finger-glass filled with water, with two or three leaves of verbenum, or bay, or sweet-smelling lime, for the persons to squeeze between their fingers. In a hot climate like India this is very pleasant and refreshing.

When a man in India, I mean a European gentleman, wants a wife, he says to his friend, "I should like to get married." "Well," says he, "why don't you?" and forthwith he applies for leave of absence for a month. A month consists of thirty days, of which, say five are occupied in his journey to Calcutta, and another five on his journey back, leaving him just twenty days in which to make his selection, get introduced, make himself agreeable, propose, court, and be married. A nice prospect he has for future happiness. But there is one curious result in this sort of marriage, and a result, too, which spreads among other people also. After a few years the wife loses her health and is ordered to England. The husband cannot afford to go with her, but he allows her about half his salary. At the end of two or three years, or whatever time may have been fixed, he writes to his wife to make arrangements for her return to India; and I have known two instances in which the husband was obliged to stop the allowance in order to compel the wife to return.

I have often wished to have some peacocks in my compound, but every one told me that they would fly away; however, I found that those who had tried to keep them had obtained the young birds from the jungle. I thought I would try another plan, and therefore I got some eggs and set them under a hen. I have three young ones coming on nicely, perfectly tame, and which, I think, will look very well among the trees in front of my house. Two are peacocks, the other a peahen.

Cuttack, September 14, 1844.

My wife and I were sitting, after tea, playing at backgammon and enjoying the cool breeze that came through the open Venetians, when suddenly it began to rain. In an instant the room swarmed with insects of all sorts. There was the beautiful large green mantis; and, as we were watching his almost human motions, a grasshopper and a large brown cricket flew against my face, while a great cockroach, full three inches long, came on my wife's neck, and began running about her head and face and dress; the flying-ant, which emits a most nauseous effluvia; and the flying-bug, black, and about the size of an English one, which, if you crush him, will make your fingers smell most dreadfully for many hours;—and with these our clothes were covered, and we were obliged to keep brushing them away from our faces, but with very gentle handling; and then came two or three hornets, which sent Mrs. Acland to bed to get under the mosquito-curtains, where none of these horrid creatures can get at her. I sat up trying to read, but buzz came a mosquito on the side of my face, up went my hand a tremendous slap on the cheek to kill the tormentor, and buzz he went on again. Then I felt something big burying itself in my hair, and then came buzz on the other side, and then all around.

Presently, with a loud hum, a great rhinoceros-beetle dashed into my face. I now began to take some of the animals out of my hair; and the first that I touched was a flying-bug: the stench was dreadful. I rushed out of the room, brushing the horrible creatures from my hair with both hands. I nearly fell over a toad on which I trod, and reached my bed-room to find eighteen or twenty great toads croaking in different parts of the room, and five large bats were whirling round and round the bed. Having washed my hands in eau-de-cologne, I quickly undressed and fell asleep.

In the course of the night a troop of jackals surrounded the house, and by their frightful yells soon drove away all idea of rest; and then, about four o'clock, as we were just dozing off again, comes the roll of the drum and the loud voice of the trumpet, the tramp of the soldiers, the firing, and all the bustle of the parade; and, as soon as that is over, comes the changing guard, and the "*shoulder harrm*," and the "*quick marrch*," near our house; and so we got up.

Then comes the bath, the greatest luxury of the day (the water just cooler than the air), into which I get with a book, lie there an hour reading, get out and partly dress, and then admit my man to wash my feet in cold water, and to shampoo me and brush my hair, whilst another brings me a cup of delicious coffee or a glass of sherbet; and then breakfast, with an enormous fan swinging to and fro over our heads; and the heat, and the discomfort, and languor till five o'clock, agreeably diversified only by a bottle of beer cooled with saltpetre and water; and then a drive, and tea, and mosquitoes again, and so on.

Cuttack, October 13, 1844.

I HAD to make a five days' journey at the worst season of the year to marry a couple, and I returned with a bad cough, which became more violent after the cold had left me. I am very weak, so that I walk like an old man. The doctors here are paid by the Government for attending all persons in the service. The Company also find medicines, but not the bottles, which sometimes leads to curious circumstances. The other day I wanted some medicine, and sent to the doctor for it; presently my man brought me back a black-draught in an old eau-de-cologne bottle, with a roll of paper by way of cork, and a request that I would return the bottle, as it was the only one he had.

I am about to apply for leave of absence. I shall go up to Calcutta, spend a fortnight with my friends there, Mr. and Mrs. S.; they will then come down here, when Mrs. Acland will join us, and we shall go to the Chelka Lake and the black pagodas.

I have another monkey now, which is kept at the stable; it is a horrible animal, about a foot and a half high, of a light greenish brown colour, no hair on its head, and very much inclined to be savage. I keep it to please my stable-people, who have a superstition that this kind of monkey prevents the horses getting unwell. Not long ago a young officer turned a very savage one loose; it took up its abode in my compound. In one night it killed three of my fan-tailed pigeons, and it chased my goats backward and forward so incessantly, that one of them died of fatigue. I told my stable-people to catch the animal, and get rid of him. This they did not do; so I then gave them notice, that, if the monkey was not in the jungle on the other side of the river by seven o'clock the next morning, I would cut them all a month's pay. This is the best method of punishing the natives, and in the present instance it was most effectual, for I have not seen the fiendish-looking face of the exile since that day.

In India the cow's milk is very bad, poor, and thin; that of the buffalo is of a bad colour and rank; but what is furnished by the goat is delicious, and many people, ourselves among the number, keep flocks of goats. I flatter myself that mine (twelve goats and seven kids) are very handsome. The male kids we eat when they are old enough to leave their mother; they are very nice indeed. Our goats are much larger than those in England, but all other animals are very small. I have heard it said at table, "Will you take a shoulder or leg of lamb?" Beef and veal in this bigoted part of the country are quite forbidden things. Yet how curious this is! No animals are worse treated than the bullocks, which are here the only beasts of burden. They are starved and ill-used in every way. I have seen a man dislocate several joints successively of his bullock's tail; yet, if I were to fire my gun at the poor animal to put it out of its misery, I should probably have my house burnt over my head.

I saw a most extraordinary sight last night. It was in the evening very hot, and a great deal of electricity in the air. There were two very heavy clouds, one at a considerable distance above the other Suddenly some vapour separated itself with a whirling motion from the upper, assuming the shape of a waterspout until the point touched the lower; then a commotion began, the lower cloud rushing in large white masses up the sides of the spout and uniting with the upper. This continued for nearly forty minutes, until the lower was absorbed.

Cuttack, November 14, 1844.

I SOWED some melon-seed one Friday morning; on the Monday when I went into the garden most of the melon-plants were two inches in height. In three days, in the open ground, from being mere dry seeds they had germinated and sprung up into strong healthy plants. The same rapidity of growth is remarkable in almost all vegetation in this country. I sowed some English peas the day before yesterday; this morning they are all above the ground. Thus we see that the effect of the climate is to hurry all these things forward, so that they naturally decay and die much earlier than they would in Europe.

Now just put man in the place of a vegetable, and the case is precisely the same. A native boy has generally good-sized mustachios by the time he is fourteen, and a girl becomes a woman at eleven or twelve; then, again, at thirty the woman is old and shrivelled, and at forty the man is white-haired and decrepit. Who can wonder, then, that a climate like this should have such serious effects on Europeans, or that our constitutions should be soon worn out by the burning sun?

However, this month I have no right to complain; I am far better than I have been for some time. The weather is delightful; we are glad of a thick blanket and counterpane at night; at six, when I get up, the thermometer is rarely above 72°. I have no objection to a cloak when I am sowing seeds in the morning. The thermometer now, two o'clock P.M., is in my room exactly 80°, but there is a delightful cool breeze.

I have before observed that I did not feel satisfied with my medical man. As the East India Company do not allow above one doctor to every fifty miles, I wrote to a friend of mine in whom I have much confidence, detailing all my symptoms and requesting his advice. I could not think it of any use to put blisters and leeches on my throat for a cough and sickness which I felt to proceed from my stomach, and as I was very unwell I thought it best to consult another person. In the wisdom of his advice I perfectly agree, although it is more difficult to act up to it in India: "Employ your mind and stint your body." Any amusement, anything that could interest or excite or rouse, he recommended, but to avoid all unnatural stimulants as much as possible (I mean wine and spirits), and take plenty of exercise. If I do this, he says, he thinks I may leave all physic in the bottles and the leeches in the ponds. In accordance with this advice I am occupying myself in various ways. Books it is impossible to procure, so I have been training a horse for my wife —a beautiful little thing. I have made arrangements too for going to Calcutta in the course of the cold weather; and I have enclosed about an acre of my ground, and am making a vegetable or rather a kitchen garden of it.

I get up about six, dress in my old clothes, go out, and find one of the horses, or rather ponies, at the door waiting for me. I must ride him through the long grass, which by the bye is very nearly fit to cut, to look at a number of my trees scattered here and there in the compound, which I have been planting; then, when I am down at the farther end I take a glance at the large pond, or tank as we call it, where, sheltered by the most beautiful flowering trees, two men are catching fish for our breakfast. Then I ride along inside the hedge, watching the soldiers at parade, until I come to the goat-house; then see the pigs fed, and ride back to the house.

By this time my wife is up, and she goes into the flower-garden, and I into the kitchen-garden, to sow seeds and superintend the gardeners. And here is the most curious scene; seven black men at work, their only dress a cloth round the loins, their long black hair wound up in a knot at the back of the head, their only tools a sort of broad pickaxe with a very short handle and a small sickle, these are their only gardening implements; and two men are watering with gurrahs, a sort of narrow-necked jar made of black clay, which they let down into a well by a rope. In the flower-garden are the beautiful balsams, of many colours, and as large as gooseberry-bushes; the splendid coxcombs, eight or ten feet high, whose great thick flowers measure twelve or fourteen inches by six or eight; the varieties of the hybiscas, with many others; and a few of the more precious European rarities—at least to us—such as the heliotrope, verbenum, lark-spur, and many others. Our borders are mostly of the sweet-scented grass from the Neilghur hills, which is always covered with a beautiful small white flower.

In the vegetable-garden, besides the precious peas, beans, celery, cress, &c., which will only grow at this time of the year, are the pine-apple, the plantain, the guava, the lime, the orange, the custard-apple, with many other native plants and trees; and in the hedges are some of the beautiful palms, from the sap of which the Indians make an intoxicating drink called toddy. In the compound are some very fine mango-trees and beeches.

The other evening I was sitting alone writing at about eleven o'clock, when I heard the sentry call out loudly to my servants who were sleeping in the verandah. I jumped up to see what was the matter. "A leopard-tiger!" was the answer; and the man said he had seen a leopard creeping stealthily along the compound. He leapt over the wall into the garden of the Colonel who lives in the next house, and the following day footsteps were found in various parts of the cantonment, which the natives said were too large for a leopard, and must have been the marks of a regular tiger. I did not see the animal myself; but if the men were correct, it must have been an extraordinary occurrence, as our little island is entirely free from wild beasts; and although it is at this time of the year joined to the main by a narrow neck of sand, yet no large beast will cross unless pressed either by hunger or by hunters.

A few days ago a man brought me an animal which he had caught in the jungle on the hills. At first sight I said it was an armadillo, but now I feel some doubt whether it was not some unknown animal. I wanted to buy it, in order to send the skin, or rather the shell, home, but the man asked ten rupees for it, which

I could not afford. It was nearly three feet long, covered with thick hard scales of a dirty yellow colour, the tail the same length as the body, and equally broad, which I do not think is the case with the armadillo. The shape of its whole back was a long oval. When frightened it rolled itself up into a ball, but it appeared very lethargic and stupid. The feet were armed with long, powerful claws, but it walked with the lower joints turned down under the feet, as if I were to walk on my ankles with the feet and toes turned under and behind. It burrowed a hole in a wall, pulling out the bricks and mortar very easily. I tried it with various kinds of food, but the only thing I could get it to eat was white ants. The man who brought it said he had never seen one like it before.

Not long ago the doctor at Pooree saw a number of natives running to the beach. He inquired what was the matter: "A great fish, sir." So down he went to join the crowd, and there he found a large fish indeed: a whale, measuring forty-eight feet in length, had been washed on shore; the body was rolling about in the surf, with great numbers of the natives clinging to it.

Then the doctor and the only other European present took off their shoes and stockings, turned up their trowsers, and climbed on the enormous animal's back; they got well wetted for their pains. The other gentleman that I mentioned is not a very learned man, and he said that their climbing up the sides of the whale reminded him of the "Lally prussians" climbing on to Gulliver. This same person once said that his wife had had a "historical" fit, in consequence of eating "aromatically" sealed salmon.

Khoutah, 30 miles from Cuttack, December 16, 1844.

I AM now writing in a tent in which, with the exception of Christmas week, I expect to spend the next month or two, travelling in search of health. The cool weather has refreshed me much, and I feel far better than I did. A question has been asked me respecting the antiquity of the religions of this country.

I believe the Bhuddist religion to be more ancient than the Brahminical in India ; though I think that the latter is the older in reality, as I imagine it to have existed almost in its present form in ancient Egypt. The Hindus burn their dead, the Mohammedans bury them: but there are very many of the former who are too poor to purchase wood; in this case the bodies are simply thrown out for the jackals and vultures.

Jenkia, about 44 miles south of Cuttack, January 4, 1845.

FROM Khoulah I returned to Cuttack for Christmas. Early on Christmas morning Mr. G., the collector and magistrate of Pooree, came in to spend the day with us. Poor man! he and a cousin of his were almost brought up together, and they became much attached even in childhood. When he obtained an appointment in India, it was agreed that he should return to England and marry her as soon as he should have attained sufficient rank in the service to give him an adequate income. After about five years' residence in this country he went home and was married. This was ten years ago, and from that time his life seems to have been as happy as a human life can be. Latterly they became anxious to go home on furlough, in order that they might see their children settled in England, but they had not saved money enough; so, in April, Mr. G. applied for a better appointment, and was consequently nominated to Pooree. On their way down, as they passed through Calcutta, both were seized with cholera; he recovered, but she died; he sent his children home, but arrived at Pooree a solitary man. He is still in a very desponding state, but I do all I can to arouse him, both by bodily amusement and religious converse.

At about one o'clock of the night of Christmas-day, or rather of the following morning, my wife, Mr. G., and myself got into our palanquins, and started for Khoordagurree, which we visited last year. We arrived at our tent by about ten o'clock on Thursday morning, bathed, dressed, breakfasted, and prepared to start for the caves; but, alas! it began to rain, and the water continued to fall in torrents for upwards of eighteen hours. We might have expected this, for in India it is almost invariably the case in Christmas week. The seasons are very regular; it generally rains every day from the 15th of June to the 15th of October, that is, in this part of India; the next showers are in Christmas-week, and then rarely any more till June. Now, this thorough drenching was both unpleasant and dangerous: for, although the tents kept out the water very effectually, yet everything was so thoroughly damp that we began to be afraid of the deadly jungle-fevers.

Just outside one of the doors of each tent we lighted a large wood fire, and allowed as much of the smoke to come in as we could possibly bear; this warmed us, and dried up the damp and purified the air; and we retired to bed and put out the fires: we closed the doors of the tents, and found ourselves in a comparatively dry healthy atmosphere.

Tanghi, 56 miles south of Cuttack, January 5, 1845.

THE following afternoon we were able to revisit the caves. But I will first describe our journey. On the Monday and Tuesday we had plenty of shooting; the Wednesday, New-Year's day, we spent in-doors. At six o'clock on the morning of Thursday, the 2nd, we started for Jonkia. We went on horseback, riding fourteen miles before breakfast. Our manner of travelling is most delightfully independent: we encamp at any place we wish to see; Mr. G. transacts his necessary business as magistrate and revenue-collector; then we have one, two, or three days' exercise in hunting and shooting, the time depending chiefly on the abundance of game.

When we feel inclined to start we send forward an order to the principal man at the next place, say twelve or fifteen miles distant, to build one room, about thirty feet square, in a shady place, for ourselves; for the walls we use cocoa-nut and palm leaves, bound together with bamboos, and the ceiling is made of the same material with a few pieces of matting to keep out the sun. The evening before we start we send on a cart with some of our chairs, tables, and other necessaries and provisions, which it would be very awkward to forget, under charge of some of our followers: we have about one hundred and twenty of them with us.

Then, in the morning, we get up at five; we have a bit of toast, an egg, and a cup of coffee or a glass of sherry; give orders for the tents to be struck and everything to be brought on as quickly as possible, and then we mount our horses; a groom runs by the side, and a little way behind come our palanquins and tonjons.

We are also attended by men carrying our guns and powder, by many other servants, and about half the inhabitants of the last village through which we passed. If we feel tired we get into our tonjons; if the sun is too hot we call for our palanquins. Every now and then we see five or six peacocks feeding in a rice-field, or we come to a place where there are plain tracks of deer. Then we give our horses to the grooms, and creep along gently with our heads down and our guns in our hands, whilst my wife either watches the sport or trots gently on. At last we arrive at our encamping-place; there we find our leafy house ready, and similar ones provided for the servants and horses; eat a hearty breakfast, at which we sometimes substitute beer for tea, and by the time that is over the tents are arrived.

We have them put up, arrange them comfortably, perhaps have a game at chess, and then go out for a stroll about our new ground. Our dinner-hour varies, but is generally between seven and eight. We are usually up about five, and often walk from ten to twenty miles a-day. This has done me a great deal of good: I feel already quite a different person from what I did when I was in Cuttack. I have not, however, lost my cough.

Sunday is a day of rest with us; we have service and spend the day very quietly. At Jonkia we remained until Saturday the 4th; then came on to Tanghi; on Thursday, the 9th, proceeded to Soonercollee, on the 10th to Bampoor, and yesterday, the 11th, we arrived at this place. So much for our actual route; now I will give some account of what we have seen.

When we came to Jonkia we agreed that we had never seen anything to compare with the scenery there; but as we came into Soonercollee we quite forgot Jonkia in the new splendours that met our eyes. Yet these were again eclipsed in the beauties of Chelka Lake, to which we took one evening's ride from Soonercollee. It is utterly impossible to convey any idea of the scenery either by the pen or the pencil; yet I will try what I can do.

In approaching the small village of Soonercollee you ascend a hill some 200 or 300 feet high by a steep winding road or rather path. At the top of the eminence it is cut through the solid rock, which rises about thirty feet on each side. Suddenly, at a turn in the road, the whole country in the front becomes visible, and I doubt whether any one could repress a cry of admiration at the sight. The spectator is (as I said before) at the summit of a lofty hill; beneath him is a plain of some ten or twelve miles across, bounded on every side by a lofty range and masses of rock. Peering up behind are to be seen a succession of noble mountains. The sides of the hills, where they do not consist of rocky precipices, are covered with a dense jungle: the plain below is cultivated, except where, in three places, abrupt rocky masses, interspersed with jungle, rise to a height of 300 or 400 feet. It looks as if some mighty convulsion had taken place, and the earth had thrown up large bubbles of rock from the surface of the plain.

The scenery on the Chelka Lake, a piece of water some forty miles long by from ten to twenty in breadth, is very similar to the above, if you substitute water for the level plain of the rice-fields. Here the hills rise abruptly from the lake, and many of them are quite inaccessible. The islands are inhabited by animals, but not by man; and it is rather curious that each islet appears to have its own peculiar race. Thus, one is inhabited by the beautiful spotted deer, another by the enormous Indian elk, another by goats and fowls (this one is sacred to the goddess Khalee), another by wild pigs, and another by pigeons. With some difficulty I landed on one of the pigeon islands: its greatest height did not exceed thirty feet, and in circumference it may have been near a quarter of a mile; but its structure was most extraordinary. It was composed entirely of enormous masses of rock piled together without the appearance of order or arrangement: it appeared as if some earthquake had destroyed some giant dwelling-place, and left the ruins in one vast heap. Some of the stones, larger than a man's body, had fallen upon one end; they gave way beneath my foot, but returned to their position as soon as relieved of the extra weight which had destroyed the balance. The blue pigeons rose in clouds from every crevice, and fluttered about until I left the neighbourhood of their nests.

The lake lay all around—so calm, so beautiful, with the green mountains rising here and there from its surface, dotted all over with myriads of ducks, geese, teal, and many other aquatic birds: and this reminded me of one thing which I should have related before. As we approached the shores of the lake we were surprised to see a long line of tall white and red creatures standing just within the water. We looked at them through Mr. G.'s glass, and found that they were birds; we got out of our tonjons, crept towards them with loaded guns, fired, and missed them, when they all rose and flew away.

The next morning Mr. G. and I returned to the spot: we each took a separate boat, as Mrs. Acland was not with us; mine, like the others, was about thirty feet long, and formed of a single piece of wood, a tree scooped out. Mr. G. was very anxious to obtain some game, and in the course of about two hours shot a couple of large bare-headed geese and nineteen ducks of various sorts; indeed, they sat in such masses on the water as to resemble rather a low wall than a number of birds. At one shot he killed five ducks, and I three: I did not care much about them, but I was anxious to see again some of my friends of the previous evening.

At last I came in sight of a flock of them near the shore. I sat down in the bottom of the boat, whilst the men pushed it gently along. I was nearly within shot, when Mr. G. fired his gun at the distance of about a mile from my boat: up and away flew all the birds. I was very much annoyed: however, after some time, I saw about half a dozen nearly two miles from me.

On we went again, but they had become shy: they raised their heads and looked about them as we approached, and presently they rose. I did not think I was sufficiently near, but I might not have another chance, so I fired, and down fell one of the birds. I pushed one of the boatmen over to fetch it, though he hardly needed pushing, for they appeared quite as anxious as I was.

I will try to describe my prize: I believe the bird to have been a flamingo; and yet, if so, the usual descriptions are very erroneous. The beak is pink, and furnished with a double row of teeth on each side of the lower mandible—one row on the beak, and dark coloured; the other very white and sharp, close to the tongue, which is large. The eyes are pale, and surrounded by a thick yellow ring; the wings are of a beautiful rose-colour, edged with black; the legs pink; the rest of the body is white. When standing upright it is about five feet high: the body is extremely small, neck and legs very long; it has three toes in front and is web-footed, also a claw behind; the beak very large.

Midnapore, February 14, 1845.

This is Friday, and on Sunday night I start for Calcutta to spend a month with our friends; there I shall have plenty of occupation for the mind, and shall, I hope, get rid entirely of the oppression under which I have recently suffered.

Fancy yourself standing with me on that little rising ground, near the foot of that large hill: it is near Bunool, on the banks of the Chelka Lake. Keep out of sight behind that bush. Hark! there are the beaters climbing the rocks on the opposite side of the hill. There are 400 extended along the whole side, and every tenth man has a drum or trumpet. Some of them have guns, curious native matchlocks; others have swords or spears; and every one has a thick bamboo about eight feet long. Listen! they are beginning to beat. As they force their way through the jungle they strike the bushes with their sticks, and from one end of the lake to the other resound the most unearthly noises.

The horrid yells of the natives, the screaming of the trumpets, the constant beating of the tom-toms and drums—you can hardly imagine such horrid discord. See: there is Mr. G. hiding himself behind that clump of trees a quarter of a mile off. Hold your gun ready, you cannot tell what may rush out of the jungle. Don't show yourself. Listen again to those yells. They must nearly have reached the top of the hill. Hush! there is a rustling in those bushes close to you. What is it? Keep close, but up with your gun. Here it comes! Bah! don't fire at that; it is only a civet-cat. What a beautiful animal it is, with its grey sides, and tail striped with that glossy black. But the skin is of no use; the stench from it is so exceedingly powerful that you could not possibly bear it in the house. Look out! there's another rush! Here it comes! a pig! no; what can it be? Why, it's a porcupine. Don't fire. Here, you messenger, catch it. Fancy the man's look of dismay when ordered to catch a porcupine. However, another of my men jumped up and stabbed the animal with his sword.

Oh, what a clash in the jungle at the top of the hill! See! that must be some large animal coming down. Don't let him see you; peep through that bush. How he plunges through the jungle! He has stopped: look now! he leaves the beaters behind him, but he suspects danger in front. You can see his head by the side of that tree, just below that high rock. He is standing still and gazing at us. What a splendid pair of antlers! He must be one of the largest sambres (Indian elk) I ever saw. I am afraid he is hardly within shot; however, I'll try. He is down; the ball struck him just in the centre of his forehead, and one of my men rushes forward to despatch him with his sword.

But look there! Mr. G. is running as fast as he can, and all his men running too. What can be the matter? Quick! see! there is an enormous bear pursuing them. Here, give me my gun; make haste. Look! G. has stumbled, and is rolling head over heels down the hill. Bang! I hit him! See, he turns back. G. shot the female, and was immediately attacked by the male, whilst his gun was not loaded, for he foolishly had but one. We got the body of the female, and brought it to our tents in triumph. It was a black bear, measuring five feet seven inches in length, and its teeth quite worn out.

Cuttack, April 2, 1845.

THE Government of India orders me to go from Cuttack to Midnapore and back again four times a-year, to Balasore and back twice a-year, and to Pooree and back four times a-year. The distance from Cuttack to Midnapore is one hundred and eighty miles, from Cuttack to Balasore one hundred and three miles, and from Cuttack to Pooree forty-nine miles. I travel about forty-seven miles a-day on the average. The Government allows me twelve annas and two pice per mile for travelling expenses; it costs me four annas and two pice—an anna being one-sixteenth part of a rupee, and a pice one-fourth part of an anna.

I must now mention some of my adventures in the jungle. One day we went with a native Rajah to hunt antelopes. Suppose the shore of the Chelka Lake on one side and the sea on the other, with a strip of sand between them rather more than a mile wide. The antelopes live entirely on the sandy plain, and feed on the scanty plants which grow among the sand. Across this flat a net about seven feet in height and a mile long was staked, and 100 men were stationed along it as guards. About 500 men were then sent out with a similar net about a mile and a half in length, which they stretched at perhaps five miles from the other. These 500 men then walked slowly towards the first net, carrying the other in front of them, and driving lots of antelopes before them. When they came within a mile of the first net they staked the second, and there were perhaps fifty or sixty antelopes enclosed in a space of about a mile square. Mr. G., the Rajah, and myself, went inside with our guns. It was barbarous sport. In two days we killed fifteen, which our servants ate most gladly. But the interesting thing was to see twenty or thirty bound, one after the other, over the net and the men's heads, giving tremendous leaps; the black men striking at them with their swords and spears, and cowering to avoid their sharp-cutting hoofs, and all hallooing and jabbering, and swearing; whilst every now and then the crack of one of our guns would be heard, and the whizz of the bullet as it passed near.

Another day we expected some danger. When we arrived at the ground, which consisted of thick patches of jungle, with open spaces between, we got out of our tonjons and took our guns. There we found a number of men looking for traces of deer, wild boars, tigers, or any other animals. As soon as they found the track of one they followed it until it led into the jungle, and exactly at that spot they pushed in amongst the bushes an enormous bag made of net of thick rope. Its mouth was kept open by a few twigs, whilst a running rope went round the entrance and was fastened to a stake on one side. If then any animal should make a rush along this track, he must go head foremost into the net: the twigs would fall down, the neck would be drawn tight, and the poor creature would be a prisoner. All these preparations were at length concluded, and the Rajah then advised us to mount the elephants, as he said two tigers had been seen in these jungles the day before. We at once asked him whether his elephants had been trained to stand the charge of a tiger, which always springs at its head. He said he did not know; and we agreed that we would rather stand the advance of a tiger on foot ourselves than be on the back of a mad elephant scampering at random through the jungle. So we built up an artificial hedge in front of us, and crouched down with our guns pointed through some loopholes we had left in our fence.

This arrangement was hardly completed before we began to hear the sounds of the drums and the trumpets, and the yells of the people, as nearly a thousand of them marched through the jungle towards us, driving before them every sort of game. I should tell you that we kept our elephants close at hand in case of the worst. You cannot imagine the excitement in such watching as this. Two or three miles off the most fearful yells from 1000 men, close around you utter silence; your eyes roaming in every direction, not knowing at what point a deer or a tiger may break out.

Ha! listen! there's a crack among the branches, and out rushes a noble stag. Bang goes G.'s gun. We had agreed that he should have the first shot. He 's down! "Hush! here 's something else in this patch of jungle." "Where?" he whispers, as he loads. "There, I see it now: look out; here it comes!" And sure enough out rushed seven pigs, followed almost immediately by three others. Now a wild boar is a most awkward animal to fight on foot, and we had agreed we should not fire at them. However, they rushed right towards us. What 's to be done? "Get on the elephant," says G. "No time," said I; "follow me:" and we both fairly turned tail, pursued by a herd of pigs until we came to a bush, or rather a patch of bushes, round which we could make a short turn to escape them, and then back to our own station, laughing as hard as we could. But really a wild boar is no laughing matter as he rushes along tearing up the earth. If he charges, as he almost invariably does, with one movement of his head he could cut both legs to the bone, dividing the arteries, and probably killing the man.

Presently a young stag rushed into one of the bags with such force as to break both his horns close off. There we found him when we examined the nets. We were sitting watching for what should come next, when G., raising his finger, whispered to me, "What 's that down there in the plain? That 's a deer: no, it can't be: do you see how it slouches along? Depend upon it it 's not a deer." "Well, at any rate it 's coming this way; we shall soon get a look at it." Another pause of half a minute and the beast was concealed in a little patch of jungle a few hundred yards from us. I now had time to examine it. "I 'll tell you what, G.; that brute 's a regular tiger." "Well, so I thought, but I hardly liked to say so: what shall we do if he comes this way?" "I say keep close where we are." "But suppose he should make a spring over the hedge in front of us?" "Lie flat down, and let him go over us: yet I think I could hardly resist having a shot while he was in the air." "Oh! pray don't fire; what in the world could we two do on foot against a wounded tiger?" However, our fears were needless: as the beaters advanced, the animal slunk away into a more distant piece of jungle, and we saw no more of him. Two of our people were rather hurt to-day—one by a deer leaping over him, and cutting his head with his hoof; a rupee, however, made him quite happy again: the other was a man who, as a large stag rushed past, made a spring at its horns, thinking to pull it down, whereby he got a severe fall and prevented us from firing.

Pooree, April 26, 1845.

I HAVE had another attack similar to last year; it came on in the same way and whilst I was in the pulpit. In the midst of the sermon my teeth began to chatter; I could not speak; my face became perfectly white; a cold blast seemed to enter my left side and spread over the surface of my body, and then gradually penetrate to the very innermost part, whilst I was obliged to cling to the sides of the pulpit for support. It did not last above a minute and a half, and I managed to finish my sermon; but it was enough to astonish the congregation and to warn me of what was coming. All my old symptoms returned, though not so strongly as before—utter restlessness at night and heavy sleepiness during the day, a painful cough when I lay down, and other alarming signs. We came down to Pooree, where my favourite doctor lives, and I already feel much better.

There is a billiard-table in the house where we are now staying, and the doctor desires me to play as much as I can every day. Of course playing for money is never allowed. The game of billiards is about the best exercise for India. It is not too violent, yet it gives a man about three miles of walking in the hour, and brings all the limbs into play.

May 8, 1845.

I am too weak to write much, and shall therefore continue at another time.

[Note.—On the 17th of May the author's life was closed.]

THE END.

THE

CAMPAIGNS OF THE BRITISH ARMY

AT

WASHINGTON AND NEW ORLEANS,

IN

THE YEARS 1814—1815.

BY

THE AUTHOR OF "THE SUBALTERN;" AND
"A TRUE STORY OF THE BATTLE OF WATERLOO."

A NEW EDITION.

LONDON:
JOHN MURRAY, ALBEMARLE STREET.

1847.

ADVERTISEMENT.

The following Narrative contains, it is believed, the only connected and authentic account, which has yet been given, of the expedition directed against Washington and New Orleans, towards the close of the late American war. It has been compiled, not from memory alone, but from a journal kept by the author whilst engaged in the enterprise; and as the adventures of each day were faithfully noted down as they occurred, and such remarks made upon passing events as suggested themselves to his mind at the moment, the public may rely with confidence upon the general correctness of the details. The issues of the expedition were not, indeed, of the most gratifying nature, but it is hoped that a plain relation of the proceedings of those to whom it was intrusted, will not, on that account, prove uninteresting; whilst nothing can be more evident than that the portion of our history which it embraces ought not to be overlooked because it is little conducive to the encouragement of national vanity. It was chiefly, indeed, upon this account, as well as with a view to redeem from an oblivion which they hardly merit, the actions and sufferings of a few brave men, that the Narrative now submitted to the public was written.

CONTENTS.

THE

BRITISH ARMY

AT

WASHINGTON AND NEW ORLEANS.

CHAPTER I.

A REVOLUTION must occur in the condition and sentiments of mankind more decided than we have any reason to expect that the lapse of ages will produce, before the mighty events which distinguished the spring of 1814 shall be spoken of in other terms than those of unqualified admiration. It was then that Europe, which during so many years had groaned beneath the miseries of war, found herself at once, and to her remotest recesses, blessed with the prospect of a sure and permanent peace. Princes, who had dwelt in exile till the very hope of restoration to power began to depart from them, beheld themselves unexpectedly replaced on the thrones of their ancestors; dynasties, which the will of one man had erected, disappeared with the same abruptness with which they had arisen; and the influence of changes, which a quarter of a century of rapine and conquest had produced in the arrangements of general society, ceased, as if by magic, to be felt, or at least to be acknowledged. It seemed, indeed, as if all which had been passing during the last twenty or thirty years, had passed not in reality, but in a dream; so perfectly unlooked for were the issues of a struggle, to which, in whatever light we may regard it, the history of the whole world presents no parallel.

At the period above alluded to, it was the writer's fortune to form one of a body of persons in whom the unexpected cessation of hostilities may be supposed to have excited sensations more powerful and more mixed than those to which the common occurrences of life are accustomed to give birth. He was then attached to that portion of the Peninsular army to which the siege of Bayonne had been intrusted; and on the 28th of April beheld, in common with his comrades, the tri-coloured flag, which, for upwards of two months, had waved defiance from the battlements, give place to the ancient *drapeau blanc* of the Bourbons. That such a spectacle could be regarded by any British soldier without stirring up in him strong feelings of national pride and exultation, is not to be imagined. I believe, indeed, that there was not a man in our ranks, however humble his station, to whose bosom these feelings were a stranger. But the excitation of the moment having passed away, other and no less powerful feelings succeeded; and they were painful, or the reverse, according as they ran in one or other of the channels into which the situations and prospects of individuals not unnaturally guided them. By such as had been long absent from their homes, the idea of enjoying once more the society of friends and relatives, was hailed with a degree of delight too engrossing to afford room for the occurrence of any other anticipations; to those who had either no homes to look to, or had quitted them only a short time ago, the thoughts of revisiting England came mixed with other thoughts, little gratifying, because at variance with all their dreams of advancement and renown. For my own part I candidly confess, that though I had just cause to look forward to a return to the bosom of my family with as much satisfaction as most men, the restoration of peace excited in me sensations of a very equivocal nature. At the age of eighteen, and still enthusiastically attached to my profession, neither the prospect of a reduction to half-pay, nor the expectation of a long continuance in a subaltern situation, were to me productive of any pleasurable emotions; and hence, though I entered heartily into all the arrangements by which those about me strove to evince their gratification at the glorious termination of the war, it must be acknowledged that I did so, without experiencing much of the satisfaction with the semblance of which my outward behaviour might be marked.

Such being my own feelings, and the feelings of the great majority of those immediately around me, it was but natural that we should turn our views to the only remaining quarter of the globe in which the flame of war still continued to burn. Though at peace with France, England, we remembered, was not yet at peace with the United States; and reasoning, not as statesmen but as soldiers, we concluded that she was not now likely to make peace with that nation till she should be able to do so upon her own terms. Having such an army on foot, what line of policy could appear so natural or so judicious as that she should employ, if not the whole, at all events a large proportion of it, in chastising an enemy, than whom none had ever proved more vindictive or more ungenerous? Our view of the matter accordingly was, that some fifteen or twenty thousand men would be forthwith embarked on board of ship and transported to the other side of the Atlantic; that the war would there be carried on with a vigour conformable to the dignity and resources of the country which waged it; and that no mention of peace would be made till our general should be in a situation to dictate its conditions in the enemy's capital.

Whether any design of the kind was ever seriously entertained, or whether men merely asserted as a truth what they earnestly desired to be such, I know not; but the white flag had hardly been hoisted on the citadel of Bayonne, when a rumour became prevalent that an extensive encampment of troops, destined for the American war, was actually forming in the vicinity of Bordeaux. A variety of causes led me to anticipate that the corps to which I was attached would certainly be employed upon that service. In the progress of the war which had been just brought to a conclusion, we had not suffered so severely as many other corps; and though not excelling in numbers, it is but justice to affirm that a more effective or better organized battalion could not be found in the whole army. We were all, moreover, from our commanding officer down to the youngest ensign, anxious to gather a few more laurels, even in America; and we had good reason to believe that those in power were not indisposed to gratify our inclinations. Under these circumstances we clung with fondness to the hope that our martial career had not yet come to a close; and employed the space which intervened between the eventful 28th of April and the 8th of the following month, chiefly in forming guesses as to the point of attack towards which it was likely that we should be turned.

Though there was peace between the French and British nations, the form of hostilities was so far kept up between the garrison of Bayonne and the army encamped around it, that it was only by an especial treaty that the former were allowed to send out parties for the purpose of collecting forage and provisions from the adjacent country. The foraging parties, however, being permitted to proceed in any direction most convenient to themselves, the supplies of corn and grass, which had heretofore proved barely sufficient for our own horses and cattle, soon began to fail, and it was found necessary to move more than one brigade to a distance from the city. Among others, the brigade of which my regiment formed a part, received orders on the 7th of May to fall back on the road towards Passages. These orders we obeyed on the following morning, and after an agreeable march of fifteen or sixteen miles, pitched our tents in a thick wood, about half-way between the village of Bedart and the town of St. Jean de Luz. In this position we remained for nearly a week, our expectations of employment on the other side of the Atlantic becoming daily less and less sanguine, till at length all doubts on the subject were put an end to by the sudden arrival of a dispatch, which commanded us to set out with as little delay as possible towards Bordeaux.

It was on the evening of the 14th that the route was received, and on the following morning, at daybreak, we commenced our march. The country through which we moved had nothing in it, unconnected with past events, calculated in any extraordinary degree to attract attention. Behind us, indeed, rose the Pyrenees in all their grandeur, forming, on that side, a noble boundary to the prospect; and on our left was the sea, a boundary different it is true in kind, though certainly not less magnificent. But, excepting at these two extremities, there was nothing in the landscape on which the eye loved particularly to rest, because the country, though pretty enough, has none of that exquisite richness and luxuriance which we had been led to expect as characteristic of the South of France. The houses, too, being all in a ruinous and dilapidated condition, reminded us more forcibly of the scenes of violence and outrage which had been lately acted among them, than of those ideas of rural contentment and innocence which various tales and melodramas had taught us to associate in our own minds with thoughts of the land of the vine.

Regarded, however, in connexion with past events, the scene was indeed most interesting; though to a stranger fresh from England—a man, we will suppose, of retired and peaceful habits, I can readily imagine that it would have been productive of much pain; for on each side of the road, in whatever direction we cast our eyes, and as far as the powers of vision extended, we beheld cottages unroofed and in ruins, châteaux stripped of their doors and windows, gardens laid waste, the walls demolished, and the fruit-trees cut down; whole plantations levelled, and vineyards trodden under foot. Here and there, likewise, a redoubt or breastwork presented itself; whilst caps, broken firelocks, pieces of clothing, and accoutrements scattered about in profusion, marked the spots where the strife had been most determined, and where many a fine fellow had met his fate. Our journey lay over a field of battle, through the entire extent of which the houses were not only thoroughly gutted (to use a vulgar but most expressive phrase), but for the most part were *riddled* with cannon shot. Round some of the largest, indeed, there was not a wall nor a tree which did not present evident proofs of its having been converted into a temporary place of defence, whilst the deep ruts in what had once been lawns and flower-gardens, showed that all their beauty had not protected them from being destroyed by the rude passage of heavy artillery.

Immediately beyond the village of Bedart such spectacles were particularly frequent. It was here, it may be remembered, that in the preceding month of December there had been fighting for four successive days; and the number of little hillocks now within our view, from under most of which legs and arms were beginning to show themselves, as well as the other objects which I have attempted to describe, sufficiently attested the obstinacy with which that fighting had been maintained.

In the bosom of a man of peace it is very conceivable that all this would have excited feelings exceedingly painful; in ours, such feelings were overborne by others of a very different nature. If we gazed with peculiar interest upon one hovel more than upon another, it was because some of us had there maintained ourselves; if we endeavoured to count the number of shot-holes in any wall, or the breaks in any hedge, it was because we had stood behind it when "the iron hail" fell thick and fast around us. Our thoughts, in short, had more of exultation in them than of sorrow; for though now and then, when the name of a fallen comrade was mentioned, it was accompanied with a "poor fellow!" the conversation soon returned again to the exploits and hair-breadth escapes of the survivors. On the whole, therefore, our march was one of deep interest and high excitement, feelings which did not entirely evaporate when we halted, about two hours after noon, at the village of Anglet.

We found this village in the condition in which it was to be expected that a place of so much importance during the progress of the late siege would be found,—in other words, completely metamorphosed into a chain of petty posts. Being distant from the outworks of Bayonne not more than a mile and a half, and standing upon the great road by which all the supplies for the left of the British army were brought up, no means, as may be supposed, had been neglected, which art or nature could supply, towards rendering it as secure against a sudden excursion of the garrison as might be. About one hundred yards in front of it felled trees were laid across the road, with their branches turned towards the town, forming what soldiers, in the language of their profession, term an abattis. Forty or fifty yards in rear of this a ditch was dug, and a breastwork thrown up, from behind which a party might do great execution upon any body of men struggling to force their way over that impediment. On each side of the highway again, where the ground rises into little eminences, redoubts and batteries were erected, so as to command the whole with a heavy flanking fire; while every house and hovel lying at all within the line of expected operations was loop-holed, and otherwise put in a posture of defence. But upon the fortification of the church a more than ordinary degree of care seemed to have been bestowed. As it stood upon a little eminence in the middle of the hamlet, it was no hard matter to convert it into a tolerably regular fortress, which might serve the double purpose of a magazine for warlike stores and a post of defence against the enemy. With this view the churchyard was surrounded by a row of stout palings, called in military phraseology stockades, from certain openings in which the muzzles of half a dozen pieces of light artillery protruded. The walls of the edifice itself were, moreover, strengthened by an embankment of earth to the height of perhaps four or five feet from the ground, above which narrow openings were made, in order to give to its garrison an opportunity of levelling their muskets; while on the top of the tower a small howitzer was mounted, from which either shot or shell could be thrown with effect into any of the lanes or passes near. It is probably needless to add that the interior arrangements of this house of God had undergone a change as striking as that which affected its exterior. Barrels of gunpowder, with piles of balls of all sizes and dimensions, now occupied the spaces where worshippers had often crowded; and the very altar was heaped up with spunges, wadding, and other implements necessary in case of an attack.

I have been thus minute in my description of Anglet, because what has been said of it will apply more or less exactly to every village, hamlet, or cluster of cottages, within the compass of what were called the lines. It is true that neither here nor elsewhere, excepting at one particular point, and that on the opposite side of the river, were any serious intentions entertained of breaching or storming the place; and that the sole object of these preparations was to keep the enemy within his works, and to cut him off from all communication with the surrounding country. But to effect even this end, the utmost vigilance and precaution were necessary, not only because the number of troops employed on the service was hardly adequate to discharge it, but because the garrison hemmed in was well known to be at once numerous and enterprising. The reader may accordingly judge what appearance a country presented which, to the extent of fifteen or twenty miles round, was thus treated; where every house was fortified, every road blocked up, every eminence crowned with fieldworks, and every place swarming with armed men. Nor was its aspect less striking by night than by day. Gaze where he might, the eye of the spectator then rested upon some portion of one huge circle of fires, by the glare of which the white tents or rudely constructed huts of the besiegers were from time to time made visible.

While things continued thus, the condition of the peaceful inhabitant of this district could hardly fail to be one of extreme discomfort. Of these the greater number had indeed fled on the advance of the British army, leaving their houses and effects a prey to the conquerors; but there were some who, having probably no place of refuge to retire to, remained in their homes, and threw themselves upon our mercy for protection. It is not requisite that I should now inform the reader of the strict discipline which Lord Wellington preserved in every division of his army; his first step, on entering France, had been to inform the people that against them no violence was intended; and the assurance thus given, was in no instance, at least wantonly, violated. But, however orderly the conduct of an invading force may be, their very presence must occasion a thousand inconveniences to those upon whom they are quartered; not the least distressing of which is, perhaps, the feeling of degradation which the consciousness of being in the power of armed foreigners can hardly fail to produce. Then there is the total destruction of all domestic comfort, which the occupation of a man's house by large bodies of soldiers produces; the liability to which the females, in particular, are exposed to insult from the common troopers; and the dread of vengeance from any delinquent on whom their complaints may have brought down chastisement,—all these things must and do create a degree of misery, of which the inhabitants of Great Britain may thank God that they know nothing except by name. In the vicinity of Bayonne, moreover, the country people lived in daily and nightly expectation of finding themselves involved in all the horrors and dangers of a battle. Sorties were continually looked for, and however these might terminate, the non-combatants felt that they must be equally the sufferers. Nay, it was no uncommon ground of complaint among them, that even the total defeat of our forces would bring with it no relief, because, by remaining to receive us, they had disobeyed the proclamations of Marshal Soult, and were consequently liable to punishment as traitors.

CHAPTER II.

As soon as the bustle of encamping was over, and my time absolutely at my own disposal, I took advantage of an offered passport, and proceeded into Bayonne. It will be readily believed that I entered this city with feelings very different from those of a common traveller. Having lain before it as a besieger for upwards of two months, its shops, its trade, its public buildings and places of amusement were to me objects of, comparatively speaking, little interest or curiosity. Its fortifications and means of defence were, in truth, what I was principally anxious to examine. Hitherto I could judge of them only from outward appearances and vague reports; and now that an opportunity was offered of so doing with greater accuracy, I confess that my inclination prompted me to embrace that opportunity, rather than to hunt for pictures which I could not value, or fatigue my imagination by endeavouring to discover fine specimens of architecture amidst heavy and ill-built churches.

It is not my intention to attempt any scientific or technical review of the works which a very natural curiosity tempted me to examine; partly because I confess myself little competent to the task, and partly because, were the contrary the case, I am inclined to believe that such a review would not prove very interesting to the public in general. Enough is done if I endeavour to impress my reader with as many of the feelings which I then experienced, as may be done by detailing them; and, at the same time, enable him to form some general idea of a place before whose walls no trifling quantity of British blood has been spilt.

The city of Bayonne stands, as everybody knows, upon the Adour, about six or eight miles from the point where that river falls into the sea. On the southern or Spanish bank, where the whole of the city, properly so called, is built, the country, to the distance of two or three miles from the walls, is perfectly flat and the soil sandy, and apparently not very productive. On the opposite bank the ground rises rather abruptly from the brink of the stream, sloping upwards likewise from the sea, till you arrive at the pinnacle upon which the citadel is erected, and which hangs immediately over the town. Thus, though the Adour in fact separates the city from the suburbs and citadel, yet as the ramparts of the former extend to the water's edge on both sides, and as those of the latter continue the sweep from points immediately opposite, the general appearance presented is that of one considerable town, with a broad river flowing through the middle of it.

It will be seen, even from this short and imperfect sketch, that its situation gives to Bayonne, considered as a military post, a superiority over most cities; inasmuch as it affords peculiar facilities towards rendering it a place of great strength. On one side there is a plain, always accounted by engineers the most convenient for the construction of fortifications; on the other an eminence, lofty enough to command the surrounding country, and at the same time sufficiently level at the summit to receive the walls of a fortress, powerful at once from its position and regularity. But the great strength of Bayonne arose at this juncture not so much from its original defences as from the numerous outworks which had been lately added to it. It was along the course of the Adour, as the reader will probably recollect, or rather between the Adour and the Nieve, that Soult formed his famous intrenched camp. The right of this chain of stupendous works rested upon the city, the importance of which was consequently much increased; and as the capture of it would have occasioned not only the loss of a town, but the turning of the whole position, no pains were spared in rendering it as nearly impregnable as possible. That I may convey some notion to the minds of others of the nature of these works, I will describe the aspect which they presented to myself, as I rode from Anglet towards the city.

When I had proceeded about a mile and a half beyond our advanced posts, I found myself in front of the first line of defence. This consisted of a battery mounting three eighteen-pounders, upon the road, flanked by other batteries, one on each side; all so placed as that whichsoever of them should be attacked, it might be defended by a cross-fire from the rest. These were of course additionally strengthened by ditches and felled trees; but they were open in the rear; and though very formidable to an assailing party, yet, when taken, could have been of small service to the conquerors, being themselves exposed to the fire of the second line. The situation of the second line, again, was similar in every respect to that of the first, being, like it, open in the rear, and placed under the guns of the town. Thus, after having forced two powerful lines of defence, the besiegers would find themselves almost as far as ever from the attainment of their object, being then only arrived at the point where the labours of a siege could commence.

But the maintenance of Bayonne must at all times depend upon keeping possession of the citadel. The city lying upon a plain, and the castle standing upon an eminence immediately above it, it is clear that, were the latter taken, the former must either surrender or be speedily reduced to ruins. It is true that, by destroying the bridge which connects them, all communication between the two places would be cut off; but the distance from the one to the other being not more than half-musket shot, and the guns of the fort pointing directly down upon the streets and houses of the city, any attempt to hold out could cause only the destruction of the town, and the unavenged slaughter of its garrison. Of the truth of this the French were as much aware as their enemies, nor did they neglect any means which an accurate knowledge of engineering could point out, for the defence of what they justly considered as the key of the entire position. In addition to its own very regular and well-constructed fortifications, two strong redoubts were thrown up, on two sides of the fort, upon the only spots of ground calculated for the purpose; both of which, I was informed by my guide, were undermined and loaded with gunpowder, ready to be sprung as soon as they should fall into our hands. They had judged, and judged correctly, that if ever the place should be invested, it would be here that the trenches would be opened and the breaching batteries erected; and they made every preparation to meet the danger, which great prudence and military skill could suggest.

Bayonne, though a populous place, does not cover so much ground as a stranger would be led to suppose. Like most walled towns, its streets, with the exception of one or two, are in general narrow, and the houses lofty: but it is compact, and, on the whole, clean, and neatly built. The number of inhabitants I should be inclined to estimate at somewhere about thirty thousand, exclusive of the garrison, which at this time amounted to fourteen or fifteen thousand men; but as most of the families appear to live in the style of those in the old town of Edinburgh, that is to say, several under the same roof, though each in a separate story or flat, it is not difficult to conceive how they contrive to find sufficient room, within a compass apparently so narrow. Of its commerce and manufactures I can say little, except that I should not imagine either to be extensive. I am led to form this opinion, partly from having seen no shipping at the wharfs, and partly because the Adour, though here both wide and deep, is rendered unnavigable to vessels of any size, by a shallow or bar at its mouth. There was, indeed, a sloop of war close to the town, but how it got there I am at a loss to conceive, unless it were built upon the river, and kept as an additional protection against a surprise from the water. The shops are, however, good, particularly those where jewellery is sold; an article in the setting and adorning of which the French, if they do not excel us in really substantial value, undoubtedly surpass us in elegance.

When I had taken as complete a survey of the town as I felt disposed to take, I crossed the bridge with the intention of inspecting the interior of the citadel. Here, however, I was disappointed, no strangers being admitted within its gates; but as there was no objection made to my reconnoitring it from without, I proceeded towards the point where our trenches had been dug, and where it had been designed to breach and storm the place. To this I was urged by two motives, partly from the desire of obtaining the best view possible of the fort, and partly that I might examine the ground upon which the desperate affair of the 14th of April took place. The reader cannot have forgotten, that some hours before daylight on the morning of that day, a vigorous and well-arranged sortie was made by the garrison, and that it was not without hard fighting and a severe loss on both sides that the attack was finally repulsed.

Mounting the heights, I soon arrived at St. Etienne, a little village nearly on a level with the citadel, and not more than a quarter of a mile from its walls. From this point I could satisfy my curiosity to the full, and as the account may not, perhaps, be uninteresting, I shall describe, as well as I am able, the scene which here met my eyes.

The ridge of little hills upon which the fort and village are built, though it rises by gentle gradation from the sea, towards the spot where I now stood, is nevertheless intersected and broken here and there by deep glens or ravines. Two of these glens, one to the right, the other to the left, chance to occur immediately under the ramparts of the fortress, supplying, in some measure, the purposes of a ditch, and leaving a sort of table or elevated neck of land between them, the extremity of which is occupied by the village. On this neck of land the besieged had constructed one of the redoubts to which I alluded as having been lately thrown up; whilst on another table, at the opposite side of the left ravine, which winds round in the direction of the wall, as nearly as if it were the work of art, stands the other redoubt. Beyond this, again, there is a perpendicular precipice, the hills there abruptly ending; so that on two sides the walls of the fort skirt the extremity of a bare rock. It was along the outer ridges of these ravines, and through the churchyard of St. Etienne, that our trenches were drawn, the village itself being the most advanced British post; and it was along these ridges, and in the street of this village, that the action of the 14th of April was fought.

It is not my business, neither indeed is it my intention, to relate here the particulars of that affair. The French, having contrived, in a dark night, to elude the vigilance of our sentinels, came upon the piquets unperceived, and took them completely by surprise. The battle was maintained on both sides with great determination, and had it not been for the unfortunate capture of Sir John Hope and the fall of General Hay, the assailants would have had little cause to rejoice at the result: for though the loss of the English was certainly great, that of the French was at least not inferior. Yet the business was an unfortunate one to both parties, since, before it took place, Buonaparte had already abdicated, and the preliminaries of peace were already signed between the two nations.

I found the village, in which the fighting had been most obstinately maintained, in the condition of most villages where such dramas have been acted. The street had been barricaded, but the barricade was almost entirely torn down; the houses, trees, and church, like those we had passed upon the march, were covered with the marks of cannon and musket balls, whilst quantities of round and grape shot, of musket and pistol bullets, broken bayonets, swords, &c. &c., lay scattered about in every direction. Nor were these the only evidences of strife discernible. In many places—on the pavement of the street, in the churchyard, but above all, on the floor of the church itself, —the traces of blood were still distinctly visible. Beside the remains of the barricade there stood a solitary six-pounder, which had been taken and re-taken nine times during the struggle; and a sprinkling of what looked like a mixture of blood and brains still adhering to its carriage and breech, showed that it had never been given up without the most desperate resistance. The mounds, too, under which the dead were buried, presented a peculiarly striking appearance; for the field of action having been narrow, those that fell, fell in heaps together, and being buried in the same way, one was led to form an idea of greater slaughter than if double the number of graves had been distinguishable in a more extended space.

Having now accomplished my wishes as far as I could, and beginning to feel somewhat fatigued with strolling about, I adjourned to an hotel in the city, from whence, in the evening, I went to the play. The house was poor and the performance miserable, consequently there was no great inducement to sit out the whole of the piece. After witnessing an act or two, therefore, I returned to the inn, where I slept, and at an early hour next morning rejoined my regiment, already under arms and making preparations for the continuance of the march.

As it would have been considerably out of our way to go round by the floating bridge,* permission was applied for and granted, to pass directly through Bayonne. With bayonets fixed, band playing, and colours flying, we accordingly marched

* The bridge here alluded to was thrown across the Adour by the Duke of Wellington at the commencement of the siege. It was composed of a number of small fishing vessels fastened together with cords, and planked from one to another, the whole firmly moored about three miles below Bayonne. Whether the daringness of the attempt, or the difficulties surmounted in its completion, be considered, the construction of this bridge may be looked upon as one of the most extraordinary actions of that extraordinary man.

along the streets of that city; a large proportion of the garrison being drawn up to receive us, and the windows crowded with spectators, male and female, eager to behold the troops from whom not long ago they had probably expected a visit of a very different nature. The scene was certainly remarkable enough, and the transition from animosity to good-will as singular as it was sudden; nor do I imagine that it would be easy to define the sensations of either party, on being thus strangely brought in contact with the other. The females, indeed, waved their handkerchiefs, whilst we bowed and kissed our hands; but I thought I could discover something like a suppressed scowl upon the countenances of the military. Certain it is, that in whatever light the new state of affairs might be regarded by the great bulk of the nation, with the army it was by no means popular; and at this period they appeared to consider the passage of British troops through their lines as the triumphal entrance of a victorious enemy.

As soon as we had cleared the entrenchments of Bayonne, and got beyond the limits of the allied camps, we found ourselves in a country more peaceful and more picturesque than any we had yet traversed. There were here no signs of war or marks of violence. The cottages were covered with honeysuckle and roses, the gardens were blooming in the most perfect order; the corn was growing in great plenty and richness, and the vines were clustering round their poles like the hops in the gardens of Kent. It is impossible to describe the feeling of absolute refreshment which such a sight stirred up in men who, for so long a time, had looked upon nothing but ruin and devastation. It is true that with respect to grandeur, or even beauty, the scenery through which we now travelled was not to be compared with the sublime passes of the Pyrenees, or with many other spots which we had beheld; but in truth, a hamlet uninjured and tenanted by its own rude peasantry, a field of Indian corn exhibiting no wasteful track of foragers, nay, a single cottage with its flowers and evergreens budding around it, was at this time a more welcome object to our eyes than the wildest mountains or most romantic valleys displaying no habitations except white tents and no inhabitants except soldiers. For my own part, I felt as if I had once more returned into the bosom of civilized and domestic life, after having been for many months a wanderer and a savage.

The road along which we proceeded had been made by Napoleon, and was remarkably good. It was sheltered, on each side, from the rays of the sun, by groves of cork-trees mingled with fir; by which means, though the day was overpoweringly hot, we did not suffer so much as we should otherwise have done. Our march was, therefore, exceedingly agreeable, and we came in, about noon, very little fatigued, to the village of Ondres, where the tents were pitched, and we remained till the morrow.

CHAPTER III.

THE dawn was just beginning to appear, when the bugles sounded, and the tents were struck. For the first few leagues, our route to-day resembled that of yesterday, in almost every particular. There was the same appearance of peaceful quiet, the same delightful intermingling of woods, corn-fields, vine-yards, and pasture; but we had not proceeded far, when a marked difference was perceptible; every step we trod, the soil became more and more sandy, the cultivation less frequent, and the wood more abundant, till at last we found ourselves marching through the heart of an immense forest of pines. We had diverged, it appeared, from the main road, which carries the traveller through a rich and open country, and were pursuing another through the middle of those deserts and savannahs which lie towards the coast, a district known by the name of *les Landes*. There was something, if not beautiful, at least new and striking in the scenery now around us. Wherever the eye turned, it was met by one wide waste of gloomy pine-trees; diversified, here and there, by the unexpected appearance of a modest hamlet, which looked as if it were the abode of some newly arrived settlers in a country hitherto devoid of human habitations.

Were I to continue the detail of a long march through these barren regions, I should soon fatigue, without amusing my reader: I shall, therefore, content myself with observing, that day after day the same dreary prospect presented itself, varied by the occasional occurrence of huge uncultivated plains, which apparently chequer the forest, at certain intervals, with spots of stunted and unprofitable pasturage; upon these there were usually flocks of sheep grazing, in the mode of watching which, the peasants fully evinced the truth of the old proverb, that necessity is the mother of invention. I do not know whether the practice to which I allude be generally known, but as it struck me as very remarkable, I shall offer no apology for relating it.

The whole of this district, as well where it is wooded, as where it is bare, is perfectly flat, containing scarcely a knoll or eminence of any sort, as far as the eye can reach. In addition to this, the vast plains where the sheep are fed, many of which extend two or three leagues in every direction, produce not so much as a fir-tree, by climbing which, a man might see to any of its extremities: and the consequence is, that the shepherds are constantly in danger of losing their sheep, as one loses sight of a vessel at sea, in the distance. To remedy this evil, they have fallen upon a plan not more simple than ingenious; they all walk upon stilts,* exactly similar to those with which our school-boys amuse themselves; the only difference lying here, that whereas the school-boys' stilts are with us seldom raised above ten or twelve inches from the ground, those of the French peasants are elevated to the height of six or eight feet.

When we first caught a glimpse of these figures, it was in the dusk of the morning, and for awhile we were willing to persuade ourselves that the haze had deceived us, by seeming to enlarge bodies beyond their real dimensions. But when we looked at the trees, we saw them in their own proper size, nor could we suppose that the atmosphere would have an effect upon one object, which it had not upon another; yet there appeared to be no other way of accounting for the phenomenon, unless indeed this wild country were the parent of a race of giants, for the men whom we saw resembled moving towers rather than mortals. I need not observe that our astonishment was very great; nor, in fact, was it much diminished when, on a nearer approach, we discovered the truth, and witnessed the agility with which they moved, and the ease with which, aided by the poles which each carried in his hand, they would stoop to the ground, pick up the smallest article, and stand upright again. But if we admired the skill of one or two individuals, our admiration rose to a still higher pitch when we saw crowds of them together, all equally skilful; till they informed us that the thing was not an amusement, but universally practised for the purpose I have stated.

Besides this, I know of nothing in the customs of this isolated people at all worthy of notice, unless, indeed, it be their method of supplying themselves with lights. Being completely cut off from the rest of the world, it is not in their power, except when once or twice a-year they travel to the nearest towns with their wool, to purchase candles; and as they have no notion how these can be made, they substitute in their room a lamp fed with the turpentine extracted from the fir-trees. The whole process is simple and primitive: to obtain the turpentine they cut a hole in the tree, and fasten a dish in it to catch the sap as it oozes through; and as soon as the dish is filled, they put a wick of cotton into the midst of the liquor, and burn it as we do a lamp. The light is not indeed of the most brilliant nature, but it is at least better than none; and as they have fir-trees in abundance within their reach, there is no danger of their oil being quickly exhausted.

In this manner was an entire week expended, each succeeding day introducing us to a repetition of the same adventures, and a renewal of the same scenery, which had amused us during the day before; nor was it till the morning of the twenty-third that we at last began to emerge from the forests, and to find ourselves once again in a more open country. At first, however, it cannot be said that, with respect to beauty, the change was greatly for the better. Upon the borders of the deserts there is a little village called Le Barp, where we spent the night of the twenty-second; from whence, till you arrive at a place called Belle-Vue, the country is exactly in that state which land assumes when nature has begun to lose ground, and art to gain it—when the wild simplicity of the one is destroyed, and the rich luxuriance of the other has not yet been superinduced. So far, therefore, we proceeded, regretting, rather than rejoicing, that we had quitted the woods; but no sooner had we attained that point, than there burst upon us, all on a sudden, a prospect as gloriously fertile as ever delighted the eyes of a weary traveller.

Instead of boundless forests of pine, the whole face of the

country was now covered with vineyards, interspersed, in the most exquisite and tasteful manner, with corn-fields and meadows of the richest pasturage. Nor was there any deficiency of timber; a well-wooded château, with its lawn and plantations, here and there presenting itself, while quiet hamlets and solitary cottages, scattered in great abundance over the scene, gave to it an appearance of life and prosperity exceedingly bewitching. Had there been but the addition of a fine river flowing through the midst of it, and had the ground been somewhat more broken into hill and dale, I should have pronounced it the most enchanting prospect of the kind I had ever beheld; but, unfortunately, both these were wanting. Though the effect of a first view, therefore, was striking and delightful, and though to the last we could not help acknowledging the richness of the land and its high state of cultivation, its beauty soon began to pall. The fact is, that an immense plain, however adorned by the labour of man, is not an object upon which it is pleasing to gaze for any length of time; the eye becomes wearied with the extent of its own stretch, and as there is no boundary but the horizon, the imagination is left to picture a continuance of the same plain, till it becomes as tired of fancying as the eye is of looking. Besides, we were not long in discovering that the vineyards were unworthy to be compared, in point of luxuriant appearance, with those of Spain and the more southern regions of France. In this neighbourhood, the vine is not permitted to grow to a greater height than three or four feet from the ground; whereas in Spain, and on the borders, it climbs, like the hop-plant in England, to the top of high poles, and hangs over from one row to another, in the most graceful festoons. In spite of these objections, however, no one could do otherwise than admit that the change we had experienced was agreeable, and we continued to move on with greater alacrity, till it was evident, from the increasing number of seats and villas, that we were rapidly approaching the vicinity of Bordeaux.

Nor was it long before the towers and buildings of that magnificent city began to be discernible in the distance. Prompted by I know not what impulse, we almost involuntarily quickened our pace at the sight, and in a short time reached the suburbs, which, like those of most French towns, are composed of low houses, inhabited by the poorest and meanest of the people. Here we halted for a few minutes to refresh the men, when having again resumed the line of march, we advanced under a triumphal arch, originally erected in honour of Napoleon, but now inscribed with the name of the Duke d'Angoulême, and ornamented with garlands of flowers. Passing under this, we proceeded along one or two handsome streets, till we reached the Military Hospital, a large and commodious structure fitted up for the reception of several thousands of sick, where it was arranged that we should spend the night.

The city of Bordeaux has been too often described, and is too well known to my countrymen, in general, to render any particular account of it at all necessary from me; and were the case otherwise, I confess that my opportunities of examining it were not sufficient to authorize my entering upon such an attempt. The whole extent of our sojourn was only during the remainder of that day (and it was past noon before we got in) and the ensuing night; a space of time which admitted of no more than a hurried stroll through some of the principal streets, and a hasty visit to such public buildings as are considered most worthy of attention. The palace of the Duke d'Angoulême, the Military Hospital, the Theatre, and the Cathedral, are all remarkably fine of their kind; whilst the public gardens, the Exchange, and fashionable promenades, are inferior only to those of Paris itself.

I have said that our sojourn in Bordeaux was limited to the short space of a few hours. We could have wished indeed to prolong it, but to wish was needless, for at an early hour next morning we were again in motion, and proceeded to an extensive common, near the village of Macau, about three leagues from Bordeaux, where we found a considerable force already assembled. Judging from the number of tents upon the heath, I conceive that there could not be fewer than eight or ten thousand men in that camp, the whole of whom, we naturally concluded, were destined for the same service with ourselves. The sight was at once pleasing and encouraging, because there could be no doubt that such a force, ably commanded, would carry everything before it.

In this situation we continued, without the occurrence of any incident deserving of record, till the 27th, when an order arrived for the officers to dispose of their horses without delay. This was necessarily done at an enormous loss; and on the morning of the 28th, we set forward towards the point of embarkation. But, alas! in the numbers allotted for the trans-Atlantic war, we found ourselves grievously disappointed, since, instead of the whole division, only two regiments, neither of them surpassingly numerous, were directed to move; it was not our business, however, to question the wisdom of any measure adopted by our superiors, and we accordingly marched on in as high spirits as if we had been followed by the entire Peninsular army.

The remainder of our journey occupied two days, nor do I often remember to have spent a similar space of time with greater satisfaction; our route lay through some of the most fertile districts in France, passing Château Margaux, famous for its wine, with other places not inferior to it either in richness of soil or in beauty of prospect. The weather was delightful, and the grapes, though not yet ripe, were hanging in heavy bunches from the vines, giving promise of much wealth to come; the hay season had commenced, and numerous groups of happy-looking peasants were busy in every field; in short, it was a march upon which I shall never look back without pleasure.

The close of the first day's progress brought us to a village called La Moe, beautifully situated within view of the majestic waters of the Garonne. Here, for the first time since we quitted Bayonne, were we quartered upon the inhabitants—a measure which the loss of our tents rendered necessary. They received us with so much frankness, and treated us with so much civility, I had almost said kindness, that it was not without a feeling of something like regret that we parted from them. The second day carried us to Pauliac, an inconsiderable town upon the banks of the same river, where we found boats ready to convey us to the shipping, which lay at anchor to receive us.

To embark the troops in these boats, and to huddle them on board two dirty little transports, occupied some time, and the provoking part of the business was, that all this trouble was to be gone through again. The men-of-war in which we were to cross the Atlantic, could not come up so high for want of water; and on this account it was that transports were sent as passage-boats to carry us to them. But the wind was foul, and blew so strong that the masters would not venture to hoist a sail; so we were obliged to endure the misery of a crowd in a small vessel for two nights and a day; nor was it till past noon on the 31st, that the regiment to which I was attached found itself finally settled in His Majesty's ship ——— of 64 guns.

CHAPTER IV.

The land army, destined for the invasion of the United States, which took shipping at this period in the Garonne, consisted but of three battalions of infantry, the 4th, 44th, and 85th regiments; the two former mustering each about eight hundred bayonets, the last not more than six hundred. In addition to these, there were two officers of engineers, a brigade of artillery, a detachment of sappers and miners, a party of artillery drivers, with a due proportion of officers belonging to the Medical and Commissariat departments. The whole together could not be computed at more than two thousand five hundred men, if indeed it amounted to so great a number; and was placed under the command of Major-General Ross, a very gallant and experienced officer.

The fleet, again, consisted of the Royal Oak, of 74 guns, bearing the flag of Rear-Admiral Malcolm; the Diadem and Dictator, two sixty-fours, armed *en flûte;* the Pomone, Menelaus, Trave, Weser, and Thames, frigates, the three last armed in the same manner as the Diadem and Dictator; the Meteor and Devastation, bomb-vessels; together with one or two gun-brigs, making in all a squadron of eleven or twelve ships of war, with several store-ships and transports.

On board the Royal Oak were embarked the General, with his staff, and the artillery; the Trave and Weser were filled with the 4th; the 44th were divided between the Dictator and the Thames, in the first of which ships were also the engineers; the 85th occupied the Diadem; and the rest were scattered through the fleet, partly in the men-of-war and partly in the transports.

As soon as the troops, with all their baggage, were finally settled in the vessels allotted for their accommodation, the signal was made to weigh; but the wind being adverse, and the navigation of the Garonne far from simple, it could not be obeyed with safety. Every thing, therefore, remained quiet till the evening of the 2nd of June, when the gale moderating a little, the anchors were raised and the sails hoisted. The tide was beginning to ebb when this was done, favoured by which the ships drifted gradually on their course; but before long, the breeze shifting, blew directly in their sterns, when they stood gallantly to sea, clearing the river before dark; and, as there was no lull during the whole of the night, by daybreak the coast of France was not to be discerned. All was now one wide waste of waters, as far as the eye could reach, bounded on every side by the distant horizon; a scene which, though at first it must strike with awe and wonder a person unaccustomed to it, soon becomes insipid, and even wearisome, from its constant sameness.

The fair wind which carried us out of the Garonne continuing to blow without any interruption till the 19th of June, it was that day calculated, by consulting the log and taking observations, that the Azores, or Western Islands, could not be very distant. Nor, as it turned out, were these calculations incorrect; for, on ascending the deck next morning, the first object that met our eyes was the high land of St. Michael's rising, like a collection of blue clouds, out of the water. With such a prospect before us our consternation may be guessed at, when we found ourselves deserted by the breeze which had hitherto so uniformly favoured us, and lying as motionless as logs, under the influence of a dead calm.

But the complaints to which we had begun to give utterance, were speedily changed again into rejoicings, for before mid-day the breeze once more freshened, and we approached every moment nearer and nearer to the object of our wishes. As soon, too, as we contrived to double the projecting headland which had attracted our attention in the morning, our course became productive of much interest and pleasure. We had neared the shore considerably, and were moving at a rate sufficiently rapid to prevent further repining, and at the same time slow enough to permit a distinct and calm survey of the beach, with the numerous villages, seats, and convents that adorned it.

The island of St. Michael is mountainous, even to the very edge of the water, but the heights, though lofty, do not present a rugged or barren appearance. Here and there, indeed, bare rocks push themselves into notice, but in general the ascent is easy, and the hills are covered to the tops with groves of orange-trees and beautiful green pasturage. Like other Portuguese settlements, this island abounds in religious houses, the founders of many of which do not appear to have been deficient in taste when they pitched upon situations for building. There was one of these in particular that struck me: it stood upon a sort of platform or terrace, about half-way between the sea and the summit of the mountain; above it were hanging woods, whether natural or artificial I cannot say, broken in upon here and there by projecting rocks; and round it were plantations of orange-trees loaded with fruit, and interspersed with myrtles and other odoriferous shrubs. Being greatly pleased with the mansion and the surrounding scenery, I naturally inquired from the pilot (for one had already come off to us) as to its use, and the quality of its owner; and from him I learnt that it was a convent, I forget of what order,—a piece of intelligence which was soon confirmed by the sound of bells distinctly audible as we passed.

In this manner we continued to coast along, being seldom at a greater distance than four or five miles from the land, till we came opposite to a small town called Villa Franca. Here, as the wind threatened to die away, several others and myself agreed to go on shore: a boat was accordingly lowered, and we pushed off from the ship; but the operation of landing did not prove to be altogether so simple as we had expected. An immense reef of rocks, some under water, others barely above it, but none distinguishable till we had almost run against them, opposed our progress; and it was not without considerable difficulty, and the assistance of the country people, who made signals to us from the beach, that we contrived to discover a narrow channel leading up to the strand.

Having at length so far attained our wishes as to tread once more upon firm ground, the next thing to be done was to find out some inn, or house of public entertainment, where we might pass the night, a measure which the increasing darkness rendered necessary. In this, however, we were disappointed, the town of Villa Franca boasting of no such convenience on any scale. But we were not on that account obliged to bivouac; for the

Alcalde, or mayor of the place, politely insisted upon our accompanying him home, and entertained us with great hospitality; nor, in truth, had we any cause to regret the unsuccessful issue of our inquiries, since, in addition to the good cheer with which we were presented, our host, being an intelligent person, did not fail to render himself an agreeable companion; and what contributed in no slight degree to the facility of our intercourse was, that though he assured us he had never quitted St. Michael's in his life, he spoke English with the fluency of a native. Among other pieces of information we learnt from him that the reef which impeded our progress towards the land, had formerly been an island. It appeared, he affirmed, one morning, in the most sudden and extraordinary manner, as if it had been thrown up by an earthquake during the night, and having continued so long above water as to embolden a single family of fishers to settle upon it, it disappeared again as suddenly as it had come, leaving no trace of its existence except the rocks which we had found so troublesome. Whether there be truth in this story, I cannot pretend to determine; and yet I see no reason to doubt the word of a man of respectability, who could have no motive whatever for deceiving us. But this was not all that we learnt from him respecting the reef. He declared that previous to the appearance of the island, the water in that very spot was unfathomable; and it was not till after it had sunk, that a single rock stood in the way to prevent the largest ship of war from anchoring within a stone's throw of the beach.

Finding our new acquaintance so civil and obliging, we naturally informed him of our intention to proceed next morning to Ponto del Gada, the principal town in St. Michael's, and requested his assistance in procuring some mode of conveyance; but we were startled by the intelligence that nothing of the kind could be had, and that there were not even horses or mules to be hired at any place nearer than the very town whither we were going. This was rather an alarming piece of news, for our boat had left us, the weather was too hot for walking, and the distance to be travelled full fifteen miles. Had we been prudent enough to detain our boat, the matter would have been easily managed, because we might have sailed round to the point where the fleet was to anchor; but this was no longer in our power, and being rather unwilling to pursue our journey on foot, we were altogether at a loss upon what course to determine. Whilst we thus hesitated, the Alcalde suggested that if we would condescend to ride upon asses, he thought he could obtain a sufficient number for our party; a proposal with which we gladly closed, prudently determining that any mode of being carried was better than walking. Leaving the arrangement of this affair, therefore, to our obliging friend, we retired to rest upon clean comfortable mattresses spread for us on the floor; and on waking in the morning, we found that he had not been negligent in the charge assigned to him. Our party consisted of five officers, with five servants, for whose accommodation we found ten asses at the door, each attended by its driver, who wielded a long pole tipped with an iron spike, for the purpose of goading the animal whenever it should become lazy.

It was not without a good deal of laughing that the cavalcade, after bidding adieu to the hospitable Mayor, began to move forward. Our asses, of no larger size than ordinary English donkeys, were uncaparisoned, at least with bridles; and the saddles were neither more nor less than the pack-saddles upon which goods are transported to market. For our own comfort, therefore, we were obliged to sit *à la femelle*, and having no command over the heads of our steeds, we were content to be guided by the hallooing and punching of the drivers. In spite, however, of these inconveniences, if so they may be called, I shall never cease to congratulate myself on having been of the party, because the ride proved to be one of the most agreeable I remember at any time to have taken.

The road from Villa Franca to Ponto del Gada quits the water's edge, and turns, for a little way, inland, carrying you through a region as romantic and beautiful as can well be imagined. There are here no level plains, no smooth paths over which a landau or tilbury might glide, but, on the contrary, a rugged and stony track, sometimes leading down the face of steep hills, sometimes scaling heights which at the distance of a mile appear to be almost perpendicular, and sometimes winding along the side of a cliff, and by the edge of a fearful precipice. Except when you reach the summit of a mountain, the road is in general shaded by the richest underwood, hanging over it from above;

but the whole aspect of the country is decidedly that of a volcanic production: the rocks seem to have been cast up and torn asunder by some prodigious violence, and hurled, by a force which nothing but a volcano could possess, into the most grotesque and irregular shapes. It is no uncommon thing to pass under a huge crag, leaning almost horizontally over the road, and bedded in the earth by a foundation apparently so slight, as to appear liable to fall every moment, precipitating the enormous mass upon the luckless wretch beneath. Nay, the very colour of the stones, and the quantity of what bears every resemblance to vitrification, scattered about, all tend to induce the belief that the main island owes its formation to the same cause which doubtless produced the smaller one that has now disappeared.

It is not, however, to be inferred from the above description that St. Michael's is nothing but a barren rock; far from it. There is, indeed, in this direction at least, a fair proportion of that commodity; but tracts of cultivated ground are not therefore wanting. I should not certainly suppose that the soil was remarkably rich in any part of the island; but it produces the fig, the orange-tree, and a grape from which the inhabitants make very tolerable wine; and there is excellent pasture for sheep, and a competent supply of grain. But that in which the Azores, and St. Michael's among the number, particularly excel, is the extreme salubrity of the climate. Lying in nearly the same degree of latitude with Lisbon, the intense heat which oppresses in that city is here alleviated by refreshing sea-breezes; by which means, though I believe there is no occasion at any season to complain of cold, it is only in the very height of the dog-days, if then, that a person, not actually engaged in violent exercise, is justified in complaining of sultriness.

The trade of St. Michael's, as far as I could learn, is confined exclusively to fruit: the fig and the orange are the staple commodities; and being both very abundant, they are, of course, proportionably cheap. Into the praise of a St. Michael's orange it is unnecessary for me to enter, because it is generally allowed to be the best with which the English market is supplied; but of the excellence of the St. Michael's fig, I am not sure that my countrymen in general are so much aware. It might be, that not having seen a fig for a considerable lapse of time, my appetite was peculiarly sharpened towards its good qualities, but it struck me that I never before tasted any so highly flavoured or so delicate. Besides these, they sell to vessels putting in, as we did, for water, some of the wine made in this and the neighbouring islands; but the quantity thus disposed of must be too inconsiderable to entitle it to be classed among the articles of merchandise.

I find, however, that I am entering upon subjects in which I am but little versed, and digressing from my narrative. Let me return, then, to self, that beloved idol of all travellers, and state that, after we had ridden about six miles, the road, which had hitherto conducted us along a narrow glen, where the vision was intercepted on both sides, now carried us to the summit of a lofty mountain, from whence we enjoyed the satisfaction of an extensive prospect, both of the sea and of the interior. Looking towards the former, we beheld our own fleet bearing down majestically upon Ponto del Gada, and fast approaching the anchorage. Turning our eyes inland again, we were delighted with a view of mountain and valley, rock and culture, wood and pasturage, intermingled in the most exquisite degree of irregularity; but what principally attracted our attention was a thick dark smoke rising slowly from the summit of a high hill that bounded the prospect. Our curiosity being excited by this phenomenon, we inquired from our guides into its cause, and were informed that the mountain in question was a volcano, and that at its base and along its sides were hot springs of water, of a temperature sufficient to boil an egg in three minutes. This piece of intelligence confirmed me in my former opinion relative to the operative cause in the production of these islands; though, indeed, had such evidence been wanting, I should have equally concluded, either that they were thrown up, in their present form, from the bottom of the sea, or at least that they were torn asunder from one another by the force of fire. It must be confessed, however, that mine is the opinion of one who has devoted little of his attention to geology; but I would by all means advise the disciples of Werner to come hither, if they desire further helps in the prosecution of that very interesting and practically useful study.

CHAPTER V.

DESCENDING the mountain, on which we had paused for a few minutes to feast our eyes and satisfy our curiosity, we arrived at a small hamlet, or rather a group of two or three hovels, as romantically situated as it is possible for the imagination of man to conceive. They stood at the further end of a sort of recess, formed by the hills, which are here broken into a circular valley, cut off, to all appearance, from the rest of the habitable world; behind them rose a towering crag, as perpendicular as the drop of a plummet, from the top of which a little rivulet came tumbling down, giving to the scene an appearance of the most delightful coolness, and amusing the ear with the unceasing roar of a waterfall. From the very face of the cliff, where there seemed to be scarcely soil enough to nourish a thistle, numerous shrubs and dwarf trees protruded themselves; whilst above it, and on every side of the area, the hills were covered with wood, interrupted now and then by the bald forehead of a blackened rock. In front of the hamlet again, there was an opening sufficient to admit the most delicious glimpse of the ocean; and through this the stream, after boiling for awhile in a little basin, which it has excavated for itself out of what resembles the foundation of the cliff, makes its way, brawling over a clear pebbly bottom, till it joins the sea.

This paragon of valleys burst upon us as such scenes, to be witnessed with advantage, ought to do, without the slightest warning or expectation. The road by which we approached it, being completely shut in with wood, and winding considerably to aid the descent, brought us out nearly at the gorge of the vale, so as to throw the hamlet, the cliff, and the waterfall into the background; and as the whole was of such extent as to be taken in at one glance, the effect was striking beyond anything of the kind I ever witnessed. It is but natural to suppose that we had no desire to hurry through such a glen as this; and needed not the additional motive which the weariness of our donkeys afforded, to persuade us to a temporary halt. Giving the animals, therefore, to the care of their owners, we dismounted, and went into some of the cabins, the inhabitants of which appeared to be as simple as the situation of their abodes had prepared us to expect. The men were all goatherds, and the women seemed to be as idle as their countrywomen in Portugal, sitting at the doors of their houses, surrounded by groups of half-naked and filthy-looking children. If it be fair to judge from their dress and the furniture of their hovels, they were miserably poor, though perfectly contented; they did not ask us for money, but astonished, I suppose, at the glaring colour of our coats, they were very inquisitive to know who we were and whence we had come. The English, the French, and the Portuguese seemed to be the only three nations of whose existence they had any knowledge; and having been assured, in answer to their first question, that we were not French, they immediately added, "Then you must be English." They did not appear, however, to be without some degree of cunning, for as long as we paused in replying to their query, they were silent; but no sooner had we answered in the negative, than they launched forth into the most violent invectives against the French; convincing us that the animosity of the mother-country towards its barbarous invaders was not more implacable than that of the colonies.

Having loitered away half an hour in this romantic spot, and distributed a few dollars among its inhabitants, we remounted our steeds and continued our journey. The remainder of the ride carried us through scenery very similar to what we had already passed; the only difference was, that the nearer we approached to Ponto del Gada the more frequent became the spots of cultivation, the width and smoothness of the road improving in proportion; till at last, when we had attained the brow of an eminence, from whence the town with its port and bay were distinguishable, we looked down upon an extensive valley, richly covered with fields of standing corn. Quickening our pace, we soon entered the capital of St. Michael's, and were conducted by the drivers to a good hotel, kept by an Englishwoman of the name of Currie, where we found every accommodation which we could desire, at a very moderate expense.

As we had started at an early hour from Villa Franca, the clocks were just striking ten when we alighted at Mrs. Currie's hotel; consequently, there was a long day yet before us, in which we might see everything that was to be seen in the place. Having discharged our muleteers, therefore, who seemed overjoyed at the receipt of one dollar a-piece, swallowed a hasty breakfast, and made ourselves somewhat comfortable, we lost no time in setting out upon a stroll of examination and discovery.

Ponto del Gada is, on the whole, rather a neat town, containing from twelve to fourteen thousand inhabitants; but being built, especially in the outskirts, without much regard to compactness, it covers more ground than many places of double the amount in population. It stands upon a little bay, formed by two projecting headlands, and can boast of a tolerable harbour and excellent roadstead. In its immediate vicinity the country is more uniformly level than any I had yet observed; the vale extending to the distance of four or five miles on every side, and ending in an amphitheatre of low green hills, which resemble, in appearance, the downs as they are seen from Eastbourne in Sussex. The whole of this flat is in a state of high cultivation, being cleared, perhaps too completely, of wood, and portioned off into different fields and parks by hedges and stone walls. Judging from the appearance of the crops, I should conceive that the soil was here of some depth, as well as fertility, the whole valley being covered with wheat, barley, and Indian corn. And in truth, if the aspect of the country beyond the downs, where rocks tower one above another in rude and barren grandeur, furnish a legitimate criterion by which to determine respecting the general fertility of the island, I should be almost tempted to believe that the whole industry of its people has been expended upon this spot, simply because it was the only one capable of rewarding it. I was assured, however, by the natives, that such is not the case; and that, in the interior, and towards the opposite coast, the rugged magnificence of mountain scenery gives place to a more profitable though less picturesque champaign.

The principal streets of Ponto del Gada are paved, and kept at once cool and clean by a constant sprinkling of water, which it is the business of two or three men stationed at pumps within a certain distance of one another, to scatter over them. Of the by-streets little can be said in praise, they being, like those of other Portuguese towns, composed of mean cottages, unpaved, and extremely dirty. There is, however, an air of elegance given to the town, particularly when looked at from a distance, by the intermixture of orange-groves among the houses; the largest of these, wherever they happen to stand, being, in general, surrounded by extensive gardens, all of which are abundantly stocked with that graceful and odoriferous plant. Add to this the number of towers and spires with which its numerous churches and convents are supplied, and the first aspect of the whole may be conceived to be extremely striking and imposing.

As soon as we had taken a hurried survey of the streets, the next object of attention was the religious houses. In these there was but little to admire, the architecture being of the plainest kind, and even the chapels as much wanting in ornament as can be imagined. There were, indeed, in most of them some trifling attempts at carved work and gilding upon the roof, a little stained glass, neither rich nor ancient, in the windows, and a few tawdry pictures suspended above the altars; but the general appearance was decidedly that of buildings which did not even aim at beauty or grandeur. The monks we found a good-natured, obliging set of men, very willing to give us any information in their power; by one of whom we were fortunate enough to be conducted through a convent of Augustine friars. Into their mode of living it is not to be supposed that we could obtain much insight. It seemed, however, to be less indolent than that of some convents which we had visited in the old country, and approached proportionably nearer to a college life among ourselves; though it must be admitted that the fellows and undergraduates of Oxford and Cambridge have a better notion of both comfort and elegance than the Augustine friars of St. Michael's. Of the nuns we of course saw nothing, excepting through the grates. We found them full of curiosity, and eager to know as much as they could learn of the world from which they were excluded; but quite as fond of flirting as any set of young ladies at a boarding-school. It was amusing to observe their mode of begging, for all the nuns in this part of the world are licensed beggars. The younger and fairer members of the sisterhood came to the grate first; chatted, sung, and presented us with artificial flowers, and then retiring, made way for the old and the ugly, who requested a little money for the good of our souls and their bodies. To solicitations thus expressed it was impossible to turn a deaf ear, and the consequence was, that we soon discovered it to be quite as expensive an amusement to flirt with a nun, as with any other belle in London or elsewhere.

Besides the churches and convents, amounting in all to not fewer than nine, there is a fort erected for the protection of the harbour, which we likewise endeavoured to see, but were prevented by the sentinel at the gate, who refused us admittance. The disappointment, however, was not great, as it was easy to perceive, from its outward appearance, that the fort could possess few points worthy of observation; and, indeed, we attributed the reluctance evinced in admitting strangers to its utter uselessness as a place of defence.

To describe all this occupies but a small portion of time; but to see it was the laborious employment of an entire day. Wearied out at length with my exertions, and not feeling much rewarded, at least for the latter part of my trouble, I returned in the evening to the hotel, where, as the ships were still at anchor, taking on board water and fresh provisions, I ventured to spend the night.

Having thus discovered that there was little in the works of art, and a great deal in those of nature, throughout St. Michael's, to interest the traveller, a friend and myself determined to set off next morning on a visit to the volcano. With this design we ordered asses, for asses are the only animals for hire, to be in readiness by daybreak; and finding them in waiting at the time appointed, we took a guide with us and pushed forward in the direction of the dark smoke. The mountain with its crater being distinctly visible from Ponto del Gada, we took it for granted that the distance between the two places could not exceed twelve or fourteen miles; but, on inquiring of our guide, we learned that the nearest road would carry us at least twenty-seven miles from the town. This was at once a startling and unpleasant piece of intelligence, affecting our arrangements in no trifling degree. To proceed was dangerous, because, mounted as we were, to go and return in one day was impossible; and, if we remained so far from the shipping during the night, the fleet might sail before we should be able to get back. On the other hand, to give up our design, and quit a country where a volcano was to be seen, without seeing it, appeared rather a mortifying prospect. After weighing for a few minutes the chances on both sides,—I shall not say with the utmost impartiality, curiosity finally prevailed over apprehension; and, in order to prevent any further repentance and consequent change of mind, we put our donkeys into a gallop, and hurried on as fast as they could carry us. But the speed of the asses and our own venturous determination proved, after all, equally unavailing; for, on gaining the summit of the downs, and looking back upon the fleet, we beheld, to our great sorrow, the signal for sailing displayed at the topmasts of all the ships. Mortified at our disappointment, and at the same time rejoicing that we had got no farther on our journey, we were compelled to turn our asses' heads, and to retrace our steps towards Ponto del Gada, where we found everything in the bustle and confusion of a re-embarkation. The beach was covered with sailors, soldiers, bullocks, and casks of fresh water, hurrying, and being hurried, indiscriminately into the boats which had arrived to take them off. The townspeople were running about upon the strand, some offering their skiffs to convey the officers on board the ships, some helping to swing the bullocks into the barges, and others shouting and hallooing apparently from the disinterested love of noise. In short, it was a scene of great liveliness and bustle, perhaps rather too much so to be agreeable.

Seeing this universal eagerness to reach the fleet, we, like the rest, threw ourselves into the first boat we could approach, and in a short time found ourselves on board our own ship. But here a very tantalizing piece of intelligence awaited us, for we learnt that, in spite of all this show of preparation, the Admiral had not begun to weigh anchor; and that no intention of moving was entertained, at soonest, before the morrow. The opportunity, however, was lost; it could not be recovered, and we were obliged to submit as cheerfully as we could, though it was impossible to help regretting, what had at first been a source of consolation, the circumstance of our having caught a view of the signal at the time we did. But, as the event proved, all had turned out for the best; for on the day following the signal was again repeated; and by way of giving additional weight to it, the

Admiral began to shake loose his topsails. Nor did it prove, like that of yesterday, a false alarm. By mid-day, the victualling and watering being complete, the fleet immediately began to get under weigh; and, as the wind blew fair and fresh, before dark the mountains of St. Michael's could be seen only like a thin vapour in the sky. Next morning nothing but the old prospect of air and water met the gaze, as we stood our course, at a rapid rate, towards Bermuda.

The voyage from St. Michael's to Bermuda occupied the space of almost an entire month, the first having been lost sight of on the 27th of June, and it being the 24th of July before the low shores of the last could be discerned. It was, however, a passage of more interest and productive of more variety than that from Bordeaux to the Azores. We had now arrived within the influence of the tropical climate, and were not unfrequently amused with water-spouts, and other phenomena peculiar to warm regions. The flying-fish, likewise, and its pursuer, the dolphin, afforded at least something to look at; whilst many idle hours were whiled away in attempts to catch or strike the latter with harpoons. In these we were not always unsuccessful, consequently we enjoyed several opportunities of watching the change of colour which that fish undergoes whilst it is dying; and though the description generally given of it is certainly indebted in some degree to the imagination of voyagers, I must confess that the transitions from blue to purple, and from purple to green, with all their intermediate shades, are extremely beautiful. When the fish is in the water, it is by no means remarkable for brilliancy of hue, and as soon as it is dead it returns to its original colour—a dingy sea-green; but whilst it is floundering and flapping upon the deck, it is impossible to say what is its real appearance, so many and so different are the hues which it assumes. Nor did we escape without the occasional occurrence of a less agreeable species of variety; I mean squalls, thunder-storms, and whirlwinds. As we approached Bermuda, indeed, these became too frequent to excite any interest beyond an earnest desire that they would cease: but while we were yet a good way off, and the incident rare, they were witnessed with more of admiration than terror.

Besides these amusements with which nature supplied us, we were not backward in endeavouring to amuse ourselves. Being now pretty well accustomed to the atmosphere of a ship, we began to consider ourselves at home, and to give balls and other public entertainments through the fleet. One of these I shall take leave to describe, because I am sure it must interest from its novelty.

On the 19th of July, at an early hour in the morning, a signal was made from the Royal Oak, that the Admiral would be happy to see the officers of the fleet on board his ship that evening. Boats were accordingly sent off from the different vessels, loaded with visitors; and on mounting the gangway, a stage, with a green curtain before it, was discovered upon the quarter-deck. The whole of the deck, from the poop to the mainmast, was hung round with flags, so as to form a moderate-sized theatre; and the carronades were removed from their port-holes, in order to make room for the company. Lamps were suspended from all parts of the rigging and shrouds, casting a brilliant light upon this singular playhouse; and the crew, arrayed in their best attire, crowded the booms, yards, and fore part of the deck; whilst the space from the mainmast to the foot of the stage was set with benches for the more genteel part of the audience.

At seven o'clock the curtain drew up, and discovered a scene painted with such taste as would not have disgraced any theatre in London. The play was the 'Apprentice,' with the 'Mayor of Garret' as an afterpiece, performed by the officers of the ship and of the artillery, and went off in high style, applauded, as it deserved to be applauded, with the loudest acclamations. The quarter-deck of a British line-of-battle ship has often enough been a stage for the exhibition of bloody tragedies; but to witness a comedy and a farce upon that stage, and in the middle of the Atlantic Ocean, was delightful from its very singularity. When the performance came to an end, the stage was knocked down, the seats removed, and everything cleared for dancing. The music was excellent, being composed of the band of the Royal Oak; and the ball was opened by Admiral Malcolm and the Honourable Mrs. Mullens, in a country dance, followed by as many couples as the space would permit; the greater number of officers dancing, as necessity required, with one another. In this amusement every person, from the Admiral and General, down to the youngest ensign and midshipman, joined, laying aside for the time all restraint or form of discipline; and having kept it up with great spirit till considerably beyond midnight, a blue light was hoisted as a signal for the different boats to come off for the strangers, and each returned to his own ship highly gratified with the evening's entertainment.

CHAPTER VI.

By employing ourselves in this manner, and by keeping up what is emphatically called a good heart, we contrived to pass our time agreeably enough. As often as the weather would permit, and the fleet lay well together, we made parties of pleasure to the different ships; when the wind was too high, and the fleet too much scattered for such proceedings, we remained at home, and amused ourselves in the best way we could. Some of the captains, and ours among the number, were possessed of very tolerable libraries, the doors of which they politely threw open for the benefit of their military guests; and thus, by reading, fishing, and boating, we were enabled to make head, with some success, against the encroachments of ennui. It must be confessed, however, that in spite of strenuous efforts to the contrary, that determined enemy of all idle persons was beginning to gain ground upon us, when, about mid-day on the 24th of July, a cry of land was heard from the mast-head. All eyes were immediately turned in the direction to which the sailor pointed, and as the wind blew fair and moderately fresh, no great length of time elapsed before the same object was distinguishable from the deck. A signal was immediately hoisted for a pilot, who lost no time in coming off to us; and before dark we were at anchor opposite to the tanks in Bermuda.

The appearance of Bermuda is altogether as different from that of St. Michael's as one thing can be from another. Whilst the last, with its lofty mountains and bold shores, can be seen at the distance of many leagues, a ship must be within a few miles of the first before the slightest symptom of land is discernible. On this account it is that mariners find greater difficulty in making Bermuda than perhaps any other island or continent in the known world; the most experienced seaman frequently sailing past it, and not a few suffering shipwreck every year upon its numerous shoals and rocks. For not only is the land itself low, and thus apt to be run against by vessels which may have approached in stormy weather too near to put about, but for many miles round, reefs of sunken rocks stretch out into the sea in every direction; insomuch, that even the approach to the principal anchorage is no more than a narrow channel between two reefs, in many places scarcely exceeding a mile or a mile and a half in width. The navigation, even in calm weather, is therefore attended with considerable danger; the idea of which is greatly heightened by the remarkable clearness of the water and the peculiar brightness of the rocks. In some places this is so much the case, that the bottom may be seen at the depth of six or seven fathoms; whilst the aspect of the reefs which lie on each side, as you steer towards the anchorage, is such, as almost to persuade you, contrary to the evidence of reason, that a man might leap upon them from a boat without incurring the danger of being wet above the knees. Yet these very reefs are seldom covered with less than six, and sometimes with fourteen and fifteen feet of water.

Low as they are, the shores of Bermuda are nevertheless extremely beautiful. They are covered with cedar, a tree which here, at least, seldom exceeds the height of twenty feet, and from which, before the sun has risen and after he has set, the land-breeze comes loaded with the most delicious perfume. Under the wood there grows a rich short turf, apparently struggling to spread itself over the chalky rocks, of which the entire island, or rather islands, seem to be composed; and, as the houses of the better orders are chiefly built within reach of the cool air from the water, they, with their little lawns and gardens, produce a lively and pleasing effect.

As darkness had come on before the ship could be properly moored, no boats were permitted to leave her that night; but at an early hour next morning I embraced the first opportunity of going on shore. To reach St. George's, the capital of the colony, you are obliged to row for several miles up a narrow frith called the ferry, immediately on entering which the scenery becomes in the highest degree picturesque. Though still retaining its character of low, the ground on each side looks as if it were broken into little swells, the whole of them beautifully shaded with groves of cedar, and many of them crowned with country-houses as white as the drifted snow. But the fact is, that this appearance of hill and dale is owing to the prodigious number of islands which compose the cluster; there being in all, according to vulgar report, not fewer than three hundred and sixty-five, of which the largest exceeds not seven or eight miles in diameter. Yet it is only when you follow what at first you are inclined to mistake for a creek or the mouth of a river, that you discover the absence of valleys from between these hills; and even then you are more apt to fancy yourself upon the bosom of a lake studded with islets, than steering amid spots of earth which stand, each of them distinct, in the middle of the Atlantic Ocean.

In the town of St. George's there is nothing to be seen at all worthy of record. It consists of about fifty or sixty houses, the glare from which, as they are all built of the chalk stone, is extremely dazzling to the eyes. It is called the capital, because here the court-house stands and the magisterial sittings are held; but in point of size, and, as far as I could learn, in every other respect, it is greatly inferior to Hamilton, another town at the opposite extremity of the cluster, which I did not visit. A little way from St. George's, and on the summit of a bare rock, stand the barracks, fitted up for the accommodation of a thousand men; and about a mile and a half beyond them are the tanks, well worth the notice of travellers. The object of this work is to catch and preserve the rain—a measure which the total deficiency of fresh springs throughout the colony renders absolutely necessary. There are, indeed, wells dug upon the beach, but the water in these is nothing more than sea-water, filtered and rendered brackish in making its way through the sand, and by no means fit to be used, at least in any quantity. To supply this deficiency, the bad effects of which were experienced in the unhealthiness of many of the crews upon the American station, Government was induced to build these tanks; consequently the water contained in them is the property of the king, and none but king's ships, with the troops in garrison, are permitted, except in extreme cases, to be supplied from thence.

The climate of Bermuda has been extolled by many, and

among the rest by Mr. Moore in his odes and epistles, as salubrious and delightful. It is possible that he, and the rest of its eulogists, may have visited these islands at a season of the year different from that in which I visited them, but to me the heat was beyond measure oppressive. Lying, as they do, under the influence of a vertical sun, and abounding in all directions with cliffs of white chalk, it is obvious that the constant reflection of the sun's rays thereby occasioned must be quite overpowering. If these panegyrists mean to say, that as long as you contrive to keep in the shade, and take care not to stir abroad till after sunset, you will find the Bermudas deserving of their title of summer-islands, then I will agree with them; but I believe there is no man who ever walked the street of St. George's at noon, or any other spot where the sun-beams could reach him, that did not consider the heat as anything rather than temperate.

But whatever may be thought of the climate, there can, I think, be but one opinion as to the soil. It is generally admitted that there is no more unproductive spot of earth upon the face of the deep than Bermuda. The only animals which appear to thrive are the goat and the duck; the cedar and a few calabash-trees are the only wood, and, except the most common kinds of vegetables, such as cabbages, onions, and sweet potatoes, I know of hardly another thing brought to perfection, even in the gardens. The fruits which a stranger may meet with are no doubt delicious, since among them he will find the shaddock and the pine-apple; but for these, as well as for almost all their other comforts and luxuries, the Bermudians are indebted to the continent of America or to the West Indies. Whether this be owing to the natural sterility of the soil, or to the extreme indolence of the inhabitants, I cannot pretend to decide; though I should be inclined to suspect that both were, in some degree, to blame; but its consequences are felt by all visitors, in a very sensible manner, every article of living being here sold for thrice its intrinsic value. That provisions should be dear in this country cannot surprise, when it is considered that this small colony is the general depôt and place of resort for repairs and stores to a large proportion of the British navy, scattered along the coast of America; but, surely, if the natives were a little more industrious, they might afford to sell their goods at a cheaper rate, and at the same time secure an equal, if not a greater profit. But their indolence is beyond all conception, and can be attributed only to, what I believe is its real cause, the facility with which they acquire fortunes, from men who are necessitated to give whatever they demand for the most trifling article. The poorest and meanest freeman upon the island never dreams of applying his own hand, or even his own head, to the cultivation of the ground; and being abundantly supplied with negro slaves, they leave everything, even the care of providing necessaries for themselves, to the industry of that ill-used race. I may perhaps be considered as expressing myself with too much severity towards the Bermudians, but, in truth, I repeat only what I was told by some of themselves; nor did I, from my own personal observation, discover any cause to question the veracity of my informers.

In the praise bestowed by Mr. Moore upon the beauty of these regions, I do, however, most cordially join. There is something bewitchingly pretty, for pretty is perhaps the most appropriate epithet to be used, in every one of the many views which you may obtain from different points. The low and elegant cedar, the green short turf, the frequent recurrence of the white and dazzling rock, the continual rise and fall of the numerous small islands, but above all, the constant intermingling of land and water, seem more like a drawing of fairy land than a reality. There is nothing grand, nothing imposing, or calculated to excite any feeling bordering upon the awful, throughout the whole; but it is soft, gentle, and exquisitely pleasing.

Having spent the day at St. George's, I returned on board to sleep; and on the morrow removed, with my baggage, to a transport then lying at anchor within the ferry, which was thenceforth to be my head-quarters. Thither my friend Grey also removed, and as our ship was well stored, and its commander civil and accommodating, we had no reason to complain of any suffering consequent upon our change of residence.

It will be readily believed that a very small portion of our time was now wasted on board ship; for economy's sake we usually slept there, because at the inn the charge for beds, as well as for everything else, was enormous; but all the hours of daylight were devoted to rowing round the different islands, and climbing the different eminences, from whence the most extensive prospects were to be obtained. Among other curiosities, we were informed of two caves in one of the little isles, distant about four or five miles from the place where we lay. Being assured that they were highly deserving of notice, we determined to visit them; and setting off one evening for that purpose, we reached the spot which had been pointed out to us a little before dark. We fastened the boat to the stump of a tree, and were proceeding towards the caves, when a fine manly voice, singing one of the Irish melodies, attracted our attention. Being rather curious to discover who, in this extramundane place, had learnt to sing with so much taste, we followed the direction of the sound, till we came upon a party sitting under the shade of a tent, and, like ourselves, enjoying the cool of the evening; on perceiving us, some of them came forward, and the satisfaction was mutual when we recognised one another as old acquaintances. They urged us to relinquish our design, and to partake of their good cheer, with which, as the hour was late, we had small reluctance in complying; and it was agreed, that instead of going on without proper guides, and at so unseasonable a time, we should breakfast together at the same spot in the morning, and proceed in a body to examine the caverns. Here, therefore, we remained till the moon had risen, when we returned to our boat, and sailed back to the ship.

Next morning everything was prepared for the expedition, but a heavy squall coming on, prevented us from setting out as early as we had intended; as soon, however, as this blew over, we took to our boat, and reached the place of rendezvous in time to share the remains of a good breakfast which our friends had prepared for themselves and us. When our meal was finished, we supplied ourselves with torches from some dry branches of the calabash-tree, and, headed by a guide, moved towards the mouth of the nearest and largest of the two caves. We descended into this by a ladder of sixteen steps, and arrived upon a broad ledge of rock, where we halted for a few minutes to light the torches, and accustom our vision to the gloom; when, both of these ends being attained, we advanced a few paces into the cave, and a sight of the most indescribable sublimity burst upon us. The appearance was that of a huge Gothic cathedral, having its roof supported upon pillars of spar, moulded into the most regular shapes, and fluted and carved after the most exact models of architecture. The roof itself was indeed too lofty to be discerned, nor could the eye penetrate to anything like an extremity, all beyond a certain extent being wrapped in the most profound darkness; but the flashes of light which at intervals streamed out, as the glare of the torches fell upon pieces of spar as clear as crystal, and the deep echo of our own voices as we spoke, inspired us with a feeling of awe bordering upon superstition. It is in such a situation as this, that the poverty of the mightiest monument of human art becomes conspicuous. The most magnificent churches and abbeys, with their sculptured pillars and vaulted ceilings, were thought of as mean in comparison of what was now before us; indeed, I for one could not help imagining that these very churches and abbeys had been built in humble imitation of this, which looked like a temple reared by some beings more powerful than men. It seemed a shrine worthy of the genii of old, while yet they were in the zenith of their glory, ere they had been driven from their thrones and oracles of darkness by the light of Christianity.

As we moved onward we found the sides of the cave gradually narrow upon us, and the roof become lower and lower. There was, however, a continuance of the same fane-like appearance to the last, though growing more and more contracted; till, finally, we were compelled to advance one by one, and to stoop in order to prevent our heads from coming into contact with the rock. We had proceeded as far as it was possible to proceed with any degree of comfort, and were informed by the guide that we were upwards of three hundred yards from the entrance, when we found it expedient to wheel about, and to return to the open air. But the effect of so sudden a change from darkness to light was exceedingly disagreeable; insomuch that we hastened into the smaller cave, as well for the purpose of deferring the moment of suffering as to continue our search after the sublime.

The entrance to this cavern is extremely dangerous, and not to be ventured upon without either a trusty guide or a thorough knowledge of the ground. After descending a ladder, not quite so deep as that which leads into the larger cave, we arrived at the brink of a fearful chasm, across which a flat stone, about two feet in width, was laid, connecting the edges by a bridge four or five feet in length. To what depth the chasm may reach, the guide could not inform us; but that it is considerable we discovered by dropping a large stone, which we could hear for some time as it dashed against the projecting edges of the rock, and at length splashed with a tremendous echo into water. The man maintained that the sea beat under the foundation of the island as far as the spot where we now stood, and his story was rendered at least probable by the number of pools of salt water which we met with in the interior of the cave.

After having visited the larger cavern, this certainly appeared to disadvantage; though in truth it is in its dimensions only that the one can be pronounced inferior to the other. The spar is equally clear and proportionably as abundant in both: the pillars are quite as regularly formed, and the lesser has an advantage over its rival in two or three broken columns, which give to it the semblance of a temple in ruins. There is also in this cave a strange propinquity of salt and fresh water pools, the situation of two of which struck me as peculiarly curious. They were divided from each other by a piece of rock not much thicker than a man's hand; and yet the water from the one tasted as if it had been taken from the German Ocean, whilst that from the other was as fresh and pleasant as possible.

We had by this time fully gratified our curiosity, and once more ascended to the world of sunshine, the splendour of which was at first almost insupportable. By degrees, however, our eyes became accustomed to the change and recovered their original tone, when we separated, each party returning to its respective ship in high good humour with the day's employment.

But to dine quietly on board was no longer endurable. A tent was accordingly carried on shore, and having sought out the most shady and agreeable nook within a moderate distance of the vessel, our dinner was brought thither, and we spent the evening, as we had done the morning, among the works of nature. Here we remained till a late hour, talking over the adventures of the day, and occasionally attempting a blind peep into futurity, till our friend the moon having risen, we again pulled on board by her light, and lay down to dream of sparry domes and enchanted temples.

CHAPTER VII.

SOME apology is due to the reader, whose attention has been thus long withdrawn from other and more important matters, to follow the adventures of an humble individual like myself. The fault, however, of which I have been guilty may be at once repaired, when I inform him that on our arrival at Bermuda we found Sir Alexander Cochrane, in the Tonnant, of eighty guns, waiting to receive us, and to take the command of the whole fleet. The secret of our destination likewise, which up to that moment had been kept, transpired almost as soon as we cast anchor off the island; and it was publicly rumoured that our next point of debarkation would be somewhere on the shores of the Bay of Chesapeake. Nor are these the only interesting public occurrences of which no notice has as yet been taken. On the 4th of June our little army was reinforced by the arrival of the 21st Fusiliers, a fine battalion, mustering nine hundred bayonets, under the command of Colonel Patterson. On the evening of the 29th a squadron of four frigates and several transports appeared in the offing, which by mid-day on the day following were all at anchor in the roads. They proved to be from the Mediterranean, having the 21st, 29th, and 62nd Regiments on board, of which the two latter were proceeding to join Sir George Prevost's army in Canada, whilst the former attached itself to that under the command of General Ross. By this very acceptable reinforcement, our numbers were increased to upwards of three thousand effective men, and a greater confidence in themselves, as well as a better grounded hope of success in whatever they might undertake, was at the same time given to the troops.

Having already dwelt sufficiently upon my own personal adventures at Bermuda, I shall not waste time by a particular detail of the various preparations which during this interval were making throughout the fleet. Stores of provisions, fresh water, ammunition, clothing, &c., were provided, and magazines for the future supply of the expedition established; when, on the 3rd of August, all things being complete, the ships once more got under weigh, and stood towards America.

During the whole of this day the wind was light and unsteady, consequently little progress was made, nor did the white rocks of Bermuda disappear till darkness concealed them; but towards morning a fresher and more favourable breeze springing up, the rest of the voyage was performed in reasonable time, and without the occurrence of any incident worthy of notice. The heat, indeed, became more and more oppressive every day, and the irksomeness of renewed confinement was more sensibly experienced from the long holiday which we had enjoyed on shore; but, in other respects, everything returned to its former state, till towards evening on the 14th, when a signal was made by the Admiral that land was in sight. As yet, however, there was no appearance of it from the deck of our transport, nor for a full half-hour could our anxious gaze be rewarded by the slightest trace of what it sought; but at the end of that time the low sandy point of Cape Charles began to show itself, and we rejoiced in the prospect of a speedy release from the ennui of a seafaring life.

The coast of America, at least in this quarter, is universally low and uninteresting; insomuch, that for some time before the land itself can be discerned, forests of pines appear to rise, as it were, out of the water. It is also dangerous from the numerous shoals and sandbanks which run out in many places to a considerable extent into the sea, and which are so formidable that no master of a vessel, unless he chance to be particularly well acquainted with the navigation, will venture to approach after dark. The fleet was accordingly anchored within a few miles of the shore, but no sooner had the day begun to break than the sails were again hoisted, and the ships, steering under the influence of a leading wind, between the Capes Charles and Henry, stood in gallant style up the Chesapeake.

This noble bay is far too wide, and the land on each side too flat, to permit any but an indistinct glimpse of the shore from the deck of a vessel which keeps well towards the middle. On the present occasion we could distinguish nothing, on either hand, except the tops of trees, with occasionally a windmill or a lighthouse; but the view of our own fleet was in truth so magnificent as to prevent any murmuring on that account. Immediately on entering, we were joined by Admiral Cockburn with three line-of-battle ships, several frigates, and a few sloops of war and gun-brigs, by which means the squadron could now muster above twenty vessels entitled to display the pendant, besides an equal if not a greater number of victuallers and transports. Nor were we strengthened by this addition in the naval part of the expedition alone. On board these ships was embarked a powerful reinforcement for the army, consisting of a battalion of seven hundred marines, a hundred negroes lately armed and disciplined, and a division of marine artillery, so that we could now calculate on landing a corps of at least four thousand men. The spectacle was therefore as agreeable and imposing as might be; because we could not help remembering that this magnificent fleet was sailing in an enemy's bay, and that it was filled with troops for the invasion of that enemy's country. Thus, like a snowball, we had gathered as we went on, and from having set out a mere handful of soldiers, were now become an army, formidable as well from its numbers as its discipline.

The shoals and sandbanks which abound on the outside of the bay, continue to encumber the navigation after it is entered, and the fleet was in consequence compelled to anchor every night. This proceeding unavoidably occasioned much delay. The first day's sail carried us only to the mouth of the James river, and the second to the mouth of the Potomac; but, on both occasions, we brought up at too great a distance from the beach to permit a perfect or distinct view of either of these rivers. Opposite to the latter, indeed, we remained for a night and a considerable part of the following day, and the sky being remarkably clear, we saw something more of it than we had been able to see of the other river. It appeared to be a fine piece of water making its way through the centre of huge forests, and, though the current is in reality strong, flowing on without any apparent motion. But it would have been impossible to trace its course, even had we been nearer to the shore, above a few miles, on account of its numerous windings, the first of which, overshadowed as it is with wood, shuts it out from further observation. By continuing here so long, we had begun to conjecture that a landing somewhere on the banks of this river was in contemplation. In this, however, we were deceived, for about one o'clock the fleet was again under sail, and moving towards the Patuxent, a river which empties itself into the bay, several miles above the Potomac.

It was singular enough, that the ships had scarcely begun to lift their anchors, when the sky, which had hitherto continued clear and serene, became suddenly darkened and overcast with heavy clouds: and the water, which before had been as smooth and bright as a mirror, began to rise in black waves tipped with foam, though there was not a breath of air to fill the sails. Hurricanes are, I believe, not unfrequent in this part of the world, and it was expected that these changes in the sea and sky foreboded the arrival of one; but they passed by without producing any violent results, and when we brought up, which was done in the evening, the clouds had dispersed, and the water was again like a glassy lake.

The 18th of August had now arrived, and as yet we had advanced no farther than to the mouth of the Patuxent. There we lay, as we had done the day before, anxiously expecting a breeze; till about noon, the wind beginning to blow fair, the fleet entered the river and made its way slowly and majestically against the stream. The voyage soon became picturesque and interesting in the highest degree. Fields of Indian corn, with meadows of the most luxuriant pasture, stretched along the margin of the stream on either hand; whilst the neat wooden houses of the settlers, all of them painted white, and surrounded with orchards and gardens, presented a striking contrast to the boundless forests which formed a background to the scene. Of the prodigious extent and gloomy appearance of these forests, it is impossible for any language to convey an adequate conception. There is nothing, at least nothing which I have seen, in the Old World, at all resembling or to be compared with them; and hemming in, as they do, on every side, the tiny spots of cultivation, they certainly convey no very enlarged idea of the power of human industry. The cleared fields on the banks of the Patuxent, for example, could in no direction measure above half a mile across,—in many places their breadth fell short of that, from the river to the woods; and then all was one vast forest, through which no eye could penetrate, nor any traveller venture to seek his way. We were, as may be imagined, greatly taken by scenery so novel; and we continued to gaze upon it with the liveliest interest, till our attention was drawn away to other and more important matters.

We had not proceeded many miles from the river's mouth when a telegraph from the Admiral gave orders for the troops to be in readiness to land at a moment's notice. Everything was forthwith put in a state of forwardness; provisions for three days, that is to say, three pounds of pork, with two pounds and a half of biscuit, were cooked and given to the men; the cartouch-boxes were supplied with fresh ammunition, and the arms and accoutrements handed out. The fleet, however, continued to move on, without showing any inclination to bring to; till at length, having ascended to the distance of ten leagues from the bay, the ships of the line began to take the ground; and in a little while after, even the frigates could proceed no farther. But by this time the sun had set, and darkness was coming on; consequently, there was no possibility, for that day, of getting the troops on shore without much confusion, if not danger. All therefore remained quiet for the night, with this exception, that the soldiers were removed from the large ships into such as drew least water; which running up as high as prudence would permit, under convoy of the gun-brigs and sloops of war, there cast anchor.

As soon as the dawn began to appear, on the morning of the 19th, there was a general stir throughout the fleet. A gun-brig had already taken her station within a hundred and fifty yards of a village called St. Benedict's, on the left bank of the river, where it was determined that the disembarkation should be effected. Her broadside was turned towards the shore, and her guns, loaded with grape and round shot, were pointed at the beach, to cover the landing of the boats; and being moored fore and aft with spring-cables, she was altogether as manageable as if she had been under sail. The rest of the ships were several miles lower down the stream, some of them being aground at the distance of four leagues from this point; but the boats were quickly hoisted out from every one of them, and the river was covered in a trice with a well-manned and warlike flotilla. The disembarkation was conducted with the greatest regularity and dispatch. Though the stream ran strong against them, and some of them were obliged to row fourteen or fifteen miles backwards and forwards, so strenuously did the sailors exert themselves, that by three o'clock in the afternoon the whole army was landed, and occupied a strong position about two miles above the village.

From what I have stated respecting the gun-brig, it will be seen that all things were in readiness to meet and repel opposition, should such be offered. Her broadside being pointed directly towards the village, whilst it hindered the enemy from bringing down troops in that direction, gave to our people an opportunity of forming, and being able to meet, in good order, whatever force might be posted to check their advance up the country. Had a few pieces of artillery been mounted, indeed, upon the high ground, afterwards taken possession of by us, some execution might have been done upon the boats as they drew towards the beach; but even that would have been trifling, because, unless they had had leisure to heat their shot, no artillery in the open country could have long stood before the fire of even a gun-brig, armed as this was for the occasion with long thirty-two pounders. Each boat-load of soldiers, likewise, drew up the moment they stepped on shore, forming line without any regard to companies or battalions; whilst parties were instantly dispatched to reconnoitre, and to take possession of every house, as well as to line every hedge, in front of the shore where their comrades were arriving. But these preparations, though no more than common prudence required, were unnecessary; since there was not only no opposition to the landing, but, apparently, no enemy within many miles of the place.

So much time was unavoidably expended in establishing the different regiments on the ground allotted to them, in bringing up the hospital and commissariat stores, and arranging the matériel, that when all things were ready, the day appeared too far spent to permit an advance into a country, of the nature and military situation of which we were of course ignorant. The afternoon was accordingly devoted to a proper distribution of the force; which was divided into three brigades, in the following order:—

The first, or light brigade, consisted of the 85th, the light infantry companies of the 4th, 21st, and 44th regiments, with the party of disciplined negroes, and a company of marines, amounting in all to about eleven hundred men; to the command of which Colonel Thornton, of the 85th regiment, was appointed.

The second brigade, composed of the 4th and 44th regiments, which mustered together fourteen hundred and sixty bayonets, was intrusted to the care of Colonel Brooke, of the 44th; and the third, made up of the 21st, and the battalion of marines, and equalling in number the second brigade, was commanded by Colonel Patterson, of the 21st. The whole of the infantry may, therefore, be estimated at four thousand and twenty men. Besides these, there were landed about a hundred artillery-men, and an equal number of drivers; but for want of horses to drag them, no more than one six-pounder and two small three-pounder guns were brought on shore. Except those belonging to the General and staff-officers, there was not a single horse in the whole army. To have taken on shore a large park of artillery would have been, under such circumstances, absolute folly; indeed, the pieces which were actually landed, proved in the end of very little service, and were drawn by seamen sent from the different ships for the purpose. The sailors, thus employed, may be rated at a hundred, and those occupied in carrying stores, ammunition, and other necessaries, at a hundred more; and thus, by adding these, together with fifty sappers and miners, to the above amount, the whole number of men landed at St. Benedict's may be computed at four thousand five hundred.

This little army was posted upon a height which rises at the distance of two miles from the river. In front was a valley, cultivated for some way, and intersected with orchards; at the farther extremity of which the advanced piquets took their ground, pushing forward a chain of sentinels to the very skirts of the forest. The right of the position was protected by a farm-house with its enclosure and outbuildings, and the left rested upon the edge of the hill, or rather mound, which there abruptly ended. On the brow of the hill, and about the centre of the line, were placed the cannon, ready loaded, and having lighted fusees beside them; whilst the infantry bivouacked immediately under the ridge, or rather upon the slope of the hill which looked towards the shipping, in order to prevent their disposition from being seen by the enemy, should they come down to attack. But as we were now in a country where we could not calculate upon being safe in rear, any more than in front, the chain of piquets was carried round both flanks, and so arranged, that no attempt could be made to get between the army and the fleet, without due notice, and time given to oppose and prevent it. Everything, in short, was arranged with the utmost skill, and every chance of surprise provided against; but the night passed in quiet, nor was an opportunity afforded of evincing the utility of the very soldier-like dispositions which had been made.

CHAPTER VIII.

NEXT morning the troops, as is customary during a state of active warfare, were under arms an hour before daylight, and remained in position till after the sun had risen. It was then confidently expected that the column would be put in motion, though in what direction it was to proceed, or what was the object of the descent, none but the General himself appeared to know. A rumour, indeed, prevailed, that a flotilla of gun-boats upon the Patuxent, commanded by the American Commodore Barney, was the point of attack; and that while the land force advanced up the river to prevent their retreat, armed boats from the fleet were to engage them in front. That such was in reality the primary object of the landing, I have every reason to believe, though circumstances afterwards occurred to bring about a change in the plan of operations. Into these, however, I shall not now enter, because they are in no way connected with the present stage of my narrative, but shall merely observe, that in their expectations of an immediate advance the troops were disappointed. Whether it was that the arrangements had not been completed, or that intelligence respecting the state of the country and the enemy's preparations was wanting, I do not know; but the regiments returned to the ground which they had occupied during the night, and everything resumed the same face which it had worn on the evening before.

In this state affairs continued till four o'clock in the afternoon, when the General suddenly made his appearance in the camp, the bugles sounded, and the regiments formed in order for marching. Nor did many minutes elapse before the word was given, and the army began to move, taking the direction of Nottingham, a town situated on the river, where it was understood that the flotilla lay at anchor. The march was conducted with the same caution and good order that had marked the choice of ground for encamping and the disposition of the troops in position. The advanced-guard, consisting of three companies of infantry, led the way. These, however, were preceded by a section of twenty men, moving before them at the distance of a hundred yards; and even these twenty were but the followers of two files, sent forward to prevent surprise, and to give warning of the approach of the enemy. Parallel with the head of the three companies marched the flank patrols; parties of forty or fifty men, which, extending in files from each side of the road, swept the woods and fields to the distance of nearly half a mile. After the advanced guard, leaving an interval of a hundred or a hundred and fifty yards, came the light brigade; which, as well as the advance, sent out flankers to secure itself against ambuscades. Next to it, again, marched the second brigade, moving steadily on, and leaving the skirmishing and reconnoitring to those in front; then came the artillery, consisting, as I have already stated, of one six and two three-pounder guns, drawn by seamen; and last of all came the third brigade, leaving a detachment at the same distance from the rear of the column, as the advanced guard was from its front.

In moving through an enemy's country, the journeys of an army will, except under particular circumstances, be regulated by the nature of the ground over which it passes: thus, though eight, ten, or even twelve miles may be considered as a short day's march, yet if at the end of that space an advantageous position occur (that is, a piece of ground well defended by natural or accidental barriers, and at the same time calculated for the operations of that species of force of which the army may be composed), it would be the height of imprudence to push forward, merely because a greater extent of country might be traversed without fatiguing the troops. On the other hand, should an army have proceeded eighteen, twenty, or even twenty-five miles, without the occurrence of any such position, nothing except the prospect of losing a large proportion of his men from weariness ought to induce a general to stop, until he has reached some spot at least more tenable than the rest. Our march to-day was, upon this principle, extremely short, the troops halting when they had arrived at a rising ground distant not more than six miles from the point whence they set out; and having stationed the piquets, planted the sentinels, and made such other arrangements as the case required, fires were lighted, and the men were suffered to lie down.

It may seem strange, but it is nevertheless true, that during this short march of six miles a greater number of soldiers dropped out of the ranks, and fell behind from fatigue, than I recollect to have seen in any march in the Peninsula of thrice its duration. The fact is that the men, from having been so long cooped up in ships, and unused to carry their baggage and arms, were become relaxed and enervated to a degree altogether unnatural; and this, added to the extreme sultriness of the day, which exceeded anything we had yet experienced, quite overpowered them. The load which they carried, likewise, was far from trifling, since, independent of their arms and sixty rounds of ball-cartridge, each man bore upon his back a knapsack, containing shirts, shoes, stockings, &c., a blanket, a haversack, with provisions for three days, and a canteen or wooden keg filled with water. Under these circumstances, the occurrence of the position was extremely fortunate, since not only would the speedy failure of light have compelled a halt, whether the ground chanced to be favourable or the reverse, but even before darkness had come on scarcely two-thirds of the soldiers would have been found in their places.

The ground upon which we bivouacked, though not remarkable for its strength, was precisely such as might tempt a General to halt, who found his men weary and in danger of being benighted. It was a gentle eminence, fronted by an open and cultivated country, and crowned with two or three houses, having barns and walled gardens attached to them. Neither flank could be said to rest upon any point peculiarly well defended, but they were not exposed; because, by extending or condensing the line, almost any one of these houses might be converted into a protecting redoubt. The outposts, again, were so far arranged differently from those of yesterday, that, instead of covering only the front and the two extremities, they extended completely round the encampment, enclosing the entire army within a connected chain of sentinels; and precluding the possibility of even a single individual making his way within the lines unperceived.

These precautions were, however, like those of the preceding day, unnecessary; no enemy making his appearance, even to reconnoitre: and yet it cannot be said that the night was passed in uninterrupted quiet, for the troops had scarcely lain down when they were disturbed by a tremendous storm of thunder and lightning, accompanied by a heavy fall of rain. The effect of the lightning, as it glanced for a moment upon the bivouac, and displayed the firelocks piled in regular order, and the men stretched like so many corpses beside them, was extremely fine. The effect of the rain, however, was not so agreeable, for, being perfectly destitute of shelter, we were speedily wet to the skin; and the remainder of our resting-time was rendered thereby the reverse of comfortable. But the feeling of fretfulness, natural on such an occasion, lasted no longer than till the day dawned, and the line of march was again formed; when their former good-humour returning, and seasoned in some degree by the fatigues of yesterday, the troops moved on in excellent order and in the highest spirits.

The route to-day was different, in many respects, from that of yesterday. In the first place, we had now got beyond the stretch of cultivation, and were proceeding through forests of immeasurable extent; this, of itself, gave a very different aspect to all around, because hitherto we had seen houses and fields of corn on each side of the road, and now we could discover nothing but wild savannahs, apparently untenanted by a single human being. In the next place, we learnt from some of the country people, who had been impressed as guides into our service, that numerous detached bodies of riflemen lay in ambush among the thickets; and the very expectation of having something to do, created a degree of excitement which, till now, we had not experienced. In consequence of that information, the flank patrols were strengthened and commanded to extend to a greater distance; the advanced guard marched at a greater interval from the head of the column, and the whole army moved forward with more caution and circumspection than had hitherto been used.

In the course of this day's march a little adventure occurred to myself, which, in the illiberality of my heart, I could not but regard as strikingly characteristic of the character of the people to whom we were now opposed, and which, as at the time it had something in it truly comical, I cannot resist the inclination of repeating, though aware that its title to drollery must in a great measure be lost in the relation. Having been informed that in a certain part of the forest a company of riflemen had passed the night, I took with me a party of soldiers, and proceeded in the direction pointed out, with the hope of surprising them. On reaching the place, I found that they had retired, but I thought I could perceive something like the glitter of arms a little farther towards the middle of the wood. Sending several files of soldiers in different directions, I contrived to surround the spot, and then moving forward, I beheld two men dressed in black coats, and armed with bright firelocks and bayonets, sitting under a tree; as soon as they observed me, they started up and took to their heels, but being hemmed in on all sides, they quickly perceived that to escape was impossible, and accordingly stood still. I hastened towards them, and having arrived within a few paces of where they stood, I heard the one say to the other, with a look of the most perfect simplicity, "Stop, John, till the gentlemen pass." There was something so ludicrous in this speech, and in the cast of countenance which accompanied it, that I could not help laughing aloud; nor was my mirth diminished by their attempts to persuade me that they were quiet country people, come out for no other purpose than to shoot squirrels. When I desired to know whether they carried bayonets to charge the squirrels, as well as muskets to shoot them, they were rather at a loss for a reply; but they grumbled exceedingly when they found themselves prisoners, and conducted as such to the column.

But to return to the principal narrative. The army had now advanced within a few miles of Nottingham, and the men were beginning to look forward with some anxiety to a halt; whilst as yet nothing beyond the capture of a few stragglers had occurred to confirm the rumours which, in the morning, and during the whole of the march, had occasioned so much more circumspection than appeared to be requisite. The day was likewise far spent, and, as was to be expected, the ranks were beginning to be less carefully preserved, when a smart firing in the wood upon the right of the road gave new life and energy to the soldiers. It was now confidently expected that the enemy would make a stand. The column closed its order, ready to wheel into line in a moment, and everything was on the *qui vive*: but it proved to be no more than a rencounter between a party of American riflemen and the flank patrol. After firing a few shots, the enemy gave way, and our main body, which had continued to move on during the skirmish, came in without the slightest opposition to the town of Nottingham.

We found this place (a town or large village, capable of containing from a thousand to fifteen hundred inhabitants) completely deserted. Not an individual was to be seen in the streets, or remained in the houses; whilst the appearance of the furniture, &c., in some places the very bread left in the ovens, showed that it had been evacuated in great haste, and immediately before our arrival. The town itself stands upon the banks of the Patuxent, and consists of four short streets, two running parallel with the river, and two others crossing them at right angles. The houses are not such as indicate the existence of much wealth or grandeur among the owners, being in general built of wood, and little superior to cottages; but around the village are others of a far better description, which convey the idea of good substantial farm-houses, a species of mansion very common in the United States. For several miles in every direction the country was in a high state of cultivation; though, instead of the maize and wheat which we had hitherto seen, the fields were covered with an abundant and luxuriant crop of tobacco. This plant seems, indeed, to be at all times the staple commodity of that district; for, besides what was growing and unripe, we found numerous barns filled with the remains of last year's crop; the whole of which was, of course, seized in the name of His Majesty King George the Third. But in the main object of our pursuit we were disappointed. The flotilla, which had been stationed opposite to Nottingham, retired, on our approach, higher up the stream; and we were consequently in the situation of a huntsman who sees his hounds at fault, and has every reason to apprehend that his game will escape.

In this posture the army continued during the night, having its right defended by the river, and its left extending considerably beyond the town, and secured, as usual, by a connected chain of outposts; nor was it put in motion, as had been done the day before, as soon as there was sufficient light to distinguish objects. There seemed, indeed, to be something like hesitation as to the course to be pursued,—whether to follow the gun-boats, or to return to the shipping; but, at last, the former proceeding was resolved upon, and the column set forward about eight o'clock, in the direction of Marlborough, another village, about ten miles beyond Nottingham. The road by which we travelled, as well to-day as during the whole of the excursion, was remarkably good; in some places rather heavy, from being cut through a sandy soil, but in general hard, dusty, and, to use an expressive phrase, having a sound bottom. Running, as it did for the most part, through the heart of thick forests, it was also well sheltered from the rays of the sun; a circumstance which, in a climate like this, is of no slight importance. To-day, our whole journey was of this description, nor did we reach a single cultivated spot till we approached the vicinity of Marlborough; when we found ourselves in a country not more fertile than beautiful. The ground, which had been hitherto perfectly flat, was now broken into the most graceful swells, generally cleared of wood to within a short space of the summits, and then crowned with hoar and venerable forests. The village itself lies in a valley formed by two green hills; the distance from the base of one hill to the base of the other may be about two miles, the whole of which was laid out in fields of corn, hay, and tobacco; whilst the slopes themselves were covered with sheep, for whose support they furnished ample means. But Marlborough is not, like an English village, compact, and consisting of one or two lanes: the houses are scattered over the plain, and along the sides of the hills, at considerable intervals from one another, and are all surrounded by orchards and gardens, abounding in peaches and other fruits of the most delicious flavour. To add to the beauty of the place, a small rivulet makes its way through the bottom, and winding round the foot of one of these ridges, falls into the Patuxent, which flows at its back.

During our progress to-day the same caution was observed which had been practised yesterday. Nor was it altogether unnecessary, several bodies of the enemy's horse occasionally showing themselves, and what appeared to be the rear-guard of a column of infantry evacuating Marlborough, as our advance entered.

There was, however, little or no skirmishing, and we were allowed to remain in the village all night without molestation. But if we were not harassed, we were at least startled on the march by several heavy explosions. The cause of these we were at first unable to discover; but we soon learnt that they were occasioned by the blowing up of the very squadron of which we were in pursuit, and which Commodore Barney, perceiving the impossibility of preserving, prudently destroyed, in order to prevent its falling into our hands.

In Marlborough we remained not only during the night, but till past noon on the following day. The hesitation which had caused the loss of a few hours at Nottingham again interfered, and produced a delay which might have been attended with serious consequences. At length, however, orders were given to form, and we quitted Marlborough about two in the afternoon, taking the road to Washington. During this day's march there was more skirmishing than had yet occurred. We had scarcely got above three miles from the village, when the advanced guard fell in with a party of riflemen, who maintained a sharp contest before they gave way. The column, however, continued to move on without molestation, till arriving at a point where two roads meet, the one leading to Washington, the other to Alexandria, a strong body of troops, with some artillery, were observed upon the slope of a height opposite. The capture of Washington was now the avowed object of our invasion; but the General, like an experienced officer, was desirous of keeping his enemy in the dark as to his plan of operations. Whilst the advanced guard, therefore, reinforced by two additional companies, marched directly forward to dislodge the party from the heights, the rest of the army wheeled to the left, taking the road which leads, not to Washington, but to Alexandria. These movements were not lost upon the enemy, who, observing by the dust in what direction the main body had filed off, immediately began to retreat, without waiting for the approach of the detachment sent against them. As they ascended the hill, however, they made a show of halting and forming a line. Our men moved steadily on in column, covered by one company in extended order along the front; but the enemy, having merely thrown a few round shot with great precision among the skirmishers, broke once again into marching order, and were quickly hid by the rising ground. As soon as they had disappeared, the advance halted; and having remained for about an hour on a little hill to watch their motions, turned to the left, and followed the rest of the army, which they found advantageously posted at a place called Woodyard.

CHAPTER IX.

I HAD almost forgotten to state that, from the first moment of our landing, the want of cavalry, so useful in obtaining information and reconnoitring the open country, was very sensibly felt. To remedy this evil, as far as it could by such means be remedied, orders had been issued to catch and bring in all the horses that were found in the fields or stables of any houses along the road; and these orders being punctually obeyed, there were now fifty or sixty in the camp. Upon these some of the artillery-drivers were mounted, and the command of the troop being given to an officer of experience, it was found of great service during the remainder of the march.

The advanced guard having joined the main body, the whole army, with the exception of a party which had been sent to the rear to bring up a convoy of provisions, was now bivouacked upon a rising ground, well defended by hedge-rows and thickets. The night, however, was not spent in as much quietness as usual. It was late before the troops got to their ground, consequently the piquets, for want of light, could not be posted in their customary good order, neither had there been time to examine the country in the neighbourhood of the position. The outposts were, therefore, kept in a state of constant anxiety by the frequent appearance of small parties of the enemy, who hovered about, probably with the design of cutting off stragglers, or perhaps of surprising, if they could, some of the piquets themselves. But whatever their intentions might be, the vigilance of the sentries contrived to render them abortive; nor did anything occur during the night productive of serious alarm; and the following day, being joined by the convoy which came up in safety, the column was again in motion, hastening across the country into the high road, which had been deserted for no other purpose than to mislead the Americans.

Having started on the 24th at an early hour, our march was for some time both cool and agreeable. The road—if road it could be called—wound for the first five miles through the heart of an immense forest, and being, in every sense of the word, a by-path, was completely overshadowed by projecting branches of trees, so closely interwoven, as to prevent a single sunbeam from making its way, even at noon, within the arch. We continued to move on, therefore, long after the sun had risen, without being sensible that there was not a cloud in the sky to screen us from his influence; whilst a heavy moisture continually emitted from the grass and weeds on both sides of us, produced a coolness which, had it been less confined, would have proved extremely pleasant. So far, then, we proceeded without experiencing any other inconvenience than what was produced by the damp and fetid atmosphere which we breathed; but no sooner had we begun to emerge from the woods and to enter the open country, than an overpowering change was perceived. The sun, from which we had been hitherto defended, now beat upon us in full force; and the dust rising in thick masses from under our feet, without a breath of air to disperse it, flew directly into our faces, occasioning the greatest inconvenience both to the eyes and respiration. I have stated this at length, because I do not recollect a period of my military life during which I suffered more severely from heat and fatigue; and as a journey of a few miles, under such circumstances, tells more than one of thrice the distance in a cool day and along a firm wintry road, it is not surprising that before many hours had elapsed numbers of men began to fall behind from absolute inability to keep up.

Yet, in spite of all this, there was that in to-day's march which rendered it infinitely more interesting than any we had performed since the landing. We had learnt, from various quarters, that the enemy was concentrating his forces for the purpose of hazarding a battle in defence of his capital. The truth of these rumours we had no cause to doubt, confirmed as they were by what we had ourselves witnessed only the evening before; indeed the aspect of various fields on each side of the high road (which we had now regained), where smoking ashes, bundles of straw, and remnants of broken victuals were scattered about, indicated that considerable bodies of troops had passed the night in this neighbourhood. The appearance of the road itself, likewise, imprinted as it was with fresh marks of many feet and hoofs, proved that these troops could be no great way before us; whilst our very proximity to Washington, being now distant from it not more than ten or twelve miles, all tended to assure us that we should at least see an American army before dark.

It was now that we experienced the great usefulness of our badly mounted troopers, or as they were called by the private soldiers, our Cossacks. The country, from being extremely close, had become open on every side to a considerable extent, although thick groves, instead of hedges, frequently separated one field from another. This was exactly the ground on which cavalry could act with advantage; because they might lie in ambush behind these groves, totally unperceived, and when an opportunity offered, charge the column, before it had time to prepare for their reception. There were one or two places, indeed, where such events were confidently anticipated; whole rows of paling having been pulled up from the side of the road, and open spaces left, through which several squadrons of horse might gallop; and the consequence was that every man held his breath in expectation, and prepared himself to form square in a moment. It was here that the mounted drivers became peculiarly useful. They were divided into small parties of six or eight, and sent out in different directions to reconnoitre, two of them generally taking post at every suspicious corner, that one might give notice to the column, whilst the other watched the motions of an enemy.

It so happened that these precautions were unnecessary, for whatever might be the strength of the Americans in cavalry, their General did not think fit to employ it in harassing our march. But the very knowledge that every danger was provided against, and that they could not be attacked without having time to make ready, gave to the soldiers a degree of steady confidence which they would otherwise have wanted; and the want of which, had the case been different, might have been productive of disorder at a moment when good order was of vital importance.

We had now proceeded about nine miles, during the last four of which the sun's rays had beat continually upon us, and we had inhaled almost as great a quantity of dust as of air. Numbers of men had already fallen to the rear, and many more could with difficulty keep up; consequently, if we pushed on much farther without resting, the chances were that at least one half of the army would be left behind. To prevent this from happening, and to give time for the stragglers to overtake the column, a halt was determined upon, and being led forward to a spot of ground well wooded, and watered by a stream which crossed the road, the troops were ordered to refresh themselves. Perhaps no halt ever arrived more seasonably than this, or bid fair to be productive of more beneficial effects; yet so oppressive was the heat, that we had not resumed our march above an hour, when the banks by the way side were again covered with stragglers; some of the finest and stoutest men in the army being literally unable to go on.

The hour of noon was approaching, when a heavy cloud of dust, apparently not more than two or three miles distant, attracted our attention. From whence it originated there was little difficulty in guessing, nor did many minutes expire before surmise was changed into certainty: for on turning a sudden angle in the road, and passing a small plantation, which obstructed the vision towards the left, the British and American armies became visible to one another. The position occupied by the latter was one of great strength and commanding attitude. They were drawn up in three lines upon the brow of a hill, having their front and left flank covered by a branch of the Potomac, and their right resting upon a thick wood and a deep ravine. This river, which may be about the breadth of the Isis at Oxford, flowed between the heights occupied by the American forces and the little town of Bladensburg. Across it was thrown a narrow bridge, extending from the chief street in that town to the continuation of the road, which passed through the very centre of their position; and its right bank (the bank above which they were drawn up) was covered with a narrow stripe of willows and larch trees, whilst the left was altogether bare, low, and exposed. Such was the general aspect of their position as at the first glance it presented itself; of which I must endeavour to give a more detailed account, that my description of the battle may be in some degree intelligible.

I have said that the right bank of the Potomac was covered with a narrow stripe of willow and larch trees. Here the Americans had stationed strong bodies of riflemen, who, in skirmishing order, covered the whole front of their army. Behind this plantation, again, the fields were open and clear, intersected, at certain distances, by rows of high and strong palings. About the middle of the ascent, and in the rear of one of these rows, stood the first line, composed entirely of infantry; at a proper interval from this, and in a similar situation, stood the second line; while the third, or reserve, was posted within the skirts of a wood, which crowned the heights. The artillery, again, of which they had twenty pieces in the field, was thus arranged: on the high road, and commanding the bridge, stood two heavy guns; and four more, two on each side of the road, swept partly in the same direction, and partly down the whole of the slope into the streets of Bladensburg. The rest were scattered, with no great judgment, along the second line of infantry, occupying different spaces between the right of one regiment and the left of another; whilst the cavalry showed itself in one mass, within a stubble field, near the extreme left of the position. Such was the nature of the ground which they occupied, and the formidable posture in which they waited our approach; amounting, by their own account, to nine thousand men, a number exactly doubling that of the force which was to attack them.

In the mean time, our column continued to advance in the same order which it had hitherto preserved. The road, having conducted us for about two miles in a direction parallel with the river, and of consequence with the enemy's line, suddenly turned, and led directly towards the town of Bladensburg. Being of course ignorant whether this town might not be filled with American troops, the main body paused here till the advanced guard should reconnoitre. The result proved that no opposition was intended in that quarter, and that the whole of the enemy's army had been withdrawn to the opposite side of the stream, whereupon the column was again put in motion, and in a short time arrived in the streets of Bladensburg, and within range of the American artillery. Immediately on our reaching this point, several of their guns opened upon us, and kept up a quick and well-directed cannonade, from which, as we were again commanded to halt, the men were directed to shelter themselves as much as possible behind the houses. The object of this halt, it was conjectured, was to give the General an opportunity of examining the American line, and of trying the depth of the river; because at present there appeared to be but one practicable mode of attack, by crossing the bridge, and taking the enemy directly in front. To do so, however, exposed as the bridge was, must be attended with bloody consequences, nor could the delay of a few minutes produce any mischief which the discovery of a ford would not amply compensate.

But in this conjecture we were altogether mistaken; for without allowing time to the column to close its ranks, or to be joined by such of the many stragglers as were now hurrying, as fast as weariness would permit, to regain their places, the order to halt was countermanded, and the word given to attack; and we immediately pushed on at double quick time, towards the head of the bridge. While we were moving along the street, a continued fire was kept up, with some execution, from those guns which stood to the left of the road; but it was not till the bridge was covered with our people that the two-gun battery upon the road itself began to play.—Then, indeed, it also opened, and with tremendous effect; for at the first discharge almost an entire company was swept down; but whether it was that the guns had been previously laid with measured exactness, or that the nerves of the gunners became afterwards unsteady, the succeeding discharges were much less fatal. The riflemen likewise began to gall us from the wooded bank with a running fire of musketry; and it was not without trampling upon many of their dead and dying comrades that the light brigade established itself on the opposite side of the stream.

When once there, however, everything else appeared easy. Wheeling off to the right and left of the road, they dashed into the thicket, and quickly cleared it of the American skirmishers; who, falling back with precipitation upon the first line, threw it into disorder before it had fired a shot. The consequence was, that our troops had scarcely shown themselves when the whole of that line gave way, and fled in the greatest confusion, leaving the two guns upon the road in possession of the victors.

But here it must be confessed that the light brigade was guilty of imprudence. Instead of pausing till the rest of the army came up, the soldiers lightened themselves by throwing away their knapsacks and haversacks; and extending their ranks so as to show an equal front with the enemy, pushed on to the attack of the second line.—The Americans, however, saw their weakness, and stood firm, and having the whole of their artillery, with the exception of the pieces captured on the road, and the greater part of their infantry in this line, they first checked the ardour of the assailants by a heavy fire, and then, in their turn, advanced to recover the ground which was lost. Against this charge the extended order of the British troops would not permit them to offer an effectual resistance, and they were accordingly borne back to the very thicket upon the river's brink; where they maintained themselves with determined obstinacy, repelling all attempts to drive them through it; and frequently following, to within a short distance of the cannon's mouth, such parts of the enemy's line as gave way.

In this state the action continued till the second brigade had likewise crossed, and formed upon the right bank of the river; when the 44th regiment moving to the right, and driving in the skirmishers, debouched upon the left flank of the Americans, and completely turned it. In that quarter, therefore, the battle was won; because the raw militia-men, who were stationed there as being the least assailable point, when once broken could not be rallied. But on their right the enemy still kept their ground with much resolution; nor was it till the arrival of the 4th regiment, and the advance of the British forces in firm array to the charge, that they began to waver. Then, indeed, seeing their left in full flight, and the 44th getting in their rear, they lost all order, and dispersed, leaving clouds of riflemen to cover their retreat; and hastened to conceal themselves in the woods, where it would have been madness to follow them. The rout was now general throughout the line. The reserve, which ought to have supported the main body, fled as soon as those in its front began to give way; and the cavalry, instead of charging the British troops, now scattered in pursuit, turned their horses' heads and galloped off, leaving them in undisputed possession of the field, and of ten out of the twenty pieces of artillery.

This battle, by which the fate of the American capital was decided, began about one o'clock in the afternoon, and lasted till four. The loss on the part of the English was severe, since, out of two-thirds of the army, which were engaged, upwards of five hundred men were killed and wounded; and what rendered it doubly severe was, that among these were numbered several officers of rank and distinction. Colonel Thornton, who commanded the light brigade, Lieutenant-Colonel Wood, commanding the 85th regiment, and Major Brown, who led the advanced guard, were all severely wounded; and General Ross himself had a horse shot under him. On the side of the Americans the slaughter was not so great. Being in possession of a strong position, they were of course less exposed in defending, than the others in storming it; and had they conducted themselves with coolness and resolution, it is not conceivable how the battle could have been won. But the fact is, that, with the exception of a party of sailors from the gun-boats, under the command of Commodore Barney, no troops could behave worse than they did. The skirmishers were driven in as soon as attacked, the first line gave way without offering the slightest resistance, and the left of the main body was broken within half an hour after it was seriously engaged. Of the sailors, however, it would be injustice not to speak in the terms which their conduct merits. They were employed as gunners, and not only did they serve their guns with a quickness and precision which astonished their assailants, but they stood till some of them were actually bayoneted, with fuzes in their hands; nor was it till their leader was wounded and taken, and they saw themselves deserted on all sides by the soldiers, that they quitted the field. With respect to the British army, again, no line of distinction can be drawn. All did their duty, and none more gallantly than the rest; and though the brunt of the affair fell upon the light brigade, this was owing chiefly to the circumstance of its being at the head of the column, and perhaps also, in some degree, to its own rash impetuosity. The artillery, indeed, could do little; being unable to show itself in presence of a force so superior; but the six-pounder was nevertheless brought into action, and a corps of rockets proved of striking utility.

Our troops being worn down from fatigue, and of course as ignorant of the country as the Americans were the reverse, the pursuit could not be continued to any distance. Neither was it attended with much slaughter. Diving into the recesses of the forests, and covering themselves with riflemen, the enemy were quickly beyond our reach; and having no cavalry to scour even the high road, ten of the lightest of their guns were carried off in the flight. The defeat, however, was absolute, and the army which had been collected for the defence of Washington was scattered beyond the possibility of, at least, an immediate re-union; and as the distance from Bladensburg to that city does not exceed four miles, there appeared to be no further obstacle in the way to prevent its immediate capture.

CHAPTER X.

An opportunity so favourable was not endangered by any needless delay. While the two brigades which had been engaged remained upon the field to recover their order, the third, which had formed the reserve, and was consequently unbroken, took the lead, and pushed forward at a rapid rate towards Washington.

As it was not the intention of the British Government to attempt permanent conquests in this part of America, and as the General was well aware that, with a handful of men, he could not pretend to establish himself, for any length of time, in an enemy's capital, he determined to lay it under contribution, and to return quietly to the shipping. Nor was there anything unworthy of the character of a British officer in this determination. By all the customs of war, whatever public property may chance to be in a captured town, becomes, confessedly, the just spoil of the conqueror; and in thus proposing to accept a certain sum of money in lieu of that property, he was showing mercy rather than severity to the vanquished. It is true that if they chose to reject his terms he and his army would be deprived of their booty, because without some more convenient mode of transporting it than we possessed, even the portable part of the property itself could not be removed. But, on the other hand, there was no difficulty in destroying it; and thus, though we should gain nothing, the American Government would lose probably to a much greater amount than if they had agreed to purchase its preservation by the money demanded.

Such being the intention of General Ross, he did not march the troops immediately into the city, but halted them upon a plain in its immediate vicinity, whilst a flag of truce was sent forward with terms. But whatever his proposal might have been, it was not so much as heard; for scarcely had the party bearing the flag entered the street, when it was fired upon from the windows of one of the houses, and the horse of the General himself, who accompanied it, killed. The indignation excited by this act throughout all ranks and classes of men in the army, was such as the nature of the case could not fail to occasion. Every thought of accommodation was instantly laid aside; the troops advanced forthwith into the town, and having first put to the sword all who were found in the house from which the shots were fired, and reduced it to ashes, they proceeded without a moment's delay to burn and destroy everything in the most distant degree connected with Government. In this general devastation were included the Senate-house, the President's palace, an extensive dock-yard and arsenal, barracks for two or three thousand men, several large storehouses filled with naval and military stores, some hundreds of cannon of different descriptions, and nearly twenty thousand stand of small-arms. There were also two or three public ropewalks which shared the same fate, a fine frigate pierced for sixty guns, and just ready to be launched, several gun brigs and armed schooners, with a variety of gun-boats and small craft. The powder-magazines were set on fire, and exploded with a tremendous crash, throwing down many houses in their vicinity, partly by pieces of the walls striking them, and partly by the concussion of the air; whilst quantities of shot, shell, and hand-grenades, which could not otherwise be rendered useless, were cast into the river. In destroying the cannon a method was adopted which I had never before witnessed, and which, as it was both effectual and expeditious, I cannot avoid relating. One gun of rather a small calibre was pitched upon as the executioner of the rest, and being loaded with ball and turned to the muzzles of the others, it was fired, and thus beat out their breechings. Many, however, not being mounted, could not be thus dealt with; these were spiked, and having their trunnions knocked off, were afterwards cast into the bed of the river.

All this was as it should be, and had the arm of vengeance been extended no further, there would not have been room given for so much as a whisper of disapprobation. But unfortunately it did not stop here; a noble library, several printing-offices, and all the national archives were likewise committed to the flames, which, though no doubt the property of Government, might better have been spared. It is not, however, my intention to join the outcry which was raised at the time against what the Americans and their admirers were pleased to term a line of conduct at once barbarous and unprofitable. On the contrary, I conceive that too much praise cannot be given to the forbearance and humanity of the British troops, who, irritated as they had every right to be, spared, as far as possible, all private property, neither plundering nor destroying a single house in the place, except that from which the General's horse had been killed.

Whilst the third brigade was thus employed, the rest of the army, having recalled its stragglers, and removed the wounded into Bladensburg, began its march towards Washington. Though the battle came to a close by four o'clock, the sun had set before the different regiments were in a condition to move, consequently this short journey was performed in the dark. The work of destruction had also begun in the city before they quitted their ground; and the blazing of houses, ships, and stores, the report of exploding magazines, and the crash of falling roofs, informed them, as they proceeded, of what was going forward. It would be difficult to conceive a finer spectacle than that which presented itself as they approached the town. The sky was brilliantly illumined by the different conflagrations; and a dark red light was thrown upon the road, sufficient to permit each man to view distinctly his comrade's face. Except the burning of St. Sebastian's, I do not recollect to have witnessed at any period of my life a scene more striking or more sublime.

Having advanced as far as the plain, where the reserve had

previously paused, the first and second brigades halted; and forming into close column, passed the night in bivouac. At first this was agreeable enough, because the air was mild, and weariness made up for what was wanting in comfort. But towards morning a violent storm of rain, accompanied with thunder and lightning, came on, which disturbed the rest of all who were exposed to it. Yet in spite of the inconvenience arising from the shower, I cannot say that I felt disposed to grumble at the interruption, for it appeared that what I had before considered as superlatively sublime, still wanted this to render it complete. The flashes of lightning vied in brilliancy with the flames which burst from the roofs of burning houses, whilst the thunder drowned for a time the noise of crumbling walls, and was only interrupted by the occasional roar of cannon, and of large depôts of gunpowder, as they one by one exploded.

I need scarcely observe, that the consternation of the inhabitants was complete, and that to them this was a night of terror. So confident had they been of the success of their troops, that few of them had dreamt of quitting their houses or abandoning the city; nor was it till the fugitives from the battle began to rush in, filling every place as they came with dismay, that the President himself thought of providing for his safety. That gentleman, as I was credibly informed, had gone forth in the morning with the army, and had continued among his troops till the British forces began to make their appearance. Whether the sight of his enemies cooled his courage or not I cannot say, but according to my informant, no sooner was the glittering of our arms discernible, than he began to discover that his presence was more wanted in the senate than in the field; and having ridden through the ranks, and exhorted every man to do his duty, he hurried back to his own house, that he might prepare a feast for the entertainment of his officers, when they should return victorious. For the truth of these details I will not be answerable; but this much I know, that the feast was actually prepared, though, instead of being devoured by American officers, it went to satisfy the less delicate appetites of a party of English soldiers. When the detachment sent out to destroy Mr. Maddison's house, entered his dining parlour, they found a dinner-table spread, and covers laid for forty guests. Several kinds of wine in handsome cut-glass decanters were cooling on the sideboard; plate-holders stood by the fire-place, filled with dishes and plates; knives, forks, and spoons, were arranged for immediate use; everything in short was ready for the entertainment of a ceremonious party. Such were the arrangements in the dining-room, whilst in the kitchen were others answerable to them in every respect. Spits loaded with joints of various sorts turned before the fire; pots, saucepans, and other culinary utensils stood upon the grate; and all the other requisites for an elegant and substantial repast were in the exact state which indicated that they had been lately and precipitately abandoned.

The reader will easily believe that these preparations were beheld, by a party of hungry soldiers, with no indifferent eye. An elegant dinner, even though considerably over-dressed, was a luxury to which few of them, at least for some time back, had been accustomed; and which, after the dangers and fatigues of the day, appeared peculiarly inviting. They sat down to it, therefore, not indeed in the most orderly manner, but with countenances which would not have disgraced a party of aldermen at a civic feast; and having satisfied their appetites with fewer complaints than would have probably escaped their rival *gourmands*, and partaken pretty freely of the wines, they finished by setting fire to the house which had so liberally entertained them.

I have said that to the inhabitants of Washington this was a night of terror and dismay. From whatever cause the confidence arose, certain it is that they expected anything rather than the arrival among them of a British army; and their consternation was proportionate to their previous feeling of security, when an event, so little anticipated, actually came to pass. The first impulse naturally prompted them to fly, and the streets were speedily crowded with soldiers and senators, men, women, and children, horses, carriages, and carts loaded with household furniture, all hastening towards a wooden bridge which crosses the Potomac. The confusion thus occasioned was terrible, and the crowd upon the bridge was such as to endanger its giving way. But Mr. Maddison, as is affirmed, having escaped among the first, was no sooner safe on the opposite bank of the river, than he gave orders that the bridge should be broken down; which being obeyed, the rest were obliged to return, and to trust to the clemency of the victors.

In this manner was the night passed by both parties; and at daybreak next morning the light brigade moved into the city, whilst the reserve fell back to a height about half a mile in the rear. Little, however, now remained to be done, because everything marked out for destruction was already consumed. Of the Senate-house, the President's palace, the barracks, the dockyard, &c., nothing could be seen, except heaps of smoking ruins; and even the bridge, a noble structure upwards of a mile in length, was almost entirely demolished. There was, therefore, no further occasion to scatter the troops, and they were accordingly kept together as much as possible on the Capitol Hill.

Of the city of Washington I have purposely declined attempting any minute description, because it possesses no leading features, by catching which I might hope to convey to a person who has not seen it, something like an accurate notion of the whole. It was then, and is, I believe, still in its infancy, few of the streets being finished, and many containing not more than three or four houses, at wide intervals from each other. But its situation gives to it advantages such as few capitals either in the new or old world can boast of, and if it continue to be the head of the American States for another century, it will become, I doubt not, one of the most flourishing cities in existence. America is, and always will be, a commercial nation, nor can a single town throughout the whole of that vast continent boast of a better harbour than Washington. Standing upon the Potomac, one of the most navigable of all the rivers that empty themselves into the Chesapeake, the depth of which is sufficient to float a frigate for some way above the town, it possesses unrivalled facilities for the carrying on of an extensive trade; whilst its distance from the coast is such as to place it, in a great measure, beyond reach of insult from an enemy. Such an assertion, coming from one who has just detailed the particulars of its capture, may, indeed, appear to partake not slightly of the nature of a paradox; but there is no denying that the fall of Washington ought to be attributed much more to the misconduct of the Americans themselves, than to the skill or enterprise of those who effected it. Had the emergency been contemplated, and in a proper manner provided against, or had the most moderate ingenuity and courage been displayed in retarding the progress of our troops, the design, if formed at all, would have been either abandoned immediately, or must have ended in the total destruction of the invaders.

Like other infant towns, Washington is but little ornamented with fine buildings; except the Senate-house, I really know of none worthy to be noticed. This however is, or rather was, an edifice of some beauty. It stood, where its ruins now stand, upon a mound called the Capitol Hill, and near a trifling stream named the Tiber; from which circumstances these modern republicans are led to flatter themselves that the days are coming when it will rival in power and grandeur the Senate-house of ancient Rome herself. It was built entirely of freestone, tastefully worked and highly polished; and, besides its numerous windows, was lighted from the top by a large and handsome cupola. Perhaps it could not be said to belong to any decided style of architecture; but its central appearance was light, airy, and elegant. After traversing a wide and spacious entrance-hall, you arrived at the foot of a handsome spiral hanging staircase; on the right of which were two spacious apartments, one above the other, which were occupied as sitting chambers by the two houses of representatives. From these branched off several smaller rooms, fitted up as offices, and probably used as such by the various officers of state. On the right of the staircase, again, were two other apartments equal in size to those on the left, with a like number of smaller rooms branching off from them. These were furnished as a public library, the two larger being well stocked with valuable books, principally in modern languages, whilst the others, filled with archives, national statutes, acts of legislature, &c., were used as the private rooms of the librarians.

The President's house, on the other hand, though likewise a public building, was remarkable for nothing except the absence of taste exhibited in its structure. It was small, incommodious, and plain; in no respect likely to excite the jealousy of a people peculiarly averse to all pomp or parade, even in their chief magistrate. Besides these, there were also a custom-house, several banking-houses, and a school or college, all claiming to themselves the distinction of public works; but in them there was a plainness amounting almost to coarseness, and a general air of republicanism, by no means imposing. With respect to the number of inhabitants which Washington contained, I confess that I cannot pretend to give an opinion: but if any judgment may be formed from the extent of ground covered by what is considered as the town, I should say that they amounted to somewhere about sixty thousand. George Town, the quarter where the President's house stood, is compact and regular, containing, I should conceive, at least twenty thousand souls within itself; nor can the population of the other quarters be estimated at less than double that number.

Such was then the city of Washington, of which our hasty and unfriendly visit did not allow us to take a very minute survey. I return now to the movements of the British army.

I have stated above that our troops were this day kept as much together as possible upon the Capitol Hill. But it was not alone on account of the completion of their destructive labours that this was done. A powerful army of Americans already began to show themselves upon some heights, at the distance of two or three miles from the city; and as they sent out detachments of horse even to the very suburbs, for the purpose of watching our motions, it would have been unsafe to permit more straggling than was absolutely necessary. The army which we had overthrown the day before, though defeated, was far from annihilated; it had by this time recovered its panic, began to concentrate itself in our front, and presented quite as formidable an appearance as ever. We learnt, also, that it was joined by a considerable force from the back settlements, which had arrived too late to take part in the action, and the report was, that both combined amounted to nearly twelve thousand men.

Whether or not it was their intention to attack, I cannot pretend to say, because it was noon before they showed themselves; and soon after, when something like a movement could be discerned in their ranks, the sky grew suddenly dark, and the most tremendous hurricane ever remembered by the oldest inhabitant in the place came on. Of the prodigious force of the wind it is impossible for one who was not an eye-witness to its effects to form a conception. Roofs of houses were torn off by it, and whirled into the air like sheets of paper; whilst the rain which accompanied it resembled the rushing of a mighty cataract rather than the dropping of a shower. The darkness was as great as if the sun had long set, and the last remains of twilight had come on, occasionally relieved by flashes of vivid lightning streaming through it; which, together with the noise of the wind and the thunder, the crash of falling buildings, and the tearing of roofs as they were stript from the walls, produced the most appalling effect I ever have, and probably ever shall, witness. The storm lasted for nearly two hours without intermission, during which time many of the houses spared by us were blown down, and thirty of our men, besides several of the inhabitants, buried beneath their ruins. Our column was as completely dispersed as if it had received a total defeat; some of the men flying for shelter behind walls and buildings, and others falling flat upon the ground, to prevent themselves from being carried away by the tempest; nay, such was the violence of the wind, that two pieces of light cannon, which stood upon the eminence, were fairly lifted from the ground, and borne several yards to the rear.

CHAPTER XI.

When the hurricane had blown over, the camp of the Americans appeared to be in as great a state of confusion as our own; nor could either party recover themselves sufficiently during the rest of the day to try the fortune of a battle. Of this General Ross did not fail to take advantage. He had already attained all that he could hope, and perhaps more than he originally expected to attain; consequently, to risk another action would only be to spill blood for no purpose. Whatever might be the issue of the contest, he could derive from it no advantage. If he were victorious, it would not do away with the necessity which existed of evacuating Washington; if defeated, his ruin was certain. To avoid fighting was therefore his object, and perhaps he owed its accomplishment to the fortunate occurrence of the storm. Be that, however, as it may, a retreat was resolved upon; and we now only waited for night, to put the resolution into practice.

There was, however, one difficulty to be surmounted in this proceeding. Of the wounded, many were so ill as to preclude all possibility of their removal, and to leave them in the hands of an enemy whom we had beaten was rather a mortifying anticipation. But for this there was no help; and it now only remained to make the best arrangements for their comfort, and to secure for them, as far as could be done, civil treatment from the Americans.

It chanced that, among other prisoners taken at Bladensburg, was Commodore Barney, an American officer of much gallantry and high sense of honour. Being himself wounded, he was the more likely to feel for those who were in a similar condition, and having received the kindest treatment from our medical attendants, as long as he continued under their hands, he became, without solicitation, the friend of his fellow-sufferers. To him, as well as to the other prisoners, was given his parole, and to his care were our wounded, in a peculiar manner, intrusted,—a trust which he received with the utmost willingness, and discharged with the most praiseworthy exactness. Among other stipulations, it was agreed that such of our people as were left behind should be considered as prisoners of war, and should be restored to us as soon as they were able to travel; and that, as soon as they reached the ships, the Commodore and his countrymen would, in exchange, be released from their engagements.

As soon as these arrangements were completed, and darkness had come on, the third brigade, which was posted in the rear of our army, began to withdraw. Then followed the guns, afterwards the second, and last of all the light brigade, exactly reversing the order which had been maintained during the advance. Instead of an advanced guard, this last now furnished a party to cover the retreat, and the whole procession was closed by the mounted drivers.

It being a matter of great importance to deceive the enemy and to prevent pursuit, the rear of the column did not quit its ground upon the Capitol till a late hour. During the day an order had been issued that none of the inhabitants should be seen in the streets after eight o'clock; and as fear renders most men obedient, the order was punctually attended to. All the horses belonging to different officers were removed to drag the guns, no one being allowed to ride, lest a neigh, or even the trampling of hoofs, should excite suspicion. The fires were trimmed, and made to blaze brightly; fuel enough was left to keep them so for some hours; and finally, about half-past nine o'clock the troops formed in marching order, and moved off in the most profound silence. Not a word was spoken, nor a single individual permitted to step one inch out of his place, by which means they passed along the streets perfectly unnoticed, and cleared the town without any alarm being given. Our pace, it will be imagined, was none of the most tardy, consequently it was not long before we reached the ground which had been occupied by the other brigades. Here we found a second line of fires blazing in the same manner as those deserted by ourselves; and the same precautions in every respect adopted, to induce a belief that our army was still quiet.—Beyond these, again, we found two or three solitary fires, placed in such order as to resemble those of a chain of piquets. In a word, the deception was so well managed, that even we ourselves were at first doubtful whether the rest of the troops had fallen back.

When we reached the ground where yesterday's battle had been fought, the moon rose, and exhibited a spectacle by no means enlivening.—The dead were still unburied, and lay about in every direction completely naked. They had been stripped even of their shirts, and having been exposed in this state to the violent rain in the morning, they appeared to be bleached to a most unnatural degree of whiteness. The heat and rain together had likewise affected them in a different manner; and the smell which rose upon the night air was horrible.

There is something in such a scene as this extremely humbling, and repugnant to the feelings of human nature. During the agitation of a battle, it is nothing to see men fall in hundreds by your side. You may look at them, perhaps, for an instant, but you do so almost without being yourself aware of it, so completely are your thoughts carried away by the excitation of the moment and the shouts of your companions.—But when you come to view the dead in an hour of calmness, stripped as they generally are, you cannot help remembering how frail may have been the covering which saved yourself from being the loathsome thing on which you are now gazing.—For myself, I confess that these reflections rose within my mind on the present occasion; and if any one should say that, similarly situated, they would not rise in his, I should give him no credit for a superior degree of courage, though I might be inclined to despise him for his want of the common feelings of a reasonable being.

In Bladensburg the brigade halted for an hour, while those men who had thrown away their knapsacks endeavoured to recover them. During this interval I strolled up to a house which had been converted into an hospital, and paid a hasty visit to the wounded. I found them in great pain, and some of them deeply affected at the thought of being abandoned by their comrades, and left to the mercy of their enemies. Yet, in their apprehension of evil treatment from the Americans, the event proved that they had done injustice to that people; who were found to possess at least one generous trait in their character, namely, that of behaving kindly and attentively to their prisoners.

As soon as the stragglers had returned to their ranks, we again moved on, continuing to march without once stopping to rest during the whole of the night. Of the fatigue of a night march none but those who have experienced it can form the smallest conception. Oppressed with the most intolerable drowsiness, we were absolutely dozing upon our legs; and if any check at the head of the column caused a momentary delay, the road was instantly covered with men fast asleep. It is generally acknowledged that no inclination is so difficult to resist as the inclination to sleep; but when you are compelled not only to bear up against that, but to struggle also with weariness, and to walk at the same time, it is scarcely possible to hold out long. By seven o'clock in the morning, it was found absolutely necessary to pause, because numbers had already fallen behind, and numbers more were ready to follow their example; when throwing ourselves upon the ground, almost in the same order in which we had marched, in less than five minutes there was not a single unclosed eye throughout the whole brigade. Piquets were of course stationed, and sentinels placed, to whom no rest was granted, but, except these, the entire army resembled a heap of dead bodies on a field of battle, rather than living men.

In this situation we remained till noon, when we were again roused to continue the retreat. Though the sun was oppressively powerful, we moved on without resting till dark, when having arrived at our old position near Marlborough, we halted for the night. During this day's march we were joined by numbers of negro slaves, who implored us to take them along with us, offering to serve either as soldiers or sailors, if we would but give them their liberty; but as General Ross persisted in protecting private property of every description, few of them were fortunate enough to obtain their wishes.

We had now proceeded a distance of thirty-five miles, and began to consider ourselves beyond the danger of pursuit. The remainder of the retreat was accordingly conducted with more leisure; our next march carrying us no farther than to Nottingham, where we remained during an entire day, for the purpose of resting the troops. It cannot, however, be said that this resting-time was spent in idleness. A gun-brig, with a number of ships' launches and long-boats, had made their way up the stream, and were at anchor opposite to the town. On board the former were carried such of the wounded as had been able to travel, whilst the latter were loaded with flour and tobacco, the only spoil which we found it practicable to bring off.

Whilst the infantry were thus employed, the cavalry was sent back as far as Marlborough, to discover whether there were any American forces in pursuit; and it was well for the few stragglers who had been left behind that this recognizance was made. Though there appeared to be no disposition on the part of the American General to follow our steps and to harass the retreat, the inhabitants of that village, at the instigation of a medical practitioner called Bain, had risen in arms as soon as we departed; and falling upon such individuals as strayed from the column, put some of them to death, and made others prisoners. A soldier whom they had taken, and who had escaped, gave information of these proceedings to the troopers, just as they were about to return to head-quarters; upon which they immediately wheeled about, and galloping into the village, pulled the doctor out of his bed (for it was early in the morning), compelled him, by a threat of instant death, to liberate his prisoners; and mounting him before one of the party, brought him in triumph to the camp.

The wounded, the artillery, and plunder, being all embarked on the 28th, at daybreak on the 29th we took the direction of St. Benedict's, where we arrived, without any adventure, at a late hour in the evening. Here we again occupied the ground of which we had taken possession on first landing, passing the night in perfect quiet; and next day, the boats of the fleet being ready to receive us, the regiments, one by one, marched down to the beach. We found the shore covered with sailors from the different ships of war, who welcomed our arrival with loud cheers; and having contrived to bring up a larger flotilla than had been employed in the disembarkation, they removed us within a few hours, and without the occurrence of any accident, to our respective vessels.

Such is a plain impartial account of the inroad upon Washington, an affair than which the whole war produced none more brilliant or more daring. In whatever light we may regard it, whether we look to the amount of difficulties which it behoved him to overcome, the inadequacy of the force which he commanded, or the distance which he was called upon to march, in the midst of a hostile population, and through deep and trackless forests, we cannot deny to General Ross the praise which is his due, of having planned and successfully accomplished an expedition which none but a sagacious mind could have devised, and none but a gallant spirit carried into execution. Among the many important transactions which then occupied the public attention, the campaign at Washington was, I believe, but little spoken of; and even now, it is overwhelmed in the recollections of the all-engrossing Waterloo; but the time will probably come, when he who at the head of four thousand men penetrated upwards of sixty miles into an enemy's country; overthrew an army more than double his own in point of numbers; took possession of the capital of a great nation, and having held it as long as it suited his own purposes to hold it, returned again in triumph to his fleet, will be ranked, as he deserves to be ranked, among the number of those who have most successfully contributed to elevate Great Britain to the height of military glory on which she now stands.

It has been said that the entire merit of this brilliant expedition is due, not so much to the brave man who conducted it, as to Sir George Cockburn, at whose suggestion it was undertaken.

To the great gallantry and high talents of Sir George Cockburn no one who served within the compass of the Bay of Chesapeake will refuse to bear testimony; nor is it improbable that in attributing to him the original design of laying Washington itself under contribution, common report speaks truly. But with whomsoever the idea first originated, to General Ross belongs the undivided fame of having carried it into effect. From Sir George Cockburn, and indeed from the whole fleet, the army received every assistance which it was in the power of the fleet to bestow; but had no Ross been at the head of the land forces, the capital of the United States would have suffered no insult. I have ventured to make these remarks, not with any design of taking away, in the slightest degree, from the well-earned reputation of the living; but merely as an act of justice towards the memory of the gallant dead, whose services have hardly received all the notice, either from the Government or the country, which they deserved.

Of the degree of military sagacity exhibited on both sides, during the progress of hostilities, it scarcely becomes me to speak. Perhaps our leader delayed something too long in making up his mind as to the ultimate end to be pursued, after the troops had penetrated so far into the interior as Marlborough. Had he pushed on at once, it is barely possible that Washington might have fallen at a less expense of human life than actually occurred. Perhaps, too, he commenced the attack at Bladensburg with a degree of precipitancy which hindered him from taking advantage of an open ford, and compelled him to expose his troops to the fire of the enemy's artillery whilst crossing a narrow bridge in a single column. But these errors, if errors they may be termed, were amply compensated by the perfect success of his operations; whilst in every other particular his conduct was beyond the reach of censure. In his choice of ground for halting, in the order both of his advance and retreat, and in the rapidity of his movements as soon as his plans had been arranged, General Ross exhibited himself in the light of an able and diligent commander. No man could possess more than he a soldier's eye in examining the face of a country; and in what little manœuvring the circumstances permitted, he displayed the proficiency of one well practised in the arts of campaigning. It will be recollected, that on the 23rd, the day previous to the battle, we fell in with a strong body of the enemy, to deceive whom we wheeled off from the main rôad, and took the direction of Alexandria. The plan was attended by the most perfect success; the party deceived being in fact the advanced guard of the main army. Thinking that Alexandria, and not Washington, was threatened, the American General abandoned a strong position, which he had seized on the main road, harassed his troops by a needless march towards that town; and discovered his mistake only time enough to occupy the heights of Bladensburg a very few minutes before we came in sight.

With respect to the Americans, again, criticism necessarily degenerates into unqualified censure. From the beginning to the end of the affair, they acted in no one instance like prudent or sagacious men. In the first place, they ought on no account to have risked a general action in an open country, however strong and steep; and, secondly, they deserved to suffer much more severely than they did suffer, for permitting an enemy's army to penetrate beyond Nottingham. In allowing us to land without opposition, they were perhaps guilty of no great mistake; but having done so, instead of concentrating their forces in one place, they ought to have harassed us with continual skirmishing; felled trees on each side, and thrown them across the road; dug deep ditches at certain intervals; in a word, it was their wisdom to adopt the mode of warfare to which their own habits, as well as the nature of their country, invited them.

In America, every man is a marksman from his very boyhood, and every man serves in the militia; but to bring an army of raw militia-men, however excellent they might be as marksmen, into a fair field against regular troops, could end in nothing but defeat. When two lines oppose each other, very little depends upon the accuracy with which individuals take aim. It is then that the habit of acting in concert, the confidence which each man feels in his companions, and the rapidity and good order in which different movements can be executed, are alone of real service. But put these raw militia-men into thick woods, and send your regular troops to drive them out, and you will immediately lose all the advantages of discipline, and reduce your battle to so many single combats.

Here, therefore, lay their principal error: had they left all clear, and permitted us to advance as far as Nottingham, then broken up the roads, and covered them with trees, it would have been impossible for us to go a step beyond. As soon as this was effected, they might have skirmished with us in front, and kept our attention alive with part of their troops, till the rest, acquainted as they doubtless were with every inch of the country, had got into our rear, and, by a similar mode of proceeding, cut off our retreat. Thus we should have been taken in a snare, from which it would have been no easy task to extricate ourselves, and might, perhaps, have been obliged in the end to surrender at discretion.

But so obvious and so natural a plan of defence they chose to reject; and determining to trust all to the fate of a battle, they were guilty of a monstrous error again. Bladensburg ought not to have been left unoccupied. The most open village, if resolutely defended, will cost many men before it falls; whereas Bladensburg, being composed of substantial brick houses, might have been maintained for hours against all our efforts. In the next place, they displayed great want of military knowledge in the disposition of both their infantry and artillery. There was not, in the whole space of their position, a single point where an enemy would be exposed to a cross fire. The troops were drawn up in three straight lines, like so many regiments upon a gala parade; whilst the guns were used as connecting links to a chain, being posted in the same order, by ones and twos, at every interval.

In maintaining themselves, likewise, when attacked, they exhibited neither skill nor resolution. Of the personal courage of the Americans there can be no doubt; they are, individually taken, as brave a nation as any in the world. But they are not soldiers; they have not the experience nor the habits of soldiers. It was the height of folly, therefore, to bring them into a situation where nothing except that experience and those habits will avail; and it is on this account that I repeat what I have already said, that the capture of Washington was more owing to the blindness of the Americans themselves than to any other cause.

CHAPTER XII.

WHILST the army was thus actively employed, the fleet did not remain idle. A squadron of frigates, with two bomb-ships, under the command of Captain Gordon, of the Sea-horse, penetrated up the Potomac, and appeared before Alexandria. The whole of the militia of the district was at this time called away for the defence of the capital, consequently no place could be less prepared to resist an invader than that city. A party accordingly landed from the ships without opposition, and having destroyed the barracks, public works, and all the cannon which they found on shore, they seized a number of schooners and other small craft then lying in the harbour, and loading them with flour and tobacco to a considerable amount, prepared to rejoin the fleet in the bay.

But by this time the country was alarmed; a detachment was sent from the main army, and being joined by the reserve of militia, it was determined to intercept the squadron on its return. With this view, several pieces of heavy cannon were mounted upon a steep part of the bank, where the river, in making an angle, narrows considerably in its channel. Thither also hastened large bodies of infantry; and before the frigates had begun to weigh anchor nearly 5000 men were assembled to prevent their passage.

Of these preparations Captain Gordon did not long remain ignorant; nor was he backward in making the best arrangements possible to meet the danger. By shifting the ballast in each of the vessels entirely to one side, he caused them to lean in such a manner as that their artillery could be elevated to a surprising degree, and the shot rise even to the summit of the hill. The guns were then stuffed, rather than loaded, with grape and musket-balls; and the ships, taking their stations according to their draft of water, the lightest keeping nearest to the enemy's shore, set sail, and, favoured by a leading breeze, stood leisurely down the river.

As soon as they arrived within tangible distance, a brisk cannonade was opened upon them from the heights, and the whole of the infantry appeared in line along the brow of the eminence. Regardless of these formidable salutations, the ships continued to hold their course without changing their order or returning a shot, till they reached the base of the hill upon which the infantry stood, and received a volley of musketry into their decks. Then, indeed, they answered the fire; and with such effect, that at the first broadside the enemy's guns were abandoned, and their infantry took to flight. The Americans had persuaded themselves that no ship could point her guns so as to sweep the top of the hill; and under this idea had drawn up their troops along the ridge, with the intention of overawing the squadron by a display of their numbers. But in the event they found themselves mistaken, for so well had Captain Gordon arranged matters, that not a single shot fell under its mark; and as the ships' artillery had been loaded for the occasion, a shower of balls of every size and description came amongst them, such as it was impossible to withstand. A single broadside was sufficient to secure the safe passage of his squadron; but with this Captain Gordon was not contented. Seeing the enemy driven from their cannon, he immediately landed his marines, spiked the guns, and blew up the expense magazines; when, having received them all safely on board again, he continued his voyage, and regained the Chesapeake without further molestation.

Nor was this the only operation in which the navy were employed. Cruising about in every direction, they threatened the whole line of coast, from the entrance to the very bend of the bay; and thus kept the Americans in a constant state of alarm. Whenever a favourable opportunity presented itself, parties landed, plundered or destroyed the Government stores, laid towns and districts under contribution, and brought off all the shipping which could be reached. In a word, the hostilities carried on in the Chesapeake resembled the expeditions of the ancient Danes against Great Britain, rather than a modern war between civilized nations. But these hasty excursions, though generally successful, were not always performed without loss to the invaders. Many men and some officers were killed and wounded, among whom was Captain Sir Peter Parker, of the Menelaus frigate, an officer distinguished for his gallantry and knowledge of naval tactics. Having learnt that an encampment of 300 men and six pieces of cannon had been formed, at the distance of a few miles from the banks of the Potomac, and about nine leagues below Alexandria, he determined, with part of his ship's crew, to surprise it, and to capture the guns. Running his frigate with this view up the river, he cast anchor opposite to the place where the American forces lay; and leaving on board only a sufficient number of sailors to manage the ship, and to guard against surprise, with the rest, amounting to 200 seamen and marines, he landed, and marched rapidly towards the enemy's camp. But intelligence of his proceedings had already reached them; patrols of horse hovering continually along the coast for the purpose of watching the motions of our fleet. When, therefore, he arrived at the point of destination, he found the bivouac deserted, and the rear-guard in full retreat. With these a little skirmishing ensued, and he received a rifle-ball in the thigh. Not suspecting that the wound was dangerous, he continued to push forward, till he fell exhausted from loss of blood; when, on examining the hurt, it was found that the femoral artery had been cut; and before any proper assistance could be afforded, he literally bled to death. Seeing their leader killed, and the enemy retiring, apparently with the design of drawing them away from the coast, the sailors now halted; and taking up their dead commander, returned to the river without being able to effect anything which might, in any degree, console them for their loss.

In the meantime the army continued, for some days, quietly on board the ships in the Patuxent. The wounded whose cases appeared most desperate were removed to vessels fitted up for their reception, and sailed, some for Halifax, and others for England. The dispatches were likewise made out and sent off in the Iphigenia, whilst a sort of breathing-time was given to those who had been of late so actively employed. Whilst this sabbath continued, I amused myself by landing; and under the pretext of shooting, strolled sometimes farther up the country than prudence exactly warranted. The houses and villas, upon the immediate banks of the river, I found universally deserted, and thoroughly plundered. The corn, however, was uninjured; and even flocks of sheep were seen grazing within a short distance of the water, protected only by negro slaves. Of these none were taken without an equivalent being as faithfully paid as if they had been sold in the market-place of New York; a circumstance which favoured the belief that the houses had been ransacked, not by the British troops, but by the inhabitants themselves. Whether it was really so or not I cannot say, but this I know, that from the time of our arrival in the Chesapeake, all acts of individual plunder or violence were strictly prohibited, and severely punished.

But this appearance of ruin and desertion extended not more than a mile or two from the coast. Beyond that, I found the cottages occupied by their owners, and everything remaining as if no enemy were within a hundred miles. The young men, indeed, were generally absent, because every man fit to bear arms was now serving with the army; but the old men and the women seemed to live as comfortably as if the most profound peace had reigned throughout the State. Nor did I find them altogether so hostile to our interest as I had expected. They professed to be Federalists; and though they regretted the events of the war, they blamed their own rulers for its commencement. Tempted by this show of quietness, I one day continued my walk to a greater distance from the fleet than I had yet ventured to do. My servant was with me, but had no arms, and I was armed only with a double-barrelled fowling-piece. Having wearied myself with looking for game, and penetrated beyond my former landmarks, I came suddenly upon a small hamlet, occupying a piece of cleared ground in the very heart of a thick wood. With this, to confess the truth, I was by no means delighted, more especially as I perceived two stout-looking men sitting at the door of one of the cottages. To retire unobserved was, however, impossible, because the rustling which I had made among the trees attracted their attention, and they saw me, probably, before I had seen them. Perceiving that their eyes were fixed upon me, I determined to put a bold face upon the matter; and calling aloud, as if to a party to halt, I advanced, with my servant, towards them. They were dressed in sailors' jackets and trowsers, and rose on my approach, taking off their hats with much civility. On joining them, I demanded to be informed whether they were not Englishmen, and deserters from the fleet, stating that I was in search of two persons very much answering their description. They assured me that they were Americans, and no deserters, begging that I would not take them away; a request to which, after some time, I assented. They then conducted me into the house, where I found an old man and three women, who entertained me with bread, cheese, and new milk. While I was sitting here, a third youth, in the dress of a labourer, entered, and whispered to one of the sailors, who immediately rose to go out, but I commanded him to sit still, declaring that I was not satisfied, and should certainly arrest him if he attempted to escape. The man sat down sulkily; and the young labourer coming forward, begged permission to examine my gun. This was a request which I did not much relish, and with which I, of course, refused to comply; telling the fellow that it was loaded, and that I was unwilling to trust it out of my own hand, on account of a weakness in one of the locks.

I had now kept up appearances as long as they could be kept up, and therefore rose to withdraw; a measure to which I was additionally induced by the appearance of two other countrymen at the opposite end of the hamlet. I therefore told the sailors that, if they would pledge themselves to remain quietly at home, without joining the American army, I would not molest them; warning them, at the same time, not to venture beyond the village, lest they should fall into the hands of other parties, who were also in search of deserters. The promise they gave, but not with much alacrity, when I rose, and keeping my eye fixed upon them, and my gun ready cocked in my hand, walked out, followed by my servant. They conducted us to the door, and stood staring after us till we got to the edge of the wood; when I observed them moving towards their countrymen, who also gazed upon us, without either advancing or flying. The reader will readily believe, that as soon as we found ourselves concealed by the trees, we lost no time in endeavouring to discover the direct way towards the shipping; but plunging into the thickets, ran with all speed, without thinking of aught except an immediate escape from pursuit. Whether the Americans did attempt to follow, or not, I cannot tell. If they did, they took a wrong direction, for in something more than an hour I found myself at the edge of the river, a little way above the shipping, and returned safely on board, fully resolved not again to expose myself to such risks, without necessity.

In this manner the time was spent till daybreak on the 6th of September, when the whole fleet got under weigh, and stood towards the Chesapeake. The wind was fair, and we speedily cleared the river; but instead of standing up the bay, as we had expected, we ran down a few miles below the mouth of the Patuxent, and there anchored. A signal was then made by telegraph for all ships to send in a return of the number of seamen whom, in addition to marines, they could land with small-arms. Every ship's crew was accordingly mustered, and it was found that, besides the numbers necessary for conveying stores and dragging guns, one thousand sailors could be spared from the fleet. Thus, in spite of our loss at Bladensburg, we were enabled on our next debarkation to bring into the field about five thousand fighting men.

Next morning we again weighed, and directed our course towards the Potomac. We entered this river soon after midday, and continued to stem the stream during the night, and till dusk on the following evening, when we again brought up. Here we were joined by Admiral Cockburn, who had quitted the anchorage some days before the rest of the fleet, with a large flotilla of prizes and small craft; and having on the 9th once more set sail, and steered for a few hours in the direction of Alexandria, we suddenly put about, and, favoured by a fresh breeze, ran down to the bay, turning our heads upwards towards the Patapsco. Baltimore, it was now understood, was the point of attack; and towards the river upon which that town is built we hastened under a heavy press of sail.

The object of this manœuvring was evidently to deceive the enemy, and by keeping him in suspense as to the place threatened, to prevent his concentrating his forces, or throwing up works for its defence. But in the attainment of our object, the event proved that we were but partially successful. Certain it is, however, that the utmost consternation prevailed in every town or village opposite to which we made our appearance. In passing Anapolis, a considerable town built upon the bay, and possessing a tolerable harbour, we stood in so close as to discern the inhabitants flying from their houses; carts and waggons loaded with furniture hurrying along the roads, and horsemen galloping along the shore, as if watching the fearful moment when the boats should be hoisted out, and the troops quit the vessels. Wherever a lighthouse or signal station was erected, alarm-guns were fired and beacons lighted. In a word, all the horrors of doubt and apprehension seemed to oppress the inhabitants of this devoted district.

The fair wind continuing to blow without interruption, on the 11th we came in sight of the projecting headland, where it was designed to disembark the troops. It was a promontory washed by the Patapsco on one side, and a curvature of the bay itself on the other. It was determined to land here, rather than to ascend the river, because the Patapsco, though broad, is far from deep. It is, in fact, too shallow to admit a line-of-battle ship; and, as no one could guess what impediments might be thrown in the way to obstruct the navigation, prudence forbade that five thousand men should be intrusted to the convoy of the smaller vessels alone. Besides, the distance from the point to Baltimore did not exceed fourteen or fifteen miles, a space which might easily be traversed in a day.

But while the land forces moved in this direction upon Baltimore, it was resolved that the frigates and bomb-ships should endeavour to force their way through every obstacle, and to obtain possession of the navigation of the river, so as, if possible, to co-operate with the army by bombarding the place from the water. A frigate was accordingly dispatched to try the depth, and to take soundings of the channel, whilst the remainder of the fleet came to an anchor off the point. In the meantime all was again bustle and preparation on board the troop-ships and transports. Three days' provisions were cooked, as before, and given to the men; and as we were now to carry everything by a *coup-de-main*, twenty rounds of ammunition were added to the sixty with which soldiers are usually loaded; whilst a smaller quantity of other baggage was directed to be taken on shore. A blanket, with a spare shirt and pair of shoes, was considered enough for each man on an expedition of so rapid a nature; whilst brushes and other articles of that description were divided between comrades, one carrying what would suffice for both. Thus the additional load of twenty cartridges was more than counterbalanced by the clothing and necessaries left behind.

It was dusk when we reached the anchorage, consequently no

landing could take place before the morrow. But as the boats were ordered to be in readiness at dawn, every man slept in his clothes, that he might be prepared to start at a moment's warning. There was something in this state of preparation at once solemn and exciting. That we should obtain possession of a place so important as Baltimore without fighting was not to be expected; and, therefore, this arming and this bustle seemed in fact to be the prelude to a battle. But no man of the smallest reflection can look forward to the chance of a sudden and violent death without experiencing sensations very different from those which he experiences under any other circumstances. When the battle has fairly begun, I may say with truth that the feelings of those engaged are delightful; because they are in fact so many gamblers playing for the highest stake that can be offered. But the stir and noise of equipping, and then the calmness and stillness of expectation, these are the things which force a man to think. On the other hand, the warlike appearance of everything about you, the careless faces and rude jokes of the private soldiers, and something within yourself, which I can compare to nothing more seemly than the mirth which criminals are said sometimes to experience and to express previous to their execution; all these combine to give you a degree of false hilarity, I had almost said painful from its very excess. It is an agitation of the nerves, such as we may suppose madmen feel, which you are inclined to wish removed, though you are not unwilling to admit that it is agreeable.

And yet, as if in mockery of these deadly preparations, I do not recollect to have seen a more heavenly night than the present. The heat of the day was past, a full clear moon shone brightly in a sky where not a cloud could be discerned, and a heavy dew falling appeared to refresh the earth, which had been parched and burnt up by the sun. We lay at this time within two miles of the shore, consequently every object there was distinctly visible. Around us were moored numerous ships, which, breaking the tide as it flowed gently onwards, produced a ceaseless murmur like the gushing of a mountain stream. The voices of the sentinels too, as they relieved one another on the decks, and the occasional splash of oars, as a solitary boat rowed backwards and forwards to the Admiral's ship for orders, sounded peculiarly musical in the perfect stillness of a calm night. Though I am far from giving the preference, in all respects, to a sailor's life, it must nevertheless be confessed that it has in it many moments of exquisite enjoyment, and the present seemed to me to be of the number.

CHAPTER XIII.

But the stillness of night soon passed away, and at three o'clock in the morning every ship in the fleet began to lower her boats, and the soldiers were roused from their slumbers. The same precautions which had been formerly used to cover the landing were again adopted, several gun-brigs laying themselves within cable's length of the beach, and the leading boats in every division being armed with carronades, loaded and ready for action. But, as had been the case at St. Benedict's, they were unnecessary, for the troops reached the shore without opposition, and leisurely formed in an open field close to the river.

It was seven o'clock before the whole army was disembarked and in order for marching. The same arrangements which had been made on the late expedition were, as far as circumstances would permit, again adopted on this. The light brigade, now commanded by Major Jones of the 4th regiment, led the advance; then followed the artillery, amounting to six field-pieces and two howitzers, all of them drawn by horses; next came the second brigade, then the sailors, and last of all the third brigade. Flank patrols and reconnoitring parties were likewise sent out; in short, the same admirable dispositions regulated the present march which had governed our march to Washington.

The column being put in motion, advanced, without the occurrence of any incident deserving of notice, for about an hour, when it arrived at a piece of ground which appeared as if it had been lately in possession of the enemy. It was a narrow neck of land, confined between the river on one side, and the head of a creek on the other, measuring, perhaps, a mile across. From the river to the creek a breastwork had been begun, and was partly completed. In front of it there were lines drawn, apparently for the purpose of marking out the width of a ditch;

in some places the ditch itself was dug, and the commencement of what resembled an enfilading battery in the centre, showed that a considerable degree of science had been displayed in the choice of this spot as a military position. And, in truth, it was altogether such a position as, if completed, might have been maintained by a determined force against very superior numbers. Both flanks were completely protected, not only by water, but by thick wood, while a gentle eminence in the very middle of the line offered the most desirable situation for the projecting battery which had been begun; because a fire from it would have swept the whole, both to the right and left. In its present state, however, it was untenable, unless by a force as able to attack as to defend; consequently the Americans, who acted solely on the defensive, did wisely in choosing another.

But the aspect of the ground was such as led us to conclude that the enemy could not be very distant. The troops were accordingly halted, that the rear might be well up, and the men fresh and ready for action. Whilst this was done part of the flank patrol came in, bringing with them three light-horsemen, as prisoners. These were young gentlemen belonging to a corps of volunteers, furnished by the town of Baltimore, who had been sent out to watch our motions, and convey intelligence to the American General. Being but little accustomed to such service, they had suffered themselves to be surprised; and, instead of reporting to their own leader as to the number and dispositions of their adversaries, they were now catechized by General Ross respecting the strength and preparations of their friends. From them we learned that a force of no less than twenty thousand men was embodied for the defence of Baltimore; but as the accounts of prisoners are generally over-rated, we took it for granted that they made their report only to intimidate.

Having rested for the space of an hour, we again moved forward, but had not proceeded above a mile when a sharp fire of musketry was heard in front, and shortly afterwards a mounted officer came galloping to the rear, who desired us to quicken our pace, for that the advanced guard was engaged. At this intelligence the ranks were closed, and the troops advanced at a brisk rate, and in profound silence. The firing still continued, though, from its running and irregular sound, it promised little else than a skirmish; but whether it was kept up by detached parties alone, or by the outposts of a regular army, we could not tell; because, from the quantity of wood with which the country abounded, and the total absence of all hills or eminences, it was impossible to discern what was going on at the distance of half a mile from the spot where we stood.

We were already drawing near to the scene of action, when another officer came at full speed towards us, with horror and dismay in his countenance, and calling loudly for a surgeon. Every man felt within himself that all was not right, though none was willing to believe the whispers of his own terror. But what at first we would not guess at, because we dreaded it so much, was soon realized; for the aide-de-camp had scarcely passed, when the General's horse, without its rider, and with the saddle and housings stained with blood, came plunging onwards. Nor was much time given for fearful surmise as to the extent of our misfortune. In a few moments we reached the ground where the skirmishing had taken place, and beheld General Ross laid by the side of the road, under a canopy of blankets, and apparently in the agonies of death. As soon as the firing began, he had ridden to the front, that he might ascertain from whence it originated, and, mingling with the skirmishers, was shot in the side by a rifleman. The wound was mortal: he fell into the arms of his aide-de-camp, and lived only long enough to name his wife, and to commend his family to the protection of his country. He was removed towards the fleet, but expired before his bearers could reach the boats.

It is impossible to conceive the effect which this melancholy spectacle produced throughout the army. By the courteousness and condescension of his manners, General Ross had secured the absolute love of all who served under him, from the highest to the lowest; and his success on a former occasion, as well as his judicious arrangements on the present, had inspired every one with the most perfect confidence in his abilities. His very error, if error it may be called, in so young a leader—I mean that diffidence in himself which had occasioned some loss of time on the march to Washington, appeared now to have left him. His movements were at once rapid and cautious; nay, his very countenance indicated a fixed determination, and a perfect security of success. All eyes were turned upon him as we passed, and a sort of involuntary groan ran from rank to rank, from the front to the rear of the column.

By the fall of our gallant leader, the command now devolved upon Colonel Brook, of the 44th regiment, an officer of decided personal courage, but, perhaps, better calculated to lead a battalion than to guide an army. Being informed of his unexpected and undesired elevation, he came to the front, and under him we continued to move on; sorrowful, indeed, but not dejected. The skirmishing had now ceased, for the American riflemen were driven in; and in a few minutes we found ourselves opposite to a considerable force, drawn up with some skill, and occupying a strong position. Judging from appearances, I should say that the corps now opposed to us amounted to six or seven thousand men. They covered a neck of land, very much resembling that which we had passed; having both flanks defended by little inland lakes; the whole of their position was well wooded, and in front of their line was a range of high palings, similar to those which intersected the field of Bladensburg. About the centre, though some way advanced, was a farm-house, with its outbuildings and stack-yard; and near to the right ran the main road. Their artillery, which could not greatly exceed our own, either in weight of metal or number of guns, was scattered along the line of infantry in nearly the same order as had been preserved at Bladensburg, and their reserve was partly seen, and partly hid by a thick wood.

The whole of this country is flat and unbroken. About half a mile in rear of the enemy's position were some heights, but to occupy these as they should be occupied would have required a much greater number of men than the American army could muster. Their General, therefore, exhibited some judgment in his choice of ground, but, perhaps, he would have exhibited more had he declined a pitched battle altogether. Yet, to do him justice, I repeat that the ground was well chosen; for, besides the covering of wood which he secured for his own people, he took care to leave open fields in his front; by which means we were of necessity exposed to a galling fire, as soon as we came within range. Of one error, however, he was guilty.

Either he did not possess himself of the farm-house at all, or he suffered it to be taken from him with very little resistance; for on the arrival of the column at the ground where it was to form, it was in the occupation of our advanced guard. He was likewise to blame in not filling the wood upon our left with skirmishers. In short, he acted unwisely in merely attempting to repel attacks, without ever dreaming that the most effectual mode of so doing is to turn the tables, and attack the assailants.

As our troops came up they filed off to the right and left, and drew up just within cannon shot in the following order. The light brigade, consisting, as I have formerly stated, of the 85th regiment and the light companies of the other corps, in extended order, threatened the whole front of the American army. The 21st remained in column upon the road; the 4th moved off to the right, and advanced through a thicket to turn the enemy's left; and the 44th, the seamen and marines, formed line in rear of the light brigade.

While this formation was going on, the artillery being brought up, opened upon the American army, and a smart cannonade ensued on both sides. That our guns were well served I myself can bear witness; for I saw the Shrapnel shells which were thrown from them strike among the enemy, and make fearful gaps in the line. Our rockets likewise began to play, one of which falling short, lighted upon a haystack in the barn-yard belonging to the farm-house, and immediately set it on fire. The house itself, the stables, barns, and outhouses, as well as all the other stacks, one after another caught the flames, and were quickly in a state of conflagration; and the smoke and blaze which they emitted, together with the roar of cannon and flashes of the guns, produced altogether a very fine effect.

In the meantime the American artillery was not idle. Pushing forward two light field-pieces upon the road, they opened a destructive fire of grape upon the 21st regiment, and such of the sailors as occupied that point. Three other guns were directed against our artillery, between which and several of our pieces a sort of duel was maintained; and the rest played without ceasing upon the 85th and the light companies, who had lain down while the other regiments took up their ground. Neither was their infantry altogether quiet. They marched several strong bodies from the right to the left, and withdrew others from the left to the right of their line, though for what end this marching and countermarching was undertaken I am at a loss to conceive. While thus fluctuating it was curious to observe their dread of every spot where a cannon-ball had struck. Having seen the shots fall, I kept my eye upon one or two places, and perceived that each company as it drew near to those points hung back; and then assuming as it were a momentary courage, rushed past, leaving a vacancy between it and the company which next succeeded.

All this while the whole of our infantry, except the 4th regiment, lay or stood in anxious expectation of an order to advance. This, however, was not given till that corps had reached the thicket through which it was to make its way; when Colonel Brook, with his staff, having galloped along the line to see that all was ready, commanded the signal to be made. The charge was accordingly sounded, and echoed back from every bugle in the army, when, starting from the ground where they had lain, the troops moved on in a cool and orderly manner. A dreadful discharge of grape and canister shot, of old locks, pieces of broken muskets, and everything which they could cram into their guns, was now sent forth from the whole of the enemy's artillery, and some loss was on our side experienced. Regardless of this, our men went on without either quickening or retarding their pace, till they came within a hundred yards of the American line. As yet not a musket had been fired, nor a word spoken on either side, but the enemy, now raising a shout, fired a volley from right to left, and then kept up a rapid and ceaseless discharge of musketry. Nor were our people backward in replying to these salutes; for giving them back both their shout and their volley, we pushed on at double-quick, with the intention of bringing them to the charge.

The bayonet is a weapon peculiarly British; at least it is a weapon which in the hands of a British soldier is irresistible. Though they maintained themselves with great determination, and stood to receive our fire till scarcely twenty yards divided us, the Americans would not hazard a charge. On the left, indeed, where the 21st advanced in column, it was not without much difficulty and a severe loss that any attempt to charge could be made; for in that quarter seemed to be the flower of the enemy's infantry, as well as the main body of their artillery; towards the right, however, the day was quickly won. The only thing to be regretted, indeed, was that the attack had not been for some time longer deferred; because the Americans were broken and fled, just as the 4th regiment began to show itself upon the brink of the water which covered their flank; and before a shallow part could be discovered, and the troops were enabled to pass, they had time to escape.

As soon as their left gave way, the whole American army fell into confusion; nor do I recollect on any occasion to have witnessed a more complete rout. Infantry, cavalry, and artillery were huddled together, without the smallest regard to order or regularity. The sole object of anxiety seemed to be, which should escape first from the field of battle; insomuch, that numbers were actually trodden down by their countrymen in the hurry of the flight. Yet, in spite of the short duration of the action, which lasted little more than two hours from its first commencement, the enemy's loss was severe. They stood in some respects better than at Bladensburg, consequently we were more mingled with them when they gave way, and were thus enabled to secure some prisoners, an event which their more immediate flight had on the other occasion prevented. In the capture of guns, however, we were not so fortunate. Their pieces being light, and well supplied with horses, they contrived to carry off all except two; both of which would have also escaped but for the shooting of the leaders.

I have said that the number of killed and wounded in the American army was very great; in ours, on the other hand, the casualties were fewer by far than might have been expected. The 21st and seamen suffered a good deal, the 85th and light companies a little; but had our gallant General been spared, we should have pronounced this a glorious, because a comparatively bloodless day. In the loss of that one man, however, we felt ourselves more deeply wounded than if the best battalion in the army had been sacrificed.

In following up the flying enemy the same obstacles which presented themselves at Bladensburg again came in the way. The thick woods quickly screened the fugitives, and as even our mounted drivers were wanting, their horses having been taken for the use of the artillery, no effectual pursuit could be attempted. We accordingly halted upon the field of battle, of necessity content with the success which we had obtained; and having collected the stragglers and called in the pursuers, it was resolved to pass the night in this situation. Fires were speedily lighted, and the troops distributed in such a manner as to secure a tolerable position in case of attack; and the wounded being removed into two or three houses scattered along the ground, the victors lay down to sleep under the canopy of heaven.

Having thus given a distinct and connected detail of this affair, I shall beg leave to finish the present chapter with one or two anecdotes, which may not be unamusing. It is said that when Admiral Cockburn, who accompanied the army, and attended General Ross with the fidelity of an aide-de-camp, was in the wood where the latter fell, he observed an American rifleman taking deliberate aim at him from behind a tree. Instead of turning aside, or discharging a pistol at the fellow, as any other man would have done, the brave Admiral, doubling his fist, shook it at his enemy, and cried aloud, "O you d—d Yankee, I'll give it you!" upon which the man dropped his musket in the greatest alarm, and took to his heels.

It is likewise told of an officer of engineers, that having overtaken an American soldier, and demanded his arms, the fellow gave him his rifle very readily, but being ordered to resign a handsome silver-hilted dagger and silver-mounted cartouch-box, which graced his side, he refused to comply, alleging that they were private property, and that, by our own proclamations, private property should be respected. This was an instance of low cunning which reminded me of my own adventure with the squirrel-hunters, and which was attended with equal success.

One other anecdote, of a different nature, and for the truth of which I can myself answer, may likewise be related. In strolling over the field of battle, I came unexpectedly upon a wounded American, who lay among some bushes with his leg broken. I drew near to offer him assistance, but on seeing me the wretch screamed out, and appeared in the greatest alarm; nor was it without some difficulty that I could persuade him he had nothing to fear. At last, being convinced that I intended him no harm, the fellow informed me that it was impressed upon the minds of the American levies that from the British they might expect no quarter; and that it was consequently their determination to give no quarter to the British troops. The fellow might belie his countrymen, and I hope and believe he did, but such was his report to me. To convince him of the erroneousness of his notions, I removed him to one of our hospitals, where his leg was amputated; and he saw himself, as well as many others of his wounded comrades, treated with the same attention which was bestowed upon our own soldiers.

CHAPTER XIV.

At an early hour on the 13th the troops were roused from their lairs, and forming upon the ground, waited till daylight should appear. A heavy rain had come on about midnight, and now fell with so much violence, that some precautions were necessary, in order to prevent the firelocks from being rendered useless by wet. Such of the men as were fortunate enough to possess leathern cases, wrapped them round the locks of their muskets, whilst the rest held them in the best manner they could, under their elbows; no man thinking of himself, but only how he could best keep his arms in a serviceable condition.

As soon as the first glimmering of dawn could be discerned, we moved to the road, and took up our wonted order of march; but before we pushed forward, the troops were desired to lighten themselves still further, by throwing off their blankets, which were to be left under a slender guard till their return. This was accordingly done; and being now unencumbered, except by a knapsack almost empty, every man felt his spirits heightened in proportion to the diminution of his load. The grief of soldiers is seldom of long duration, and though I will not exactly say that poor Ross was already forgotten, the success of yesterday had reconciled at least the privates to the guidance of their new leader; nor was any other issue anticipated than what would have attended the excursion had he still been its mainspring and director.

The country through which we passed resembled, in every particular, that already described. Wood and cultivation succeeded each other at intervals, though the former surpassed the latter in tenfold extent; but instead of deserted villages and empty houses, which had met us on the way to Washington, we found most of the inhabitants remaining peaceably in their homes, and relying upon the assurance of protection given to them in our proclamations. Nor had they cause to repent of that confidence. In no instance were they insulted, plundered, or ill-treated; whereas every house which was abandoned fell a prey to the scouts and reconnoitring parties.

But our march to-day was not so rapid as our motions generally were. The Americans had at last adopted an expedient which, if carried to its proper length, might have entirely stopped our progress. In most of the woods they had felled trees, and thrown them across the road; but as these abattis were without defenders, we experienced no other inconvenience than what arose from loss of time; being obliged to halt on all such occasions till the pioneers had removed the obstacle. So great, however, was even this hinderance, that we did not come in sight of the main army of the Americans till evening, although the distance travelled could not exceed ten miles.

It now appeared that the corps which we had beaten yesterday was only a detachment, and not a large one, from the force collected for the defence of Baltimore; and that the account given by the volunteer troopers was in every respect correct. Upon a ridge of hills, which concealed the town itself from observation, stood the grand army, consisting of twenty thousand men. Not trusting to his superiority in numbers, their General had there entrenched them in the most formidable manner, having covered the whole face of the heights with breastworks, thrown back his left so as to rest it upon a strong fort erected for the protection of the river, and constructed a chain of field redoubts which covered his right and commanded the entire ascent. Along the side of the hill were likewise *flèches* and other projecting works, from which a cross fire might be kept up; and there were mounted throughout this commanding position no less than one hundred pieces of cannon.

It would be absurd to suppose that the sight of preparations so warlike did not in some degree damp the ardour of our leader;

at least it would have been madness to storm such works without pausing to consider how it might best be attempted. The whole of the country within cannon-shot was cleared from wood, and laid out in grass and corn-fields; consequently there was no cover to shelter an attacking army from any part of the deadly fire which would be immediately poured upon it. The most prudent plan, therefore, was to wait till dark; and then, assisted by the frigates and bombs, which he hoped were by this time ready to co-operate, to try the fortune of a battle.

Having resolved thus to act, Colonel Brook halted his army; and, secured against surprise by a well-connected line of piquets, the troops were permitted to light fires and to cook their provisions. But though the rain still fell in torrents, no shelter could be obtained; and as even their blankets were no longer at hand, with which to form gipsy-tents, this was the reverse of an agreeable bivouac to the whole army.

Darkness had now come on, and as yet no intelligence had arrived from the shipping. To assail such a position, however, without the aid of the fleet, was deemed impracticable; at least our chance of success would be greatly diminished without their co-operation. As the left of the American army extended to a fort built upon the very brink of the river, it was clear that could the ships be brought to bear upon that point, and the fort be silenced by their fire, that flank of the position would be turned. This once effected, there would be no difficulty in pushing a column within their works; and as soldiers entrenched always place more reliance upon the strength of their entrenchments than upon their own personal exertions, the very sight of our people on a level with them would in all probability decide the contest. At all events, as the column was to advance under cover of night, it might easily push forward and crown the hill above the enemy, before any effectual opposition could be offered; by which means they would be enclosed between two fires, and lose the advantage which their present elevated situation bestowed. All, however, depended upon the ability of the fleet to lend their assistance; for without silencing the fort, this flank could scarcely be assailed with any chance of success, and, therefore, the whole plan of operations must be changed.

Having waited till it was considered imprudent to wait longer, without knowing whether he was to be supported, Colonel Brook determined, if possible, to open a communication with the fleet. That the river could not be far off we knew, but how to get to it without falling in with wandering parties of the enemy was the difficulty. The thing, however, must be done; and as secrecy, and not force, was the main object, it was resolved to dispatch for the purpose a single officer without an escort. On this service a particular friend of mine chanced to be employed. Mounting his horse, he proceeded to the right of the army, where, having delayed a few minutes till the moon rising gave light enough through the clouds to distinguish objects, he pushed forward at a venture, in as straight a line as he could guess at. It was not long before his progress was stopped by a high hedge. Like knight-errants of old, he then gave himself up to the guidance of his horse, which taking him towards the rear, soon brought him into a narrow lane, that appeared to wind in the direction of the enemy's fort: this lane he determined to follow, and holding a cocked pistol in his hand, pushed on, not perhaps entirely comfortable, but desirous at all hazards of executing his commission. He had not ridden far, when the sound of voices through the splashing of the rain arrested his attention. Pulling up, he listened in silence, and soon discovered that they came from two American soldiers, whether stragglers or sentinels it was impossible to divine; but whoever they were, they seemed to be approaching. It now struck him that his safest course would be to commence the attack, and having therefore waited till he saw them stop short, as if they had perceived him, he rode forward, and called out to them to surrender. The fellows turned and fled, but galloping after them, he overtook one, at whose head he presented a pistol, and who instantly threw down his rifle, and yielded himself prisoner; whilst the other, dashing into a thicket, escaped, probably to tell that he had been attacked by a whole regiment of British cavalry. Having thus taken a prisoner, my friend resolved to make him of some use; with this view he commanded him to lay hold of his thigh, and to guide him directly to the river, threatening, if he attempted to mislead or betray him into the hands of the Americans, that he would instantly blow out his brains. Finding himself completely in my friend's power, the fellow could not refuse to obey; and accordingly, the man resting his hand upon the left thigh of the officer, they proceeded along the lane for some time, till they came to a part where it branched off in two directions. My friend here stopped for a moment, and again repeated his threat, swearing that the instant his conduct became suspicious should be the last of his life. The soldier assured him that he would keep his word, and moreover informed him that some of our ships were almost within gun-shot of the fort; a piece of information which was quickly confirmed by the sound of firing, and the appearance of shells in the air. They now struck to the right, and in half an hour gained the brink of the river: where my friend found a party just landed from the squadron, and preparing to seek their way towards the camp. By them he was conducted to the Admiral, from whom he learnt that no effectual support could be given to the land force; for such was the shallowness of the river, that none except the very lightest craft could make their way within six miles of the town; and even these were stopped by vessels sunk in the channel, and other artificial bars, barely within a shell's longest range of the fort. With this unwelcome news he was accordingly forced to return; and taking his unwilling guide along with him, he made his way, without any adventure, to our advanced posts; where, having thanked the fellow for his fidelity, he rewarded it more effectually by setting him at liberty.

Having brought his report to head-quarters, a council of war was instantly summoned to deliberate upon what was best to be done. Without the help of the fleet, it was evident that, adopt what plan of attack we could, our loss must be such as to counterbalance even success itself; whilst success, under existing circumstances, was, to say the least of it, doubtful. And even if we should succeed, what would be gained by it? We could not remove anything from Baltimore, for want of proper conveyances. Had the ships been able to reach the town, then, indeed, the quantity of booty might have repaid the survivors for their toil, and consoled them for the loss of comrades; but as the case now stood, we should only fight to give us an opportunity of reacting the scenes of Washington. To distress an enemy is, no doubt, desirable, but, in the present instance, that distress, even if brought upon the Americans, would cost us dear; whereas, if we failed, it was hardly possible to avoid destruction.

Such was the reasoning which influenced the council of war to decide that all idea of storming the enemy's lines should be given up. To draw them from their works would require manœuvring, and manœuvring requires time; but delays were all in their favour, and could not possibly advantage us. Every hour brought in reinforcements to their army, whereas ours had no source from which even to recruit its losses; and it was, therefore, deemed prudent, since we could not fight at once, to lose no time in returning to the shipping.

About three hours after midnight the troops were accordingly formed upon the road, and began their retreat, leaving the piquets to deceive the enemy, and to follow as a rear-guard. The rain, which had continued with little interruption since the night before, now ceased, and the moon shone out bright and clear. We marched along, therefore, not in the same spirits as if we had been advancing, but feeling no debasement at having thus relinquished an enterprise so much beyond our strength.

When the day broke, our piquets, which had withdrawn about an hour before, rejoined us, and we went on in a body. Marching over the field where the battle of the 12th had been fought, we beheld the dead scattered about, and still unburied; but so far different from those which we had seen at Bladensburg, that they were not stripped, every man lying as he had fallen. One object, however, struck me as curious. I saw several men hanging lifeless among the branches of trees, and learnt that they had been riflemen, who chose, during the battle, to fix themselves in these elevated situations, for the combined purposes of securing a good aim and avoiding danger. Whatever might be their success in the first of these designs, in the last they failed; for our men soon discovered them, and, considering the thing as *unfair*, refused to give them quarter, and shot them on their perches.

Here we paused for about an hour, that the soldiers might collect their blankets and refresh themselves; when we again moved forward, passing the wood where the gallant Ross was killed. It was noon, and as yet all had gone on smoothly without any check or alarm. So little indeed was pursuit dreamt of, that the column began to straggle, and to march without much regard to order; when suddenly the bugle sounded from the rear, and immediately after some musket shots were heard. In an instant the men were in their places, and the regiments wheeled into line, facing towards the enemy. The artillery turned round and advanced to the front; indeed I have never seen a manœuvre more coolly or more steadily performed on a parade in England than this rally. The alarm, however, turned out to be groundless, being occasioned only by the sudden appearance of a squadron of horse, which had been sent out by the American General to track our steps. These endeavoured to charge the rear-guard, and succeeded in making two prisoners; but a single Shrapnel checked their farther advance, and sent them back at full speed to boast of the brave exploit which they had performed.

Seeing that no attack was seriously intended, the army broke once more into the line of march, and proceeded to a favourable piece of ground, near the uncompleted position which I have already described, where we passed the night under little tents made with blankets and ramrods. No alarm occurring, nor any cause of delay appearing, at daybreak we again got under arms, and pushed on towards the shipping, which in two hours were distinguishable.

The infantry now halted upon a narrow neck of land, while the artillery was lifted into boats, and conveyed on board the fleet. As soon as this was done, brigade after brigade fell back to the water's edge and embarked, till finally all, except the light troops, were got off. These being left to cover the embarkation, were extended across the entire space which but a little before contained the whole army; but as no attempt was made to molest them, they had only the honour of being the last to quit the shore.

Were I to enter into a review of the military proceedings in this expedition, I should be condemned to repeat, almost word for word, the remarks which I ventured to make upon the operations previous to the capture of Washington. On the present occasion, however, neither hesitation nor precipitancy was displayed by the British General. He threw his valuable life away, indeed, by exposing his person unnecessarily in a trifling skirmish; but who will blame a soldier for excess of courage, or a leader for excess of alertness? Like other able men, he was unwilling to trust to the report of his subalterns, when it was in his power to ascertain what he sought to know by personal observation; and, like other brave men, he would not be deterred from prosecuting his design by the apprehension of danger. In the plan of the expedition here, he displayed both skill and resolution. Instead of wasting time by an attempt to ascend the river, he chose to land where he was least likely to meet with immediate opposition; and such was the celerity of his motions, that, had he lived, the chances are that we should have fought two battles in one day. But of what a man might have done, I have nothing to say; let me rather do justice to his successor and his advisers. Of these latter, there is one whom it would be improper not to mention by name—I mean Lieutenant Evans, Deputy-Assistant Quartermaster-General. The whole arrangement of our troops in order of battle was committed to him; and the judicious method in which they were drawn up, proved that he was not unworthy of the trust. With respect to the determination of the council of war, I choose to be silent. Certain it is, that the number of our forces would hardly authorise any desperate attempt; yet had the attempt been made, I have very little doubt that it would have been made successfully.

On the part of the Americans, again, the same blunders were committed which marked their proceedings during the incursion to Washington, with this exception, that more science was displayed now than formerly in the distribution of their forces along their principal position. At Bladensburg, indeed, there existed no works, and the troops were badly arranged in an open country: here there were not only fortifications, but fortifications constructed in a scientific manner, and troops drawn up in such order, as that, even without their works, many cross fires would have protected their front. But they neglected numerous favourable opportunities of harassing both our advance and retreat. They felled trees, but left no guards to keep them from being removed, and took no advantage of the delays which their removal created. They risked a battle with a part of their army, when there was no necessity for it; in a word, they committed all those errors which men generally commit who are not soldiers, and yet love war.

CHAPTER XV.

HAVING once more received the troops on board, the fleet remained quietly at anchor till the 17th, when, at an early hour, we set sail and stood towards the Patuxent. In this voyage we passed close to Kent Island, and again threw the inhabitants of Anapolis into alarm by approaching almost within gun-shot of their town; but at neither place were hostilities attempted, and on the 19th we arrived, without any adventure, at our former anchorage in the river. Here we brought up, and parties were sent on shore to dig wells in the sand, to which the boats resorted in great numbers for water. Cattle and sheep were likewise purchased from the natives; some of the flour which had been captured was converted into biscuit; and every preparation seemed to be making for a long voyage.

To facilitate these operations, the fleet now separated, part remaining here, and part proceeding under Admiral Malcolm to the Potomac; whilst Sir Alexander Cochrane, in the Tonnant, with several frigates and gun-brigs, quitted us altogether, and set sail, as it was given out, for Halifax. But our situation was by no means agreeable. The climate of this part of America is, at certain seasons, far from healthy; and the prevalence of dysentery through the armament proved that the unhealthy season had already commenced. Neither did there appear to be any prospect of further employment. No one talked of a future enterprise, nor was the slightest rumour circulated as to the next point of attack. The death of General Ross seemed to have disorganized the whole plan of proceedings, and the fleet and army rested idle, like a watch without its main spring.

Whilst things were in this state, whilst the banks of the rivers continued in our possession, and the interior was left unmolested to the Americans, a rash confidence sprang up in the minds of all, insomuch that parties of pleasure would frequently land without arms, and spend many hours on shore. On one of these occasions, several officers from the 85th regiment agreed to pass a day together at a farm-house, about a quarter of a mile from the stream; and taking with them ten soldiers, unarmed, to row the boat, a few sailors, and a young midshipman, not more than twelve years of age, they proceeded to put their determination into practice. Leaving the men, under the command of their youthful pilot, to take care of the boat, the officers went on to the house; but they had not remained there above an hour, when they were alarmed by a shout, which sounded as if it came from the river. Looking out, they beheld their party surrounded by seventy or eighty mounted riflemen; the boat dragged upon the beach, and set on fire. Giving themselves up for lost, they continued for an instant in a sort of stupor; but the master of the house, to whom some kindness had been shown by our people, proved himself grateful, and, letting them out by a back door, directed them to hide themselves in the wood, whilst he should endeavour to turn their pursuers on a wrong scent. As they had nothing to trust to except the honour of this American, it cannot be supposed that they felt much at ease; but, seeing no better course before them, they resigned themselves to his guidance, and plunging into the thicket, concealed themselves as well as they could among the underwood. In the mean time the American soldiers, having secured all that were left behind, except the young midshipman, who fled into the wood in spite of their fire, divided into two bodies, one of which approached the house, whilst the other endeavoured to overtake the brave boy. It so chanced that the party in pursuit passed close to the officers in concealment, but by the greatest good fortune failed to observe them. They succeeded, however, in catching a glimpse of the midshipman, just as he had gained the water's edge, and was pushing off a light canoe which he had loosened from the stump of a tree. The barbarians immediately gave chase, firing at the brave lad, and calling out to surrender; but the gallant youth paid no attention either to their voices or their bullets. Launching his little bark, he put to sea with a single paddle, and, regardless of the showers of balls which fell about him, returned alone and unhurt to the ship.

Whilst one party was thus employed, the other hastened to the house in full expectation of capturing the British officers. But their host kept his word with great fidelity, and, having directed his countrymen towards another farm-house at some distance from his own, and in an opposite quarter from the spot where his guests lay, he waited till they were out of sight, and then joined his new friends in their lurking-place. Bringing with him such provisions as he could muster, he advised them to keep quiet till dark, when, their pursuers having departed, he conducted them to the river, supplied them with a large canoe, and sent them off in perfect safety to the fleet.

On reaching their ship, they found the 85th regiment under arms, and preparing to land, for the purpose of either releasing their comrades from captivity, or inflicting exemplary punishment upon the farmer by whose treachery it was supposed that they had suffered. But when the particulars of his behaviour were related, the latter alternative was at once abandoned; and it was determined to force a dismissal of the captives, by advancing up the country, and laying waste every thing with fire and sword. The whole of the light brigade was accordingly carried on shore, and halted on the beach, whilst a messenger was sent forward to demand back the prisoners. Such, however, was the effect of his threatening, that the demand was at once complied with, and they returned on board without having committed any ravages, or marched above two miles from the boats.

Besides this trifling debarkation, another little excursion was made by the second and third brigades, the light troops being left most unaccountably on board of ship. Colonel Brook, having heard that an encampment was formed a few miles from the left bank of the Potomac, determined, if possible, to come up with and engage the force there stationed. With this view, two brigades were landed on the night of the 4th of October, and pushed forward at a brisk pace; but the enemy, being on the alert, had timely notice of the movement, and retired; by which means our people returned on the 5th, without effecting anything.

By this time the whole fleet was once more collected together, and crowded the Potomac with their keels. The Diadem being an old ship and a bad sailer, it was determined to remove from her the troops which she had formerly carried, to fill her with American prisoners, and to send her to England. The Menelaus was likewise dispatched with such officers and soldiers as required the benefit of their native air to complete the cure of their wounds; and the rest, getting under weigh on the 6th, stood directly towards the mouth of the Chesapeake. When we reached the James River, we anchored, and were joined by an American schooner bearing a flag of truce. She brought with her Colonel Thornton, Lieut.-Colonel Wood, with the rest of the officers and men who had been left behind at Bladensburg, and, being under the guidance of Commodore Barney, that gentleman was enabled to discharge his trust even to the very letter.

It may readily be supposed that the meeting between friends thus restored to each other was very agreeable. But there was another source of comfort which this arrival communicated, of greater importance than the pleasure bestowed upon individuals. In Colonel Thornton we felt that we had recovered a dashing and enterprising officer; one as well calculated to lead a corps of light troops, and to guide the advance of an army, as any in the service. On the whole, therefore, the American schooner was as welcome as if she had been a first-rate man-of-war filled with reinforcements from England.

The wounded being now sent off, and Colonel Wood among the number, the remainder of the fleet again set sail, and reached the mouth of the bay without interruption. Here they were met by a frigate and two brigs, which spoke to the Admiral, and apparently communicated some important intelligence; for we immediately put about and stood once more up the Chesapeake. The wind, however, blew with great violence, and directly against us. After beating about, therefore, for some time, without making any progress, we turned our heads towards the ocean, and flying between the Capes with amazing velocity, stood out to sea, directing our course towards the S.S.E., and proceeding at the rate of seven miles an hour under bare poles. The sea ran tremendously high, and the sky was dark and dreary; insomuch that by a landsman the gale might safely be accounted a storm. Under these circumstances, the ship rolling as if she would dip her topmasts in the water, and the waves breaking in at the back windows of the cabin, nothing remained to be done but to go to bed. Thither most of us accordingly repaired, and holding ourselves in our berths by clinging to the posts, we amused ourselves by watching the motions of stools, books, trunks, and other articles, as they floated majestically from one side of the cabin to the other. But the effects of the gale were not in every respect ludicrous. Two small schooners, which had been captured at Alexandria and converted into tenders, foundered and went down, without an opportunity being afforded of saving an individual of their crews.

At length the wind began to moderate, and on the 18th there was a dead calm. In point of comfort, however, I cannot say that much change was experienced; for though the gale had ceased, the swell still continued; and the motion produced by a heavy sea after a storm is even more disagreeable than that occasioned by the storm itself. But on this day the minds of all were set at ease as to the place whither we were going, a telegraph signal being made to steer for Jamaica. It was likewise understood that we should be there joined by strong reinforcements, and proceed upon a secret expedition against some place on the southern borders of the United States.

The calm which had succeeded the storm did not last long, for on the 19th a fair breeze sprang up, and sent us at a moderate and agreeable rate upon our course. The heat, however, was most oppressive; even awnings being unable to afford sufficient shelter. We were fast approaching the tropic of Cancer, and every day experienced a greater degree of sultriness; till at length, on the 25th, we crossed that imaginary boundary. Here we were visited, according to custom, by Neptune and his wife; and as the ceremony of shaving may be unknown to some of my readers, I shall beg leave to relate the particulars of that operation.

A clever active seaman, dressed up grotesquely in party-coloured rags, adorned with a long beard made of the stuff which sailors call spun-yarn, and armed with a tri-pronged harpoon, personates the God of the Ocean. Another seaman, arrayed in like manner, except that, instead of a beard, he wears a hideous mask, performs the part of the lady. These are attended by a troop of sea-gods and nymphs, similarly equipped; and advancing from the bow of the vessel, as if just stepped on board, they come forward to the mainmast, and summon before them all such persons as have never sworn the oaths or previously visited their capital. At the foot of the mast is placed a large tub full of sea-water, and covered by a piece of canvas, which is held tight by four of their attendants. Upon this unsteady throne is the luckless wight, whom they design to initiate, compelled to sit;

and being asked several questions, which he cannot answer, and taking several oaths, very much resembling those said to be administered at Highgate, Neptune proceeds to confer upon him the honour of filiation, by rather an extraordinary process. Two of the sea-nymphs, generally tall stout fellows, pinion his arms to his sides; and another, bringing a bucket filled with grease and slops from the kitchen, sets it down at his godship's feet, putting a small painting-brush into his hand. Neptune now dips his brush into the filth, and proceeds to spread a lather over the face of the novice, taking care to ask questions during the whole process; and if the adopted be simple enough to reply, the brush is instantly thrust into his mouth. As soon as a sufficient quantity of grease is laid upon the face, Neptune seizes a piece of rusty iron, generally the broken hoop of some water-cask, with which he scrapes off all that has been applied. If the novice take all this patiently, his face is washed, and he is permitted to descend from his throne in peace; but if he lose his temper, which most men are apt to do, a bucket of sea-water is poured upon his head. If this be sufficient to cool his wrath, he suffers no more; but if it only increase his indignation, bucket after bucket is emptied over him, and at last, the holders of the sail-cloth suddenly retiring, he is plunged overhead into the tub. To crown all, the unfortunate wretch who has endured these miseries is fined by his tormentor in a gallon of rum; a fine which the force of custom compels him to pay. It must be confessed that this is a barbarous amusement, much resembling that of the boys in the fable of the boys and the frogs. Though very agreeable to those who act and to the lookers on, it is not so to him that suffers.

In this manner many persons were treated, till at length Neptune, growing weary from the number of novices, was content to admit the rest to the privileges of initiation, on condition that the fines should be punctually paid; an agreement into which most of us very thankfully entered.

Next morning, the first object which met our eyes was the land of Caycos island. We were so close to the shore, when daylight discovered it, that had the wind been at all adverse we must unquestionably have struck; but being assisted by a fair and gentle breeze, the ships put about immediately, and escaped the danger. Standing out to sea, the fleet now doubled the promontory, and steering round by the other side, sailed on without losing sight of the land till late in the evening.

On the following day, a signal was made from the Admiral's ship, that the Golden Fleece transport, under convoy of the Volcano bomb, should proceed to Port Royal, whilst the rest of the fleet held their course towards Negril Bay. These two vessels accordingly set all sail, and pushed forward by themselves; the others keeping on at a more moderate rate, that none might stray from the convoy: for the West India seas at this time swarmed with American privateers, and it was of great consequence to keep the store-ships and heavy transports in the middle of the squadron.

It so chanced that I took my passage in one of the two ships which proceeded forward by themselves. The wind was fair, and we made great progress, insomuch that before dark the high land of St. Domingo on one side, and the mountains of Cuba on the other, were discernible. In spite of the heat, therefore, our voyage soon became truly delightful. Secure of getting on under the influence of the trade winds, we had nothing to distract our thoughts, or keep us from feasting our eyes upon the glorious shores of these two islands; whilst in addition to the sight of land, which of itself was cheering, we were amused with water-spouts, apparently playing about us in every direction. One of these, however, began to form within a little distance of the ship, and as they are dangerous as well as interesting, a cannon was got ready to break it before it should reach us. But it did not complete its formation, though I cannot tell why; for, after one spout had risen into the air some height, and another bent down from the clouds to meet it, they were suddenly carried away in different directions, and fell into the sea with the noise of a cataract.

Among other sources of amusement, our attention was drawn, on the 29th, to a shark, which made its appearance at the stern of the vessel. A strong hook was immediately prepared, and baited with a piece of salt pork, which being thrown over, was instantly gulped by the voracious monster. But as soon as he felt the pain occasioned by the hook in his jaws, he plunged towards the bottom of the sea with such violence, as to render the very tafferel hot, by the rapidity of the cord gliding over it.

I 2

Having permitted him to go a certain length, he was again hauled up to the surface, where he remained without offering further resistance, till a boat was lowered, and a strong noose thrown over his head. Being thus made fast to the gunwale of the boat, he was brought round to the gangway, when the end of the noose being cast over the main-yard, he was lifted out of the sea and swung upon the ship's deck. Hitherto he had suffered quietly enough, in apparent stupefaction from the pain of his jaw; but he began now to convince us that neither life nor strength had deserted him; lashing his tail with such violence as speedily to clear the quarter-deck, and biting in the most furious manner at everything within his reach. One of the sailors, however, who seemed to understand these matters more than his comrades, took an axe, and watching his opportunity, at one blow chopped off his tail. He was now perfectly harmless, unless, indeed, one had chosen to thrust one's hand into his mouth; and the same sailor accordingly proceeded to lay him open, and to take out his entrails. And now it was that the tenacity of life, peculiar to these animals, displayed itself. After his heart and bowels were taken out, the shark still continued to exhibit proofs of animation, by biting with as much force as ever at a bag of carpenter's tools that happened to lie within his reach.

Being cut up, he was distributed in portions among the soldiers and the ship's crew. The tail part only was reserved as the chief delicacy for our cabin, which, though dry and hard, with little flavour or taste, was on the present occasion considered as agreeable food, because it was fresh.

CHAPTER XVI.

But what I principally relished, in this part of our voyage, was the exquisite beauty of its night-scenery. To an inhabitant of Great Britain, the splendour of a night-scene in these climates is altogether unknown. Shining broad and full in a sky perfectly clouuless, the moon sends forth a clear and mellow lustre, little inferior, in point of brilliancy, to the full twilight in England. By this means you never lose sight of land, either by night or day, as long as your course lies between Cuba and St. Domingo; whilst the delicious coolness, which follows the setting of the sun, tempts you, in spite of all the whispers of prudence, to expose yourself to dews and damps, rather than forego the pleasures of which they are the bane. Besides, you have constantly the satisfaction of observing yourself move steadily on at the most agreeable of all rates, about five or six miles an hour; a satisfaction far from trifling in a sea-life. Then the ocean is so smooth, that scarcely a ripple is seen to break the moon-beams as they fall; whilst the quiet dash of little waves against the ship's side, and the rushing noise occasioned by the moving of her bow through the water, produce altogether an effect which may, without affectation, be termed absolutely refreshing. It was my common practice to sit for hours after night-fall upon the tafferel, and strain my eyes in the attempt to distinguish objects on shore or strange sails in the distance.

It happened that, on the 30th, I was tempted to indulge in this idle but bewitching employment, even beyond my usual hour for retiring, and did not quit the deck till towards two o'clock in the morning of the 31st. I had just entered my cabin, and was beginning to undress, when a cry from above, of an enemy in chase, drew me instantly to the quarter-deck. On looking astern, I perceived a vessel making directly after us, and was soon convinced of the justice of the alarm, by a shot which whistled over our heads. All hands were now called to quarters, the small sails were taken in, and having spoken to our companion, and made an agreement as to position, both ships cleared for action. But the stranger, seeing his signal obeyed with so much alacrity, likewise slackened sail, and, continuing to keep us in view, followed our wake without approaching nearer. In this state things continued till daybreak, we still holding our course, and he hanging back; but as soon as it was light, he set more sail and ran to windward, moving just out of gun-shot, in a parallel direction with us. It was now necessary to fall upon some plan of deceiving him, otherwise there was little probability that he would attack. In the bomb, indeed, the height of the bulwark served to conceal some of the men; but in the transport no such screen existed. The troops were, therefore, ordered below, and only the sailors, a few blacks, and the officers, kept the deck. The same expedient was likewise adopted, in part, by Captain Price, of the Volcano; and in order to give to his ship a still greater resemblance than it already had to a merchantman, he displayed an old faded scarlet ensign, and drew up his fore and mainsail in what sailors term a lubberly manner.

As yet the stranger had shown no colours, but, from her build and rigging, there was little doubt as to her country. She was a beautiful schooner, presenting seven ports on a side, and apparently crowded with men,—circumstances which immediately led us to believe that she was an American privateer. The Volcano, on the other hand, was a clumsy strong-built ship, carrying twelve guns; and the Golden Fleece mounted eight; so that, in point of artillery, the advantage was rather on our side; but the American's sailing was so much superior to that of either of us, that this advantage was more than counterbalanced.

Having dodged us till eight o'clock, and reconnoitred with great exactness, the stranger began to steer gradually nearer and nearer, till at length it was judged that she had arrived within range. A gun was accordingly fired from the Volcano, and another from the transport, the balls from both of which passed over her and fell into the sea. Finding herself thus assaulted, she instantly threw off her disguise, and hung out an American ensign; when, putting her helm up, she poured a broadside, with a volley of musketry, into the transport; and ran alongside of the bomb, which sailed to windward.

As soon as her flag was displayed, and her intention of attacking discerned, all hands were ordered up, and she received two well-directed broadsides from the Volcano, as well as a warm salute from the Golden Fleece. But such was the celerity of her motion, that she was alongside of the bomb in less time than can be imagined; and actually dashing her bow against the other, attempted to carry her by boarding. Captain Price, however, was ready to receive them. The boarders were at their posts in an instant, and the enemy discovering, when it was too late, the mistake into which he had fallen, left about twenty of his men upon the Volcano's bowsprit, all of whom were thrown into the sea; and filling his sails, sheered off with the same speed with which he had borne down. In attempting to escape, he unavoidably fell somewhat to leeward, and exposed the whole of his deck to the fire of the transport. A tremendous discharge of musketry saluted him as he passed; and it was almost laughable to witness the haste with which his crew hurried below, leaving none upon deck except such as were absolutely wanted to work his vessel.

The Volcano had by this time filled, and gave chase, firing with great precision at the privateer's yards and rigging, in the hope of disabling him. But as fortune would have it, none of his important ropes or yards were cut; and we had the mortification to see him, in a few minutes, beyond our reach.

In this affair, a marine officer and two men were killed on board the bomb; and some of the tackling was shot away. The transport suffered nothing in killed or wounded, having been in a great degree protected from the enemy's fire by her commodore; and only one rope, not, I believe, an important one, was destroyed.

The battle having ended, and the chase being given up as fruitless, we continued our course without any other adventure; and before dark were able to distinguish the blue mountains of Jamaica. St. Domingo and Cuba had both disappeared, and this was now the only land visible; but it was not till the 1st of November that we could obtain a distinct view of it. Then, indeed, we found ourselves within a few miles of the shore, and seldom has landscape appeared more attractive to the eyes of a voyager, than the romantic shores of Jamaica now appeared to ours.

Jamaica is in general a bold and mountainous island, but on this side it is peculiarly so. It appeared to me that even the Pyrenees, magnificent as they are, were not to be compared, in point of altitude, to the hills now before me; and early in the morning, while yet the mists hung upon their summits and concealed them, no prospect can be imagined more sublime than that which they presented. It was, in truth, a glorious scene; and as the wind blew light and uncertain, we were permitted, from the slowness of the ship's progress, to enjoy it to the full. Towards evening, indeed, the breeze died entirely away, which compelled us to anchor about eight miles from the harbour of Port Royal.

In spite of the little rest which I had procured during the two preceding nights, having sat up till an early hour this morning, to watch several strange sails that hovered about us, I could not bring myself to quit the deck till after midnight, so beautiful, in all respects, were the objects around me. The moon shone with her accustomed brilliancy, and exhibited every crag and tree upon the land, changed and confounded in shape, but still plainly; whilst the perfume, borne off upon the breeze, was odoriferous in the highest degree. The sound of the waves, likewise, breaking upon the rocks, and the occasional cry of seamen, as they adjusted ropes and sails, together with the sight of several vessels which took advantage of the night-wind and stood to sea, with canvas glittering in the moonbeams, produced so delightful a combination, as completely riveted me to my seat; nor was it without much reluctance that I at length yielded to the drowsy god, and descended to my cabin.

Next morning, the ship got under weigh at an early hour, but, owing to the unsteadiness of the breeze, it was ten o'clock before we made any satisfactory progress. As we approached the bay which forms the harbour of Port Royal, a novel and pleasing sight presented itself. The hills dying gradually away, gave place to gentle slopes and green knolls, till, towards the entrance, the coast became perfectly level. Pushing forward, we soon found ourselves in a narrow channel between two projecting headlands, beautifully ornamented with cocoa-nut trees, and so near to each other, that I could with ease have thrown a biscuit from the ship's deck upon either. At the extremity of these necks, just where the bay begins its sweep, stand two well-built forts, bristling with cannon; and at the opposite side may be seen a third, ready to sink whatever hostile fleet should be fortunate enough to force an entrance. But these were not the most striking parts of the scene. The water in this strait is remarkably clear, and exhibits with great distinctness the tops and chimneys of houses at the bottom. It will be recollected, that many years ago, an earthquake not only demolished great part of the town of Port Royal, but likewise covered it with the sea; by which means, the site of the harbour was completely changed, and that which was formerly dry land, and a town, became part of the entrance of the bay.

Having doubled the promontories, a rich and extensive prospect meets the eye. You find yourself, as it were, in a large inland lake, the banks of which are covered with plantations of sugar-cane, groves of cocoa-nut and plantain trees, and other woods peculiar to these regions, beautifully interspersed with seats and villages. On your right is the town of Port Royal, lying almost on a level with the water, and strongly protected by fortifications, whilst in various other directions are castles and batteries, adding an appearance of security to that of plenty. The banks, though not lofty, slope gently upwards, with occasional falls or glens, and the background is composed in general of the rugged tops of distant mountains.

Having waited till the ship dropped anchor, I put myself into a sort of barge rowed by four negroes, and proceeded to Kingston. Though not the capital of the island, Kingston is the largest town in Jamaica. It stands upon the brink of a frith, about nine miles above Port Royal, and thence enjoys all the advantages of the chief mart in this trading country. Like most other mercantile seaports, it is built without much regard to regularity. The streets, though wide, are in general the reverse of elegant, being composed almost entirely of wooden houses, and by no means remarkable for cleanliness. Of public buildings it possesses none worthy of notice. Its inns are, however, excellent; and though certainly not moderate in their charges, they are at least more so than those of Bermuda. In a word, it is exactly such a town as one would expect to find holding the principal commercial rank in a colony where men's minds seldom aspire beyond the occupations of trade.

Of the intense heat in this place, none but those who have experienced it can form a notion. It is impossible to walk out with any comfort, except before the sun has risen, or after he has set; and even within doors, with the aid of thorough draughts and all the other expedients usually adopted on such occasions, it is with the utmost difficulty that you can contrive to keep your blood in a moderate degree of temperature. In the town itself, therefore, few of the higher classes reside, the closeness produced by a proximity of houses being in this climate peculiarly insupportable. These inhabit for the most part little villas, called Pens, about three or four miles in the country, the master of each family generally retaining a suite of apartments, or perhaps an entire mansion, in some open street, for his own use, when business obliges him to exchange the comfort of fresh air for the suffocating atmosphere of Kingston. Towards the outskirts, indeed, in one direction, a few genteel families inhabit one or two handsome houses, surrounded by extensive gardens and shrubberies; but these are not numerous, and they are so far removed from the heart of the town, as to be in great measure beyond the influence of its smoke and other nuisances.

During our sojourn in this place we received the most hospitable attention from several persons of the first distinction. Balls and other entertainments were given, at which all the beauty and fashion in this part of the island attended; and for some days I had little leisure or inclination for any other pursuit than the enjoyment of civilized pleasure, a pursuit which, from long disuse, possessed more than ordinary zest. But at length having seen as much of Kingston and its vicinity as I desired to see, I determined to take advantage of the opportunity which fortune had placed within my reach, and to make an excursion into the heart of the Blue Mountains. To this I was additionally induced by an invitation from an old friend to visit him at Annotto Bay; and as, along with his letter, he sent a horse for my own conveyance, and a mule for the conveyance of my baggage, no difficulty respecting a mode of being transported stood in the way to obstruct my design.

Having made up my mind to this journey, I waited till sunset on the 9th, when, starting in the cool of the evening, I reached a little tavern called the Plum Tree, about half an hour after dark. My ride carried me through an open and fertile country covered with sugar-canes, coffee, and such other plants as are cultivated in the low grounds of Jamaica. It was a short one, not more than twelve miles in extent; but I was forced to halt where I did, because I had gained the foot of the mountains; and if I had passed the Plum Tree, well known as a sort of half-way house on such tours, I might have travelled all night without finding any place of accommodation.

As darkness set in, one of the beautiful peculiarities of a tropical climate, which I had not previously witnessed, came under my observation. The air was filled with fire-flies, which, emitting a phosphoric light something similar to the light of the glow-worm, only more red and brilliant, danced around me like sparks from a smith's anvil when he is beating a bar of red-hot iron. These creatures flutter about with a humming noise, and frequently settle in large swarms upon branches of trees, giving them the semblance of so many pieces of timber taken newly out of a fire. When viewed by daylight they are in no way remarkable for their elegance, resembling in the shape of the body a long beetle which may be seen in the fields after sunset, without wings or scales. In colour they are a dingy brown, and, like the glow-worm, carry their light in the tail.

As I had not before chanced to see anything of the kind, and forgot at the moment that such an insect as the fire-fly existed, I was for a few minutes at a loss to what cause to attribute the phenomenon, and was at last indebted to my negro guide for refreshing my memory on the subject. The effect, however, cannot be conceived without being witnessed. A cluster of two or three glow-worms shine so brilliantly, that they will furnish subject for the commendatory eloquence of any one fortunate enough to perceive them together; but their brilliancy is as a farthing candle to the sun, when compared with that of the fire-fly. Not two or three, but thousands of these creatures dance around, filling the air with a wavering and uncertain glimmer, of the extreme beauty of which no words can convey an adequate conception.

Having passed the night at this tavern, a small cottage kept by a free negro and his wife, I rose two hours before dawn, and prosecuted my journey. From the moment I quitted the Plum Tree I began gradually to ascend, till at daybreak I found myself in the midst of the most glorious scenery that the imagination of man can conceive. Everything around was new and romantic. The hills, towering into the very sky, were covered from top to bottom with the richest herbage and the most luxuriant wood. Rarely could a barren crag be discerned, and when it did appear it was only a sharp point, or a bold projection pushing itself forward from the midst of the thickest foliage. But what to me formed the most bewitching part of the prospect was the elegance of the trees and their perfect dissimilitude to any which I had previously beheld. The cocoa-nut and plantain were mingled with the wild pine and lime-tree; while the cashew and wild coffee, with numberless other shrubs, loaded at once with fruit and blossom, formed the underwood to these graceful forests.

As yet I had been favoured with a wide and good road, but now it began gradually to narrow, till at last it ended in a path little more distinct than the sheep-tracks over the hills in Scotland. Winding along the sides of the mountains, it brought me frequently to spots where the wood parting, as if artificially, displayed deep ravines, to look down which, without becoming dizzy, required no little strength of head; whilst above, the same hill continued to stretch itself to a height far beyond any I had before gazed upon. Presently after it conducted me gently down into valleys completely shut out from the rest of the world; and as I descended I could hear the roar of water, though neither the stream nor the bottom of the glen could be perceived. On one of these occasions, after passing through a thick grove, I beheld a river of some width dashing along the glen, and chafing so as to produce the noise of a mighty waterfall. Towards the brink of this river my guide conducted me; when, plunging in, we made our way with some difficulty to the opposite bank, and again began to ascend.

For several hours, the same scenery surrounded me, only varied by the occasional appearance of clusters of negro huts. Than these, it is impossible to imagine any species of huts or dwellings more beautifully picturesque. They are constructed of strong limbs of trees, thatched over with straw, and usually ending in a cone; having no windows, but only two, or sometimes four doors, for the purpose of admitting a free current of air. The spots chosen for their erection, are generally small platforms or terraces in the sides of the hills. A little path, similar to that along which I travelled, winds down from their doors to the bottom of the valley, and conducts to the edge of the river, from whence the inhabitants are supplied with water. Other tracks likewise branch off in different directions, some towards the summit, and others along the sides of the mountains; leading, probably, to the fields or spots where the inhabitants labour. These huts have no chimney, but only a large hole in the roof, to give free passage to the smoke; and I could perceive, by its rise at present, that fires were now burning.

It would be labour lost, were I to attempt any more minute description of this delightful journey. Every step I took presented something new, and something more grand and sublime than I had just quitted; whilst the continual fording of the swollen river (for I crossed the same stream no fewer than eight-and-twenty times) gave an additional interest to the scene, arising from the sense of danger. The rainy season having just ended, this stream, the Wag-water, a most appropriate name, had not as yet returned to its natural size; but at the fords, which in general would not cover a horse's knees, the depth was such as to moisten the saddle-girths. So great a quantity of water, in a furious mountain-torrent, pouring on with all the violence produced by a steep descent, occasioned no slight pressure upon my steed; nor was it without considerable floundering on his part, and some anxiety on mine, that once or twice we succeeded in making good our passage.

CHAPTER XVII.

NOON was approaching when my sooty fellow-traveller directed my attention to a neat cottage, romantically situated on the top of a low mound, which stood alone in the middle of stupendous mountains. It commanded one of the most exquisite prospects that fancy can represent. A sort of glen surrounded it on every side, richly and beautifully wooded; behind, rose some of the most lofty of the Blue Mountains; on the right there was an opening, which admitted a fine view of Annotto Bay; whilst in the other direction, the hills sloping gradually upwards, presented an inclined plane, covered with fields of sugar-cane, and ending, at a considerable distance, in one abrupt and broken ridge.

The cottage in question was the residence of my friend, and the resting-place whither my steps were turned; nor did I experience any regret at finding myself so near my journey's end. The heat had for some time been almost intolerable, and having eaten nothing since the night before, nature began to cry out for repose and repletion; and, in truth, the welcome which I experienced, was of a nature to take away all desire of wandering farther. We had not met for several years—not, indeed, since I was a child—and in the interval, some melancholy changes had occurred in the family of my host; but he received me with the cordial hospitality which a warm heart produces, and forgot his private sorrows for a time, that he might not throw a damp upon my enjoyments.

The remainder of this day I spent, as a powerful sensation of fatigue warned me to spend it, within doors; but on the following morning I set out at an early hour, for the purpose of gratifying my curiosity on a number of points which had frequently exercised it. In this excursion, and indeed in all the excursions which I undertook during my residence at his Pen, my friend accompanied me; and an excellent and most intelligent guide he proved to be. We made the tour of several estates, saw the process of making sugar, visited the sugar and coffee plantations, and inspected several hospitals, with one of which each estate is supplied, for the accommodation and cure of sick negroes. In the course of these rambles, I made it my business to inquire into the condition and treatment of the slave population; inspecting their huts, and even examining their provisions; and I frankly confess that, though I began my researches under the influence of as many prejudices as, on such a subject, are wont to be entertained by Englishmen in general, the result of the whole was to convince me that I had done glaring injustice to the character of the Jamaica planters, as well as fostered notions of the wretchedness of the negroes, utterly and iniquitously erroneous. It is no business of mine, and, if it were, this is no proper place to take part in what has of late been termed the West-Indian controversy; but, as an eye-witness, I may venture to speak out on one point, by affirming, that a countless proportion of the stories with which the British public is amused, touching the barbarous treatment of slaves by owners and overseers, are, if not absolute fables, at all events gross exaggerations. I am aware that my residence in the island was too brief, and my acquaintance with it too limited, to entitle my opinions to the weight which a more protracted sojourn might have obtained for them; but it is but justice to state, that whilst I was there, I enjoyed opportunities of seeing the negro at all times, and under all circumstances, such as few casual visitors can boast of. My host was not a planter, but a medical practitioner; and one prejudiced rather against the slave system than in favour of it: there was therefore no disposition on his part to cast dust into my eyes, or to present to them only the bright side of the picture. Under his guidance, I beheld the negro at work in the fields, in the bosom of his family, in the sick ward, and at market; and I never saw him other than a contented and light-hearted being. No doubt there are instances of cruelty on the part of overseers in Jamaica, exactly as there are instances of tyranny on the part of parish officers and county magistrates in England; but had these been as numerous, or as flagrant, as they are represented to be, I cannot doubt but that something of the kind must have passed under my eyes, even within the space of one week. No such event, however, took place; and, as far as I could learn, no such event was to be expected.

Far be it from me to stand forward as the advocate of personal bondage in the abstract—it is a grievous evil; and wherever men are so far civilized as to render its abolition desirable, it is an evil which ought to be abolished. But it is an evil of long standing, authorized in the Bible, and therefore, we may presume, not without its counterbalancing benefits. He, therefore, who would seek, at all hazards and under all circumstances, to dissolve the tie which binds a master to his slave, and a slave to his master—whilst he would be doing that which the Apostles never did, and which Christians are nowhere commanded to do—would run no slight hazard of causing a quantity of mischief to both parties, for which the benefits bestowed upon either would not compensate. With respect to our own colonies, in particular, it is manifest that the whole matter resolves itself into one consideration. If the negroes be in such a state, as that the boon of universal freedom would be productive to them of universal benefit, by all means let it be bestowed at once, even though it be attended by so much national expense, as the fair demands of the proprietors for compensation shall impose upon us. If they be not thus situated, let every practicable method be adopted to advance them on the scale of civilization; but till they be advanced far beyond their present station, let no false hopes be excited that the moment of their liberation is at hand. Many measures for their improvement have been adopted since the year 1814, and many more are in daily process of adoption ; but it is greatly to be apprehended that much of the benefit which these measures promised to bring about, has been obstructed by the indiscreet zeal of those who profess, and probably feel, the liveliest interest in their welfare.

Besides adding to my stock of knowledge as to the cultivation of the sugar-cane, the making of sugar, rum, &c. &c., I had an opportunity of seeing something of the Maroons, or free Negroes, who inhabit the mountains. These people dwell apart from the European settlers, holding very little intercourse with them, though a single European generally resides in each of their villages, as a sort of chief or magistrate. They struck me to be a lazy, indolent, and harmless race of human beings; and they formed, in all their habits, a striking contrast with their enslaved brethren. Whilst the latter devote their spare hours to the culture of their own little spots, to cudgel-playing, dancing, or other gambols, the former appear to spend their whole time in a state between sleeping and waking, at the doors of their huts, or under the shelter of trees. Some of the Maroon females, I observed, were really handsome, their features being high, and their persons elegantly formed; but in general they differed nothing from the other negroes, from whom, indeed, they are principally descended.

I heard that the men carry on a petty trade in feathers, but that their principal occupation, at least that from which they derive the largest emolument, consists in apprehending, and leading back to their masters, run-away slaves. For their services in this department, they were wont to receive a pension from the Government; and they are still, I believe, supplied with muskets and ammunition at the expense of the colonial authorities. But enough of these details.

My sojourn in St. Mary's having extended considerably beyond the limits which prudence would have imposed upon it, I set out on the morning of the 13th, on my return towards Kingston. The country through which I travelled differed in many respects from that which I had crossed in my way hither: it was in general less wild, and less mountainous; but it possessed features of striking beauty, rich corn-fields being interspersed amidst graceful forests, and here and there a wild hill-side rising as a contrast to both. The most remarkable variety, and not perhaps the least agreeable, was, however, to be found in the absence of the Wag-water; my guide having led me in a direction by which its tortuous course was avoided.

As it was late before I started, my ride soon became toilsome on account of the heat, and I was fain to stop short for the night at a place called Stoney Hill, about twelve miles from Kingston. Here I was hospitably entertained by the officers of the 102nd regiment; and, rising at an early hour on the following morning, I contrived to complete my journey before breakfast. And it was well that no further time had been expended in my progress. The ships, I found, were preparing to put to sea; the stock was all embarked, and the crews on board; nothing therefore remained for me but to follow the general example, and to establish myself with as little delay as possible in my cabin.

In spite of these preparations, the 15th and 16th of November both passed away without any movement being made. It was, however, my custom not to neglect any opportunities which chanced to come in my way of viewing strange places, and obtaining an acquaintance with strange people; neither on the present occasion did I fail to make the most of the interval, by landing and wandering over the town of Port Royal. But to describe minutely a place so little deserving of description, would hardly repay me for the labour of writing, or the reader for the toil of perusing what I write. It is sufficient to observe, that except to him who takes delight in beholding a well-constructed military work, there is nothing in the busy, bustling town of Port Royal which will at all compensate for the heat and fatigue which he must undergo who, like myself, traverses its streets and lanes at noon-day.

The long looked-for signal to weigh was hung out at last; and at an early hour on the 17th we put to sea. Our point of destination was Negril Bay, the appointed place of rendezvous for the whole armament; and we reached it without the occurrence of mishap or adventure on the evening of the 19th. We found here a large fleet already assembled; but the horses were all landed, many officers were dwelling in tents on the shore, and everything gave indication that some further delay might be expected. To say the truth, I experienced no degree of satisfaction at this prospect; for the point of the island opposite to which we now lay was neither remarkable for its natural beauty nor very thickly inhabited; and had the contrary been the case, I had seen as much of Jamaica and its people as I was at all desirous to see. Besides, it was impossible not to feel that whatever the object of our expedition might be, it was not likely to be furthered by this tardy mode of entering upon it; and rumours already began to spread abroad, of discoveries incautiously and untimely made. It was, therefore, with no slight degree of pleasure that, on the morning of the 24th, the topmasts of a numerous squadron were seen over the eastern promontory, in full sail towards us; and it was with still greater delight that in a short time we were able to discern the flags of Sir Alexander Cochrane and Admiral Malcolm floating in the breeze. By and bye the Tonnant and Royal Oak showed their hulls in the offing; and a short while afterwards, these ships, followed by a large fleet of troopers and transports, majestically entered the bay. As may be imagined, our curiosity was strongly excited to learn what reinforcements they contained, and what intelligence they brought; insomuch, that they had scarcely dropped anchor when they were boarded from almost every one of the ships which they came to join.

It appeared that this powerful reinforcement consisted of the following corps:—the 93rd regiment, a fine battalion of Highlanders, mustering nine hundred bayonets; six companies of the 95th rifle corps; two West India regiments, each eight hundred strong; two squadrons of the 14th Dragoons dismounted; detachments of artillery, rockets, sappers, and engineers; recruits for the different corps already in this part of the world; and though last, not least, Major-General Keane to take upon himself the command of the whole. The intelligence brought was likewise interesting, for it informed us of the point whither we were to proceed; and it was soon known throughout the fleet, that the conquest of New Orleans was the object in view.

But before I pursue my narrative further, having arrived, as it were, at a second commencement, it may be well if I state in full the number of men of which the army now consisted. In the first place, then, there were the 4th, 44th, and 85th regiments, originally dispatched from Bordeaux, and the 21st, which joined the expedition at Bermuda. These battalions, being considerably reduced by past service, could not at present muster conjunctly above two thousand two hundred men; and being likewise deprived of the Marine battalion, which had fought beside them in the Chesapeake, they retained no followers except the artillery, sappers, &c. which had accompanied them from the first. The whole amount of this corps may, therefore, be estimated at two thousand five hundred men.

Without computing the individual strength of each detachment now arrived, I will venture to fix the aggregate at two thousand five hundred; and thus the whole, taken collectively, will amount to five thousand combatants. That it might somewhat exceed or fall under this computation, I do not deny; but neither the excess nor deficiency could be considerable; and therefore my statement may be received as correct, with very little allowance.

This, it must be confessed, was a formidable force, and such as, had all its parts been trustworthy, might have done much. But on the black corps little reliance could be placed, especially if the climate should prove colder than was anticipated; consequently, there were not more than three thousand four hundred men upon whom a General could fully depend.

Together with these forces were brought out abundant stores of ammunition, some clothing for the troops, and tents to be used when an opportunity should offer. There were also numerous additions to the commissariat and medical departments; in short, the matériel of the army was increased in proportion to its increase in number.

To find himself in the chief command of the army, exceeded the expectation, and perhaps the desire, of General Keane. Being a young and dashing officer, he had been selected as most fit to serve under General Ross; and having sailed from England before the death of that gallant chief was known, he reached Madeira before his elevation was communicated to him. Young as he was, however, his arrival produced much satisfaction throughout the armament; for though no one entertained a doubt as to the personal courage of Colonel Brook, it was felt that a leader of more experience was wanted on the present expedition.

As soon as the newly-arrived squadron had anchored, the Bay was covered with boats, which conveyed parties of officers from ship to ship, hastening to salute their comrades, and to inquire into the state of things at home. Greetings and hearty embraces were interchanged between friends thus again brought together; and a few passing ejaculations of sorrow bestowed upon those who could not now take part in the meeting. Many questions were put, relative to persons and places in England; in a word, the day was spent in that species of employment, which can be completely known only to those who have been similarly situated.

CHAPTER XVIII.

But the period granted for such indulgence was not of long duration, for on the following morning the Tonnant, Ramilies, and two brigs stood to sea; and on the 26th the rest of the fleet got under weigh and followed the Admiral. It is impossible to conceive a finer sea-view than this general stir presented. Our fleet amounted now to upwards of fifty sail, many of them vessels of war, which shaking loose their topsails, and lifting their anchors at the same moment, gave to Negril Bay an appearance of bustle such as it has seldom been able to present. In half an hour all the canvas was set, and the ships moved slowly and proudly from their anchorage, till, having cleared the headlands, and caught the fair breeze which blew without, they bounded over the water with the speed of eagles, and long before dark the coast of Jamaica had disappeared.

There is something in rapidity of motion, whether it be along a high road or across the deep, extremely elevating; nor was its effect unperceived on the present occasion. It is true that there were other causes for the high spirits which now pervaded the armament, but I question if any proved more efficient in their production than the astonishing rate of our sailing. Whether the business we were about to undertake would prove bloody or the reverse entered not into the calculations of a single individual in the fleet. The sole subject of remark was the speed with which we got over the ground, and the probability that existed of our soon reaching the point of debarkation. The change of climate, likewise, was not without its effect in producing pleasurable sensations. The farther we got from Jamaica, the more cool and agreeable became the atmosphere; from which circumstance we were led to hope that, in spite of its southern latitude, New Orleans would not be found so oppressively hot as we had been taught to expect.

The breeze continuing without interruption, on the 29th we came in sight of the island of Grand Cayman. It is a small speck in the middle of the sea, lying so near the level of the water as to be unobservable at any considerable distance. Though we passed along with prodigious velocity, a canoe nevertheless ventured off from the shore, and making its way through waves which looked as if they would swallow it up, succeeded in reaching our vessel. It contained a white man and two negroes, who brought off a quantity of fine turtle, which they gave us in exchange for salt pork; and so great was the value put upon salt provisions, that they bartered a pound and a half of the one for a pound of the other. To us the exchange was very acceptable, and thus both parties remained satisfied with their bargain.

Having lain-to till our turtle-merchants left us, we again filled and stood our course. The land of Cayman was soon invisible; nor was any other perceived till the 2nd of December, when the western shores of Cuba presented themselves. Towards them we now directed the ship's head, and reaching in within a few miles of the beach, coasted along till we had doubled the promontory, which forms one of the jaws of the Mexican Gulf. Whilst keeping thus close to the shore, our sail was more interesting than usual, for though this side of Cuba be low, it is nevertheless picturesque, from the abundance of wood with which it is ornamented. There are likewise several points where huge rocks rise perpendicularly out of the water, presenting the appearance of old baronial castles, with their battlements and lofty turrets; and it will easily be believed that none of these escaped our observation. The few books which we had brought to sea were all read, many of them twice and three times through; and there now remained nothing to amuse except what the variety of the voyage could produce.

But the shores of Cuba were quickly passed, and the old prospect of sea and sky again met the gaze. There was, however, one circumstance from which we experienced a considerable diminution of comfort. As soon as we entered the gulf, a short disagreeable swell was perceptible; differing in some respects from that in the Bay of Biscay, but to my mind infinitely more unpleasant. So great was the motion, indeed, that all walking was prevented; but as we felt ourselves drawing every hour nearer and nearer to the conclusion of our miseries, this additional one was borne without much repining. Besides, we found some amusement in watching, from the cabin windows, the quantity and variety of weed with which the surface of the gulf is covered. The current being here extremely rapid, the weed sails continually in the same direction; that is to say, it goes round by the opposite side of Cuba towards the banks of Newfoundland, and is carried sometimes as far as Bermuda, and even to the Western Isles.

It is not, however, my intention to continue the detail of this voyage longer than may be interesting; I shall therefore merely state that, the wind and weather having undergone some variations, it was the 10th of December before the shores of America could be discerned. On that day we found ourselves opposite to the Chandeleur Islands, and near the entrance of Lake Borgne. There the fleet anchored, that the troops might be removed from the heavy ships into such as drew least water; and from this and other preparations it appeared that to ascend this lake was the plan determined upon.

But before I pursue my narrative further, it will be well if I endeavour to give some account of the situation of New Orleans, and of the nature of the country against which our operations were directed.

New Orleans is a town of some note, containing from twenty to thirty thousand inhabitants. It stands upon the eastern bank of the Mississippi, in 30° north latitude, and about 110 miles from the Gulf of Mexico. Though in itself unfortified, it is difficult to conceive a place capable of presenting greater obstacles to an invader; and at the same time more conveniently situated with respect to trade. Built upon a narrow neck of land, which is confined on one side by the river, and on the other by impassable morasses, its means of defence require little explanation; and as these morasses extend to the distance of only a few miles, and are succeeded by Lake Pontchartrain, which again communicates through Lake Borgne * with the sea, its peculiar commercial advantages must be equally apparent. It is by means of the former of these lakes, indeed, that intercourse is maintained between the city and the northern parts of West Florida, of which it is the capital; a narrow creek, called in the language of the country a bayo or bayouke, navigable for vessels drawing less than six feet water, running up through the marsh, and ending within two miles of the town. The name of this creek is the Bayouke of St. John, and its entrance is defended by works of considerable strength.

But to exhibit its advantages in a more distinct point of view, it will be necessary to say a few words respecting that mighty river upon which it stands. The Mississippi (a corruption of the word Mechasippi, signifying, in the language of the natives, "the father of rivers") is allowed to be inferior, in point of size and general navigability, to few streams in the world. According to the Sioux Indians it takes its rise from a large swamp, and is increased by many rivers emptying themselves into its course as far as the Fall of St. Anthony, which, by their account, is upwards of 700 leagues from its source. But this fall, which is formed by a rock thrown across the channel, of about twelve feet perpendicular height, is known to be 800 leagues from the sea; and therefore the whole course of the Mississippi, from its spring to its mouth, may be computed at little short of 5000 miles.

Below the fall of St. Anthony, again, the Mississippi is joined by a number of rivers, considerable in point of size, and leading out of almost every part of the continent of America. These are the St. Pierre, which comes from the west; St. Croix, from the east; the Moingona, which is said to run 150 leagues from the west, and forms a junction about 250 below the fall; and the

* These are, properly speaking, one and the same lake. From the entrance, however, as far as Ship Island, is called by the inhabitants Lake Borgne, whilst all above that point goes under the name of Lake Pontchartrain. They are both extremely shallow, varying from 12 to 6 feet in depth.

Illinois, which rises near the lake Michigan, 200 leagues east of the Mississippi.

But by far the most important of these auxiliary streams is the Missouri, the source of which is as little known as that of the Father of Rivers himself. It has been followed by traders upwards of 400 leagues, who traffic with the tribes which dwell upon its banks, and obtain an immense return for European goods. The mouth of this river is five leagues below that of the Illinois, and is supposed to be 800 from its source, which, judging from the flow of its waters, lies in a north-west direction from the Mississippi. It is remarkable enough that the waters of this river are black and muddy, and prevail over those of the Mississippi, which running with a clear and gentle stream till it meets with this addition, becomes from that time both dark and rapid.

The next river of note is the Ohio, which taking its rise near Lake Erie, runs from the north-east to the south-west, and joins the Mississippi about 70 leagues below the Missouri. Besides this there are the St. Francis, an inconsiderable stream, and the Arkansas, which is said to originate in the same latitude with Santa Fé in New Mexico, and which, holding its course nearly 300 leagues, falls in about 200 above New Orleans. Sixty leagues below the Arkansas, comes the Yazous from the north-east; and about 58 nearer to the city is the Rouge, so called from the colour of its waters, which are of a reddish dye, and tinge those of the Mississippi at the time of the floods. Its source is in New Mexico, and after running about 200 leagues it is joined by the Noir 30 miles above the place where it empties itself into the Mississippi.

Of all these rivers there is none which will not answer the purposes of commerce, at least to a very considerable extent; and as they join the Mississippi above New Orleans, it is evident that this city may be considered as the general mart of the whole. Whatever nation, therefore, chances to possess this place, possesses in reality the command of a greater extent of country than is included within the boundary-line of the whole United States; since from every direction are goods, the produce of East, West, North, and South America, sent down by the Mississippi to the Gulf. But were New Orleans properly supplied with fortifications, it is evident that no vessels could pass without the leave of its governor; and therefore is it that I consider that city as of greater importance to the American government than any other within the compass of their territories.

Having said so much on its commercial advantages, let me now point out more distinctly than I have yet done the causes which contribute to its safety from all hostile attempts. The first of these is the shallowness of the river at its mouth, and the extreme rapidity of the current. After flowing on in one prodigious sheet of water, varying in depth from one hundred to thirty fathoms, the Mississippi, previous to its joining the Mexican Gulf, divides into four or five mouths, the most considerable of which is encumbered by a sandbank continually liable to shift. Over this bank no vessel drawing above seventeen feet water can pass; when once across, however, there is no longer a difficulty in being floated; but to anchor is hazardous, on account of the huge logs which are constantly carried down the stream. Should one of these strike the bow of the ship, it would probably dash her to pieces; whilst, independent of this, there is always danger of drifting or losing anchors, owing to the number of sunken logs which the under-current bears along within a few feet of the bottom. All vessels ascending the river are accordingly obliged, if the wind be foul, to make fast to the trees upon the banks; because without a breeze at once fair and powerful, it is impossible to stem the torrent.

But besides this natural obstacle to invasion, the mouth of the river is defended by a fort, which from its situation may be pronounced impregnable. It is built upon an artificial causeway, and is surrounded on all sides by swamps totally impervious, which extend on both sides of the river to a place called the *Détour des Anglais*, within twenty miles of the city. Here two other forts are erected, one on each bank. Like that at the river's mouth, these are surrounded by a marsh, a single narrow path conducting from the commencement of firm ground to the gates of each. If, therefore, an enemy should contrive to pass both the bar and the first fort, he must here be stopped, because all landing is prevented by the nature of the soil; and however fair his breeze may have hitherto been, it will not now assist his further progress. At this point the Mississippi winds almost in a circle, insomuch that vessels which arrive are necessitated to make fast till a change of wind occur.

From the Détour des Anglais towards New Orleans the face of the country undergoes an alteration. The swamp does not indeed end, but it narrows off to the right, leaving a space of firm ground, varying from three to one mile in width, between it and the river. At the back of this swamp, again, which may be about six or eight miles across, come up the waters of Lake Pontchartrain, and thus a neck of arable land is formed, stretching for some way above the city. The whole of these morasses are covered as far as the Détour with tall reeds; a little wood now succeeds, skirting the open country, but the wood measures no more than one mile in depth, when it again gives place to reeds. Such is the aspect of that side of the river upon which the city is built; with respect to the other I can speak with less confidence, having seen it but cursorily. It appears, however, to resemble this in almost every particular, except that it is more wooded and less confined with marsh. Both sides are flat, containing no broken ground, nor any other cover for military movements; for on the open shore there are no trees, except a few in the gardens of those houses which skirt the river, the whole being laid out in large fields of sugar-cane, separated from one another by rails and ditches.

From the preceding brief account of the country, the advantages possessed by a defending army must be apparent. To approach by the river is out of the question, and therefore an enemy can land only from the lake. But this can be done nowhere, except where creeks or *bayos* offer conveniences for that purpose, because the banks of the lake are universally swampy; and can hardly supply footing for infantry, far less for the transportation of artillery. Of these, however, there are not above one or two which could be so used. The Bayo of St. John is one; but it is too well defended, and too carefully guarded for any attempts; and the Bayo of Catiline is another, about ten miles below the city. That this last might be found useful in an attack, was proved by the landing effected by our army at that point; but what is the consequence? The invaders arrive upon a piece of ground, where the most consummate generalship will be of little avail. If the defenders can but retard their progress—which, by crowding the Mississippi with armed vessels, may very easily be done, the labour of a few days will cover the narrow neck with entrenchments; whilst the opposite bank remaining in their hands, they can at all times gall their enemy with a close and deadly cannonade. Of wood, as I have already said, or broken ground which might conceal an advance, there exists not a particle. Every movement of the assailants must, therefore, be made under their eyes; and as one flank of their army will be defended by a morass, and the other by the river, they may bid defiance to all attempts at turning.

Such are the advantages of New Orleans; and now it is only fair that I should state its disadvantages: these are owing solely to the climate. From the swamps with which it is surrounded, there arise, during the summer months, exhalations extremely fatal to the health of its inhabitants. For some months of the year, indeed, so deadly are the effects of the atmosphere, that the garrison is withdrawn, and most of the families retire from their houses to more genial spots, leaving the town as much deserted as if it had been visited by a pestilence. Yet, in spite of these precautions, agues and intermittent fevers abound here at all times. Nor is it wonderful that the case should be so; for independent of the vile air which the vicinity of so many putrid swamps occasions, this country is more liable than perhaps any other to sudden and severe changes of temperature. A night of keen frost sufficiently powerful to produce ice a quarter of an inch in thickness, frequently follows a day of intense heat; whilst heavy rains and bright sunshine often succeed each other several times in the course of a few hours. But these changes, as may be supposed, occur only during the winter; the summer being one continued series of intolerable heat and deadly fog.

Of all these circumstances the conductors of the present expedition were not ignorant. To reduce the forts which command the navigation of the river was regarded as a task too difficult to be attempted; and for any ships to pass without their reduction seemed impossible. Trusting, therefore, that the object of the enterprise was unknown to the Americans, Sir Alexander Cochrane and General Keane determined to effect a landing somewhere on the banks of the lake; and pushing directly on, to take possession of the town, before any effectual preparation could be made for its defence. With this view the troops were removed from the larger into the lighter vessels, and these, under convoy of such gun-brigs as the shallowness of the water would float, began on the 13th to enter Lake Borgne. But we had not proceeded far, when it was apparent that the Americans were well acquainted with our intentions, and ready to receive us. Five large cutters, armed with six heavy guns each, were seen at anchor in the distances: and as all endeavours to land, till these were captured, would have been useless, the transports and largest of the gun-brigs cast anchor, whilst the smaller craft gave chase to the enemy.

But these cutters were built purposely to act upon the lake. They accordingly set sail as soon as the English cruisers arrived within a certain distance, and running on, were quickly out of sight, leaving the pursuers fast aground. To permit them to remain in the hands of the enemy, however, would be fatal, because, as long as they commanded the navigation of the lake, no boats could venture to cross. It was therefore determined at all hazards, and at any expense, to take them; and since our lightest craft could not float where they sailed, a flotilla of launches and ships' barges was got ready for the purpose.

This flotilla consisted of fifty open boats; most of them armed with a carronade in the bow, and well manned with volunteers from the different ships of war. The command was given to Captain Lockier, a brave and skilful officer, who immediately pushed off; and about noon came in sight of the enemy, moored fore and aft, with broadsides pointing towards him. Having pulled a considerable distance, he resolved to refresh his men before he hurried them into action; and, accordingly, letting fall grapplings just beyond the reach of the enemy's guns, the crews of the different boats coolly ate their dinner.

As soon as that meal was finished, and an hour spent in resting, the boats again got ready to advance. But, unfortunately, a light breeze which had hitherto favoured them, now ceased to blow, and they were in consequence compelled to make way only with the oar. The tide also ran strong against them, at once increasing their labour and retarding their progress; but all these difficulties appeared trifling to British sailors; and, giving a hearty cheer, they moved steadily onward in one extended line.

It was not long before the enemy's guns opened upon them, and a tremendous shower of balls saluted their approach. Some boats were sunk, others disabled, and many men were killed and wounded; but the rest pulling with all their might, and occasionally returning the discharges from their carronades, succeeded, after an hour's labour, in closing with the Americans. The marines now began a deadly fire of musketry; whilst the seamen, sword in hand, sprang up the vessels' sides in spite of all opposition; and sabring every man that stood in their way, hauled down the American ensign, and hoisted the British flag in its place.

One cutter alone, which bore the commodore's broad pendant, was not so easily subdued. Having noted its pre-eminence, Captain Lockier directed his own boat against it; and happening to have placed himself in one of the lightest and fastest sailing barges in the flotilla, he found himself alongside of his enemy before any of the others were near enough to render him the smallest support. But nothing dismayed by odds so fearful, the gallant crew of this small bark, following their leader, instantly leaped on board the American. A desperate conflict ensued, in which Captain Lockier received several severe wounds; but after fighting from the bow to the stern, the enemy were at length overpowered; and other barges coming up to the assistance of their commander, the commodore's flag shared the same fate with the others.

Having destroyed all opposition in this quarter, the fleet again weighed anchor, and stood up the lake. But we had not been many hours under sail, when ship after ship ran aground: such as still floated were, therefore, crowded with the troops from those which could go no farther, till finally the lightest vessel stuck fast; and the boats were of necessity hoisted out, to carry us a distance of upwards of thirty miles. To be confined for so long a time as the prosecution of this voyage would require, in one posture, was of itself no very agreeable prospect; but the confinement was but a trifling misery when compared with that which arose from the change in the weather. Instead of a constant bracing frost, heavy rains, such as an inhabitant of England cannot dream of, and against which no cloak could furnish protection, began. In the midst of these were the troops embarked in their new and straitened transports, and each division, after an exposure of ten hours, landed upon a small desert spot of earth, called Pine Island, where it was determined to collect the whole army, previous to its crossing over to the main.

Than this spot it is scarcely possible to imagine any place more completely wretched. It was a swamp, containing a small space of firm ground at one end, and almost wholly unadorned with trees of any sort or description. There were, indeed, a few stinted firs upon the very edge of the water, but these were so diminutive in size as hardly to deserve a higher classification than among the meanest of shrubs. The interior was the resort of wild ducks and other water-fowl; and the pools and creeks with which it was intercepted abounded in dormant alligators.

Upon this miserable desert the army was assembled, without tents or huts, or any covering to shelter them from the inclemency of the weather; and in truth we may fairly affirm that our hardships had here their commencement. After having been exposed all day to a cold and pelting rain, we landed upon a barren island, incapable of furnishing even fuel enough to supply our fires. To add to our miseries, as night closed, the rain generally ceased, and severe frosts set in, which, congealing our wet clothes upon our bodies, left little animal warmth to keep the limbs in a state of activity; and the consequence was, that many of the wretched negroes, to whom frost and cold were altogether new, fell fast asleep, and perished before morning.

For provisions, again, we were entirely dependent upon the fleet. There were here no living creatures which would suffer themselves to be caught; even the water-fowl being so timorous that it was impossible to approach them within musket-shot. Salt meat and ship biscuit were, therefore, our food, moistened by a small allowance of rum; fare which, though no doubt very wholesome, was not such as to reconcile us to the cold and wet under which we suffered.

On the part of the navy, again, all these hardships were experienced in a four-fold degree. Night and day were boats pulling from the fleet to the island, and from the island to the fleet; for it was the 21st before all the troops were got on shore; and as there was little time to inquire into men's turns of labour, many seamen were four or five days continually at the oar. Thus they had not only to bear up against variety of temperature, but against hunger, fatigue, and want of sleep in addition; three as fearful burdens as can be laid upon the human frame. Yet in spite of all this, not a murmur nor a whisper of complaint could be heard throughout the whole expedition. No man appeared to regard the present, whilst every one looked forward to the future. From the General, down to the youngest drum-boy, a confident anticipation of success seemed to pervade all ranks; and in the hope of an ample reward in store for them, the toils and grievances of the moment were forgotten. Nor was this anticipation the mere offspring of an overweening confidence in themselves. Several Americans had already deserted, who entertained us with accounts of the alarm experienced at New Orleans. They assured us that there were not at present 5000 soldiers in the State; that the principal inhabitants had long ago left the place; that such as remained were ready to join us as soon as we should appear among them; and that, therefore, we might lay our account with a speedy and bloodless conquest. The same persons likewise dilated upon the wealth and importance of the town, upon the large quantities of Government stores there collected, and the rich booty which would reward its capture; subjects well calculated to tickle the fancy of invaders, and to make them unmindful of immediate afflictions, in the expectation of so great a recompense to come.

CHAPTER XIX.

It is well known that, at the period to which my narrative refers, an alliance, offensive and defensive, subsisted between the Government of Great Britain and the heads of as many Indian nations or tribes as felt the aggressions of the settlers upon their ancient territories, and were disposed to resent them. On this side of the continent our principal allies were the Chaktaws and Cherokees, two nations whom war and famine had reduced from a state of comparative majesty to the lowest ebb of feebleness and distress. Driven from hunting-ground to hunting-ground, and pursued like wild beasts wherever seen, they were now confined to a narrow tract of country, lying chiefly along the coasts of the gulf and the borders of the lakes which adjoin to it. For some time previous to the arrival of the expedition, the warriors of these tribes put themselves under the command of Colonel Nickolls, of the Royal Marines, and continued to harass the Americans by frequent incursions into the cultivated districts. It so happened, however, that, being persuaded to attempt the reduction of a fort situated upon Mobile Point, and being, as might be expected, repulsed with some loss, their confidence in their leader, and their dependence upon British aid, had begun of late to suffer a serious diminution. Though not very profitable as friends, their local position and desultory mode of warfare would have rendered them at this period exceedingly annoying to us as enemies; it was accordingly determined to dispatch an embassy to their settlements, for the purpose of restoring them to good humour, or at least discovering their intentions.

Whilst the troops were assembling upon Pine Island, a cutter, having proper officers on board, and carrying presents of clothing, arms, and rum, was dispatched upon this business. It reached its place of destination in safety, and the ambassadors found very little difficulty in bringing back the fickle Indians to their wonted reliance upon British support. Several of the chiefs and warriors, indeed, requested and obtained permission to visit our Admiral and General, and to follow the fortunes of our troops; and a very grotesque and singular appearance they presented as they stood upon the quarter-deck of the Tonnant. But the costume, habits, and customs of these savages have been too frequently and too accurately described elsewhere, to render any account of them on the present occasion desirable. It is sufficient to observe, that whilst they gazed upon everything around them with a look expressive of no astonishment whatever, they were themselves objects of eager curiosity to us; and that they bore our close inspection and somewhat uncourteous deportment with the most perfect philosophy. But to my tale.

The enemy's cutters having fallen into our hands, at an early hour on the morning of the 16th the disembarkation of the troops began. So deficient, however, was the fleet in boats and other small craft fit to navigate the lakes, that it was late on the evening of the 21st before the last division took up its ground upon Pine Island, and even then the inconveniences of our descent were but beginning. The troops had yet to be arranged in corps and brigades; to each of these its proportion of Commissaries, Purveyors, and Medical attendants, &c., &c., required to be allotted; and some attempt at establishing depôts of provisions and military stores behoved to be made. In adjusting these matters the whole of the 22nd was occupied, on which day the General likewise reviewed the whole of the army. This being ended, the force was next distributed into divisions, or corps; and the following is the order it assumed.

Instead of a light brigade, the General resolved to set apart three battalions as an advanced guard. The regiments nominated to that service were the 4th, the 85th Light Infantry, and the 95th Rifles; and he selected Colonel Thornton of the 85th, as an officer of talent and enterprise, to command them. Attached to this corps were a party of rocket-men, with two light three-pounders—a species of gun convenient enough, where celerity of movement is alone regarded, but of very little real utility in the field. The rest of the troops were arranged, as before, into two brigades. The first, composed of the 21st, 44th, and one black regiment, was intrusted to Colonel Brook; and the second, containing the 93rd and the other black corps, to Colonel Hamilton, of the 7th West India regiment. To each of these, a certain proportion of artillery and rockets was allotted: whilst the dragoons, who had brought their harness and other appointments on shore, remained as a sort of body-guard to the General, till they should provide themselves with horses.

The adjustment of these matters having occupied a considerable part of the 22nd, it was determined that all things should remain as they were till next morning. Boats, in the mean time, began to assemble from all quarters, supplies of ammunition were packed, so as to prevent the possibility of damage from moisture, and stores of various descriptions were got ready. But it appeared that, even now, many serious inconveniences must be endured, and obstacles surmounted, before the troops could reach the scene of action. In the first place, from Pine Island to that part of the main towards which prudence directed us to steer, was a distance of no less than 80 miles. This, of itself, was an obstacle, or at least an inconvenience, of no slight nature; for should the weather prove boisterous, open boats, heavily laden with soldiers, would stand little chance of escaping destruction in the course of so long a voyage. In the next place, and what was of infinitely greater importance, it was found that there were not, throughout the whole fleet, a sufficient number of boats to transport above one-third of the army at a time. But to land in divisions would expose our forces to be attacked in detail, by which means one party might be cut to pieces before the others could arrive to its support. The undertaking was, therefore, on the whole, extremely dangerous, and such as would have been probably abandoned by more timid leaders. Ours, however, were not so to be alarmed. They had entered upon a hazardous business, in whatever way it should be prosecuted; and since they could not work miracles, they resolved to lose no time in bringing their army into the field in the best manner which circumstances would permit.

With this view, the advance, consisting of 1600 men and two pieces of cannon, was next morning embarked. I have already stated that there is a small creek, called the Bayo de Catiline, which runs up from Lake Pontchartrain through the middle of an extensive morass, about ten miles below New Orleans. Towards this creek were the boats directed, and here it was resolved to effect a landing. When we set sail, the sky was dark and lowering, and before long a heavy rain began to fall. Continuing without intermission during the whole of the day, towards night, it, as usual, ceased, and was succeeded by a sharp frost; which, taking effect upon men thoroughly exposed, and already cramped by remaining so long in one posture, rendered our limbs completely powerless. Nor was there any means of dispelling the benumbing sensation, or effectually resisting the cold. Fires of charcoal, indeed, being lighted in the sterns of the boats, were permitted to burn as long as daylight lasted; but as soon as it grew dark, they were of necessity extinguished, lest the flame should be seen by row-boats from the shore, and an alarm be thus communicated. Our situation was, therefore, the reverse of agreeable; since even sleep was denied us, from the apprehension of fatal consequences.

Having remained in this uncomfortable state till midnight, the boats cast anchor and hoisted awnings. There was a small piquet of the enemy stationed at the entrance of the creek by which it was intended to effect our landing. This it was absolutely necessary to surprise; and whilst the rest lay at anchor, two or three fast-sailing barges were pushed on to execute the service. Nor did they experience much difficulty in accomplishing their object. Nothing, as it appeared, was less dreamt of by the Americans than an attack from this quarter, consequently no persons could be less on their guard than the party here stationed. The officer who conducted the force sent against them, found not so much as a single sentinel posted! but having landed his men at two places, above and below the hut which they inhabited, extended his ranks so as to surround it, and closing gradually in, took them all fast asleep, without noise or resistance.

When such time had been allowed as was deemed sufficient for the accomplishment of this undertaking, the flotilla again weighed anchor, and without waiting for intelligence of success, pursued their voyage. Hitherto we had been hurried along at a rapid rate by a fair breeze, which enabled us to carry canvas; but this now left us, and we made way only by rowing. Our progress was therefore considerably retarded, and the risk of discovery heightened by the noise which that labour necessarily occasions; but in spite of these obstacles, we reached the entrance of the creek by dawn; and about nine o'clock, were safely on shore.

The place where we landed was as wild as it is possible to imagine. Gaze where we might, nothing could be seen except one huge marsh covered with tall reeds; not a house nor a vestige of human industry could be discovered; and even of trees there were but a few growing upon the banks of the creek. Yet it was such a spot as, above all others, favoured our operations. No eye could watch us, or report our arrival to the American General. By remaining quietly among the reeds, we might effectually conceal ourselves from notice; because, from the appearance of all around, it was easy to perceive that the place which we occupied had been seldom, if ever before, marked with a human footstep. Concealment, however, was the thing of all others which we required; for be it remembered that there were now only sixteen hundred men on the mainland. The rest were still at Pine Island, where they must remain till the boats which had transported us should return for their conveyance, consequently many hours must elapse before this small corps could be either reinforced or supported. If, therefore, we had sought for a point where a descent might be made in secrecy and safety, we could not have found one better calculated for that purpose than the present; because it afforded every means of concealment to one part of our force, until the others should be able to come up.

For these reasons, it was confidently expected that no movement would be made previous to the arrival of the other brigades; but, in our expectations of quiet, we were deceived. The deserters who had come in, and accompanied us as guides, assured the General that he had only to show himself, when the whole district would submit. They repeated, that there were not five thousand men in arms throughout the State: that of these, not more than twelve hundred were regular soldiers, and that the whole force was at present several miles on the opposite side of the town, expecting an attack on that quarter, and apprehending no danger on this. These arguments, together with the nature of the ground on which we stood, so ill calculated for a proper distribution of troops in case of attack, and so well calculated to hide the movements of an army acquainted with all the passes and tracks which, for aught we knew, intersected the morass, induced our leader to push forward at once into the open country. As soon, therefore, as the advance was formed, and the boats had departed, we began our march, following an indistinct path along the edge of the ditch or canal. But it was not without many checks that we were able to proceed. Other ditches, similar to that whose course we pursued, frequently stopped us by running in a cross direction, and falling into it at right angles. These were too wide to be leaped, and too deep to be forded; consequently, on all such occasions, the troops were obliged to halt, till bridges were hastily constructed of such materials as could be procured, and thrown across.

Having advanced in this manner for several hours, we at length found ourselves approaching a more cultivated region. The marsh became gradually less and less continued, being intersected by wider spots of firm ground; the reeds gave place, by degrees, to wood, and the wood to inclosed fields. Upon these, however, nothing grew, harvest having long ago ended. They accordingly presented but a melancholy appearance, being covered with the stubble of sugar-cane, which resembled the reeds which we had just quitted, in everything except altitude. Nor as yet was any house or cottage to be seen. Though we knew, therefore, that human habitations could not be far off, it was impossible to guess where they lay, or how numerous they might prove; and as we could not tell whether our guides might not be deceiving us, and whether ambuscades might not be laid for our destruction as soon as we should arrive where troops could conveniently act, our march was insensibly conducted with increased caution and regularity.

But in a little while some groves of orange-trees presented themselves; on passing which two or three farm-houses appeared. Towards these, our advanced companies immediately hastened, with the hope of surprising the inhabitants, and preventing any alarm from being raised. Hurrying on at double-quick time, they surrounded the buildings, succeeded in securing the inmates, and capturing several horses; but becoming rather careless in watching their prisoners, one man contrived to effect his escape. Now, then, all hope of eluding observation might be laid aside. The rumour of our landing would, we knew, spread faster than we could march; and it only remained to make that rumour as terrible as possible.

With this view, the column was commanded to widen its files, and to present as formidable an appearance as could be assumed. Changing our order, in obedience to these directions, we marched, not in sections of eight or ten abreast, but in pairs, and thus contrived to cover with our small division as large a tract of ground as if we had mustered thrice our present numbers. Our steps were likewise quickened, that we might gain, if possible, some advantageous position, where we might be able to cope with any force that might attack us; and thus hastening on, we soon arrived at the main road which leads directly to New

Orleans. Turning to the right, we then advanced in the direction of that town for about a mile; when, having reached a spot where it was considered that we might encamp in comparative safety, our little column halted; the men piled their arms, and a regular bivouac was formed.

The country where we had now established ourselves, answered, in every respect, the description which I have already given of the neck of land on which New Orleans is built. It was a narrow plain of about a mile in width, bounded on one side by the Mississippi, and on the other by the marsh from which we had just emerged. Towards the open ground this marsh was covered with dwarf wood, having the semblance of a forest rather than of a swamp; but on trying the bottom, it was found that both characters were united, and that it was impossible for a man to make his way among the trees, so boggy was the soil upon which they grew. In no other quarter, however, was there a single hedge-row, or plantation of any kind; excepting a few apple and other fruit trees in the gardens of such houses as were scattered over the plain, the whole being laid out in large fields for the growth of sugar-cane, a plant which seems as abundant in this part of the world as in Jamaica.

Looking up towards the town, which we at this time faced, the marsh is upon your right, and the river upon your left. Close to the latter runs the main road, following the course of the stream all the way to New Orleans. Between the road and the water is thrown up a lofty and strong embankment, resembling the dykes in Holland, and meant to serve a similar purpose; by means of which the Mississippi is prevented from overflowing its banks, and the entire flat is preserved from inundation. But the attention of a stranger is irresistibly drawn away from every other object, to contemplate the magnificence of this noble river. Pouring along at the prodigious rate of four miles an hour, an immense body of water is spread out before you; measuring a full mile across, and nearly a hundred fathoms in depth. What this mighty stream must be near its mouth, I can hardly imagine, for we were here upwards of a hundred miles from the ocean.

Such was the general aspect of the country which we had entered;—our own position, again, was this. The three regiments turning off from the road into one extensive green field, formed three close columns within pistol-shot of the river. Upon our right, but so much in advance as to be of no service to us, was a large house, surrounded by about twenty wooden huts, probably intended for the accommodation of slaves. Towards this house there was a slight rise in the ground, and between it and the camp was a small pond of no great depth. As far to the rear again as the first was to the front, stood another house, inferior in point of appearance, and skirted by no outbuildings: this was also upon the right; and here General Keane, who accompanied us, fixed his head-quarters; but neither the one nor the other could be employed as a covering redoubt, the flank of the division extending, as it were, between them. A little way in advance, again, where the outposts were stationed, ran a dry ditch and a row of lofty palings; affording some cover to the front of our line, should it be formed diagonally with the main road. The left likewise was well secured by the river; but the right and the rear were wholly unprotected. Though in occupying this field, therefore, we might have looked very well had the country around us been friendly, it must be confessed that our situation hardly deserved the title of a military position.

CHAPTER XX.

NOON had just passed, when the word was given to halt, by which means every facility was afforded of posting the piquets with leisure and attention. Nor was this deemed enough to secure tranquillity: parties were sent out in all directions to reconnoitre, who returned with an account that no enemy nor any trace of an enemy could be discerned. The troops were accordingly suffered to light fires, and to make themselves comfortable; only their accoutrements were not taken off, and the arms were piled in such form as to be within reach at a moment's notice.

As soon as these agreeable orders were issued, the soldiers proceeded to obey them both in letter and in spirit. Tearing up a number of strong palings, large fires were lighted in a moment;

water was brought from the river, and provisions were cooked. But their bare rations did not content them. Spreading themselves over the country as far as a regard to safety would permit, they entered every house, and brought away quantities of hams, fowls, and wines of various descriptions; which being divided among them, all fared well, and none received too large a quantity. In this division of good things, they were not unmindful of their officers; for upon active warfare the officers are considered by the privates as comrades, to whom respect and obedience are due, rather than as masters.

It was now about three o'clock in the afternoon, and all had as yet remained quiet. The troops having finished their meal, lay stretched beside their fires, or refreshed themselves by bathing, for to-day the heat was such as to render this latter employment extremely agreeable, when suddenly a bugle from the advanced posts sounded the alarm, which was echoed back from all in the army. Starting up, we stood to our arms, and prepared for battle, the alarm being now succeeded by some firing; but we were scarcely in order, when intelligence arrived from the front that there was no danger, only a few horse having made their appearance, who were checked and put to flight at the first discharge. Upon this information, our wonted confidence returned, and we again betook ourselves to our former occupations, remarking that, as the Americans had never yet dared to attack, there was no great probability of their doing so on the present occasion.

In this manner the day passed without any further alarm; and darkness having set in, the fires were made to blaze with increased splendour, our evening meal was eaten, and we prepared to sleep. But about half-past seven o'clock, the attention of several individuals was drawn to a large vessel, which seemed to be stealing up the river till she came opposite to our camp; when her anchor was dropped, and her sails leisurely furled. At first we were doubtful whether she might not be one of our own cruisers which had passed the fort unobserved, and had arrived to render her assistance in our future operations. To satisfy this doubt, she was repeatedly hailed; but returning no answer, an alarm immediately spread through the bivouac, and all thought of sleep was laid aside. Several musket-shots were now fired at her with the design of exacting a reply, of which no notice was taken; till at length, having fastened all her sails, and swung her broadside towards us, we could distinctly hear some one cry out in a commanding voice, "Give them this for the honour of America." The words were instantly followed by the flashes of her guns, and a deadly shower of grape swept down numbers in the camp.

Against this destructive fire we had nothing whatever to oppose. The artillery which we had landed was too light to bring into competition with an adversary so powerful; and as she had anchored within a short distance of the opposite bank, no musketry could reach her with any precision or effect. A few rockets were discharged, which made a beautiful appearance in the air; but the rocket is at the best an uncertain weapon, and these deviated too far from their object to produce even terror amongst those against whom they were directed. Under these circumstances, as nothing could be done offensively, our sole object was to shelter the men as much as possible from the iron hail. With this view, they were commanded to leave the fires, and to hasten under the dyke. Thither all accordingly repaired, without much regard to order and regularity, and laying ourselves along wherever we could find room, we listened in painful silence to the pattering of grape-shot among our huts, and to the shrieks and groans of those who lay wounded beside them.

The night was now as dark as pitch, the moon being but young, and totally obscured with clouds. Our fires deserted by us, and beat about by the enemy's shot, began to burn red and dull, and, except when the flashes of those guns which played upon us cast a momentary glare, not an object could be distinguished at the distance of a yard. In this state we lay for nearly an hour, unable to move from our ground, or offer any opposition to those who kept us there; when a straggling fire of musketry called our attention towards the piquets, and warned us to prepare for a closer and more desperate struggle. As yet, however, it was uncertain from what cause this dropping fire arose. It might proceed from the sentinels, who, alarmed by the cannonade from the river, mistook every tree for an American; and till the real state of the case should be ascertained, it would be improper to expose the troops by moving any of them from the shelter which the bank afforded. But these doubts were not permitted to continue long in existence. The dropping fire having paused for a few moments, was succeeded by a fearful yell; and the heavens were illuminated on all sides by a semicircular blaze of musketry. It was now manifest that we were surrounded, and that by a very superior force; and that no alternative remained, except to surrender at discretion, or to beat back the assailants.

The first of these plans was never for an instant thought of; the second was immediately put into force. Rushing from under the bank, the 85th and 95th flew to support the piquets, whilst the 4th, stealing to the rear of the encampment, formed close column, and remained as a reserve. And now began a battle of which no language were competent to convey any distinct idea; because it was one to which the annals of modern warfare furnish no parallel. All order, all discipline were lost. Each officer, as he succeeded in collecting twenty or thirty men about him, plunged into the midst of the enemy's ranks, where it was fought hand to hand, bayonet to bayonet, and sabre to sabre.

I am well aware that he who speaks of his own deeds in the field of battle lies fairly open to the charge of seeking to make a hero of himself in the eyes of the public; and feeling this, it is not without reluctance that I proceed to recount the part which I myself took in the affair of this night. But, in truth, I must either play the egotist awhile, or leave the reader without any details at all; inasmuch as the darkness and general confusion effectually prevented me from observing how others, except my own immediate party, were employed.

Offering this as my apology for a line of conduct which I should otherwise blush to pursue, and premising that I did nothing, in my own person, which was not done by my comrades at least as effectually, I go on to relate as many of the particulars of this sanguinary conflict as came under the notice of my own senses.

My friend Grey and myself had been supplied by our soldiers with a couple of fowls taken from a neighbouring hen-roost, and a few bottles of excellent claret, borrowed from the cellar of one of the houses near. We had built ourselves a sort of hut, by piling together, in a conical form, a number of large stakes and broad rails torn up from one of the fences; and a bright wooden fire was blazing at the door of it. In the wantonness of triumph, too, we had lighted some six or eight wax-candles; a vast quantity of which had been found in the store-rooms of the châteaux hard by; and having done ample justice to our luxurious supper, we were sitting in great splendour and in high spirits at the entrance of our hut, when the alarm of the approaching schooner was communicated to us. With the sagacity of a veteran, Grey instantly guessed how matters stood: he was the first to hail the suspicious stranger; and on receiving no answer to his challenge, he was the first to fire a musket in the direction of her anchorage. But he had scarcely done so when she opened her broadside, causing the instantaneous abandonment of fires, viands, and mirth throughout the bivouac.

As we contrived to get our men tolerably well around us, Grey and myself were among the first who rushed forth to support the piquets and check the advance of the enemy upon the right. Passing as rapidly as might be through the ground of encampment amidst a shower of grape-shot from the vessel, we soon arrived at the pond; which being forded, we found ourselves in front of the farm-house of which I have already spoken as composing the head-quarters of General Keane. Here we were met by a few stragglers from the outposts, who reported that the advanced companies were all driven in, and that a numerous division of Americans was approaching. Having attached these fugitives to our little corps, we pushed on, and in a few seconds reached the lower extremity of a sloping stubble-field, at the other end of which we could discern a long line of men, but whether they were friends or foes the darkness would not permit us to determine. We called aloud for the purpose of satisfying our doubts; but the signal being disregarded, we advanced. A heavy fire of musketry instantly opened upon us; but so fearful was Grey of doing injury to our own troops, that he would not permit it to be returned. We accordingly pressed on, our men dropping by ones and twos on every side of us, till having arrived within twenty or thirty yards of the object of our curiosity, it became to me evident enough that we were in front of the enemy. But Grey's humane caution still prevailed; he was not convinced, and till he should be convinced it was but natural that he should not alter his plans. There chanced to be near the spot where we were standing a huge dung-heap, or rather a long solid stack of stubble, behind which we directed the men to take shelter whilst one of us should creep forward alone, for the purpose of more completely ascertaining a fact of which all except my brave and noble-minded comrade were satisfied. The event proved that my sight had not deceived me: I approached within sabre's length of the line; and having ascertained beyond the possibility of doubt that the line was composed of American soldiers, I returned to my friend and again urged him to charge. But there was an infatuation upon him that night for which I have ever been unable to account: he insisted that I must be mistaken; he spoke of the improbability which existed that any part of the enemy's army should have succeeded in taking up a position in rear of the station of one of our outposts, and he could not be persuaded that the troops now before him were not the 95th Rifle corps. At last it was agreed between us that we should separate; that Grey with one half of the party should remain where he was, whilst I with the other half should make a short détour to the right, and come down upon the flank of the line from whose fire we had suffered so severely. The plan was carried into immediate execution. Taking with me about a dozen or fourteen men, I quitted Grey, and we never met again.

How or when he fell I know not; but, judging from the spot and attitude in which I afterwards found his body, I conceive that my back could have been barely turned upon him when the fatal ball pierced his brain. He was as brave a soldier and as good a man as the British army can boast of; beloved by his brother officers and adored by his men. To me he was as a brother; nor have I ceased even now to feel, as often as the 23rd of December returns, that on that night a tie was broken than which the progress of human life will hardly furnish one more tender or more strong. But to my tale.

Leaving Grey—careless as he ever was in battle of his own person, and anxious as far as might be to secure the safety of his followers—I led my little party in the direction agreed upon, and fortunately falling in with about an equal number of English riflemen, I caused them to take post beside my own men, and turned up to the front. Springing over the paling, we found ourselves almost at once upon the left flank of the enemy; and we lost not a moment in attacking it. But one volley was poured in, and then bayonets, musket-butts, sabres, and even fists, came instantly into play. In the whole course of my military career I remember no scene at all resembling this. We fought with the savage ferocity of bull-dogs; and many a blade which till to-night had not drunk blood became in a few minutes crimsoned enough.

Such a contest could not in the nature of things be of very long continuance. The enemy, astonished at the vigour of our assault, soon began to waver, and their wavering was speedily converted into flight. Nor did we give them a moment's time to recover from their panic. With loud shouts we continued to press upon them; and amidst the most horrible din and desperate carnage drove them over the field and through the little village of huts, of which notice has already been taken as surrounding the mansion on our advanced right. Here we found a number of our own people prisoners, and under a guard of Americans. But the guard fled as we approached, and our countrymen catching up such weapons as came first to hand, joined in the pursuit.

In this spot I halted my party, increased by the late additions to the number of forty; among whom were two gallant young officers of the 95th. We had not yet been joined, as I expected to be joined, by Grey; and feeling that we were at least far enough in advance of our own line, we determined to attempt nothing further except to keep possession of the village should it be attacked. But whilst placing the men in convenient situations, another dark line was pointed out to us considerably to the left of our position. That we might ascertain at once of what troops it was composed, I left my brother officers to complete the arrangements which we had begun, and walking down the field, demanded in a loud voice to be informed who they were that kept post in so retired a situation. A voice from the throng made answer that they were Americans, and begged of me not to fire upon my friends. Willing to deceive them still further, I asked to what corps they belonged; the speaker replied that they were the second battalion of the first regiment, and inquired what had become of the first battalion. I told him that it was upon my right, and assuming a tone of authority, commanded him not to move from his present situation till I should join him with a party of which I was at the head.

The conversation ended here, and I returned to the village; when, communicating the result of my inquiries to my comrades, we formed our brave little band into line and determined to attack. The men were cautioned to preserve a strict silence, and not to fire a shot till orders were given; they observed these injunctions, and with fixed bayonets and cautious tread advanced along the field. As we drew near, I called aloud for the commanding officer of the second regiment to step forward, upon which an elderly man, armed with a heavy dragoon sabre, stepped out of the ranks. When he discovered by our dress that we were English, this redoubtable warrior lost all self-command; he resigned his sword to me without a murmur, and consented at once to believe that his battalion was surrounded, and that to offer any resistance would but occasion a needless loss of blood. Nor was he singular in these respects: his followers, placing implicit reliance in our assurances that they were hemmed in on every side by a very superior force, had actually begun to lay down their arms, and would have surrendered, in all probability, at discretion, but for the superior gallantry of one man. An American officer, whose sword I demanded, instead of giving it up as his commander had done, made a cut at my head, which with some difficulty I managed to ward off; and a few soldiers near him, catching ardour from his example, discharged their pieces among our troops. The sound of firing was no sooner heard than it became general, and as all hope of success by stratagem might now be laid aside, we were of necessity compelled to try the effect of violence. Again we rushed into the middle of the throng, and again was the contest that of man to man, in close and desperate strife; till a panic arising among the Americans, they dispersed in all directions and left us masters of the field.

In giving a detail so minute of my own adventures this night, I beg to repeat what has been stated already, that I have no wish whatever to persuade my readers that I was one whit more cool or more daring than my companions. Like them I was driven to depend, from first to last, upon my own energies; and I believe the energies of few men fail them when they are satisfied that on them alone they must depend. Nor was the case different with my comrades. Attacked unexpectedly, and in the dark,—surrounded, too, by a numerous enemy, and one who spoke the same language with ourselves,—it is not to be wondered at if the order and routine of civilised warfare were everywhere set at nought. Each man who felt disposed to command was obeyed by those who stood near him, without any question being asked as to his authority; and more feats of individual gallantry were performed in this single night than many regular campaigns might furnish an opportunity to perform.

The night was far spent, and the sound of firing had begun to wax faint, when, checking the ardour of our brave followers, we collected them once more together and fell back into the village. Here likewise considerable numbers from other detachments assembled, and here we learned that the Americans were repulsed on every side. The combat had been long and obstinately contested: it began at eight o'clock in the evening and continued till three in the morning—but the victory was ours. True, it was the reverse of a bloodless one, not fewer than two hundred and fifty of our best men having fallen in the struggle: but even at the expense of such a loss, we could not but account ourselves fortunate in escaping from the snare in which we had confessedly been taken.

To me, however, the announcement of the victory brought no rejoicing, for it was accompanied with the intelligence that my friend was among the killed. I well recollect the circumstances under which these sad news reached me. I was standing with a sword in each hand—my own and that of the officer who had surrendered to me, and, as the reader may imagine, in no bad humour with myself or with the brave fellows about me, when a brother officer stepping forward abruptly told the tale. It came upon me like a thunderbolt; and casting aside my trophy, I thought only of the loss which I had sustained. Regardless of every other matter I ran to the rear, and found Grey lying behind the dung-heap, motionless and cold. A little pool of blood which had coagulated under his head, pointed out the spot where the ball had entered, and the position of his limbs gave proof that he must have died without a struggle. I cannot pretend to describe what were then my sensations, but of whatever nature they might be, little time was given for their indulgence; for the bugle sounding the alarm, I was compelled to leave him as he lay, and to join my corps. Though the alarm proved to be a false one, it had the good effect of bringing all the troops together, by which means a regular line was now, for the first time since the commencement of the action, formed. In this order, having defiled considerably to the left, so as to command the highway, we stood in front of our bivouac till dawn began to appear; when, to avoid the fire of the schooner, we once more moved to the river's bank and lay down. Here, during the whole of the succeeding day, the troops were kept shivering in the cold frosty air, without fires, without provisions, and exhausted with fatigue; nor was it till the return of night that any attempt to extricate them from their comfortless situation could be made.

Whilst others were thus reposing, I stole away with two or three men for the purpose of performing the last sad act of affection which it was possible for me to perform to my friend Grey. As we had completely changed our ground, it was not possible for me at once to discover the spot where he lay; indeed I traversed a large portion of the field before I hit upon it. Whilst thus wandering over the arena of last night's contest, the most shocking and most disgusting spectacles everywhere met my eyes. I have frequently beheld a greater number of dead bodies within as narrow a compass, though these, to speak the truth, were numerous enough, but wounds more disfiguring or more horrible I certainly never witnessed. A man shot through the head or heart lies as if he were in a deep slumber; insomuch that when you gaze upon him you experience little else than pity. But of these, many had met their deaths from bayonet wounds, sabre cuts, or heavy blows from the butt ends of muskets; and the consequence was, that not only were the wounds themselves exceedingly frightful, but the very countenances of the dead exhibited the most savage and ghastly expressions. Friends and foes lay together in small groups of four or six, nor was it difficult to tell almost the very hand by which some of them had fallen. Nay, such had been the deadly closeness of the strife, that in one or two places an English and American soldier might be seen with the bayonet of each fastened in the other's body.

Having searched for some time in vain, I at length discovered my friend lying where during the action we had separated, and where, when the action came to a close, I had at first found him, shot through the temples by a rifle bullet so remarkably small as scarcely to leave any trace of its progress. I am well aware that this is no fit place to introduce the working of my own personal feelings, but he was my friend, and such a friend as few men are happy enough to possess. We had known and loved each other for years; our regard had been cemented by a long participation in the same hardships and dangers, and it cannot therefore surprise, if even now I pay that tribute to his worth and our friendship which, however unavailing it may be, they both deserve.

When in the act of looking for him I had flattered myself that I should be able to bear his loss with something like philosophy, but when I beheld him pale and bloody, I found all my resolution evaporate. I threw myself on the ground beside him and wept like a child. But this was no time for the indulgence of useless sorrow. Like the royal bard, I knew that I should go to him, but he could not return to me, and I knew not whether an hour would pass before my summons might arrive. Lifting him therefore upon a cart, I had him carried down to head-quarter house, now converted into an hospital, and having dug for him a grave at the bottom of the garden, I laid him there as a soldier should be laid, arrayed, not in a shroud, but in his uniform. Even the privates whom I brought with me to assist at his funeral mingled their tears with mine, nor are many so fortunate as to return to the parent dust more deeply or more sincerely lamented.

Retiring from the performance of this melancholy duty, I strolled into the hospital and visited the wounded. It is here that war loses its grandeur and show, and presents only a real picture of its effects. Every room in the house was crowded with wretches mangled, and apparently in the most excruciating agonies. Prayers, groans, and, I grieve to add, the most horrid exclamations, smote upon the ear wherever I turned. Some lay at length upon straw, with eyes half closed and limbs motionless; some endeavoured to start up, shrieking with pain, while the wandering eye and incoherent speech of others indicated the loss of reason, and usually foretold the approach of death. But there was one among the rest whose appearance was too horrible ever to be forgotten. He had been shot through the windpipe, and the breath making its way between the skin and the flesh had dilated him to a size absolutely terrific. His head and face were particularly shocking. Every feature was enlarged beyond what can well be imagined; whilst his eyes were so completely hidden by the cheeks and forehead as to destroy all resemblance to a human countenance.

Passing through the apartments where the private soldiers lay, I next came to those occupied by officers. Of these there were five or six in one small room, to whom little better accommoda-tion could be provided than to their inferiors. It was a sight peculiarly distressing, because all of them chanced to be personal acquaintances of my own. One had been shot in the head, and lay gasping and insensible; another had received a musket-ball in the belly, which had pierced through and lodged in the back-bone. The former appeared to suffer but little, giving no signs of life, except what a heavy breathing produced; the latter was in the most dreadful agony, screaming out, and gnawing the covering under which he lay. There were many besides these, some severely and others slightly hurt; but as I have already dwelt at sufficient length upon a painful subject, I shall only observe, that to all was afforded every assistance which circum-stances would allow, and that the exertions of their medical attendants were such as deserved and obtained the grateful thanks of even the most afflicted among the sufferers themselves.

CHAPTER XXI.

In the mean time the rest of the troops were landing as fast as possible, and hastening to join their comrades. Though the advance had set out from Pine Island by themselves, they did not occupy all the boats in the fleet. Part of the second brigade, therefore, had embarked about twelve hours after their departure; and rowing leisurely on, were considerably more than half way across the lakes when the action began. In the stillness of night, however, it is astonishing at what distance a noise is heard.

Though they must have been at least twenty miles from the Bayo when the schooner first opened her fire, the sound reaching them roused the rowers from their indolence, who, pulling with all their might, hurried on, whilst the most profound silence reigned among the troops, and, gaining the creek in little more than three hours, sent fresh reinforcements to share in the danger and glory of the night.

Nor was a moment lost by the sailors in returning to the island. Intelligence of the combat spread like wildfire; the boats were loaded even beyond what was strictly safe, and thus, by exerting themselves in a degree almost unparalleled, our gallant seamen succeeded in bringing the whole army into position before dark on the 24th. The second and third brigades, therefore, now took up their ground upon the spot where the late battle had been fought, and, resting their right upon the woody morass, extended so far towards the river, as that the advance by wheeling up might continue the line across the entire plain.

But instead of taking part in this formation, the advance was still fettered to the bank, from which it was additionally prevented from moving by the arrival of another large ship, which cast anchor about a mile above the schooner. Thus were three battalions kept stationary by the guns of these two formidable floating batteries, and it was clear that no attempt to extricate them could be made without great loss, unless under cover of night. During the whole of the 24th, therefore, they remained in this uncomfortable situation; but as soon as darkness had well set in, a change of position was effected. Withdrawing the troops, company by company, from behind the bank, General Keane stationed them in the village of huts, by which means the high road was abandoned to the protection of a piquet, and the left of the army covered by a large château.

Being now placed beyond risk of serious annoyance from the shipping, the whole army remained quiet for the night. How long we were to continue in this state nobody appeared to know; not a whisper was circulated as to the time of advancing, nor a surmise ventured respecting the next step likely to be taken. In our guides, to whose rumours we had before listened with avidity, no further confidence was reposed. It was quite evident, either that they had purposely deceived us, or that their information was gathered from a most imperfect source; and hence, though they were not exactly placed in confinement, they were strictly watched, and treated more like spies than deserters. Instead of an easy conquest, we had already met with a vigorous opposition; instead of finding the inhabitants ready and eager to join us, we found the houses deserted, the cattle and horses driven away, and every appearance of hostility. To march by the only road was rendered impracticable, so completely was it commanded by the shipping. In a word, all things had turned out diametrically opposite to what had been anticipated; and it appeared that, instead of a trifling affair more likely to fill our pockets than to add to our renown, we had embarked in an undertaking which presented difficulties not to be surmounted without patience and determination.

Having effected this change of position, and covered the front of his army with a strong chain of outposts, General Keane, as I have said, remained quiet during the remainder of the night, and on the morrow was relieved from further care and responsibility by the unexpected arrival of Sir Edward Pakenham and General Gibbs. As soon as the death of Ross was known in London, the former of these officers was dispatched to take upon himself the command of the army. Sailing immediately with the latter as his second in command, he had been favoured during the whole voyage by a fresh and fair wind, and now arrived in time to see his troops brought into a predicament from which all his abilities could scarcely expect to extricate them. Nor were the troops themselves ignorant of the unfavourable circumstances in which they stood. Hoping everything, therefore, from a change, they greeted their new leader with a hearty cheer; whilst the confidence which past events had tended in some degree to dispel, returned once more to the bosoms of all. It was Christmas-day, and a number of officers, clubbing their little stock of provisions, resolved to dine together in memory of former times. But at so melancholy a Christmas dinner I do not recollect at any time to have been present. We dined in a barn; of plates, knives, and forks, there was a dismal scarcity; nor could our fare boast of much either in intrinsic good quality or in the way of cooking. These, however, were mere matters of merriment; it was the want of many well-known and beloved faces that gave us pain; nor were any other subjects discussed besides the amiable qualities of those who no longer formed part of our mess, and never would again form part of it. A few guesses as to the probable success of future attempts alone relieved this topic, and now and then a shot from the schooner drew our attention to ourselves; for though too far removed from the river to be in much danger, we were still within cannon-shot of our enemy. Nor was she inactive in her attempts to molest. Elevating her guns to a great degree, she contrived occasionally to strike the wall of the building within which we sat; but the force of the ball was too far spent to penetrate, and could therefore produce no serious alarm.

Whilst we were thus sitting at table a loud shriek was heard after one of these explosions, and on running out we found that a shot had taken effect in the body of an unfortunate soldier. I mention this incident because I never beheld in any human being so great a tenacity of life. Though fairly cut in two at the lower part of the belly, the poor wretch lived for nearly an hour, gasping for breath and giving signs even of pain.

But to return to my narrative. As soon as he reached the camp, Sir Edward proceeded to examine with a soldier's eye every point and place within view. Of the American army nothing whatever could be perceived except a corps of observation, composed of five or six hundred mounted riflemen, which hovered along our front and watched our motions. The town itself was completely hid; nor was it possible to see beyond the distance of a very few miles either in front or rear, so flat and unbroken was the face of the country. Under these circumstances little insight into the state of affairs could be obtained by reconnoitring. The only thing, indeed, which he could learn from it was, that while the vessels kept their present station upon the river no advance could be made; and as he felt that every moment's delay was injurious to us and favourable to the enemy, he resolved to remove these incumbrances and to push forward as soon as possible.

With this view nine field-pieces, two howitzers, and one mortar were brought down to the brink of the stream as soon as it was dark. Working parties were likewise ordered out, by whom a battery was thrown up opposite to the schooner; and having got all things in readiness, at dawn on the 26th a heavy cannonade was opened upon her with red-hot shot. It was not long before we could perceive her crew hastening into their boats, whilst the smoke which began to rise from her decks proved that the balls had taken effect. She was, in fact, on fire, and being abandoned without resistance, in little more than an hour she blew up. In itself the sight was a fine one, but to us it was peculiarly gratifying, for we could not but experience something like satiated revenge at the destruction of a vessel from which we had suffered so much damage. A loud shout accordingly followed the explosion, and the guns were immediately turned against the ship. But the fate of her companion had warned her not to remain till she herself should be attacked. Setting every inch of canvas, and hoisting out her boats, she began to stem the stream at the very instant the schooner took fire, and being impelled forward both by towing and sailing, she succeeded in getting beyond the range of shot before the guns could be brought to bear. One shell, however, was thrown with admirable precision, which falling upon her deck caused considerable execution; but excepting this, she escaped without injury, and did not anchor again till she had got too far for pursuit.

Having thus removed all apparent obstacles to his future progress, the General made dispositions for a speedy advance. Dividing the army into two columns, he appointed General Gibbs to the command of one, and General Keane to the command of the other. The left column, led on by the latter officer, consisted of the 95th, the 85th, the 93rd, and one black corps; the right, of the 4th, 21st, 44th, and the other black corps. The artillery, of which we had now ten pieces in the field, though at present attached to the left column, was designed to act as circumstances and the nature of the ground would permit; whilst the dragoons, few of whom had as yet provided themselves with horses, were appointed to guard the hospitals, and to secure the wounded from any sudden surprise or molestation from the rear.

But the day was too far spent in making these arrangements, and in clearing the way for future operations, to permit any movement before the morrow. The whole of the 26th was therefore spent in bringing up stores, ammunition, and a few heavy guns from the ships, which being placed in battery upon the banks of the river, secured us against the return of our floating adversary. All this was done quietly enough, nor was there any cause of alarm till after sunset; but from that time till towards dawn, we were kept in a constant state of anxiety and agitation. Sending down small bodies of riflemen, the American General harassed our piquets, killed and wounded a few of the sentinels, and prevented the main body from obtaining any sound or refreshing sleep. Scarcely had the troops lain down when they were roused by a sharp firing at the outposts, which lasted only till they were in order, and then ceased; but as soon as they had dispersed and had once more addressed themselves to repose, the same cause of alarm returned, and they were again called to their ranks. Thus was the entire night spent in watching, or at best in broken and disturbed slumbers, than which nothing is more trying, both to the health and spirits of an army.

With the piquets, again, it fared even worse. For the outposts of an army to sleep is at all times considered as a thing impossible; but in modern and civilized warfare they are nevertheless looked upon as in some degree sacred. Thus, whilst two European armies remain inactively facing each other, the outposts of neither are molested, unless a direct attack upon the main body be intended; nay, so far is this tacit good understanding carried, that I have myself seen French and English sentinels not more than twenty yards apart. But the Americans entertained no such chivalric notions. An enemy was to them an enemy, whether alone or in the midst of five thousand companions; and they therefore counted the death of every individual as so much taken from the strength of the whole. In point of fact they no doubt reasoned correctly, but to us at least it appeared an ungenerous return to barbarity. Whenever they could approach unperceived within proper distance of our watch-fires, six or eight riflemen would fire amongst the party that sat round them, while one or two, stealing as close to each sentinel as a regard to their own safety would permit, acted the part of assassins rather than that of soldiers, and attempted to murder him in cold blood. For the officers, likewise, when going their rounds, they constantly lay in wait, and thus, by a continued dropping fire, they not only wounded some of those against whom their aim was directed, but occasioned considerable anxiety and uneasiness throughout the whole line.

It was on this night, and under these circumstances, that I was indebted to the vigilance of my faithful dog for my life. Amid all the bustle of landing, and throughout the tumult of the nocturnal battle, she never strayed from me; at least if she did lose me for a time, she failed not to trace me out again as soon as order was restored, for I found her by my side when the dawn of the 24th came in, and I never lost sight of her afterwards. It was my fortune on the night of the 26th to be put in charge of an outpost on the left front of the army; on such occasions I seldom experienced the slightest inclination to sleep; and on the present, I made it a point to visit my sentinels at least once in every half-hour. Going my rounds for this purpose, it was necessary that I should pass a little copse of low underwood, just outside the line of our videttes; and I did pass it again and again, without meeting with any adventure. But about an hour after midnight, my dog, which, as usual, trotted a few paces before me, suddenly stopped short at the edge of the thicket, and began to bark violently, and in great apparent anger. I knew the animal well enough to be aware that some cause must exist for such conduct; and I too stopped short, till I should ascertain whether danger were near. It was well for me that I had been thus warned; for at the instant of my halting, about half a dozen muskets were discharged from the copse, the muzzles of which, had I taken five steps forward, must have touched my body. The balls whizzed harmlessly past my head; and, on my returning the fire with the pistol which I carried in my hand, the ambuscade broke up, and the party composing it took to their heels. I was Quixote enough to dash sword in hand into the thicket after them: but no one waited for me; so I continued my perambulations in peace.

Having continued this detestable system of warfare till towards morning, the enemy retired and left us at rest. But as soon as day began to break, our piquets were called in, and the troops formed in order of attack. The right column, under General Gibbs, took post near the skirts of the morass, throwing out skirmishers half way across the plain, whilst the left column drew up upon the road covered by the rifle corps, which in extended order met the skirmishers from the other. With this last division went the artillery, already well supplied with horses; and, at the signal given, the whole moved forward.

It was a clear frosty morning, the mists had dispersed, and the sun shone brightly upon our arms when we began our march. The enemy's corps of observation fell back as we advanced, without offering in any way to impede our progress, and it was impossible to guess, ignorant as we were of the position of his main body, at what moment opposition might be expected. Nor, in truth, was it matter of much anxiety. Our spirits, in spite of the troubles of the night, were good, and our expectations of success were high, consequently many rude jests were bandied about, and many careless words spoken: for soldiers are, of all classes of men, the freest from care, and on that account, perhaps, the most happy. By being continually exposed to it, danger, with them, ceases to be frightful; of death they have no more terror than the beasts that perish; and even hardships, such as cold, wet, hunger, and broken rest, lose at least part of their disagreeableness, by the frequency of their recurrence.

Moving on in this merry mood, we advanced about four or five miles without the smallest check or hindrance; when, at length, we found ourselves in view of the enemy's army, posted in a very advantageous manner. About forty yards in their front was a canal, which extended from the morass to within a short distance of the high road. Along their line were thrown up breastworks, not indeed completed, but even now formidable. Upon the road and at several other points were erected powerful batteries; whilst the ship, with a large flotilla of gun-boats, flanked the whole position from the river.

When I say that we came in sight of the enemy, I do not mean that he was gradually exposed to us in such a manner as to leave time for cool examination and reflection. On the right, indeed, he was seen for some time, but on the left a few houses built at a turning in the road entirely concealed him; nor was it till they had gained that turning, and beheld the muzzles of his guns pointed towards them, that those who moved in this direction were aware of their proximity to danger. But that danger was indeed near they were quickly taught; for scarcely had the head of the column passed the houses when a deadly fire was opened from both the battery and the shipping. That the Americans are excellent marksmen, as well with artillery as with rifles, we have had frequent cause to acknowledge; but, perhaps, on no occasion did they assert their claim to the title of good artillery-men more effectually than on the present. Scarce a ball passed over or fell short of its mark, but all striking full into the midst of our ranks, occasioned terrible havoc. The shrieks of the wounded, therefore, the crash of firelocks, and the fall of such as were killed, caused at first some little confusion; and what added to the panic was, that from the houses beside which we stood bright flames suddenly burst out. The Americans, expecting this attack, had filled them with combustibles for the purpose; and directing against them one or two guns, loaded with red-hot shot, in an instant set them on fire. The scene was altogether very sublime. A tremendous cannonade mowed down our ranks, and deafened us with its roar; whilst two large châteaux and their outbuildings almost scorched us with the flames, and blinded us with the smoke which they emitted.

The infantry, however, was not long suffered to remain thus exposed; but being ordered to quit the path and to form line in the fields, the artillery was brought up, and opposed to that of the enemy. But the contest was in every respect unequal, since their artillery far exceeded ours, both in numerical strength and weight of metal. The consequence was, that in half an hour two of our field-pieces and one field-mortar were dismounted: many of the gunners were killed; and the rest, after an ineffectual attempt to silence the fire of the shipping, were obliged to retire.

In the mean time the infantry having formed line, advanced under a heavy discharge of round and grape shot, till they were checked by the appearance of the canal. Of its depth they were of course ignorant, and to attempt its passage without having ascertained whether it could be forded might have been productive of fatal consequences. A halt was accordingly ordered, and the men were commanded to shelter themselves as well as they could from the enemy's fire. For this purpose they were hurried into a wet ditch, of sufficient depth to cover the knees, where, leaning forward, they concealed themselves behind some high rushes which grew upon its brink, and thus escaped many bullets which fell around them in all directions.

Thus fared it with the left of the army, whilst the right, though less exposed to the cannonade, was not more successful in its object. The same impediment which checked one column forced the other likewise to pause; and after having driven in an advanced body of the enemy, and endeavoured, without effect, to penetrate through the marsh, it also was commanded to halt. In a word, all thought of attacking was for this day abandoned; and it now only remained to withdraw the troops from their present perilous situation, with as little loss as possible.

The first thing to be done was to remove the dismounted guns. Upon this enterprise a party of seamen were employed, who, running forward to the spot where they lay, lifted them, in spite of the whole of the enemy's fire, and bore them off in triumph. As soon as this was effected, regiment after regiment stole away; not in a body, but one by one, under the same discharge which saluted their approach. But a retreat thus conducted necessarily occupied much time. Noon had therefore long passed before the last corps was brought off; and when we again began to muster twilight was approaching. We did not, however, retire to our former position; but having fallen back only about two miles from the canal, where it was supposed that we should be beyond reach of annoyance from the American artillery, we there established ourselves for the night, having suffered less during the day than, from our exposed situation and the enemy's heavy fire, might have been expected.

The ground which we now occupied resembled, in almost every particular, that which we had quitted. We again extended across the plain, from the marsh to the river; no wood or cover of any description concealing our line, or obstructing the view of either army; while both in front and rear was an open space, laid out in fields and intersected by narrow ditches. Our outposts, however, were pushed forward to some houses within a few hundred yards of the enemy's works, sending out advanced sentinels even farther; and the head-quarters of the army were established near the spot where the action of the 23rd had been fought.

In this state we remained during the 28th, the 29th, and 30th, without any efforts being made to fortify our own position, or to annoy that of the enemy. Some attempts were, I believe, set on foot to penetrate into the wood on the right of our line, and to discover a path through the morass, by which the enemy's left might be turned. But all of these proved fruitless, and a few valuable lives having been sacrificed, the idea was finally laid aside. In the meanwhile the American General directed the whole of his attention to the strengthening of his post. Day and night we could observe numerous parties at work upon his lines, whilst from the increased number of tents, which almost every hour might be discerned, it was evident that strong reinforcements were continually pouring into his camp. Nor did he leave us totally unmolested. By giving to his guns a great degree of elevation, he contrived at last to reach our bivouac; and thus were we constantly under a cannonade which, though it did little execution, proved nevertheless extremely annoying. Besides this, he now began to erect batteries on the opposite bank of the river; from which a flanking fire could be thrown across the entire front of his position. In short, he adopted every precaution which prudence could suggest, and for the reception of which the nature of his ground was so admirably adapted.

Under these circumstances it was evident that the longer an attack was delayed the less likely was it to succeed; that something must be done immediately every one perceived, but how to proceed was the difficulty. If we attempted to storm the American lines, we should expose ourselves to almost certain destruction from their artillery; to turn them was impossible; and to draw their troops by any manœuvring from behind their entrenchments was a thing altogether out of the question. There seemed therefore to be but one practicable mode of assault; which was, to treat these field-works as one would treat a regular fortification; by erecting breaching batteries against them, and silencing, if it were possible, at least some of their guns. To this plan, therefore, our leader had recourse; and, in consequence, the whole of these three days were employed in landing heavy cannon, bringing up ammunition, and making such preparations as might have sufficed for a siege.

At length, having completed his arrangements, and provided such means as were considered sufficient to ensure success, General Pakenham determined to commence operations without delay. One half of the army was accordingly ordered out on the night of the 31st, and marched to the front, passing the piquets, and halting about three hundred yards from the enemy's line. Here it was resolved to throw up a chain of works; and here the greater part of this detachment, laying down their firelocks, applied themselves vigorously to their tasks, whilst the rest stood armed and prepared for their defence.

The night was dark, and our people maintained a profound silence; by which means, not an idea of what was going on existed in the American camp. As we laboured, too, with all diligence, six batteries were completed long before dawn, in which were mounted thirty pieces of heavy cannon; when, falling back a little way, we united ourselves to the remainder of the infantry, and lay down behind some rushes, in readiness to act, as soon as we should be wanted.

In the erection of these batteries, a circumstance occurred worthy of notice, on account of its singularity. I have already stated that the whole of this district was covered with the stubble of sugar-cane; and I might have added, that every storehouse and barn, attached to the different mansions scattered over it, was filled with barrels of sugar. In throwing up these works, the sugar was used instead of earth. Rolling the hogsheads towards the front, they were placed upright in the parapets of the batteries; and it was computed that sugar to the value of many thousand pounds sterling was thus disposed of.

CHAPTER XXII.

THE infantry having retired, and the gunners taken their station, dawn was anxiously expected. But the morning of the 1st of January chanced to be peculiarly gloomy. A thick haze obscured for a long time the rays of the sun, nor could objects be discerned with any accuracy till a late hour.

But at length the mist gave way, and the American camp was fully exposed to view. Being at this time only three hundred yards distant, we could perceive all that was going forward with great exactness. The different regiments were upon parade; and being dressed in holiday suits, presented really a fine appearance. Mounted officers were riding backwards and forwards through the ranks, bands were playing, and colours floating in the air; in a word, all seemed jollity and gala; when suddenly our batteries opened, and the face of affairs was instantly changed. The ranks were broken; the different corps dispersing, fled in all directions, whilst the utmost terror and disorder appeared to prevail. Instead of nicely-dressed lines, nothing but confused crowds could now be observed; nor was it without much difficulty that order was finally restored. Oh, that we had charged at that instant!

Whilst this consternation prevailed among the infantry, their artillery remained silent; but as soon as the former rallied, they also recovered confidence, and answered our salute with great rapidity and precision. A heavy cannonade quickly commenced on both sides, and continued during the whole of the day; till, towards evening, our ammunition began to fail, and our fire in consequence to slacken. The fire of the Americans, on the other hand, was redoubled: landing a number of guns from the flotilla, they increased their artillery to a prodigious amount; and directing at the same time the whole force of their cannon on the opposite bank against the flank of our batteries, they soon convinced us that all endeavours to surpass them in this mode of fighting would be useless. Once more, therefore, were we obliged to retire, leaving our heavy guns to their fate; but as no attempt was made by the Americans to secure them, working parties were again sent out after dark, and such as had not been destroyed were removed.

Of the fatigue undergone during these operations by the whole army, from the General down to the meanest sentinel, it would be difficult to form an adequate conception. For two whole nights and days not a man had closed an eye, except such as were cool enough to sleep amidst showers of cannon-ball; and during the day scarcely a moment had been allowed in which we were able so much as to break our fast. We retired, therefore, not only baffled and disappointed, but in some degree disheartened and discontented. All our plans had as yet proved abortive; even this, upon which so much reliance had been placed, was found to be of no avail; and it must be confessed that something like murmuring began to be heard through the camp. And, in truth, if ever an army might be permitted to murmur, it was this. In landing they had borne great hardships, not only without repining, but with cheerfulness; their hopes had been excited by false reports, as to the practicability of the attempt in which they were embarked; and now they found themselves entangled amidst difficulties from which there appeared to be no escape, except by victory. In their attempts upon the enemy's line, however, they had been twice foiled; in artillery they perceived themselves to be so greatly overmatched, that their own could hardly assist them; their provisions, being derived wholly from the fleet, were both scanty and coarse; and their rest was continually broken. For not only did the cannon and mortars from the main of the enemy's position play unremittingly upon them both by day and night, but they were likewise exposed to a deadly fire from the opposite bank of the river, where no less than eighteen pieces of artillery were now mounted, and swept the entire line of our encampment. Besides all this, to undertake the duty of a piquet was as dangerous as to go into action. Parties of American sharpshooters harassed and disturbed those appointed to that service from the time they took possession of their post till they were relieved; whilst to light fires at night was impossible, because they served but as certain marks for the enemy's gunners. I repeat, therefore, that a little murmuring could not be wondered at. Be it observed, however, that these were not the murmurs of men anxious to escape from a disagreeable situation by any means. On the contrary, they resembled rather the growling of a chained dog, when he sees his adversary and cannot reach him; for in all their complaints, no man ever hinted at a retreat, whilst all were eager to bring matters to the issue of a battle, at any sacrifice of lives.

Nor was our gallant leader less anxious to fight than his followers. To fight upon something like equal terms was, however, his wish; and for this purpose a new scheme was invented, worthy, for its boldness, of the school in which Sir Edward had studied his profession. It was determined to divide the army, to send part across the river, who should seize the enemy's guns, and turn them on themselves; whilst the remainder should at the same time make a general assault along the whole entrenchment. But before this plan could be put into execution, it would be necessary to cut a canal across the entire neck of land from the Bayo de Catiline to the river, of sufficient width and depth to admit of boats being brought up from the lake. Upon this arduous undertaking were the troops immediately employed. Being divided into four companies, they laboured by turns, day and night; one party relieving another after a stated number of hours, in such order as that the work should never be entirely deserted. The fatigue undergone during the prosecution of this attempt no words can sufficiently describe; yet it was pursued without repining, and at length, by unremitting exertions, they succeeded in effecting their purpose by the 6th of January.

Whilst these things were going on, and men's minds were anxiously turned towards approaching events, fresh spirit was given to the army by the unexpected arrival of Major-General Lambert, with the 7th and 43rd; two fine battalions, mustering each 800 effective men. By this reinforcement, together with the addition of a body of sailors and marines from the fleet, our numbers amounted now to little short of 6000 men; a force which, in almost any other quarter of America, would have been irresistible. Of the numbers of the enemy, again, various reports were in circulation; some stating them at 20,000, others at 30,000; but I believe that I come nearer the truth when I suppose their whole force to have comprised 12,000 men of all arms. It is, at least, certain that they exceeded us in numbers as much as they did in resources; and that scarcely an hour passed which did not bring in new levies to their camp.

The canal, as I have stated, being finished on the 6th, it was resolved to lose no time in making use of it. Boats were accordingly ordered up for the transportation of 1400 men; and Colonel Thornton, with the 85th regiment, the marines, and a party of sailors, was appointed to cross the river. But a number of untoward accidents occurred, to spoil a plan of operations as accurately laid down as any in the course of the war. The soil through which the canal was dug being soft, part of the bank gave way, and, choking up the channel, prevented the heaviest of the boats from getting forward. These again blocked up the passage, so that none of those which were behind could proceed; and thus, instead of a flotilla for the accommodation of 1400 men, only a number of boats sufficient to contain 350 was enabled to reach their destination. Even these did not arrive at the time appointed. According to the preconcerted plan, Colonel Thornton's detachment was to cross the river immediately after dark. They were to push forward, so as to carry all the batteries, and point the guns before daylight; when, on the throwing up of a rocket, they were to commence firing upon the enemy's line, which at the same moment was to be attacked by the main of our army.

In this manner was one part of the force to act, whilst the rest were thus appointed:—Dividing his troops into three columns, Sir Edward directed that General Keane, at the head of the 95th, the light companies of the 21st, 4th, and 44th, together with the two black corps, should make a demonstration, or sham attack, upon the right; that General Gibbs, with the 4th, 21st, 44th, and 93rd, should force the enemy's left, whilst General Lambert, with the 7th and 43rd, remained in reserve, ready to act as circumstances might require. But in storming an entrenched position, something more than bare courage is required. Scaling ladders and fascines had, therefore, been prepared, with which to fill up the ditch and mount the wall; and since to carry these was a service of danger, requiring a corps well worthy of dependence, the 44th was for that purpose selected, as a regiment of sufficient numerical strength, and already accustomed to American warfare. Thus were all things arranged on the night of the 7th, for the 8th was fixed upon as the day decisive of the fate of New Orleans.

Whilst the rest of the army lay down to sleep till they should be roused up to fight, Colonel Thornton, with the 85th, and a corps of marines and seamen, amounting in all to 1400 men, moved down to the brink of the river. As yet, however, no boats had arrived; hour after hour elapsed before they came; and when they did come, the misfortunes which I have stated above were discovered, for out of all that had been ordered up, only a few made their appearance. Still it was absolutely necessary that this part of the plan should be carried into execution. Dismissing, therefore, the rest of his followers, the Colonel put himself at the head of his own regiment, about fifty seamen, and as many marines, and with this small force, consisting of on more than 340 men, pushed off. But, unfortunately, the loss of time nothing could repair. Instead of reaching the opposite bank at latest by midnight, dawn was beginning to appear before the boats quitted the canal. It was in vain that they rowed on in perfect silence, and with oars muffled, gaining the point of debarkation without being perceived. It was in vain that they made good their landing and formed upon the beach, without opposition or alarm; day had already broke, and the signal-rocket was seen in the air, while they were yet four miles from the batteries, which ought hours ago to have been taken.

In the mean time, the main body armed and moved forward some way in front of the piquets. There they stood waiting for daylight, and listening with the greatest anxiety for the firing which ought now to be heard on the opposite bank. But their attention was exerted in vain, and day dawned upon them long before they desired its appearance. Nor was Sir Edward Pakenham disappointed in this part of his plan alone. Instead of perceiving everything in readiness for the assault, he saw his troops in battle array, but not a ladder or fascine upon the field. The 44th, which was appointed to carry them, had either misunderstood or neglected their orders; and now headed the column of attack, without any means being provided for crossing the enemy's ditch or scaling his rampart.

The indignation of our brave leader on this occasion may be imagined, but cannot be described. Galloping towards Colonel Mullens, who led the 44th, he commanded him instantly to return with his regiment for the ladders, but the opportunity of planting them was lost, and though they were brought up, it was only to be scattered over the field by the frightened bearers. For our troops were by this time visible to the enemy. A dreadful fire was accordingly opened upon them, and they were mowed down by hundreds, while they stood waiting for orders.

Seeing that all his well-laid plans were frustrated, Pakenham gave the word to advance, and the other regiments, leaving the 44th with the ladders and fascines behind them, rushed on to the assault. On the left, a detachment under Colonel Rennie, of the 21st regiment, stormed a three-gun battery, and took it. Here they remained for some time in expectation of support; but none arriving, and a strong column of the enemy forming for its recovery, they determined to anticipate the attack, and pushed on. The battery which they had taken was in advance of the body of the works, being cut off from it by a ditch, across which only a single plank was thrown. Along this plank did these brave men attempt to pass; but being opposed by overpowering numbers, they were repulsed; and the Americans, in turn, forcing their way into the battery, at length succeeded in recapturing it with immense slaughter. On the right, again, the 21st and 4th, supported by the 93rd, though thrown into some confusion by the enemy's fire, pushed on with desperate gallantry to the ditch; but to scale the parapet without ladders was a work of no slight difficulty. Some few, indeed, by mounting one upon another's shoulders, succeeded in entering the works, but these were speedily overpowered, most of them killed, and the rest taken; whilst as many as stood without were exposed to a sweeping fire, which cut them down by whole companies. It was in vain that the most obstinate courage was displayed. They fell by the hands of men whom they absolutely did not see; for the Americans, without so much as lifting their faces above the rampart, swung their firelocks by one arm over the wall, and discharged them directly upon their heads. The whole of the guns, likewise, from the opposite bank, kept up a well-directed and deadly cannonade upon their flank; and thus were they destroyed without an opportunity being given of displaying their valour, or obtaining so much as revenge.

Sir Edward saw how things were going, and did all that a general could do to rally his broken troops. Riding towards the 44th, which had returned to the ground, but in great disorder, he called out for Colonel Mullens to advance; but that officer had disappeared, and was not to be found. He therefore prepared to lead them on himself, and had put himself at their head for that purpose, when he received a slight wound in the knee from a musket-ball, which killed his horse. Mounting another, he again headed the 44th, when a second ball took effect more fatally, and he dropped lifeless into the arms of his aide-de-camp.

Nor were Generals Gibbs and Keane inactive. Riding through the ranks, they strove by all means to encourage the assailants and recall the fugitives; till at length both were wounded, and borne off the field. All was now confusion and dismay. Without leaders, ignorant of what was to be done, the troops first halted and then began to retire; till finally the retreat was changed into a flight, and they quitted the ground in the utmost disorder. But the retreat was covered in gallant style by the reserve. Making a forward motion, the 7th and 43rd presented the appearance of a renewed attack; by which the enemy were so much awed, that they did not venture beyond their lines in pursuit of the fugitives.

Whilst affairs were thus disastrously conducted in this quarter, the party under Colonel Thornton had gained the landing-place. On stepping ashore, the first thing they beheld was a rocket thrown up as a signal that the battle was begun. This unwelcome sight added wings to their speed. Forming in one little column, and pushing forward a single company as an advanced guard, they hastened on, and in half an hour reached a canal, along the opposite bank of which a detachment of Americans was drawn up. To dislodge them was the work of a moment: a boat, with a carronade in her bow, got upon their flank, gave them a single discharge of grape, whilst the advanced guard extended its ranks, and approached at double-quick time. But they scarcely waited till the latter were within range, when, firing a volley, they fled in confusion. This, however, was only an outpost: the main body was some way in rear, and amounted to no fewer than 1500 men.

It was not long, however, before they likewise presented themselves. Like their countrymen on the other side, they were strongly entrenched, a thick parapet with a ditch covering their front; whilst a battery upon their left swept the whole position, and two field-pieces commanded the road. Of artillery the assailants possessed not a single piece, nor any means beyond what nature supplied of scaling the rampart. Yet nothing daunted by the obstacles before them, or by the immense odds to which they were opposed, dispositions for an immediate attack were made. The 85th, extending its files, stretched across the entire line of the enemy; the sailors in column prepared to storm the battery, whilst the marines remained some little way in rear of the centre as a reserve.

These arrangements being completed, the bugle sounded, and our troops advanced. The sailors raising a shout, rushed forward, but were met by so heavy a discharge of grape and canister that for an instant they paused. Recovering themselves, however, they again pushed on; and the 85th dashing forward to their aid, they received a heavy fire of musketry, and endeavoured to charge. A smart firing was now for a few minutes kept up on both sides, but our people had no time to waste in distant fighting, and accordingly hurried on to storm the works, upon which a panic seized the Americans, they lost their order, and fled, leaving us in possession of their tents and of eighteen pieces of cannon.

In this affair our loss amounted to only three men killed and about forty wounded, among the latter of whom was Colonel Thornton. Nor could the loss on the part of the enemy greatly exceed our own. Had they stood firm, indeed, it is hardly conceivable that so small a force could have wrested an entrenched position from numbers so superior; at least it could not have been done without much bloodshed. But they were completely surprised. An attack on this side was a circumstance of which they had not dreamed; and when men are assaulted in a point which they deem beyond the reach of danger, it is well known that they defend themselves with less vigour than where such an event was anticipated.

When in the act of storming these lines the word was passed through our ranks that all had gone well on the opposite bank. This naturally added to the vigour of the assault; but we had not followed our flying enemy above two miles when we were commanded to halt. The real state of the case had now reached us, and the same messenger who brought the melancholy news brought likewise an order to return.

The place where we halted was in rear of a canal, across which was thrown a wooden bridge, furnishing apparently the only means of passing. At the opposite end of this bridge stood a collection of wooden cottages and one château of some size. Here a company was stationed to serve the double purpose of a piquet and a rear-guard; whilst the main body, having rested for half an hour, began their march towards the point where they had landed.

As soon as the column had got sufficiently on their way the piquet likewise prepared to follow. But in doing so it was evident that some risk must be run. The enemy having rallied, began again to show a front; that is to say, parties of sixty or a hundred men approached to reconnoitre. These, however, must be deceived, otherwise a pursuit might be commenced, and the re-embarkation of the whole corps hindered or prevented. It so happened that the piquet in question was this day under my command; as soon, therefore, as I received information that the main body had commenced its retreat, I formed my men, and made a show of advancing. The Americans perceiving this, fled; when, wheeling about, we set fire to the château, and under cover of the smoke destroyed the bridge and retreated. Making all haste towards the rear, we overtook our comrades just as they had begun to embark; when the little corps being once more united, entered their boats, and reached the opposite bank without molestation.

CHAPTER XXIII.

As soon as the whole army was re-united, and the broken regiments had recovered their order, a flag of truce was dispatched with proposals for the burial of the dead. To accomplish this end a truce of two days was agreed upon, and parties were immediately sent out to collect and bury their fallen comrades. Prompted by curiosity, I mounted my horse and rode to the front; but of all the sights I ever witnessed, that which met me there was beyond comparison the most shocking and the most humiliating. Within the narrow compass of a few hundred yards were gathered together nearly a thousand bodies, all of them arrayed in British uniforms. Not a single American was among them; all were English; and they were thrown by dozens into shallow holes, scarcely deep enough to furnish them with a slight covering of earth. Nor was this all. An American officer stood by smoking a cigar, and apparently counting the slain with a look of savage exultation, and repeating over and over to each individual that approached him, that their loss amounted only to eight men killed and fourteen wounded.

I confess that when I beheld the scene I hung down my head, half in sorrow and half in anger. With my officious informant I had every inclination to pick a quarrel; but he was on duty, and an armistice existed, both of which forbade the measure. I could not, however, stand by and repress my choler, and since to give it vent would have subjected me to more serious inconvenience than a mere duel, I turned my horse's head and galloped back to the camp.

But the change of expression visible there in every countenance no language can portray. Only twenty hours ago, and all was life and animation; wherever you went you were enlivened by the sound of merriment and raillery; whilst the expected attack was mentioned in terms indicative not only of sanguine hope, but of the most perfect confidence as to its result. Now gloom and discontent everywhere prevailed. Disappointment, grief, indignation, and rage, succeeded each other in all bosoms; nay, so completely were the troops overwhelmed by a sense of disgrace, that for awhile they retained their sorrow without so much as hinting at its cause. Nor was this dejection occasioned wholly by the consciousness of laurels tarnished. The loss of comrades was to the full as afflicting as the loss of honour; for out of more than 5000 men brought on this side into the field, no fewer than 1500 had fallen. Among these were two generals (for Gibbs survived his wound but a few hours), and many officers of courage and ability; besides which, hardly an individual survived who had not to mourn the loss of some particular and well-known companion.

Yet it is most certain that amidst all this variety of conflicting passions no feeling bordering upon despair or even terror found room. Even among the private soldiers no fear was experienced; for if you attempted to converse with them on the subject of the late defeat, they would end with a bitter curse upon those to whose misconduct they attributed their losses, and refer you to the future, when they hoped for an opportunity of revenge. To the Americans they would allow no credit, laying the entire blame of the failure upon certain individuals among themselves; and so great was the indignation expressed against one corps, that the soldiers of other regiments would hardly exchange words with those who chanced to wear that uniform. Though deeply afflicted, therefore, we were by no means disheartened, and even yet anticipated, with an eagerness far exceeding what was felt before, a renewal of the combat.

But General Lambert, on whom the chief command had devolved, very prudently determined not to risk the safety of his army by another attempt upon works evidently so much beyond their strength. He considered, and considered justly, that his chances of success were in every respect lessened by the late repulse. In the first place, an extraordinary degree of confidence was given to the enemy; in the next place, the only feasible plan of attack having been already tried, they would be more on their guard to prevent its being again put in execution; and lastly, his own force was greatly diminished in numbers, whilst theirs continued every day to increase. Besides, it would be casting all upon the hazard of a die. If again defeated, nothing could save our army from destruction, because unless it retreated in force no retreat could be effected. A retreat, therefore, whilst yet the measure appeared practicable, was resolved upon, and towards that end were all our future operations directed.

To the accomplishment of this desirable object, however, one great obstacle existed: by what road were the troops to travel, and in what order were they to regain the fleet? On landing we had taken advantage of the creek or bayo, and thus come up by water within two miles of the cultivated country. But to adopt a similar course in returning was impossible. In spite of our losses there were not throughout the armament a sufficient number of boats to transport above one-half of the army at a time. If, however, we should separate, the chances were that both parties would be destroyed; for those embarked might be intercepted, and those left behind would be obliged to cope with the entire American force. Besides, even granting that the Americans might be repulsed, it would be impossible to take to our boats in their presence, and thus at least one division, if not both, must be sacrificed.

To obviate this difficulty prudence required that the road which we had formed on landing should be continued to the very margin of the lake; whilst appearances seemed to indicate the total impracticability of the scheme. From firm ground to the water's edge was here a distance of many miles, through the very centre of a morass where human foot had never before trodden. Yet it was desirable at least to make the attempt; for if it failed we should only be reduced to our former alternative of gaining a battle or surrendering at discretion.

Having determined to adopt this course, General Lambert immediately dispatched strong working parties, under the guidance of engineer officers, to lengthen the road, keeping as near as possible to the margin of the creek. But the task assigned to them was burthened with innumerable difficulties. For the extent of several leagues no firm footing could be discovered on which to rest the foundation of a path; nor any trees to assist in forming hurdles. All that could be done, therefore, was to bind together large quantities of reeds, and lay them across the quagmire; by which means at least the semblance of a road was produced, however wanting in firmness and solidity. But where broad ditches came in the way, many of which intersected the morass, the workmen were necessarily obliged to apply more durable materials. For these, bridges composed in part of large branches brought with immense labour from the woods, were constructed; but they were, on the whole, little superior in point of strength to the rest of the path, for though the edges were supported by timber, the middle was filled up only with reeds.

To complete this road, bad as it was, occupied the space of nine days, during which time our army remained in position without making any attempt to molest the enemy. The Americans, however, were not so inactive. In the course of two days six guns were again mounted upon the bank of the river, from which a continual fire was kept up upon our camp. The same mode of proceeding was adopted in front, and thus, night and day, were we harassed by danger against which there was no fortifying ourselves. Of the extreme unpleasantness of our situation it is hardly possible to convey any adequate conception. We never closed our eyes in peace, for we were sure to be awakened before many minutes elapsed, by the splash of a round shot or shell in the mud beside us. Tents we had none, but lay, some in the open air, and some in huts made of boards, or any materials that could be procured. From the first moment of our landing not a man had undressed excepting to bathe; and many had worn the same shirt for weeks together. Besides all this, heavy rains now set in, accompanied with violent storms of thunder and lightning, which lasting during the entire day, usually ceased towards dark, and gave place to keen frosts. Thus were we alternately wet and frozen: wet all day, and frozen all night. With the outposts again there was constant skirmishing. With what view the Americans wished to drive them in I cannot tell; but every day were they attacked, and compelled to maintain their ground by dint of hard fighting. In one word, none but those who happened to belong to this army can form a notion of the hardships which it endured and the fatigue which it underwent.

Nor were these the only evils which tended to lessen our numbers. To our soldiers every inducement was held out by the enemy to desert. Printed papers, offering lands and money as the price of desertion, were thrown into the piquets, whilst individuals made a practice of approaching our posts, and endeavouring to persuade the very sentinels to quit their stations. Nor could it be expected that bribes so tempting would always be refused. Many desertions began daily to take place, and became before long so frequent, that the evil rose to be of a serious nature.

There occurred, however, one instance of magnanimous fidelity on the part of a British soldier, which I cannot resist the inclination of repeating. A private of the 95th, whose name I should have joyfully mentioned had I not forgotten it, chanced one day to stand sentinel, when he was addressed by an American officer. The American offered him a hundred dollars and a quantity of land if he would come over; representing, at the same time, the superiority of a democratical government, and railing, as these persons generally do, against the title of king. Though the Englishman heard what was said distinctly enough, he nevertheless pretended to be deaf, and begged his tempter to come a little nearer, that, in his own words, "he might tell him all about it." Jonathan, exulting at the prospect of drawing this fine fellow from his duty, approached within twenty paces of where he stood, when just as he had opened his mouth to renew his offer, the sentinel levelled his piece and shot him through the arm. Nor was he contented with inflicting this punishment. Walking forward, he seized his wounded enemy, and reproaching him with dishonourable dealings, brought him in a prisoner to the camp. But, unhappily, conduct such as this was rare; in the course of a week many men quitted their colours, and fled to the enemy.

In the mean time the whole of the wounded, except such as were too severely hurt to be removed, were embarked upon the canal, and sent off to the fleet. Next followed the baggage and stores, with the civil officers, commissaries, purveyors, &c.; and last of all, such of the light artillery as could be withdrawn without trouble or the risk of discovery. But of the heavy artillery, of which about ten pieces were mounted in front of the bivouac, and upon the bank of the river, no account was taken. They were ship's guns, of little value, and extremely cumbersome; consequently their removal, had it been practicable, would scarcely have rewarded the trouble. It was therefore determined to leave them behind; and they were accordingly permitted to retain their stations to the last.

These preparations being continued for some days, on the 17th no part of our force remained in camp except the infantry. Having therefore delayed only till the abandoned guns were rendered unserviceable, on the evening of the 18th it also began its retreat. Trimming the fires, and arranging all things in the same order as if no change were to take place, regiment after regiment stole away, as soon as darkness concealed their motions; leaving the piquets to follow as a rear-guard, but with strict injunctions not to retire till daylight began to appear. As may be supposed, the most profound silence was maintained; not a man opening his mouth, except to issue necessary orders, and even then speaking in a whisper. Not a cough or any other noise was to be heard from the head to the rear of the column; and even the steps of the soldiers were planted with care, to prevent the slightest stamping or echo. Nor was this extreme caution in any respect unnecessary. In spite of every endeavour to the contrary, a rumour of our intended movement had reached the Americans: for we found them of late watchful and prying, whereas they had been formerly content to look only to themselves.

For some time, that is to say, while our route lay along the high road and beside the brink of the river, the march was agreeable enough; but as soon as we began to enter upon the path through the marsh all comfort was at an end. Being constructed of materials so slight, and resting upon a foundation so infirm, the treading of the first corps unavoidably beat it to pieces; those which followed were therefore compelled to flounder on in the best way they could; and by the time the rear of the column gained the morass all trace of a way had entirely disappeared. But not only were the reeds torn asunder and sunk by the pressure of those who had gone before, but the bog itself, which at first might have furnished a few spots of firm footing, was trodden into the consistency of mud. The consequence was, that every step sank us to the knees, and frequently higher. Near the ditches, indeed, many spots occurred which we had the utmost difficulty in crossing at all; and as the night was dark, there being no moon, nor any light except what the stars supplied, it was difficult to select our steps, or even to follow those who called to us that they were safe on the opposite side. At one of these places I myself beheld an unfortunate wretch gradually sink till he totally disappeared. I saw him flounder in, heard his cry for help, and ran forward with the intention of saving him; but before I had taken a second step, I myself sank at once as high as the breast. How I contrived to keep myself from smothering is more than I can tell, for I felt no solid bottom under me, and continued slowly to go deeper and deeper till the mud reached my arms. Instead of endeavouring to help the poor soldier, of whom nothing could now be seen except the head and hands, I was forced to beg assistance for myself: when a leathern canteen strap being thrown to me, I laid hold of it, and was dragged out just as my fellow-sufferer became invisible.

Over roads such as these did we continue our journey during the whole of the night: and in the morning reached a place called Fisherman's huts, upon the margin of the lake. The name is derived from a clump of mud-built cottages, situated in as complete a desert as the eye of man was ever pained by beholding. They stand close to the water, upon a part of the morass rather more firm than the rest. Not a tree or bush of any description grows near them. As far as the eye could reach a perfect ocean of reeds everywhere presented itself, except on that side where a view of the lake changed without fertilizing the prospect. Were any set of human beings condemned to spend their lives here, I should consider their fate as little superior to that of the solitary captive: but during many months of the year these huts are wholly unoccupied, being erected, as their name denotes, merely to shelter a few fishermen while the fishing season lasts.

Here at length we were ordered to halt; and perhaps I never rejoiced more sincerely at any order than at this. Wearied with my exertions, and oppressed with want of sleep, I threw myself on the ground without so much as pulling off my muddy garments, and in an instant all my cares and troubles were forgotten. Nor did I wake from that deep slumber for many hours, when I rose cold and stiff, and creeping beside a miserable fire of reeds, addressed myself to the last morsel of salt pork which my wallet contained.

The whole army had now come up, the piquets having escaped without notice, or at least without annoyance. Forming along the brink of the lake, a line of outposts was planted, and the soldiers were commanded to make themselves as comfortable as they could. But, in truth, the word comfort is one which cannot in any sense be applied to people in such a situation. Without tents or huts of any description (for the few from which the place is named were occupied by the General and other heads of departments), our bed was the morass, and our sole covering the clothes which had not quitted our backs for upwards of a month. Our fires, upon the size and goodness of which much of a soldier's happiness depends, were composed solely of reeds; a species of fuel which, like straw, soon blazes up, and soon expires again, almost without communicating any degree of warmth. But, above all, our provisions were expended, and from what quarter to obtain an immediate supply it defied the most inventive genius to discover. Our sole dependence was upon the boats. Of these a flotilla lay ready to receive us, in which were embarked the black corps, with the 44th; but they had brought with them only food for their own use. It was therefore necessary that they should reach the fleet and return again before they could furnish us with what we so much wanted. But the distance to the nearest of the shipping could not be less than eighty miles; and if the weather should become boisterous or the winds obstinately adverse, we might starve before any supply could arrive.

These numerous grievances were, however, without remedy, and we bore them with patience; though for two whole days the only provisions issued to the troops were some crumbs of biscuit and a small allowance of rum. For my own part I did not fare so badly as many others. Having been always fond of shooting, I took a firelock and went in pursuit of wild ducks, which abounded throughout the bog. Wandering along in this quest I reached a lake, by the margin of which I concealed myself and waited for my prey; nor was it long before I had an opportunity of firing. Several large flocks flew over me, and I was fortunate enough to kill three birds. But, alas, those birds, upon which I had already feasted in imagination, dropped into the water: my dog, more tired than her master, would not fetch them out, and they lay about twenty yards off, tantalizing me with the sight of a treasure which I could not reach. Moving off to another point, I again took my station where I hoped for better fortune; but the same evil chance once more occurred, and the ducks fell into the lake. This was too much for a hungry man to endure; the day was piercingly cold, and the edge of the pool was covered with ice; but my appetite was urgent, and I resolved at all hazards to indulge it. Pulling off my clothes, therefore, I broke the ice and plunged in; and though shivering like an aspen-leaf, I returned safely to the camp with a couple of birds. Next day I adopted a similar course with like success, but at the expense of what was to me a serious misery. My stockings of warm wool were the only part of my dress which I did not strip off, and to-day it unfortunately happened that one was lost. Having secured my ducks, I attempted to land where the bottom was muddy; but my leg stuck fast, and in pulling it out off came the stocking; to recover it was beyond my power, for the mud closed over it directly, and the consequence was that till I regained the transport only one of my feet could be warm at a time. To those who can boast of many pairs of fine cotton and woollen hose, this misfortune of mine may appear light, but to me, who had only two stockings on shore, the loss of one was very grievous; and I therefore request that I may not be sneered at when I record it as one of the disastrous consequences of this ill-fated expedition.

CHAPTER XXIV.

As soon as the boats returned, regiment after regiment embarked and set sail for the fleet; but the distance being considerable and the wind foul, many days elapsed before the whole could be got off. Excepting in one trifling instance, however, no accident occurred, and by the end of the month we were all once more on board our former ships. But our return was far from triumphant. We, who only seven weeks ago had set out in the surest confidence of glory, and I may add of emolument, were brought back dispirited and dejected. Our ranks were wofully thinned, our chiefs slain, our clothing tattered and filthy, and even our discipline in some degree injured. A gloomy silence reigned throughout the armament, except when it was broken by the voice of lamentation over fallen friends; and the interior of each ship presented a scene well calculated to prove the short-sightedness of human hope and human prudence.

The accident to which I allude was the capture of a single boat by the enemy. About thirty men of the 14th dragoons having crowded into an unarmed barge, were proceeding slowly down the lake, when a boat mounting a carronade in its bow suddenly darted from a creek and made towards them. To escape was impossible, for their barge was too heavily laden to move at a rate of even moderate rapidity; and to fight was equally out of the question, because of the superiority which their cannon gave to the Americans. The whole party was accordingly compelled to surrender to six men and an officer; and having thrown their arms into the lake, their boat was taken in tow and they were carried away prisoners.

This, however, was the only misfortune which occurred. Warned by the fate of their comrades, the rest kept together in little squadrons, each attended by one or more armed launches; and thus rowing steadily on, they gained the shipping without so much as another attempt at surprisal being made.

On reaching the fleet, we found that a considerable reinforcement of troops had arrived from England. It consisted of the 40th foot, a fine regiment, containing nearly a thousand men, which, ignorant of the fatal issue of our attack, had crossed the lakes only to be sent back to the ships without so much as stepping on shore. The circumstance, however, produced little satisfaction. We felt that the coming of thrice the number could not recover what was lost or recall past events; and therefore no rejoicing was heard, nor the slightest regard paid to the occurrence. Nay, so great was the despondency which had taken possession of men's minds, that not even a rumour respecting the next point of attack obtained circulation; whilst a sullen carelessness, a sort of indifference as to what might happen, seemed to have succeeded all our wonted curiosity and confidence of success in every undertaking.

In this state we remained wind-bound till the 4th of February, when, at length getting under weigh, the fleet ran down as far as Cat Island. This is a spot of sandy soil at the mouth of the lake, remarkable for nothing except a solitary Spanish family which possesses it. Completely cut off from the rest of the world, an old man, his wife, two daughters, and a son, dwell here in apparent happiness and contentment. Being at least one hundred and twenty miles from the main, it is seldom that their little kingdom is visited by strangers; and I believe that till our arrival the daughters, though grown up to womanhood, had seen few faces besides those of their parents and brother. Their cottage, composed simply of a few boughs, thatched and in-woven with straw, is beautifully situated within a short distance of the water. Two cows and a few sheep grazed beside it; whilst a small tract of ground covered with stubble, and a little garden well stocked with fruit-trees and vegetables, at once gave proof of their industry, and showed the source from whence they supplied themselves with bread.

Having remained here till the 7th, we again took advantage of a fair wind and stood to sea. As soon as we had cleared the lake, we directed our course towards the east, steering, as it was rumoured, upon Mobile; nor was it long before we came in sight of the bay which bears that name. It is formed by a projecting headland called Point Bayo, and a large island called Isle Dauphin. Upon the first is erected a small fort, possessing the same title with the promontory which commands the entrance; for though the island is at least five miles from the main, there is no water for floating a ship of any burthen except within a few hundred yards of the latter. The island is, like Cat Island, uninhabited, except by one family, and unprovided with any works of defence.

As the attack of Mobile was professedly our object, it was clear that nothing could be done previous to the reduction of the fort. The ships accordingly dropped anchor at the mouth of the bay, and immediate preparations were made for the siege. But the fort was too inconsiderable in point of size to require the employment of all our forces in its investment. Whilst one brigade, therefore, was allotted to this service, the rest proceeded to establish themselves on the island, where, carrying tents and other conveniences on shore, the first regular encampment which we had seen since our arrival in this hemisphere was formed.

The spot of ground, of which we had now taken possession, extended twelve miles in length, and from one to three in width. Its soil is in general dry and sandy, well covered with grass, and ornamented by continued groves of pine, cedar, oak, and laurel. On one side only is there a swamp, but not of sufficient size to contaminate the atmosphere of the whole, which is considered so peculiarly healthy, that the place is generally used as a depôt for the sick in the American army. At present, as I have said, it was tenanted by no more than a single family, the master of which was a midshipman in the American navy, and banished hither for some misdemeanor; but what was to us of much greater importance, it was likewise stocked with cattle resembling in appearance the black cattle of the Highlands of Scotland, and not behind them in point of wildness.

Whilst the remainder of the army spent their time here, the 4th, 21st, and 44th, being landed above the fort, were busied in the siege. This small work stands, as I have stated, at the extremity of a promontory. Towards the sea its fortifications are respectable enough, but on the land side it is little better than a blockhouse. The ramparts being composed of sand, not more than three feet in thickness, are faced with plank barely cannon-proof; whilst a sand-hill rising within pistol-shot of the ditch, completely commands them. Within, again, the fort is as much wanting in accommodation as it is in strength. There are no bomb-proof barracks, nor any hole or arch under which men might find protection from shells; indeed, so deficient is it in common lodging-rooms, that a great part of the garrison slept in tents. To reduce this place, therefore, occupied but a short time. The troops having assembled on the 8th, drove the enemy within their lines on the 9th, and broke ground the same evening. On the 10th, four eighteen-pounders with two howitzers were placed in battery upon the top of the sand-hill; on the 11th, the fort surrendered; and on the 12th, the garrison, consisting of four hundred men of the second American regiment, marched out with all the honours of war, and laid down their arms upon the glacis.

With the reduction of this trifling work ended all hostilities in this quarter of America, for the army had scarcely re-assembled when intelligence arrived from England of peace. The news reached us on the 14th, and I shall not deny that it was received with general satisfaction. Though war is the soldier's harvest, yet it must be confessed, that when carried on as it had of late been conducted, it is a harvest of which men in time become weary; and many of us having been absent for several years from our native shores, experienced absolute delight at the prospect of returning once more to the bosom of our families. The communication was therefore welcomed with unfeigned joy, nor could any other topic of conversation gain attention throughout the camp, except the anticipated re-embarkation.

But as the preliminaries only had been signed, and as Mr. Maddison's approval was required before we should be at liberty to depart, our army still continued stationary upon the island. Of the President's conduct, however, no doubts were entertained; all thoughts of future military operations were in consequence laid aside; and the sole aim of every individual thenceforth was to make himself as comfortable as circumstances would permit. To effect this end various expedients were adopted. Among others a theatre was erected, in which such officers as chose to exhibit performed for their own amusement and the amusement of their friends. In shooting and fishing, likewise, much of our time was spent; and thus, by adopting the usual expedients of idle men, we contrived to pass some days in a state of tolerable comfort.

Occupations such as these, however, soon grew insipid, and it was with sincere rejoicing that on the 5th of March we were made acquainted with Mr. Maddison's agreement to the terms proposed. All was now hope and exultation, an immediate departure was anticipated, and those were pitied as unfortunate whose lot, it was supposed, might detain them even a day behind their fellows. But as yet no movement took place; our provisions were not sufficient to authorize the undertaking so long a voyage as we must undertake, did we attempt to run for the nearest British settlement; we were therefore compelled to remain where we were, till a frigate should return, which had been sent forward to solicit supplies from the Governor of Cuba.

During this interval, the same occupations were resorted to; and others of a less agreeable nature undertaken. As summer came on, the island sent forth multitudes of snakes from their lurking-places, which infested the camp, making their way in some instances into our very beds. This was bad enough, but it was not the only nuisance to which we were subject. The alligators, which during the winter months lie in a dormant state, now began to awaken, and prowling about the margin of the pool, created no little alarm and agitation. Apparently confounded at our invasion of their territories, these monsters at first confined themselves to the marshy part of the island, but becoming by degrees more familiar, they soon ventured to approach the very precincts of the camp. One of them at length entered a tent, in which only a woman and child chanced to be, and having stared round as if in amazement, walked out again without offering to commit any violence. But the visit was of too serious a nature to be overlooked. Parties were accordingly formed for their destruction, and it was usual on the return of each from an excursion, instead of asking how many birds, to demand how many snakes and alligators they had shot. Of the former, indeed, great numbers were killed, and of the latter not a few, the largest of which measured about nine feet from the snout to the tail.

Another employment, also, deserves to be noted, because it is truly characteristic of the boyish jollity of young soldiers. Wearied with a state of idleness, the officers of the 7th, 43rd, and 14th dragoons made an attack with fir-apples upon those of the 85th, 93rd, and 95th. For the space of some days they pelted each other from morning till night, laying ambuscades, and exhibiting, on a small scale, all the stratagems of war; whilst the whole army, not even excepting the Generals themselves, stood by and spurred them on.

But to continue a detail of such proceedings would only swell my narrative, without amusing my reader; I shall therefore content myself with observing, that things remained in this state till the 14th of March, when the long-looked for frigate at length arrived, and on the 15th, the first division of the army embarking, set sail for England. The wind, however, was foul, nor did the ships make any way till the 17th, when a fresh breeze springing up, we stood our course, and by ten o'clock on the 21st could distinguish the high land of Cuba. But the violence of the gale having driven us considerably to leeward, we were forced to bear up, and beat along the coast, on which account it was not till the 23rd that we came opposite to the port of Havannah.

Than the approach to this city, and its first appearance from the water, it is impossible to conceive anything more grand and imposing. A little bay, extremely narrow at the entrance, forms the harbour. On each side of it stand forts of prodigious strength, particularly those on the left, where the ground is considerably elevated, whilst the city itself, with its ramparts and towers, its numerous steeples, spires, and public buildings, gives an assurance of wealth and magnificence peculiarly striking. When we entered, every tower was surmounted by a national banner half-mast high, a circumstance which did not at least diminish the effect of a first view; and the guns from the forts answering our salute, showed us how desperate must be the condition of an enemy that should venture within their range. Why the flags should thus indicate a general mourning, we were at a loss to guess, till the pilot informed us that this was Holy week. Then, indeed, we remembered that we had returned to a Roman Catholic country, and rejoiced at the lucky accident which had brought us thither at such a season.

As it was late before we anchored, I was prevented from landing that night, but on the morrow I went on shore at an early hour, with the intention of seeing as much as my time would allow. But in my proposed visits to the different points worthy of attention I was interrupted. It was Good-Friday, consequently all public places were shut, and neither guides nor carriages could be procured. But if I was disappointed in this, my disappointment was amply compensated by a view of the religious ceremonies peculiar to that day.

Walking into the largest church in the city, I beheld beside the altar a figure of our Saviour as large as life nailed to a cross. Beside this figure stood a number of monks, one of whom presented a rod with a sponge affixed to its mouth, while a second thrust a spear into its side, from which came out a liquor having the colour of blood and water. This being carefully caught in a golden dish, the figure was taken down from the cross, wrapped round with white linen clothes, and laid upon a bier, when an imposing procession began in the following order: First marched a military band playing slow and solemn music; next came a guard of soldiers with heads bent down and arms reversed; then followed about two hundred monks belonging to different orders, arrayed in their dark robes, with hands and feet bare, and crucifixes suspended from their necks. A short interval now succeeded, and another party of monks dressed in white appeared, singing hymns in honour of the Virgin. Next came a splendid couch surmounted by a canopy covered with white silk and sparkling with gold and jewels, upon which sat a waxen image of the *Mother of God*, clothed in gorgeous apparel. Following this was another party of white-robed monks, chanting a requiem for a departed soul, and then a second interval. At the distance of perhaps twenty yards from these came two monks bearing two large silver nails, then two others bearing a spear and a rod, and then the body of our Saviour stretched at full length upon the bier. After the bier came two monks bearing two other nails, and then another two bearing a small cross and a ladder. Here, again, there was another interval, which was succeeded by a third white-robed party likewise chanting a requiem. Next to these came about twenty canons arrayed in scarlet; then another couch covered with crimson velvet, which supported a figure of Mary Magdalen, likewise in a sitting posture; then a second body of canons, succeeded by about two hundred monks in black; after these another guard of soldiers, and last of all a second military band.

In spite of prejudice I could not avoid being deeply struck

by this solemn procession. The airs performed by the bands were slow and mournful, the voices of the singers were deep and musical, the dresses were rich to a degree of splendour, and the whole was gone through with much apparent devotion. No doubt, when regarded with the eye of reflection, the whole may seem something worse than ludicrous, but it is impossible to witness the scene and to reason on its propriety at the same time. As long as the pageant is before your eyes you cannot avoid being powerfully impressed by it; nor is it till after it has disappeared that you are inclined to ask yourself why you gave way to feelings of that nature. Yet among the natives I thought I could observe a considerable degree of levity. It is true that as many as were in the streets or at the windows dropped upon their knees while the procession passed, but their careless looks and suppressed smiles sufficiently proved that they knelt only because they were obliged to kneel.

Commencing at the door of the church where the representation of the crucifixion had been exhibited, the funeral party (for it was neither more nor less) proceeded through the principal streets in the town with a slow and measured pace. As all except the soldiers walked two and two, it covered, I should conceive, little less than a mile in extent, and after winding from lane to lane and from square to square, directed its steps towards a particular convent, where the waxen image was solemnly deposited in a vault. It is said, but with what truth I cannot pretend to determine, that a different image is made use of every year, and that the vault is now so full of waxen corpses, that it will be necessary before long to have some of them destroyed.

Having now got rid of the most sacred part of their burthen, the monks, bearing only the two couches, returned in procession by the same route and in the same order as they had proceeded, only the bands struck up lively airs and the singers chanted hymns of rejoicing and hallelujahs. Instead of walking at a slow pace likewise, they stepped out almost in a sort of dance, and reaching the door of the great church they there separated, each party hastening to its own house to celebrate mass.

Into one or two of the convent chapels I likewise entered, and was present during the performance of their very striking service. I found them ornamented in the most magnificent manner, the rafters of many being gilded over and all the windows crowded with stained glass. Of pictures, and what struck me as something better than mere daubs, there were also great numbers. In a word, it seemed as if I had reached the heart and capital of Roman Catholic splendour. Nothing that I had beheld in the mother-country could at all compare with what was now before me, and I returned in the evening to my ship, not indeed a convert to the principles of that religion, but decidedly astonished and confounded at the solemn magnificence of its ceremonies.

CHAPTER XXV.

At an early hour next morning I returned to the city, and found that the face of affairs had undergone a complete revolution. No more melancholy countenances, no closed shops and vacant streets were now to be seen; all was bustle and rejoicing, bells ringing, carriages rattling along, flags flying, and guns firing. The solemnity of Good-Friday ends, it appeared, at ten o'clock on Saturday morning, and from that time the merriments of Easter have their commencement.

The whole of this day I spent in strolling over the different walks and points of view from whence the town and surrounding country may be seen to most advantage; and I certainly must pronounce it to be by far the most magnificent colonial capital which I have visited. The streets are in general wide, clean, and airy; the houses, except in the suburbs, are composed entirely of stone, and being occasionally intermingled with convents, churches, and other public buildings, produce a very striking and handsome effect. Though surrounded by a rampart, Havannah has little of the confined and straitened appear ance by which fortified towns are generally disfigured. The works being of great extent, have left within their circumference abundant room for the display of elegance and neatness in its construction, an advantage which has not been neglected; whilst from their situation they command as glorious a prospect as can well be imagined.

When you ascend a bastion which overhangs the harbour, the

city, with all its towers and spires, lies immediately and distinctly beneath your gaze. Beyond it, again, you perceive a winding of the bay, which washes three sides of the promontory where the city stands; numerous fields of sugar-cane and Indian corn succeed, intersected by groves of orange and other fruit trees, which extend for some miles in a sort of inclined plane, and are at length bounded by lofty and rugged mountains. On your left, again, is the creek or entrance to the bay, separating you from the Moro, a line of castles remarkable for their strength and extent. Behind sweep the waters of the Gulf of Mexico; and on the right is another view much resembling that which lies before you, only that it is more narrowed; the high ground bearing in this direction closer upon the city. On the whole I do not remember to have been more forcibly struck by any scenery than that which I beheld from this bastion; so well were town and country, castles and convents, land and water, hill and valley combined.

Having spent some hours in wandering through the city, I endeavoured to make my way into the forts, and to examine the state of the works. But in both of these attempts I was interrupted. Without an order from the Governor, I was informed, that none, even of the natives, are permitted to enter the Moro, and all applications on the part of foreigners are uniformly refused. There was a degree of jealousy in this, as needless as it was illiberal; but indeed the whole conduct of the Spanish authorities gave proof of their reluctance to admit their old allies, even to the common rites of hospitality. From the moment we entered the harbour the militia of the island were called out, many of the guns which commanded our shipping were shotted, and artillerymen with lighted fuzes stood constantly beside them. An order was likewise issued, prohibiting more than two persons to land at the same time from each vessel, and many other precautions were taken, little complimentary to the good faith of those to whom Spain must feel that she owes her very existence. In spite of these drawbacks, however, I contrived to spend a week in this city with much satisfaction. The opera and theatre opening on Easter Sunday, and continuing open during the remainder of our stay, furnished sufficient amusement for the evenings, whilst in walking or riding about, in examining the different churches and chapels, and in chatting with nuns through the grate, or monks within their cells, my mornings passed away more quickly than I desired.

At length our victualling and watering being complete, on the 9th of April we bade adieu to the shores of Cuba, and running along with the Gulf-stream, took our course towards Bermuda. The wind favoured us greatly, and on the 17th we again reached these islands; where we delayed till the 23rd, when, once more setting sail, we steered directly for England. During the remainder of the voyage nothing of importance occurred till the 7th of May, when, reaching in towards the shores of Brest, we were astonished by beholding the tri-coloured flag floating from the citadel. Of the mighty events which had taken place in Europe, we were as yet in perfect ignorance. Though surprised, therefore, at the first view of that beacon of war, we naturally concluded it to be no more than a signal, and passed on without inquiry. As we ascended the channel, however, we were hailed by a schooner, which professed to communicate some news concerning Buonaparte; but the wind being high, we could not distinctly tell what was said; nor was it till the 9th, when we had anchored off Spithead, that the reappearance of that wonderful man was made known.

The effect of this intelligence it would be difficult to describe. At first it was received with acclamations, but by and bye those who had dreamed of home began to perceive in it the destruction of their visions. Yet we considered that we were soldiers, and certainly no regret was experienced when we were ordered to re-embark, and sail for the Downs.

Having thus brought my narrative to a conclusion, I cannot lay aside my pen without offering a few remarks upon the events of this busy year, and the nature of an American war in general. In doing so, I shall begin with the unfortunate attack upon New Orleans, and endeavour, in as few words as possible, to assign the true causes of its failure.

From the account which I have given of this affair, it will appear that, from its very commencement, it was replete with error, and gave promise of no better result than actually occurred. I do not here allude to the spot fixed upon for landing, because that was as appropriate as could be chosen. Neither do I refer to the groundless rumours brought in by deserters; for to such all assailants are liable; but the error lay in the steps subsequently taken; in the unhappy advance of the first division from a place of concealment into the open country, without pushing forward to the extent required. The fact is, that having reached the main land in safety, one out of two plans might have been selected by General Keane; which, in all probability, would have been equally attended with success. Either he might have remained in the morass till the whole army was assembled, or, if this were deemed too dangerous, he ought to have advanced upon the city with the first division alone. If it be objected that a force of 1600 men was incompetent for an undertaking so important as the latter, I reply that there could be no more hazard in it than in the course actually pursued. New Orleans is not a regular fortification requiring a large army and a powerful battering train for its reduction. In obtaining possession of such a place there would have been no difficulty, because it has since been ascertained that the American troops were, at the time of our landing, some miles above the city; and surely it would not have been more difficult to repulse an attack within a town than in the open country. But neither of these courses was adopted. The advance was drawn from concealment, and halted just where it became most exposed, as if it had been our design to warn the American General of his danger; the consequence of which was a well-directed attack upon our bivouac, and an immediate commencement of those works which afterwards resisted and repelled all our efforts.

The second error evident in this business was the selection of the schooner instead of the ship for destruction. Had the latter, which lay farther up the stream been destroyed, the former never could have passed our battery, nor been of further annoyance to us; whereas, the schooner being burnt, the ship was only removed out of the reach of danger, and posted where she could be infinitely more advantageous to her friends and detrimental to her enemies. This in itself was a grave error, which beyond all doubt contributed, in some degree, to our repulse on the 29th of December.

The third error, and one which continued to exert its influence throughout the whole compaign, was the delay in bringing on a general action. Why our troops fell back on the 29th I confess is to me a mystery. It was not to be supposed that an officer who had shown so much judgment as the American General, Jackson, in his first endeavours to check our advance, would lose the advantage which the nature of his position afforded. That he would fortify the neck of land, indeed, was exactly what might have been expected: and, therefore, every hour during which an attack was deferred, contributed so much to his strength and to our weakness. It is true that we should have suffered, and perhaps suffered severely; but our chances of suffering were certainly not diminished by delay. We ought, therefore, instead of falling back, to have pursued our operations with vigour on that day; because the American lines, being then incomplete, would have assisted rather than retarded our progress.

It has been said, and perhaps truly, that the movement on the 29th was never intended for more than a reconnoissance: and that the scheme subsequently adopted, of overpowering the enemy's fire by a superior artillery brought from the fleet, was a wise one. All this may be true; but as we did not succeed in silencing the enemy's batteries, who, on the contrary, put ours to silence, either the project was faulty in its design, or some grievous error was committed in its execution. As far as our position was affected by it, the results were these:—Three days more were lost in making preparations, which ended in nothing; while, by the enemy, these same days were judiciously and indefatigably employed to improve their deficiency and recruit their force.

At last came the idea of digging a canal from the lakes to the river, by means of which a portion of our army might be thrown to the other side; a project which is said to have been suggested by Sir Alexander Cochrane; but which, wheresoever originating, was at once bold and judicious. The canal was accordingly formed; not, however, with sufficient attention to the rules of art in like cases, as was shown by the falling in of the banks, and the consequent impossibility of bringing up boats to transport the whole detachment. Still there it was, and 350 men, instead of 1400, made good their landing on the right bank of the river. It is deeply to be regretted that Sir Edward Pakenham did not delay his own advance with the main body till this fact had been ascertained. His plan of battle was to carry the enemy's works on the right bank, to turn their own guns from that flank against themselves, and to alarm them for their communications, ere he should attack the main position on the left. Nor can it be doubted, that had the detached corps arrived at the hour first named, an easy triumph would have been achieved. But Pakenham was too fiery to restrain his troops, after they had assumed their ground on his own side. Instead, therefore, of causing the columns to fall back out of gun-shot, and wait quietly till the battle began on the left, he hurried them into action as soon as the day dawned; and they became exposed to the whole of that volume of fire which it was one main object of his movement across the Mississippi to destroy. Moreover, from all the moral effects of a partial defeat the enemy were saved; and I need not say how serious such things are to irregular and undisciplined bodies. I do not mean to assert that, in spite of all this, the American lines ought not to have been carried. On the contrary, had every officer and man done his duty, the victory would have been complete, though purchased, beyond a doubt, at a severe cost. Yet it is absurd to deny that, speaking of the movement as an operation of war, the attack on the right ought to have been withheld till that on the left had either failed or succeeded. So far, therefore, the General is liable to censure; and chivalrous and high-minded as he was, it is just that he should receive it. But there were other causes of defeat than this; among which, the gross misconduct of one individual deserves to be especially noticed.

To Lieutenant-Colonel Mullens, with the 44th regiment, of which he was in command, was intrusted the arduous and therefore honourable duty of carrying the fascines and ladders. The orders were given in good time over night; and Colonel Mullens received them as if they had conveyed a sentence of death. He stated, in the hearing of the private soldiers, that his corps was devoted to destruction; and conducted himself, in every respect, like a condemned criminal on the night previous to his execution. When the troops got under arms, instead of bringing his battalion to the redoubt, where he had been instructed to find the ladders, he marched directly past it, and led them into the field without a single ladder or fascine. When the day dawned, and he was sent back for these instruments, he headed his corps in its retrograde movement, but left it to return as it could to the front; and when sought for to guide the attack, he was nowhere to be found. That a regiment thus abused and deserted by its commanding officer should fall into confusion, cannot occasion any surprise; it would have been surprising indeed, had a different result ensued. But the melancholy effect of such confusion was, that other regiments were likewise broken; and before order could be restored, all the Generals were borne dead or wounded from the field. A large share, therefore, of the blame attachable to this failure must rest where fidelity of narration has obliged me to place it.

Again, the recall of the victorious detachment from the left to the right bank of the Mississippi, and the consequent abandonment of that complete command of the river which this partial success had obtained, was a military error of the gravest kind. Great as our numerical loss had been in the principal action of the 8th, the advantages of position were at the close of the day so decidedly with us, that for General Jackson to maintain himself any longer in front of New Orleans was physically impossible. His own dispatch, indeed, addressed to the Secretary-at-War, shows that he felt the truth so forcibly, that he had actually issued orders for a retreat, when the removal of the English from his menaced flank was reported to him; and his battalions, which had begun to get under arms, were directed to resume their places. It is, however, but just to state, that such was the miserable condition of our commissariat, that the fleet contained not provisions enough to feed the people on half rations during a quick passage to Cuba; and General Lambert did not feel that he would be justified in risking the total loss of his army, which, had the campaign been prolonged another fortnight, must under such circumstances have taken place. That he erred in this supposition is certain; but his was probably an error into which most men similarly circumstanced would have fallen.

But the primary cause of all our disasters may be traced to a source even more distant than any yet mentioned; I mean, to the disclosure of our designs to the enemy. How this occurred I shall not take it upon me to declare, though several rumours bearing at least the guise of probability have been circulated. The attack upon New Orleans was professedly a secret expedition; so secret, indeed, that it was not communicated to the inferior officers and soldiers in the armament till immediately previous to our quitting Jamaica. To the Americans, however, it appears to have been known long before; and hence it was that, instead of taking them unawares, we found them fully prepared for our reception. Nor is this all. It appears difficult to account for the degree of negligence which affected the naval heads of the present expedition, as far as the providing a competent number of boats and small craft to transport the troops is concerned. Throughout the whole fleet, barges enough to carry one-half of the army could not be found; whereas there ought to have been a sufficient quantity to contain not only the entire force, but all its stores and ammunition. To this neglect, indeed, more perhaps than to any other circumstances, is the failure of the attempt to be attributed; since not a doubt can exist that, if General Keane had been enabled to bring the whole of his army to land on the morning of the 23rd, he would have reached New Orleans, without firing a shot, before nightfall. But the opportunity is past, it cannot be recalled, and therefore to point out errors on the part of my countrymen can serve no good end. That the failure is to be lamented no one will deny, since the conquest of New Orleans would have proved beyond all comparison the most valuable acquisition that could be made to the British dominions throughout the whole western hemisphere. In possession of that post we should have kept the entire southern trade of the United States in check, and furnished means of commerce to our own merchants of incalculable value.

The fact, however, is, that when we look back upon the whole series of events produced by the late American war, we shall find little that is likely to flatter our vanity or increase our self-importance. Except a few successes in Canada at its very commencement, and the brilliant inroad upon Washington, it will be found that our arms have been constantly baffled or repulsed on shore; whilst at sea, with the exception of the capture of the Chesapeake and one or two other affairs towards its conclusion, we have been equally unsuccessful. From what cause does this proceed? Not from any inferiority in courage or discipline, because in these particulars British soldiers and sailors will yield to none in the world. There must, then, be some other cause for these misfortunes, and the cause is surely one which has continually baffled all our plans of American warfare.

We have long been habituated to despise the Americans as an enemy unworthy of serious regard. To this alone it is to be attributed that frigates half manned were sent out to cope with ships capable of containing them within their hulls; and to this also the trifling handfuls of troops dispatched to conduct the war by land. Instead of fifteen hundred, had ten thousand men sailed from the Garonne under General Ross, how differently might he have acted! There would have been then no necessity for a re-embarkation after the capture of Washington, and consequently no time given for the defence of Baltimore; but, marching across the country, he might have done to the one city what he did to the other. And it is thus only that a war with America can be successfully carried on. To penetrate up the country amidst pathless forests and boundless deserts, and to aim at permanent conquest, is out of the question. America must be assaulted only on her coasts. Her harbours destroyed, her shipping burned, and her seaport towns laid waste, are the only evils which she has reason to dread; and were a sufficient force embarked with these orders, no American war would be of long continuance.

A melancholy experience has now taught us that such a war must not be entered into, unless it be conducted with spirit; and there is no conducting it with spirit, except with a sufficient numerical force. To the plan proposed of making desert the whole line of coast, it may be objected, that by so doing we should distress individuals, and not the Government. But they who offer this objection, forget the nature both of the people whose cause they plead, and of the Government under which they live. In a democratical Government, the voice of the people must at all times prevail. The members of the House of Representatives are the very persons who, from such proceedings, would suffer most severely, and we all know how far private suffering goes to influence a man's public opinions. Besides, the principle upon which the advocates for the sacredness of private property proceed, is erroneous. Every one will allow that, in absolute monarchies, where war is more properly the pastime of kings than the desire of subjects, non-combatants ought to be dealt with as humanely as possible. Not so, however, in States governed by popular assemblies. By compelling the constituents to experience the real hardships and miseries of warfare, you will compel the representatives to a vote of peace; and surely that line of conduct is, upon the whole, most humane, which puts the speediest period to the cruelties of war. There are few men who would not rather endure a raging fever for three days, than a slow and lingering disease for three months. So it is with a democracy at war. Burn their houses, plunder their property, block up their harbours, and destroy their shipping in a few places; and before you have time to proceed to the rest, you will be stopped by entreaties for peace. Whereas, if you do no mischief that can be avoided, if you only fight their fleets and armies wherever you meet them, and suffer the inhabitants to live in undisturbed tranquillity, they will continue their hostilities till they have worn out the means of one party, and greatly weakened those of both.

Should another war break out between Great Britain and America, this is the course to be adopted by the former. Besides which, I humbly conceive that a second attempt might be hazarded upon New Orleans, because the importance of the conquest would authorise almost any sacrifice for its attainment; and once gained, it could easily be defended. The neck of land, upon which it is built, extends in the same form above as below the town; and the same advantages which it holds out to its present defenders would, of course, be afforded to us. A chain of works thrown across from the river to the marsh would render it inaccessible from above; whilst by covering the lakes and the Mississippi with cruisers, all attacks from below would be sufficiently guarded against.

THE END.